A Manual for Planning and Implementing the Living Standards Measurement Study Survey

The Living Standards Measurement Study

The Living Standards Measurement Study (LSMS) was established by the World Bank in 1980 to explore ways of improving the type and quality of household data collected by statistical offices in developing countries. Its goal is to foster increased use of household data as a basis for policy decisionmaking. Specifically, the LSMS is working to develop new methods to monitor progress in raising levels of living, to identify the consequences for households of past and proposed government policies, and to improve communications between survey statisticians, analysts, and policymakers.

The LSMS Working Paper series was started to disseminate intermediate products from the LSMS. Publications in the series include critical surveys covering different aspects of the LSMS data collection program and reports on improved methodologies for using Living Standards Survey (LSS) data. More recent publications recommend specific survey, questionnaire, and data processing designs and demonstrate the breadth of policy analysis that can be carried out using LSS data.

LSMS Working Paper
Number 126

A Manual for Planning and Implementing the Living Standards Measurement Study Survey

Margaret E. Grosh
Juan Muñoz

The World Bank
Washington, D.C.

Copyright © 1996
The International Bank for Reconstruction
and Development/THE WORLD BANK
1818 H Street, N.W.
Washington, D.C. 20433, U.S.A.

To present the results of the Living Standards Measurement Study with the least possible delay, the typescript of this paper has not been prepared in accordance with the procedures appropriate to formal printed texts, and the World Bank accepts no responsibility for errors. Some sources cited in this paper may be informal documents that are not readily available.

The findings, interpretations, and conclusions expressed in this paper are entirely those of the author(s) and should not be attributed in any manner to the World Bank, to its affiliated organizations, or to members of its Board of Executive Directors or the countries they represent. The World Bank does not guarantee the accuracy of the data included in this publication and accepts no responsibility whatsoever for any consequence of their use. The boundaries, colors, denominations, and other information shown on any map in this volume do not imply on the part of the World Bank Group any judgment on the legal status of any territory or the endorsement or acceptance of such boundaries.

The material in this publication is copyrighted. Requests for permission to reproduce portions of it should be sent to the Office of the Publisher at the address shown in the copyright notice above. The World Bank encourages dissemination of its work and will normally give permission promptly and, when the reproduction is for noncommercial purposes, without asking a fee. Permission to copy portions for classroom use is granted through the Copyright Clearance Center, Inc., Suite 910, 222 Rosewood Drive, Danvers, Massachusetts 01923, U.S.A.

The complete backlist of publications from the World Bank is shown in the annual *Index of Publications*, which contains an alphabetical title list (with full ordering information) and indexes of subjects, authors, and countries and regions. The latest edition is available free of charge from the Distribution Unit, Office of the Publisher, The World Bank, 1818 H Street, N.W., Washington, D.C. 20433, U.S.A., or from Publications, The World Bank, 66, avenue d'Iéna, 75116 Paris, France.

ISSN: 0253-4517

Margaret Grosh is a senior economist at the World Bank. Juan Muñoz is the Director of Sistemas Integrales, a survey research firm in Santiago, Chile.

Library of Congress Cataloging-in-Publication Data

A manual for planning and implementing the Living standards
  measurement study survey / [compiled by] Margaret E. Grosh, Juan
Muñoz.
       p.   cm. — (LSMS working paper : no. 126)
  Includes bibliographical references   (p.   )
  ISBN 0-8213-3639-8
  1. Cost and standard of living—Data processing—Planning.
  2. Household surveys—Methodology.   I. Grosh, Margaret E.
  II. Muñoz, Juan, 1947–   . III. Series.
  HD6978.M34   1996
  339.4'7'0723—dc20   96-19418
                                            CIP

Contents

Foreword

In making sound policy decisions, governments need to know how those decisions affect the populations in their countries. Answers to some of the important questions can come only from household survey data. For example — who is poor and who is rich and why? Who uses government services such as schools, clinics, agricultural extension offices, welfare programs, and old-age pensions? Are those not using government services able to get services in the private sector? How do households change their decisions about who works and how much, whether and where to send their children to school, and how many children to have? To answer these questions requires household survey data that cover many aspects of household welfare. Until a few years ago, such surveys were very rare in developing countries. The Living Standards Measurement Study (LSMS) program was launched in 1980 to help foster the collection of good data from household surveys and improve its subsequent use in policymaking. The first LSMS surveys were implemented in Côte d'Ivoire in 1985 and in Peru in 1985/86. Since then, over forty LSMS surveys have been conducted in nineteen countries and new LSMS surveys are currently in the field or being planned in nine additional countries.

LSMS surveys provide high quality, timely, and comprehensive data on most aspects of household welfare (consumption, income from activities in the labor market, household enterprises or agriculture, asset ownership, migration, health, education, nutrition, fertility, and anthropometrics). LSMS surveys have become a powerful tool for understanding household economic decisions and the effects of social and economic policies. The use of LSMS data in poverty assessments helps to ensure that the development community's efforts to reduce poverty can be guided by quantitative information on levels, causes, and consequences of poverty. The data have been used by governments in various direct and indirect ways. In Bolivia, LSMS data were used to help the government evaluate its public employment program. In Jamaica, the government used data from its LSMS survey to reformulate the food stamps program. In South Africa, the government used the data in designing their tax reform program.

LSMS surveys have evolved over time. Originally they were motivated primarily to support research; now they are much more often driven by policy needs. The contents of the questionnaires have accordingly changed over the years and from country to country. The modular design of the LSMS questionnaires has facilitated this flexibility and country-specificity. The surveys have also benefitted from developments in computer technology. The LSMS program had to design its own software to lay out the first questionnaires, but now such software is available commercially. In the first surveys in Côte d'Ivoire and Peru, it was novel to carry out data entry on personal computers in regional field offices, with electricity often provided by gas-fueled generators. In the Nepal LSMS now in the field, data entry is carried out in the field on notebook computers powered by portable solar panels. In 1995, Tanzania became the first country to allow data from its LSMS survey to be put on the Internet for easy access by scholars worldwide.

Foreword continues on next page

The interest in conducting and analyzing surveys like the LSMS has grown markedly since the early days of the project. Such surveys are now being done in many more places than the LSMS division of the World Bank can work. Since many of those now involved in the implementation of new LSMS-type surveys have little familiarity with the old surveys, it is important to ensure that the lessons from the first ten years of LSMS field work are widely available. This manual is one of a series of efforts to compile and disseminate the lessons of LSMS experience. Here the focus is on the planning of the survey and the conduct of the field work. A comprehensive review of the content of the questionnaires and the way in which the various modules can be combined is currently underway, and the documentation and dissemination of data sets from surveys already fielded have recently been upgraded.

Lyn Squire, Director
Policy Research Department

Abstract

This manual explains the planning process, technical procedures, and standards used in Living Standard Measurement Study (LSMS) household surveys, including what these procedures entail, why they are used, and how they can be implemented. The "what" is the factual description of procedures and standards. The explanation of the "why" will help the reader to understand the importance of the different procedures. Moreover, if some aspect of them is to be changed or eliminated in a particular country, knowing what they were designed to achieve may aid the survey planner in finding an alternate strategy to accomplish the same objective. The "how" comprises explicit instructions, along with examples of ways the procedures have been adapted in different countries that have implemented LSMS surveys. Although the lessons presented here are derived from LSMS surveys, many of them are applicable to surveys generally, and especially to those that are complex or especially concerned with quality control.

Topics covered in this manual include the technical aspects of questionnaire formatting and testing, ways to implement a sample design, and what fieldwork and data management procedures have been successful. Ideas about directions to pursue in analyzing the data are sketched. A brief description of how to assess local statistical capacity is included. Generic work plans and budgets are presented to give ballpark estimates of how long each process will take and what must be included in a budget.

This manual will be useful to a broad spectrum of those who collaborate on an LSMS survey, including the staffs of the statistical agency, planning agency, university, or international development agency that will design, finance, implement, and analyze the survey, and technical assistants who are not familiar with LSMS survey practice. The authors have tried to write so that persons who are not specialists can read all parts of the manual.

Acknowledgments

This document is an attempt to put on paper the oral tradition of the Living Standards Measurement Study (LSMS) surveys. As such the authors are not the creators of the thoughts presented here, but something more like scribes. The practices recorded here were developed over years of discussion and field work in which numerous people and agencies participated. We would like to acknowledge the irreplaceable contributions to defining the body of thought presented here made by the past and present staff of the LSMS Division at the World Bank, our colleagues in the academic world who have provided advice and criticism over the years, the many agencies that provided technical assistance and financing for the surveys, and, most importantly, the agencies that actually implemented the surveys.

We have also received help from many people in bringing this document about. Emmanuel Jimenez made the funds and time available and encouraged us in the importance of the task. Martha Ainsworth allowed us to crib heavily from her writings on LSMS surveys. Martha Ainsworth, Harold Alderman, Ana Maria Arriagada, Benu Bidani, Gaurav Datt, Paul Glewwe, Christiaan Grootaert, Stephen Howes, Luisa Ferreira, Emmanuel Jimenez, Dean Jolliffe, Tim Marchant, P.B.K. Murthy, Raylynn Oliver, Giovanna Prennushi, Laura Rawlings, Chris Scott, Kinnon Scott, Jacques van der Gaag, and Robert Vos provided many useful comments on drafts of this work. Martha Ainsworth, Paul Glewwe, Christiaan Grootaert, and Emmanuel Jimenez drafted synopses of their research for Chapter 7. Stephanie Faul edited the drafts. Carlo del Ninno wrote Annex X. Jim Shafer handled the desktop publishing.

Chapter 1. Introduction

A. What This Manual Covers

This manual explains the planning process, technical procedures, and standards used in Living Standard Measurement Study (LSMS) household surveys, including what these procedures entail, why they are used, and how they can be implemented. The "what" is the factual description of procedures and standards. The explanation of the "why" will help the reader to understand the importance of the different procedures. Moreover, if some aspect of the procedures is to be changed or eliminated in a particular country, knowing what they were designed to achieve may aid the survey planner in finding an alternate strategy to accomplish the same objective. The "how" comprises explicit instructions, along with examples of ways the procedures have been adapted in different countries that have implemented LSMS surveys. Although the lessons presented here are derived from LSMS surveys, many of them are applicable to surveys generally, and especially to those that are complex or especially concerned with quality control.

This manual is part of a multi-pronged effort to document, evaluate, and improve LSMS surveys. As such it is not designed to stand alone, but to fill part of the gap in available materials. The planner of any new LSMS survey will need to consult many other documents as well as the one in hand. The basics are listed in Box 1.1 and a more extensive annotated bibliography is provided in Annex II.

Topics covered in this manual include the technical aspects of questionnaire formatting and testing, ways to implement a sample design, and what fieldwork and data management procedures have been successful. Ideas about directions to pursue in analyzing the data are sketched. A brief section describes how to assess local statistical capacity. Generic work plans and budgets are presented to give ballpark estimates of how long each process will take and what must be included in a budget.

The manual does not attempt to cover institutional factors in developing the scope and design of the survey project, the content of the questionnaires, or analysis of the data. As this manual is being written, the LSMS division of the World Bank[1] is just beginning a major research effort which will culminate in a separate volume covering these themes. The final product of that effort is expected in about 1998, but draft papers should be available beginning in 1996. Moreover, this manual provides only brief summaries of some technical topics for which extensive information is already available, for example, sampling and anthropometric measurement. Suggestions for further reading are provided in Annex II.

B. Who Should Read This Manual

This manual will be useful to a broad spectrum of those who collaborate on an LSMS survey, including the staffs of the statistical agency, planning agency, or university

---

1. The name and place in the organization chart of the division that supports LSMS surveys has changed several times over the last 15 years. Currently it is the Poverty and Human Resources Division in the Policy Research Department. For simplicity, we will use the term LSMS division throughout the manual.

Box 1.1: The Minimum Package of Reference Materials

Those involved in developing a new LSMS survey will want to refer to many other documents. Some minimal suggestions are provided here. A more complete list of materials with annotations on content and complete descriptions of the references is provided in Annex II.

Materials on LSMS Surveys

The LSMS working papers are available through the World Bank Bookstore, affiliated bookstores throughout the world, and many libraries. Materials marked with an asterisk are available from the LSMS division of the World Bank for those involved in planning new LSMS surveys. Requests for these should be sent by electronic mail to LSMS@worldbank.org, by fax to LSMS Surveys at 202-522-1153, or by sending a letter to LSMS Surveys, PRDPH, World Bank, 1818 H Street, N.W., Washington, D.C. 20433.

For a discussion of strategic institutional choices:
    LSMS Working Paper 80

For help in formatting questionnaires:
    this manual

For help in designing the contents of questionnaires:
    LSMS Working Papers 24, 34, 90
    sample questionnaires from other countries[*]
    forthcoming work to revise the prototype modules[*]

For help in planning field work:
    this manual

For help in data management:
    this manual
    examples of Basic Information Documents from other countries[*]

For lessons in building analytic capacity:
    case studies from several countries[*]

Selected Manuals Produced by Allied Survey Programs

For an overview of the Social Dimensions of Adjustment Surveys:
    Delaine *et al.* (1992) on Integrated Surveys
    Marchant and Grootaert (1991) on Priority Surveys
    Wold (1995) on Community Surveys

The UN National Household Survey Capability Program produced a series of manuals that may be of interest, especially:
    UNNHSCP (1986a) on How to Conduct Anthropometric Measurements
    UNNHSCP (1982) on Non-Sampling Error
    UNNHSCP (1986b) on Sample Frames and Sample Designs

that will design, implement and analyze the survey, and of the international agencies that
finance the survey, as well as technical assistants who are not familiar with LSMS survey
practice. The authors have tried to write so that persons who are not specialists can read
all parts of the manual.

The following aids are provided to make it easier for the reader to find the parts
of this document most relevant to his or her particular purposes:

- brief suggestions are provided in Box 1.2;
- key messages are summarized in bullet form at the beginning of each
  chapter;
- the chapter's structure and potential usefulness to different audiences is
  outlined at the beginning of each chapter; and
- information that should be read by all audiences is presented first in the
  chapter, with information of interest primarily to the different specialized
  members of the technical teams presented in the latter parts.

C. Some Assumptions Implicit in the Manual

Many strategic decisions must be made when designing a survey project, more
than can be discussed in this manual. These issues are treated in other materials already
available or that are scheduled to be made available soon. However, these choices have
repercussions for the parts of planning a survey that are described in this manual, and
therefore this subsection briefly mentions the issues and choices that are implicit in the
rest of the document. These can be thought of as the "base case" for implementation of
an LSMS survey. Packages can be tailored by adding or subtracting elements from the
base case. The assumptions made here about these strategic decisions are as follows:

ONE YEAR VS MULTI-YEAR PROGRAM. This manual describes a single year of an
LSMS survey. When surveys are repeated once a year or once every two years, most
of the same steps are required for each round. Some of them may be accomplished more
easily, with less technical assistance, and with less need for new equipment. Their

3

content, however, remains the same so the manual is still fully applicable to multiyear projects.

HOW MUCH DATA ANALYSIS TO INCLUDE IN THE PROJECT. This manual focuses on the production of data, although projects often include a good deal of analysis as well. Thus the manual is a guide to what may be one component of a larger project or may be a first project to be complemented by other projects that focus on analysis of data.[2]

AMOUNT OF CAPACITY BUILDING. This manual again focuses on the narrowest likely definition of a project. Some training will take place in the scenario used here. It includes complete training for field staff, extensive training for the data manager, and some on-the-job training for the survey manager and field manager as they interact with the technical assistants. Projects that emphasize capacity building would arrange additional training for staff involved in questionnaire design and formatting, sampling, and data management and analysis.

SOURCE OF FINANCING. The term "survey project" is used throughout the manual as though a special source of funds were to be sought. This has usually been the case for LSMS surveys, although of course countries could finance them from their normal national budgets. The source of funds is largely immaterial to the information provided in this manual.

IMPLEMENTING AGENCY. This manual assumes that the survey will be carried out by the government's central statistical office, though in some countries a university or private research firm may be used instead. In the great majority of LSMS surveys, the agency chosen has been the government statistical agency.

PERMANENT VS TEMPORARY STAFF. Lastly there is the division of labor — how much should come from the permanent staff of the statistical agency and how much from people hired on short-term contracts. The first choice may be better for institution building. The second choice may be speedier and, depending on the wages that can be paid, may make it easier to ensure high-quality staff. This manual discusses the full staff necessary to carry out a survey without differentiating whether they come from inside or outside the statistical agency.

---

2. The LSMS division is sponsoring a review and evaluation of mechanisms for supporting data analysis in LSMS projects, the results of which should be available in 1996.

Chapter 2: An Overview of LSMS Surveys

- LSMS surveys are designed to produce a comprehensive monetary measure of welfare and its distribution; describe other aspects of welfare; describe patterns of access to and use of social services; allow study of the determinants of important social and economic outcomes; and allow study of how households behave in response to changes in the economic environment or government programs.

- LSMS surveys are integrated surveys covering a number of topics. The household questionnaire always produces comprehensive measures of consumption, usually comprehensive measures of income, and always covers a variety of sectoral issues, usually health, education, nutrition, and fertility. The community questionnaire describes the economic environment faced by the households in the sample. The price questionnaire gathers information on prices of basic goods in the community. Sometimes special questionnaires are used for health clinics and schools.

- LSMS surveys use an extensive set of quality control procedures to minimize errors and delays in data collection and processing. These are the topic of much of the rest of this manual.

- Many surveys in the LSMS family differ from the prototype in one or more aspects of purpose, content, or quality control. This is natural, as each is adapted to fit the circumstances of the time and place where it was developed.

This chapter describes very briefly the purpose and contents of LSMS surveys and the factors affecting their evolution. These topics are really the theme of the planned companion manual to this one. Their treatment here is therefore brief. This chapter may be skipped or skimmed by those who are already well familiar with the content of LSMS surveys, but should be read by all others.

A. The "Prototype" LSMS Survey

Here we describe a "prototype" LSMS survey. The LSMS prototype is actually a composite based on experience with a number of surveys. Throughout the manual these will be drawn upon for examples and illustrations of the concepts discussed. In fact, many of the surveys in the LSMS family have departed from the prototype in one or more ways in order to fulfill slightly different objectives or in response to institutional or budget constraints. The use of a survey to illustrate a specific point does not imply that all aspects of that survey are the same as for the LSMS "prototype."

Purpose of LSMS Surveys

The objective of LSMS surveys is to provide data adequate for the planning, monitoring, and analysis of economic policies and social programs with respect to their impact on household living standards, especially those of the poor. In order to achieve this objective, the data must by integrated, timely, and available for analysis on a variety of issues, often conducted by many analysts and using a wide range of techniques.

In terms of content, LSMS surveys provide an integrated view of household welfare and allow for the study of its determinants. The surveys are designed on the premise that quantifying and locating a problem is not enough. We need to learn how to solve it. For example, knowing how many poor there are, where they live, and what they do is only a part of the enquiry. In order to devise cost-effective solutions, planners also need to understand in greater detail the causes and consequences of poverty and the effect of changes in government policies. The same principle applies to other problems such as illiteracy or malnutrition.

LSMS questionnaires therefore provide an integrated set of information. First, they are designed to measure the distribution of welfare and the level of poverty in economies where subsistence agriculture, informal household enterprises, seasonal employment, and non-cash payments are common. Second, they describe the patterns of access to and utilization of many public services — schooling, health care, electricity, water supply, and sanitation. Third, they are designed to understand how households react to the economic environment and government programs — for example, how household welfare might be affected by changes in the prices of major agricultural commodities or how the use of government health services might change if user fees were raised. Fourth, they are designed to support complex analyses of relationships between various aspects of household welfare — such as the impact of household income on the enrollment of children in school, of the effects of education on childbearing behavior, or the impact of health status on employment.

In order to be relevant to policy analysis, survey data must be timely. The procedures designed for LSMS surveys result in data that is ready for analysis within about three months from the completion of fieldwork, as described in chapters 5 and 6.

Finally, the most important tangible product of LSMS projects is not viewed as a set of standard tabulations, but as a data set that can be used by multiple users to answer many different questions. A rich abstract that presents some of the basic findings of the multiple aspects of welfare covered in the survey is certainly a useful reference and should be produced in the survey projects. But in most cases the availability of the data in tabulated form will not be enough to carry out the kind of deeper investigations needed for poverty-related work and economic analysis in general. Some of these issues require the adoption of sophisticated calculations and modelling tools (usually of a multidimensional nature) which require direct interaction between the analyst and the data. Moreover, much of such analysis requires knowledge of specific sectoral issues that cannot be expected to reside in statistical institutes. Thus the data sets must be produced and distributed to analysts outside of the statistical institute. Only thus can the less tangible product from the surveys, the improved understanding of poverty, social policy, and household behavior, be achieved.

Some of the most common uses of LSMS data are shown in Boxes 2.1 and 2.2. Section D of Chapter 7 provides many more examples of the varied uses that have been made of LSMS data.

The reader will have noted that the LSMS questionnaires include modules on topics that are often the focus of single-purpose surveys, including some common and well respected surveys — labor force surveys, income and expenditure surveys, or demographic and health surveys. The LSMS modules do not collect the same depth of information on any single topic as do single-topic surveys and may have smaller samples so that the precision of measurement of key outcomes may be lower than for the single-topic surveys. But because LSMS surveys collect information on so many aspects of welfare, they not only provide a good multi-dimensional summary of welfare, but also allow study of the interactions between these various factors.

LSMS surveys and other surveys can be combined into a program of household surveys in various ways, depending on the needs and constraints of the country. In Jamaica, the local (modified) version of the LSMS is carried out annually and tied to one quarter of the quarterly labor force survey. Surveys on literacy, contraceptive prevalence, and income and expenditure are conducted every three to 10 years to round out the program. In several countries — Romania, Russia, Latvia, and Lithuania — one-year LSMS survey projects have been used as a way to pilot alternatives for reforms to or replacements of ongoing survey programs. Sometimes, as in Peru, a series of single-year projects has provided a time series of data. For Africa, the Social Dimensions of Adjustment project recommends Integrated Surveys (which are much the same as LSMS surveys) every three to five years with Priority Surveys (which usually cover the same general themes but with much less detailed questionnaires and larger samples) in the intervening years.

Questionnaire Content

In order to gather data consistent with their objectives, LSMS surveys normally use three different kinds of questionnaires: (1) the household

---

Box 2.1: Common Uses of LSMS Data

Measurement with reasonable accuracy of:

- number of persons in poverty

- distribution of welfare

- variables that pertain to many individuals or households in the sample, such as employment rates, rates of malnutrition, and mean consumption levels.

Description or analysis of:

- characteristics of different socio-economic groups

- access to or use of major government services (health, education, water supply, electricity, roads)

- participation in large government programs

- incidence of taxes or subsidies on commonly consumed items

- interactions between aspects of welfare, such as the effect of health on labor supply, of parent's education on children's nutrition, or of education on earnings.

Complementary data will usually be required for:

- program impact evaluations

- program cost-effectiveness studies.

LSMS samples are usually too small to allow:

- measurement of variables that pertain to only a few households or individuals, such as infant mortality, patterns of morbidity, and rates of international migration

- description or analysis of government programs that reach only a small part of the population

- description of small socioeconomic groups or geographic units.

---

questionnaire, in which household members are asked about many aspects of the household's welfare, especially consumption, income, and use of social services; (2) the community questionnaire, in which key community leaders and groups are asked about the infrastructure and services available in the community; and (3) the price questionnaire, in which vendors are asked about prices for selected

Box 2.2: Using LSMS Data to Inform Government Policy Choices

The data from LSMS surveys are designed to be used to understand living standards and the effects of government policies. Here we provide some brief examples of how governments and aid agencies are making use of them.

In 1989 the Jamaican government was considering whether to stop subsidizing the prices of basic foods and instead to expand their food stamp program. While the decision was being made, data from their LSMS became available. Analysis showed that most of the benefits from general price subsidies went to the non-poor, while most of the benefits of the food stamps program went to the poor. This helped the government to move ahead with a reform program. The government then commissioned further analysis of the LSMS data to show how many families needed help in purchasing a minimum food basket and how much help. The government used this information to decide on new eligibility thresholds and benefit levels for the food stamp program. While this is perhaps the most concrete single use the Jamaican government has made of the data, they have been used in making other decisions as well — whether to change kerosene subsidies, whether and how to establish a "drug window" in public health clinics, to study the effects of raising user fees for public health care, etc. The survey is conducted annually, and the poverty rates are monitored as well.

In South Africa, the 1993 LSMS survey provided for the first time a comprehensive, credible data set for the entire territory of South Africa, including the homelands. The survey was completed just before the last elections. The data were quickly put to extensive use by the new government and by academic researchers alike. The first product was an extensive statistical abstract, followed by a poverty profile prepared jointly by the Ministry of Reconstruction and Development and the World Bank and other studies and reports. The body of work has helped to shift the discussion in the country from debating the nature and extent of poverty to discussion of options for alleviating poverty. For example, it was decided to admit young women in rural areas to future public works schemes since the data showed that this group was often needy and could obtain child care. Also, because the survey data have revealed that the old age pension program is well targeted, attention has moved on to reforming other programs that may be less well targeted.

In Ecuador, the 1994 LSMS data were used first to produce a poverty assessment. This work was done by the World Bank in 1995 as part of an ongoing effort with the government to develop poverty alleviation strategies. The findings from the report were presented the Cabinet. Wide-ranging discussions identified a number of issues on which the government would like further policy analysis. Arrangements to conduct these will be made over the next few months. The first use will probably be to revise the poverty maps used in targeting many government programs. As is usual, the current poverty maps are based on census data because it allows disaggregation to small geographic areas (parroquias). However, the weighting of the variables used to produce the composite poverty indicator is necessarily ad hoc, since the census contains no direct information on consumption or income. Since the LSMS data contain income and expenditure measures as well as the kind of indicators available in the census, the LSMS data will be used to help select and weight indicators to be used in a revised census-based poverty map. This should enable the government to target its programs more accurately.

items. The information usually collected in these is shown in Box 2.3. A fourth set of questionnaires to collect information about schools or health facilities is sometimes used as well.

HOUSEHOLD QUESTIONNAIRES. The LSMS household questionnaires collect data on several major aspects of household well-being, as shown in Box 2.3. A more detailed summary of all the questionnaires used in Vietnam is included in Annex I. The full household questionnaire used in Côte d'Ivoire is presented and annotated in Grootaert, 1986. The household questionnaire used in Kagera region of Tanzania is presented and annotated in Ainsworth *et al.*, 1992.

Because measuring welfare is a key objective of LSMS surveys, measures of consumption are strongly emphasized in the questionnaires.[3] Detailed questions are asked about cash expenditures, the value of food items grown at home or received as gifts, and ownership of housing and durable goods (for example, cars, televisions, bicycles, and washing machines) to allow a use value to be assigned.[4]

Because understanding household behavior and determining the causes of poverty are also central LSMS objectives, the survey collects a wide range of income measures. For individuals in formal sector jobs, the surveys include detailed questions about wages, bonuses, and various forms of in-kind compensation. Information is sought on secondary as well as principal jobs. At the household level, detailed agricultural and small enterprise modules are designed to yield estimates of net household income from these activities. Other sources of miscellaneous income, such as the receipt of private transfers (e.g., child support or remittances from abroad), public transfers (in cash or in kind), miscellaneous earnings (e.g., lottery winnings), and interest income are recorded as well.

In order to analyze the relationships among different aspects of the household's quality of life, such as the impact of parents' education on child nutrition or the effect of health on employment, it is necessary to collect several

---

3. Consumption-based measures are used in most LSMS studies of welfare. The data are, however, rich enough to allow other indicators of household welfare to be used (See Glewwe and van der Gaag, 1988).

4. These goods are not completely consumed when first acquired but are used over a long period of time. Household welfare due to the ownership of such goods can be based on the estimated yearly rental values of those goods. LSMS surveys collect data that are sufficient to impute rental values for both owner-occupied housing and ownership of durable goods.

Box 2.3: Modules in LSMS Questionnaires

Module	Respondent	Subject
Household Questionnaire		
Household Composition	Head of household/principal respondent	Household roster, demographic data, information on parents of all household members
Consumption Modules		
Food expenditures	Best-informed household member	Food expenditures in the past 14 days and past 12 months; consumption of home production in past 12 months
Non-Food Expenditures	Best-informed household member	Expenditures in the past 14 days and past 12 months; remittances to other households
Housing	Head of household/principal respondent	Type of dwelling; housing and utilities expenditures
Durable Goods	Best-informed household member	Inventory of durable goods and their characteristics
Income-related Modules		
Non-farm self-employment	Best-informed household member for each of three businesses	Income, expenditures, and assets for three most important household businesses
Agro-pastoral activities	Best-informed household member	Land, crops, income, and expenditure from raising crops and animals; livestock and farm equipment inventory
Economic Activities	All household members 7 years and older (all adults must respond for themselves)	Employment, income, and time data for the main and secondary jobs in the last 7 days and the last 12 months; employment history; unemployment spells in the last 12 months; time use in the home
Other income	Best-informed household member	Income from other sources, including remittances from other households
Saving and credit	Best-informed household member	Savings and net debt the day of the interview; characteristics of outstanding loans to and from household members

Box 2.3 continues on next page

Box 2.3 (continued)

Box 2.3: *Modules in LSMS Questionnaires*		
Module	*Respondent*	*Subject*
Sectoral Modules		
Education	Head of household/principal respondent	Completed schooling and schooling expenditures for all household members 5 or older; schooling and other information of all non-member children under 30
Health	All household members (parents respond for young children)	Utilization of health services and medical expenditures for any illness in the last four weeks; utilization of and expenditures for preventive services in the last 12 months
Migration	All household members 15 years and older	Place of birth, time and current place of residence, and reasons for first and last moves
Fertility	One randomly selected woman 15 years or older	Birth history; use of maternity services and duration of breastfeeding for last live birth
Anthropometrics	—	Height and weight measurements of all household members
Community Questionnaire		
Demographics	Community leader	Size, growth, ethnic mix
Economy and Infrastructure	Community leader	Economic activities, access to roads, electricity, water, public services such as public transport, mail service, etc.
Education	Headmaster or Community leader	Location and characteristics of schools serving community
Health	Health workers or Community leader	Location and characteristics of health facilities serving community
Agriculture	Extension agent or Community leader	Farming practices, agricultural services available
Price Questionnaire		
	Market, shops	Prices on frequently purchased items

kinds of sectoral data from each household. The sectoral modules include health, education, fertility, anthropometrics, and migration. The sectoral modules are designed to measure a few key outcomes (such as nutritional status, vaccination rates, incidence of diarrhea among children, and enrollment rates), to measure the use of services that might affect those outcomes, and to supplement information from the rest of the questionnaire to study why households use those services and what factors influence the outcomes.

COMMUNITY QUESTIONNAIRES. To help limit the length of the household questionnaire, the community questionnaire gathers information on local conditions that are common to all households in the area. This questionnaire is typically used only in rural areas, where local communities are easier to define. The information covered by the questionnaire typically includes the location and quality of nearby health facilities and schools, the condition of local infrastructure such as roads, sources of fuel and water, availability of electricity, means of communications, and local agricultural conditions and practices.

PRICE QUESTIONNAIRES. In countries where prices vary considerably among regions, it is important to gather information on the prices that households actually pay for goods and services.[5] The price questionnaires compile information on the prices of the most important items that a household (particularly a poor household) must buy and that are widely available throughout the country. The prices are gathered in markets or shops in the communities where the households live.

SPECIAL FACILITY QUESTIONNAIRES. Sometimes special questionnaires are designed to gather detailed information on schools or health facilities. These have been used in at least one year of the surveys in Côte d'Ivoire, Ghana, Morocco, Jamaica, and Tanzania.

The rest of the manual refers to "the questionnaire" as though there were only one instrument instead of separate instruments for household, community, price, and facility information. This is conceptually, if not physically, accurate. In formulating the contents of each questionnaire the planners must ensure that the information serves the survey's analytical goals and is collected in an efficient manner. In formatting, the same principles apply to all the questionnaires, although some of the techniques may be more commonly used in one than another. The same principles of data processing apply. Occasionally the logistics of how questionnaires are managed may diverge, but this is done for convenience rather than because of conceptual differences.

---

5. See Ravallion and Bidani, 1994.

There has been substantial variation among the questionnaires used in different countries.[6] The features discussed here may have been changed or omitted in specific cases because the objectives of the survey or country circumstances differed. Nonetheless, there are more commonalities than differences.

Quality Control

In addition to sharing common objectives and questionnaire content, the LSMS surveys use an extensive set of procedures to minimize errors and delays in data collection and processing. The reasons why each is used and how it is implemented are discussed in detail in the rest of this manual. Briefly, quality control elements include the following:

QUESTIONNAIRE FORMAT. A single paper questionnaire is used to obtain information on the household and the different individuals and businesses within it. The questionnaires are designed to minimize errors by the interviewer and other survey staff. The questionnaires are pre-coded, with extensive use of explicit skip patterns.

SAMPLING. The need to minimize non-sampling error is given heavy weight in decisions about sample size. Coupled with the analytic objectives of the surveys, this leads to small samples — usually on the order of 2,000-5,000 households.

FIELDWORK. Fieldwork and data entry are decentralized and supervision is very strict. A small number of highly trained interviewers is used, with the fieldwork spread over a full year. Each household is visited twice, two weeks apart. In each visit, a series of "mini-interviews" with the different members of the household is conducted. Since each adult responds for him/herself, the errors that can be introduced by proxy respondents or respondent fatigue are minimized.

DATA MANAGEMENT. Data entry and editing are carried out in the field concurrently with data collection, usually in the local survey offices. As data are entered, a number of data quality checks are carried out by the data entry program. This allows errors or inconsistencies found in the first half of the questionnaire to be checked during the second visit to the household.

---

6. In addition to standard changes in vocabulary required to make a questionnaire relevant to a given country, the major differences include: (i) some modules have been excluded in some countries; (ii) the level of detail has varied widely within each module; (iii) the direct outcome measures (height, weight, upper arm circumference, cognitive skills) and the group of respondents for which they were measured have differed; (iv) the extent of price, community, or facility questionnaires has differed; and (v) a few LSMS surveys are actually linked to other surveys. In these cases, the LSMS questionnaires omit some modules for which information is gathered in the linked survey and the data sets from the two surveys must be merged for analysis.

An important hallmark of LSMS surveys, and one of the reasons for their success, is the large role that analysts play in developing the whole survey. Not only is the questionnaire content determined by analysts who will actually use the data, their input is also used in field testing, in training field workers, in sampling, and in data management.

The work program for implementing an LSMS survey is divided into three phases. The planning stage often lasts about a year, the field work is scheduled to take place over a full year, and the initial analytic phase of producing an abstract, documenting the data, and setting up other analyses may take about six months.

The survey planner (e.g. the reader of this document) must realize that the many activities involved in planning the survey take place concurrently and that decisions in one area have repercussions for other areas. How to do the most important of these activities (designing the questionnaire, designing and drawing the sample, preparing for field work, preparing the data management system, and beginning to think about data analysis) is described in the following chapters. How long each of these may take under different circumstances and how they must be interlinked in time is discussed in detail in Chapter 8.

The formal budgets for LSMS surveys have varied widely from country to country, with a range from $155,000 to about $3,000,000. There is a preponderance of formal budgets in the neighborhood of $750,000 to $1,000,000, but the "prototype" all-inclusive budget developed in Chapter 8 is for $1,300,000. The differences are so big for three reasons. First, many of the inputs used are often supplied in-kind by either the national statistical agency or the external agency helping to finance the survey, and thus are omitted from the budget. Second, the amount of various inputs may vary from country to country depending on the survey design and the existing institutional capacity. Third, the unit prices for locally supplied inputs may vary greatly from country to country.

B. Variations from the Prototype

The LSMS surveys are not a static, uniform product. Each is unique and sometimes their differences are considerable. This can be seen from Table 2.1, which lists surveys that share some or all of the characteristics of the LSMS

Table 2.1: *Description of LSMS-Type Surveys by Country*[a]

| | Basic Information | | | | | | Content | | | | |
Country	Year of First Survey	Number of Rounds Fielded to Date	Number of Households in Sample	Interview Schedule	Panel	HH Questionnaire Scope	Price Questionnaire	Community Questionnaire	Facility Questionnaire	Educational Testing[b]	Anthropometrics
Côte d'Ivoire	1985/86	4	1600	year-round	rotating	full	yes	yes	no	none	all
Peru 1985	1985/86	1	5120	year-round	no	full	yes	yes	no	none	none
Ghana	1987/88	2	3200	year-round	no	full	yes	yes	health/ed	9-55,m,r,R	all
Mauritania	1987	2	1488	year-round	no	full	yes	yes	no	none	all
Bolivia	1989	5	10,000	wave	no	truncated	no	no	no	none	no
Jamaica	1988	8	2000-6000	wave	some	truncated	no	no	sometimes	7-18,m,r	child < 5
Morocco	1990/91	1	3360	year-round	no	full	yes	no	health	9-69,r,m	< 11, parents
Pakistan	1991	1	4800	year-round	no	full	yes	yes	health, ed	none	< 5, mother
Peru 1990/91/94	1991	1	1500/2200/3500	wave	85/90/91/94 Lima; 91-94 elsewhere	full	no	no	no	none	child < 5
Venezuela	1991	3	14,000	wave	yes	truncated	no	no	no	none	child < 5
Vietnam	1992/93	1	4800	year-round	no	full	yes	yes	no	none	all, h/w/c
Nicaragua	1993	1	4200	wave	no	truncated	yes	yes	no	none	child < 5
Guyana	1992/93	1	5340	wave	no	truncated	no	no	no	none	child < 5
Tanzania - national	1993	1	5200	wave	no	truncated	yes	no	no	none	no
Tanzania - Kagera Region	1991	4	800	year round	4 period	expanded	yes	yes	health, edu, healers, NGOs	none	all
South Africa	1993	1	9000	wave	no	full	yes	yes	no	some	child < 5
Romania	1994/95	continuous	36,000	continuous	yes	full	no	no	no	none	child < 5
Ecuador	1994	1	4500	wave	no	full	no	yes	no	none	no

Note: a. Researchers interested in using data from these surveys should refer to Grosh and Glewwe (1995).
   b. In the column "Educational Testing": numbers indicate age range to which applied; codes are m = mathematics, r = reading, R = Ravens Progressive Matrices Test.

surveys.[7] More differences are expected to crop up in the future, and these may become increasingly large.

Common Variants

The most common variants on the prototype are sketched here.

TRUNCATED QUESTIONNAIRES. The questionnaire has been severely truncated in some cases. This limits the range of possible analysis. The most common case is to forgo attempts to use income as a measure of household welfare and to understand the choices that households make about income generation. Sometimes community or price questionnaires are omitted. Another less common variation is to adapt a core and rotating module design in a multi-year survey plan.[8] The core questionnaire would allow the measurement of consumption and a reduced set of other indicators of welfare and use of services. Each year a module of special emphasis studies a particular topic in depth. This maintains some, but not all, of the possibilities of intersectoral work that is one of the objectives of the prototype LSMS questionnaire.

Modifying the questionnaire always affects what analysis is possible. It does not necessarily affect how sampling, field work, or data management is done. Therefore it will not be discussed further in this manual.

SINGLE INTERVIEW. Some surveys plan for each village and household to be visited only once. Until recently, this has only been the case when the questionnaires were severely truncated, but in the Nepal survey now in the field each village will be visited once but the full questionnaire will be maintained. Each household's interview will be conducted in more than one session if necessary for convenience of the household, but not out of strict protocol for the survey.

The use of a single interview usually means that the standard checks on data quality from the first interview and correction during the second interview

---

7. There are other surveys that have objectives as similar to the LSMS "prototype" as some of those listed in this table. The Integrated Surveys in The Gambia, Guinea, Madagascar, Senegal, and Uganda, supported by the Social Dimensions of Adjustment project in the World Bank, or the RAND-sponsored Family Life Surveys in Malaysia and Indonesia, are examples. These are similar in spirit, but are omitted here because the authors do not know enough about how they were carried out to use them as illustrations in this manual. The surveys arranged by the Cornell Food and Nutrition Policy Program in Guinea and Mozambique and those carried out by the University of North Carolina Population Center in Russia and the Kyrgyz Republic are also very similar in spirit. Since we know more about how these were conducted, we will draw examples from them.

8. Discussions of core and rotating module surveys can be found in Grosh, 1991 for the case of Jamaica, and World Bank, 1993 for Indonesia.

are not possible. There are also other minor implications for field operations and data management, which will be discussed in Chapter 5. The single visit to the household also eliminates the use of the recall period bounded between the two interviews, which has implications for the measurement of consumption.

CONCENTRATED PERIOD OF FIELD WORK. In some countries the field work has been carried out in just a few weeks or months rather than spread throughout the year. With respect to analysis, this limits the ability to study seasonality and affects how to calculate annualized values of income and consumption. It also has major implications for the organization of field work and data management, which will be discussed in Chapter 5.

REFORMS OF EXISTING SURVEYS. Finally, some countries are using parts of the LSMS experience not to carry out full-fledged LSMS surveys but to reform ongoing surveys. In some cases they have added modules to questionnaires, in others they have adapted some of the features of field work or data management to improve data quality or the speed with which results are processed, and sometimes they have done both.

Evolution in LSMS Surveys

This manual presents information on what has proved useful in the surveys conducted in the last 10 years. Much of what has been learned is expected to continue to be relevant, though the way in which the principles espoused here are put into practice will evolve. The principal types of changes expected include the following:

CHANGING PURPOSE. The early LSMS surveys were carried out as research projects. Their first goal was to determine whether it was feasible to gather such comprehensive data sets. Their second goal was to conduct research to better understand household behavior and its implications for the design of government programs. Emphasis was on analysis of the determinants of welfare and their interactions, rather than on precise measurement of a few aspects of welfare. When the first surveys proved feasible and their analyses fruitful, policymakers and their advisors realized that data from the surveys could be very useful in policymaking. The descriptions of the welfare of the population and of the use of government services were especially valued. Some of the results from the more sophisticated studies of the determinants of welfare and the impact of policies were also valued by the operations audience, but perhaps less so than by the academic community.

The shift in motivation for the surveys is leading to changes in them and to considerable variation from country to country. Some of the content is being adjusted. Often there is a desire to have the estimates of indicators be accurate at sub-national levels. This requires a much larger sample and thus calls into question whether quality and comprehensiveness can be maintained. Attention is more often being given to developing local capacity, both for data collection and for data analysis.

CHANGING ACTORS. The cast of actors involved in implementing new surveys has changed greatly in the last five years. In the early years of the LSMS surveys, the LSMS division of the World Bank wore many hats simultaneously. It usually provided the impetus to carry out a survey in a particular country, often arranged and administered financing, provided all technical assistance, and was often the main user of the data. Now these hats are being worn by many different actors. Indeed, several LSMS-type surveys have been developed without any involvement at all from the LSMS division of the World Bank. Its various functions are being parceled out to the national planning agency, to operational staff in the World Bank, to other international agencies, or to technical assistants.

Since these alternative arrangements are new and varied, institutional methods that have worked in the past may need to be modified for some tasks, such as designing a questionnaire or organizing field work and data management. The survey planner who reads this manual will need an extra dose of imagination in determining how to apply the suggestions provided here to the institutional circumstances relevant for the particular country.

CHANGING TECHNOLOGICAL ENVIRONMENT. Many of the practical issues in survey implementation are heavily influenced by available technology. Every technological change has implications for survey management, for technical assistance and training, and sometimes for costs. Three changes in technology — improved data entry programs, more portable hardware, and computer-assisted interviewing — may affect how LSMS surveys are implemented in the future. These innovations are already in view, and more are surely developing.

Commercially supported data entry packages may soon supersede the customized data entry programs that have been used for LSMS surveys to date. When these packages are used, the amount of technical assistance or training required in the use of the software may be reduced, but it will still be important to ensure that there is adequate understanding of the conceptual issues of handling hierarchical file structures and determining range and consistency checks.

Hardware has evolved to the point where it would be simple to take the data entry function on the road with the interviewers rather than having the data entry operator and computer located at a base station. This will change some aspects of the day-to-day management of field work and quality control. Such a system is being used in the survey underway in Nepal as this manual is being written.

Advances in computer technology permit a still more ambitious proposition. Interviewers can enter data directly into a portable computer during the interview, thus eliminating the paper questionnaires completely. This system has been piloted already in Bolivia and is scheduled for piloting in the Indonesia Family Life Survey in 1996. The elimination of the paper questionnaire will require fundamental new approaches to how to involve all the right people in questionnaire design, how to organize and supervise field work, establish quality control systems, and manage data.

Chapter 3. Questionnaire Development

Key Messages

- The process of defining the content of the questionnaire must be driven by analysts and by policy needs.

- Formatting a questionnaire is a complex art and proper formatting is critical to survey success. It must be done by the survey planners and not relegated to lower-level or clerical staff.

- The field test is also critical to the success of the survey.

- For advice on formulating questionnaire content, survey planners must read the cited materials, especially Grootaert (1986) and Ainsworth and van der Gaag (1988) and the new set of revised questionnaire modules that should be available in final form in 1998 and in draft form sometime in 1996.

Those who have never had to analyze data from a questionnaire they have developed themselves may think that designing a questionnaire is easy. It is not. This chapter first gives an overview of the process of developing a questionnaire. It then discusses in detail how to produce a workable format. Sections A and B are recommended for all readers, while the Section C may be skimmed lightly by those who are not involved in designing a questionnaire. For those who want more background and detail on general issues in questionnaire design, UNNHSCP (1985) is a useful introductory manual.

A. Questionnaire Content

The most important issues in designing a questionnaire are the analytic objectives and measurement techniques to be used. Indeed, these are so important that they are treated separately in other LSMS documents. LSMS standards for the objectives of the surveys and information requirements stemming from them are explained in Grootaert (1986) and Ainsworth and van der Gaag (1988). The closely related Integrated Survey supported for African countries by the Social Dimensions of Adjustment project is described in Delaine *et al.* (1992). A number of LSMS working papers on measurement were written before formulation of the LSMS questionnaires. The complete list of working papers is provided in Annex III. As this manual is being drafted, the LSMS division of the World Bank is embarking on a review of the first 10 years of field experience to determine how questionnaires might need alteration, either because of changing objectives in LSMS surveys or to improve accuracy. The first results of the planned review will be available in about 1996 and are recommended to interested readers.

B. The Process of Questionnaire Development

Perhaps the most important way to ensure a successful questionnaire is to make sure that the right kinds of people are involved in its design. The second most important thing is to allow enough time and repeated iterations in the questionnaire development process. The third critical element is the field test.

The Actors

THE ANALYSTS. The importance of the analyst in questionnaire design cannot be overemphasized. Much of the success of the LSMS stems from the fact that the questionnaires are designed by analysts.

Drafting the questionnaire and coordinating inputs from others is usually best assigned to a small group of analysts who share two characteristics: First, they should know what subjects are of policy and analytic interest to the country. Second, they should have experience using data from similar surveys on a variety of topics. The team might be composed of one person from the national planning agency, one from academia, and one person who has helped analyze or design LSMS surveys in other countries.

It is crucial for the team to have extensive local expertise when designing the questionnaire. Indeed, it is preferable for local analysts to take primary responsibility. They bring an irreplaceable knowledge of the country's society and of existing programs and they know what issues should be emphasized. They may be familiar with earlier local surveys about some of the topics covered by the LSMS, which will help them design precoded questions. Further, they will know the network of people and institutions that should be contacted during the survey design process.

Sometimes it is also desirable to have international analysts involved in questionnaire design, especially where local analysts are not familiar with surveys that have objectives similar to those of the LSMS. The international analysts can bring experience about what has worked in other LSMS surveys and why. Judicious use of past experience, rather than blind replication of old questionnaires that are ill-adapted to present circumstances, is probably best ensured by this balance of local and foreign expertise.

Most LSMS surveys have probably erred on the side of having too little local input. Where local input has been obtained, it has often been provided by statisticians from the statistical agency (data producers) rather than from social policy analysts or from government and academia (data users). The statisticians often have only a limited knowledge of sectoral policy issues and programs. They can improve nomenclature and precoding, but are not necessarily qualified to help set priorities among different possible objectives.

POLICYMAKERS.   In defining the basic and subsidiary objectives of the survey, the team responsible for drafting the questionnaire must seek extensive input from policymakers and program managers. The first level is to decide what important issues should be covered. This will help establish the relative weight of the different modules in the questionnaire. Then the important issues can be identified within sectors. Once these are outlined, the question writers may also have to learn a fair amount about how specific programs work. This means that interviews with technical level people in many agencies may be needed. Once this information is available the actual drafting of the questionnaire may begin. Box 3.1 shows how progressively greater detail is required at each level of the process.

The step of ensuring adequate communication and consultation with policymakers is usually given much less attention than it deserves. People who are unfamiliar with survey work may find it difficult to read complicated

---

Box 3.1: Levels of Refinement in Determining Questionnaire Content

Writing the questionnaire involves moving from knowing the importance of broad issues to getting the details of specific questions straight. This box illustrates the successive levels of details required.

Overarching Objectives:
Define the objectives: for example, to study poverty; to understand the effects of government policies on households

Balance between Sectors
Define which issues are most important: for example, the incidence of food price subsidies; the effect of changes in the accessibility or cost of government health and education services; the effect of changes in the economic climate due to structural adjustment or transition from a centrally planned to a market economy.

Balance within Sectors
Within the education sector, define which of the following are the most important for the country and moment: the levels and determinants of enrollment, poor attendance, learning, and differences in male and female indicators; the impact of the number of years of schooling on earnings in the formal sector and agriculture and the question of how or if they differ; which children have textbooks or receive school lunches or scholarships; how much parents have to pay for schooling.

Write Questions to Study Specific Issues or Programs
In a case where it is decided that it is important to study who has access to textbooks, for example, the question writer will need to know: how many different subjects are supposed to have textbooks available; if the books to be given out by the government are to be given to each child individually or are to be shared; if they are to be taken home or used only in the classroom; if they are to be used for only one year or several; if they are to be paid for; when the books are supposed to be available; and are textbooks bought from bookshops better or worse than those provided by the school.

questionnaires and imagine what analyses will be possible. It is therefore preferable to show policymakers and program managers examples of tables or other analyses that could be produced from it along with the questionnaire itself. These may be dummy tables or examples of work done for other countries on the basis of similar questions. Where surveys are planned to be repeated in successive years, the first year's abstract is an excellent tool for obtaining feedback from policymakers for use in the future. A complementary strategy is to ask the policymakers what they want to know. Then the survey designer can translate that need into appropriate questions or modules in the questionnaire.

THE DATA PRODUCERS. Input from the data manager is essential in questionnaire design. Often the data management process can be greatly simplified by minor changes in the layout or flow of the questionnaire that do not detract from its analytic content. The data manager should comment on every draft (see Box 3.2).

It is also useful to have the input of the field manager, who will notice whether the instructions to the interviewer are clear, if the skip codes are correct, and if the format is consistent. There is, of course, a natural tension between the analysts, who want comprehensive information, and the field manager, who is likely to see all the disadvantages but few of the advantages of a lengthy, complex

---

Box 3.2: Synergy in Elements of Questionnaire Design

There is great synergy between the different aspects of questionnaire design — defining analytic content, simplifying field work, and specifying of the data and quality checks. The story of the mother/father questions on the LSMS roster illustrates how a single change can serve all purposes.

The traditional method of assembling a roster establishes who is the head of household and then asks for the relationship between the head and each household member. Where family structure is complex, this can require many codes and the relationships between various individuals often remain unclear. For example, is the sister of the head of household the mother or the aunt of the nephew of the head of household?

In Côte d'Ivoire in 1985 the writer of the data entry program suggested adding separate follow-up questions after the traditional relationship-to-head question. These asked whether the spouse, the father, and the mother of each household member was in the household and, if so, what their identification codes were. The data manager suggested these questions to allow powerful consistency checks on the age, sex, marital status, and relationship-to-head-of-household variables. The change also simplified field work by reducing the complexity of codes needed for the relationship-to-head-of-household variable. But perhaps the most important contribution has been analytic. Knowing which household members are the parents of the children in the household has proved helpful in modeling the determinants of child welfare, especially when addressing intra-household bargaining — an issue that was hardly even on the analytic agenda at the time the innovation was made. Needless to say, this system has been recommended ever since.

questionnaire because field workers do not usually analyze the information they collect.

A real life story can illustrate the risks of not having the right kinds of people involved in questionnaire design. The questionnaire for the first year of the Jamaica Survey of Living Conditions (1988) was devised largely by the international technical assistants who knew little of Jamaican social programs. Though largely successful in accomplishing its analytic objectives and well formatted, the questionnaire ended up with three important program-specific flaws. First, the consumption section lumped together one of the main subsidized staples with one of the main non-subsidized staples, making the study of the incidence of food subsidies cumbersome and probably inaccurate, although changes in food subsidy policy was one of big issues being debated at the time. Second, the reference period on receipt of food stamps was given as a month, although the stamps are only received every two months, again making difficult the study of incidence, which was an important issue at the time. Thirdly, the education module used was very similar to that used in previous LSMS surveys where the purpose was to study the determinants of enrollment in primary school. Since primary school enrollment in Jamaica is universal, nothing very interesting was learned and the opportunity to study issues important in Jamaica, such as daily attendance, the extent of the textbook or the school feeding programs, or patterns of secondary enrollment was missed. Fortunately, the Jamaican version of the LSMS is conducted annually. Thus these flaws were corrected in the second year's questionnaire. Moreover, they were pointed out in the draft abstract from the first year. They thus served as vivid examples to many of the people who were involved in managing the survey from the second year on of the importance of their input. In the end, this pedagogic purpose was quite useful.

The Iterative Process

The process of questionnaire development is an iterative one. After an initial version is drafted, it should be reviewed in detail by the various interested parties. The next draft takes the assembled criticisms into account. This process may be repeated several times. Translations may be required (see Box 3.3). A seminar may be conducted and further revisions done. Then a field test is conducted and the questionnaire revised again. Depending on the extent of revisions, a second field test may be needed for some parts of the questionnaire.

A few concrete indicators of the extent of revisions that may be done at each stage may be useful. It is completely standard that the international technical assistants write letters of 20 or more (single spaced) pages pointing out imperfections in the substantive formulation or formatting of the questionnaires, even when these are on their third or fourth draft. Often two or more people will write such letters and only about half of their remarks will overlap, the others will relate to imperfections the other has missed. When the changes are suggested on the questionnaire itself, it is rare that a single page not be marked

25

Translation may be required for three reasons, which have different implications for logistics. Most importantly and most commonly, the survey may need to be administered in several languages. In the many countries where more than one language is spoken, good quality control for the field work requires providing written, verbatim questionnaires in as many of the languages as practical. Research reported by Scott and others (1988) demonstrates the importance of this.   They conducted an experiment to measure interviewer errors when the interviewer was asked to provide verbal field interpretations — e.g., to use a questionnaire written in English to conduct an interview in Tagalog or Cebuano or to use a French questionnaire to conduct an interview in Baoule or Dioula. Interviewer error rates were two to four times higher with oral field interpretations than with written translations of the questionnaires.

When the reason for doing translations is to administer the final questionnaire in several languages, the preliminary drafts of the questionnaire can be developed only in the official language. Ideally, the questionnaire should then be translated and field tested in each language in which it will finally be written. In fact, the field test is often done using oral interpretations of the official language version of the questionnaire only.   Thus the wording in the local language interviews during the field test may not correspond exactly to the verbatim wording worked out later for the written translations into local languages. While imperfect, this is often viewed as a reasonable tradeoff against the difficulties of field testing in each language.

When translating questionnaires, the classic practice is to translate from the language in which they were developed into the language(s) in which they will be administered and then translate them back into the original language. After the back translation, the two versions in the first language should be compared. Where the wording or meaning is different, the translation should be adjusted. The first translation should be done by a person or group of persons familiar with the purpose of the questions. The back translation should be done by someone who was not intimately involved in designing the questionnaire in order to avoid contaminating the interpretation with prior knowledge.

Most LSMS questionnaires are printed in only in the official language(s) of the country and multilingual interviewing teams are used for the most common local languages. In this case a few key questions or phrases may be translated into these languages and presented in the interviewer manual.   For less commonly spoken languages, local interpreters may have to be used. In this, the LSMS surveys have been within the range of normal survey practice, but behind the cutting edge of quality control. The cutting edge is defined by the World Fertility Survey, which used as a guideline that questionnaires should be prepared in any language that would account for more than 10 percent of the sample and that a minimum of 80 percent of the sample should be covered with a verbatim questionnaire in the language of interview.

A second reason for translations is that sometimes international technical assistants do not speak the predominant language of the country well enough to assist in designing the questionnaire directly in the official language of the country. The Vietnamese LSMS questionnaire, for example, was developed jointly in English and Vietnamese.   In the Latin

Box 3.3 continued on next page

Box 3.3 (continued)

American countries, in contrast, the LSMS questionnaires have usually been drafted directly in Spanish. When translation is required as part of questionnaire development, it becomes necessary to update the translation of each draft, which can require substantial time and money.

Finally, translating questionnaires from the local official language to one or more of the major international languages (English, Spanish, or French) for the international research community can help stimulate data analysis that may be of interest to local policymakers. These translations may be done after the final questionnaire is developed, and back translations can be omitted.

Questionnaires should always be worded in simple terms used in the language as commonly spoken rather than in academic or formal language. The gap between the spoken and written languages and the difficulty of balancing simplicity and precision may be greater in local languages, especially those that are not commonly used in writing. The translations should therefore be especially careful in finding an appropriate balance. Let us illustrate the kind of problem that may occur. The question "¿Estuvo enferma en las ultimas cuatro semanas?" literally asks, in Spanish, whether the respondent was sick in the last four weeks. But in Chilean common language, it could be understood as being a polite euphemism for asking whether a woman has had a menstrual period in the last four weeks. An even more difficult problem in wording was revealed in the field test in Nepal. Apparently the most natural Nepali phrasing for "have you been ill?" is closer to "have you been to the doctor?" The change in meaning from what was intended was revealed when several respondents answered "no, I couldn't afford to go," an inappropriate response to "have you been ill?"

in red ink on the first couple of drafts. The formulation of the Nicaraguan LSMS questionnaire, which was not subject to unusual difficulties, took nine months and produced a foot-high stack of different versions of questionnaires.

Appropriate input from all the actors can be sought through the aggressive pursuit of informal contacts. However, it is often preferable to add formal elements to the process as well.

One option is to create a user committee. It can have several roles:

- it provides a forum to balance diverse objectives of the survey;

- it provides a mechanism by which any interested individual or agency can make suggestions for the survey (either through their representative on the committee or through addressing themselves to the committee as a whole);

- the committee members can help facilitate access to individuals and information in their agencies that is required by the team drafting the questionnaire; and

- it provides one mechanism for the plans and results of the survey to be known by policymakers;[9] and

- because the members of the committee are familiar with both the policy questions and the survey's content, they are well positioned to foster data analysis.

The user committee should not assume too much authority for the technical and day-to-day management of the survey. For example, the committee should not be involved in the details of questionnaire format or the brand of computers to be purchased by the survey organization. Instead, the committee should help set the objectives of the survey, which have implications for questionnaire content, sample design, and cost.

The user committee might be chaired by the national planning agency or co-chaired by the planning and statistical agencies. Members should come from the sectoral ministries whose interests are of greatest concern in the surveys (such as health, education, welfare, agriculture, and family or women's affairs). Members of the policy research community (universities, independent research institutes, and international development agencies) should be included as well. It is ideal if the individuals who serve on the committee know about surveys, are interested in the policies to be studied by the LSMS, and come from appropriate parts of their agencies. Where that is not possible, it may be preferable to choose them based on their interest and knowledge rather than their institutional affiliation.

A formal seminar can also be a useful tool. The presentations could explain the plans for the survey, including its objectives, the questionnaires, sample plan, and approach to field work. Some general background on LSMS surveys elsewhere might also be included. The presentations should clearly define which decisions have already been firmly taken and are not open to change, and which on which elements feedback is sought. It is usually necessary to mention any refinements in the draft questionnaire have been made between the time it was circulated prior to the seminar and the date of the seminar. The bulk of the discussion should solicit feedback on the content of the questionnaires and the plans for analysis. The participants should include staff from all the concerned government agencies, several local research institutions, and international development agencies. A seminar has the advantage of being able to involve a larger number of people than informal meetings or a user committee. It also means that those providing feedback do not need to draft formal written comments and can provide input immediately.

---

9. Of course, many other complementary mechanisms should be pursued as well.

The field test is one of the most critical steps of survey preparation. Its goal is to ensure that the questionnaires are capable of collecting the information they are supposed to collect. The LSMS field test addresses the adequacy of the questionnaires at three levels:

QUESTIONNAIRE AS A WHOLE. Is the full range of required information collected? Is the information collected by different parts of the questionnaire consistent? Are there any unintentional double counts of some variables?

AT THE LEVEL OF INDIVIDUAL MODULES. Does the module collect the intended information? Have all major activities been accounted for? Are all major living arrangements, agricultural activities, and sources of in-kind and cash income accounted for? Are some questions irrelevant?

AT THE LEVEL OF INDIVIDUAL QUESTIONS. Is the wording clear? Does the question allow ambiguous responses? Are there alternative interpretations? Have all responses been anticipated?

It is important to obtain good coverage of all major socioeconomic groups in the field test. For example, sampled households should include those that are rural and those that are urban; individuals employed in the formal sector, in the informal sector, and farmers; farmers in the main agroecological regions and production schemes (independent, cooperative, and wage earners), and so forth. The households should not be selected at random. Instead, different types should be purposely included so that the various situations likely to be found during the survey are observed during the field test.

LSMS field tests usually conduct interviews in about 100 households. To get enough responses for some sections of the questionnaire, it may be necessary to visit extra households and conduct only partial interviews. For example, the original 100 households may not include enough pregnant women or people who have been ill in the month before the interview to test those modules effectively. In such a case, households with pregnant women or ill people should be located and interviewed using the health module.[10] A field test usually takes about one month to complete. More time is required if the final questionnaires are to be

---

10. An alternative approach is to stretch the reference periods during the field test. For instance, instead of asking "were you ill or injured during the last 30 days?" as in the actual survey, it may be expedient to ask "were you ill or injured in the past 12 months?" or "when was the last time you were ill or injured?" This approach will simplify the logistics of finding enough persons to put through the module, but will not test as exactly whether they have problems recalling the information since the recall period used in the field test will be longer than that in the final questionnaire.

produced in more than one language, because each version of the questionnaire should be field tested.

While a final large (100 households or so) field test is desirable, quite a lot can be learned from smaller tests. As a general rule of thumb, half of the problems will probably show up in the first ten households interviewed. In one recent field test, the international technical assistants found enough fodder after three households to write six pages of comments about a single module. Such small tests may be particularly appropriate on new or difficult modules as a preamble to a fuller test of the whole questionnaire.

The personnel involved in the field test should be the core headquarters team, a few experienced interviewers or field supervisors, and the analysts who helped design the questionnaire. It may also be helpful to include persons with experience in other LSMS surveys. The people should work in teams, and each team should include representatives with each kind of expertise.

The number of teams involved in the field test should be kept small. Mechanisms should be set up to allow contact between them during the field test so they can compare notes on problems they encounter and solutions they have tried. Perhaps the best way to accomplish this is to have all the teams involved in the field test work for the first few days in one of the main cities. This way the teams can be in contact each evening when the first and often biggest flaws in the draft questionnaire are uncovered. Agreements can be reached on modifying the questionnaire during the field test itself.

Each interview during the field test should include the respondent, the interviewer, and an analyst or senior survey specialist. During the field test, it is acceptable to tactfully interrupt the interview in order to refine the wording of a question or the responses coded for it (of course in the actual survey, the interviews should be conducted in private and the wording on the questionnaire respected).

The interviewers used for the field test should be drawn from the agency's pool of experienced staff. In training for the field test it is assumed that the participants are generally good interviewers familiar with basic interviewing practices and able to distinguish between problems caused by deficiencies in the questionnaire and problems caused by their lack of familiarity with it. Training focuses on the purpose of the survey and the structure and format of the questionnaire. Usually one week is adequate.

One to two weeks at the end of the field test should be set aside to review the results from it and to agree on what changes are required. Essentially, the group involved in the field test should go through the questionnaires module by module and discuss any issues that arose. The inevitable concern that the interviews are too long should be tempered by the knowledge that the time required for an interview falls dramatically when the interviewers are well trained and have become familiar with the questionnaire — usually to half or less of the time taken in the field test.

It is not necessary to enter the data from the field test, since the sample is so small and non-random that it is difficult to make any decisions based on the statistics produced.[11]

The *personal* participation of all senior staff (including analysts) is fundamental for both the field test and its evaluation. An anecdote will illustrate this. In one country, prior to the field test, a manager in the statistics office asserted that collecting information on family assets would be impossible because respondents would fear that the information would be used for taxation. The module was included in the field test and no unusual difficulties were encountered. But the prime opponent of the module did not witness the field test and some of those who did participate in the field test had to miss the module's evaluation. Despite the successful field experience, the module was removed from the questionnaire, largely because key decisionmakers only participated in part of the process.

Many small changes will probably result from field testing, including changes in wording of questions, the format of the questionnaire, and the answer codes. If major modifications are indicated for the questionnaire's structure or in the way concepts are measured, the modified questions must be re-tested. For this reason it is sometimes desirable to begin the field test with alternate versions of particularly difficult, contentious, or important modules of the questionnaire.

Ideally the community and price questionnaires should be field tested at the same or very nearly the same time as the household questionnaire. This allows the analysts involved to treat the resulting information as a single body and to take into account changes on one instrument that may have repercussions for other instruments. It can also reduce travel costs, since the community and price questionnaires should be tested in a variety of locations.

In fact, experience with LSMS surveys has been that field testing of the community and price questionnaires is often neglected in favor of concentrating on the household questionnaire. The community and price modules may be tested late and haphazardly or even not at all. It is probably not coincidental that users of the data seem to have more complaints about the community and price data than about the household data. If staff time constraints make it preferable that the questionnaires not be tested all at once, it is at least important to ensure that each is tested well.

---

11. The questionnaires from the field test will, however, be useful fodder for testing the data entry program.

The detailed facility questionnaires have sometimes been nearly as complex as the household questionnaire. Field testing facility questionnaires is essential and that has, in fact, been the practice. Care should be taken to visit facilities in each of the major categories expected to be of analytic interest. For example, to field test a health facility questionnaire, visits might be made to public health posts, public clinics, private doctors' offices, public hospitals, and private hospitals, each in rural and urban areas. Since facility field tests are major undertakings in their own right, it is probably best to conduct them separately from the testing of the other questionnaires.

C. Questionnaire Format

The questionnaire's format is important because it clarifies the analytic objectives. Furthermore, a good format minimizes potential interviewer and data entry errors, thus improving data quality and improving the timeliness with which the data are available. While some of the contents will need to be changed from country to country, almost all of what has been learned about questionnaire formats in LSMS surveys is applicable to new countries. This section discusses characteristics that should be replicated in all LSMS surveys (and, in fact, are good practice for other surveys as well).

UNITS OF OBSERVATION. The art of designing a complex survey questionnaire is, to a large extent, the art of choosing appropriate units of observation. Often this is simple: for example, sex and age are clearly attributes of individuals, while the roofing material of the dwelling is an attribute of the household.

Sometimes, however, it may not be obvious what the most natural level of observation is. To collect information on animal assets for a rural household, for instance, one could choose to observe individual animals and record things like species, breed, age, and size. Alternatively, observers could note the animal species and then ask the farmer how many of these animals are owned, what it costs to feed them, and so forth. Precise definition of units of observation is especially important in LSMS surveys because so many units are used. The Kagera Health and Development Survey, for example, uses 22 separate units of observation in the household questionnaire alone (see Box 6.1).

The choice of the unit of observation will largely be determined by the information's expected analytic use. The designer's judgement on the cost or reliability of the information obtained may also affect the choice. For example, if the objective is to study how education affects wages, income data must necessarily be collected at the individual level, since education can only be observed at the individual level. Alternatively, if the analytic objective is to describe the regional incidence of poverty, knowing income at the household level suffices. It may nonetheless be preferable to gather the information separately for each wage earner and household enterprise and then aggregate it to get household income on the grounds that this method probably yields more accurate information than a general question on total household income.

IDENTIFIERS. Each object observed in the survey must be uniquely identified. This usually requires two or three separate codes. The first code always identifies the household. The second code identifies the individual, business, or plot of land. Sometimes a third level applies, for example, all children ever born to each woman in the household or a series of assets for each business.

The importance of adequate identifiers is so obvious that it is hard to believe that mistakes can be made, but they can. In one health survey we know of, the questionnaire consisted of two sheets of paper stapled together. One had information on the household, the other on individuals. In order to facilitate data entry, the pages of the questionnaire were separated. Unfortunately, the household identifier was not put on the page for individuals, so it was impossible to link the two parts of the survey with each other.

The identifier used for each household and to link all its data should be short so as not to take up undue space and to avoid errors caused by copying or typing the same long code over and over. Statistical institutions around the world like to identify households by long series of numbers and letters representing the geographical location and sampling procedure. This method is cumbersome and expensive; often a dozen digits or more are used to number a few hundred households. It is better to use a simple serial number that is written or stamped on the front page of the questionnaire. This number should be appended to every datum collected for that household. Geographic location, urban/rural status, sampling codes, and so forth are, of course, important attributes and as such must be included in the variables recorded about each household, but they need not be used for household identification.

Possible improvements of the household serial number idea include:
- having the number pre-printed by the print shop, which will ensure that no serial number is duplicated;
- having the serial number printed on every page of the questionnaire, so that if pages become detached they can be matched with the rest of the questionnaire; and

- using a check digit[12] on the serial number to flag errors in copying the number.

Whenever possible, the identification codes for the second or third levels of observation should be pre-printed on the questionnaire pages to which they pertain. For example, the individual identification code is printed on every page for which individual data are collected. This ensures that the codes cannot be omitted and there are fewer opportunities for errors in copying. An example of these codes appears in the left-most column of Figure 3.1 .

QUESTIONNAIRE LAYOUT. The LSMS questionnaires are designed so that only one questionnaire is needed for each household. This contrasts with a system sometimes found in simpler surveys. In some such surveys there is one household questionnaire and a separate set of individual questionnaires. This requires that the recording of identity codes be perfect on all questionnaires. While perfection is always sought, it is rarely achieved, and separate questionnaires create the risk of improper matching. The extent of difficulty is illustrated in the case of the Russia Longitudinal Monitoring Survey. Care was taken to ensure accurate coding and matching, but the extent of error introduced was non-negligible. For the first round in the summer of 1992, there were 3 percent fewer individual questionnaires than expected based on the household questionnaires. By the summer of 1993, in the third round of the survey, the discrepancy had grown to about 9.5 percent.

A grid is required in cases where there may be more than one of a unit of analysis in a household. For example, a household includes several persons and may also have several plots of land or grow several different crops. A grid is designed for each of these cases so that questions are arranged across the top and the units of observation (people, plots, or crops) down the sides. Examples are shown in Figures 3.1 and 3.4 through 3.7. Note that the identification code for the unit of observation is either printed on the left side of the grid on each page or filled in by the interviewer in the first column.[13] In the grids for individuals, lines are differentiated with alternating shaded and unshaded blocks or by printing the questionnaire in color with a different color used for each row or block of rows. This helps the interviewer record the answer on the correct line.

------

12. In a code number, such as 49-601-666-3, the last number is the check digit. When an algorithm consisting of a series of arithmetic operations is performed on the code number, the result should give the check digit. An example of a check digit algorithm is as follows. Each digit is multiplied by a number determined by its place in the sequence and the results are summed. This sum is divided by a specific number and the remainder is subtracted from that number. The result is the check digit. Check digit algorithms are constructed so that common coding mistakes, such as the transposing or omitting of digits, will produce the wrong check digit.

13. The number of times the interviewer has to fill in the identification codes by hand should be minimized, as this introduces the possibility of errors.

Figure 3.1: Illustration of Individual Identification and Skip Codes

SECTION 5. WAGE EMPLOYMENT PART C.

PENSION, SOCIAL SECURITY AND UNEMPLOYMENT

FOLD-OUT ROSTER

	A	B
NAME	SEX MALE....1 FEMALE..2	AGE YEARS

IDENTIFICATION CODE

01	JOHN DOE	1	43
02	JANE DOE	2	37
03	FREDDIE DOE	1	8
04	BABY DOE	2	0
05			
06			

IDENTIFICATION CODE

1
Did you receive any pension or social security payment during the last 12 months?

YES...1
NO....2 (> 3)

2
How much money did you receive?

RUPEES
PENSION | SOCIAL SECURITY

3
Did you work for pay, profit, or family gain (cash or in-kind) during the past 7 days?

YES......1
(> NEXT PERSON)
NO.........2

4
Were you available for work during regular work hours during the past 7 days?

YES......1
NO....2

5
Were you looking for work during the past 7 days?

YES......1
(> NEXT PERSON)
NO........2

6
Why didn't you look for work?

SICK..............1
HANDICAPPED.......2
TOO OLD/RETIRED...3
DO NOT WANT TO WORK...4
STUDENT...........5
HOUSEWORK.........6
TOO YOUNG.........7
ON VACATION.......8
AWAITING REPLY OF
EMPLOYER..........9
WAITING TO START A
NEW JOB..........10
NO WORK EXISTS...11
DON'T KNOW HOW TO LOOK..12
OTHER REASONS....13
(SPECIFY:_____)

> NEXT PERSON

Note: the dotted lines indicate that the questionnaire page was truncated in this illustration

35

Figure 3.2: Format When Only One of a Unit of Analysis is Observed

S E C T I O N   2.   H O U S I N G   P A R T   A: TYPE OF DWELLING

1. What type of dwelling does your household occupy?

MAIN TYPE OF DWELLING

```
SINGLE-FAMILY ..............1
APARTMENT/FLAT..............2
ROOM IN LARGER UNIT.........3
COMPOUND....................4
PART OF A COMPOUND..........5
OTHER (SPECIFY:_____)..6
```

2. How many rooms does your household occupy, including sleeping rooms, living rooms and rooms used for household business?

(DO NOT COUNT STORAGE ROOMS, BATHROOMS, TOILETS OR KITCHENS)

No. OF ROOMS

3. Are any of the rooms also used for a household business or trade? (Excluding storage areas or housing for livestock)

```
YES.......1
NO........2 (> 5)
```

4. How many are used primarily for your business?

No. OF ROOMS

5. How long has your household been living in this dwelling?

IF MORE THAN 5 YEARS LEAVE MONTH BLANK.
IF 'FOREVER' OR 'ALWAYS', ETC. WRITE 99

YEARS:

MONTHS:

6. Do other persons who are not household members share this dwelling with you?

```
YES.......1
NO........2 (> 8)
```

7. How many such persons share with you?

INTERVIEWER: PLEASE PROVIDE THE FOLLOWING INFORMATION ON THE RESPONDENT HOUSEHOLD'S DWELLING UNIT (Q. 8-11)

8. MAIN CONSTRUCTION MATERIAL OF OUTSIDE WALLS:

```
BAKED BRICKS/
   CEMENTED BRICKS/
   STONES-CEMENT
   BONDED...................1
BAKED BRICKS/STONES-
   MUD BONDED...............2
WOOD/BRANCHES..............3
CONCRETE...................4
UNBAKED BRICKS.............5
OTHER PERMANENT
   MATERIALS................6
   (SPECIFY:_____)
NO OUTSIDE WALLS...........7
```

9. MAIN FLOORING MATERIAL:

```
EARTH......................1
WOOD.......................2
STONE/BRICK................3
CEMENT/TILE................4
OTHER......................5
   (SPECIFY:_____)
```

10. MAIN MATERIAL ROOF IS MADE OF:

```
STRAW, THATCH..............1
EARTH/MUD..................2
WOOD, PLANKS...............3
GALVANIZED IRON............4
CONCRETE, CEMENT...........5
OTHER......................6
   (SPECIFY:_____)
```

11. THE WINDOWS ARE FITTED WITH (CHECK THE FIRST THAT APPLIES)

```
NO WINDOWS/
   NO COVERING.............1
SCREENS/SHUTTERS...........2
GLASS......................3
OTHER......................4
   (SPECIFY:_____)
```

> PART B

36

Exceptionally large households sometimes have so many members that there are not enough lines in the grids for individuals. In these cases a second questionnaire for the household will be required and care should be taken to ensure that the right household and individual numbers are used. For example, the individual numbers in the second questionnaire should be changed to start with 16 instead of 1. These cases are a potential source of errors, so to minimize them, spaces for as many individuals as practical should be put in the grids. LSMS questionnaires usually have space for 12 to 15 individuals.

Where there is only one observation for a unit of analysis, the questions pertaining to that unit are arranged in a single column down the page.[14] For example, there will usually be only one dwelling per household.[15] Questions on the quality of the dwelling or its other characteristics can follow this simple format. The first page of the section on housing expenses from the Kagera Health and Development Survey questionnaire is shown in Figure 3.2. This format is often used in the community questionnaires as well, since they often have only one observation of each unit of analysis.

CONCEPTUAL STRUCTURE OF QUESTIONNAIRE. The questionnaire is divided into several parts or modules. Each module has a unifying theme, for example, labor or durable assets. Each module will also pertain to a uniform unit of observation, e.g. individuals or crops or items of expenditure.

In LSMS surveys, the roster questions are administered first, in order to establish who should be included in subsequent sections of the questionnaire. Then mini-interviews are conducted with different household members. In these, each member is asked to answer each module that applies — e.g. health, education, employment, etc., before the next mini-interview is conducted. The order of modules within the questionnaire and of questions within modules is therefore carefully thought out. It should aid in establishing rapport with the respondent, provide a structure to the interview that makes sense to the respondent, and aid in the logistics of field work. The relatively uncontroversial modules are placed early in the questionnaire — housing, health, and education. The modules for which greater rapport is needed, such as savings or fertility, are put at the end of the questionnaire. The consumption modules are administered in the second visit to the cluster so that the first visit may be used to define the beginning of the recall period for the purchase of food items.

---

14. There may in fact be two or more columns on the page to save on paper, but the columns are not related.

15. In some cultures, there may be a number of separate tents, huts, or structures that house a single household. Consideration should be given as to whether these need to be enumerated separately or whether the attributes of the housing situation as a whole are more pertinent.

FOLD-OUT ROSTER PAGE. The roster page is printed in such a way that it extends to the left of the pages that pertain to individuals in the household, with lines for individuals aligned with items on the questionnaire.[16] This has been done four different ways in LSMS surveys, as illustrated in Figure 3.3.

- In the first method the sheets in front of the roster are shorter than the cover and the sheets behind the roster, as shown in Format 1.
- The second, most common, method is shown in Format 2. The roster sheet is folded out to extend beyond the body of the questionnaire and its covers. In either of these formats, the roster is placed behind all the pages that pertain to individuals so that it is visible whenever individual questions are asked.
- An innovation in the Kagera Health and Development Survey in Tanzania was to make the rosters removable, as shown in Format 3. This was useful because the survey was designed as a four-wave panel. The roster was inserted in a pocket in the back of the questionnaire in the first wave of the survey. When the second wave started, the roster was removed from the first questionnaire and placed in the back pocket of the second questionnaire. In this way individuals retained the same identification code from wave to wave. A few follow-up questions guaranteed that individuals who moved in or out of the household or were born or died between rounds were counted appropriately. After four waves of interviews conducted over two years, none of the roster cards were lost.
- The Tunisia questionnaire is shown in Format 4. It is oriented as "portrait" (a vertical page) rather than as "landscape" (a horizontal page) and is spiral bound so it opens flat. Each questionnaire "page" is then the full 11 x 17 inches of the two-page spread. The roster folds out to the left.

There may be more than one fold-out roster per questionnaire for different units of analysis. Any time there will be several pages of questions on the same level of analysis, and especially where there are many rows on the grid, a fold-out roster will be useful. For example, rosters might be made for crops grown, or for the list of landholdings.

PRECODING. Potential responses to almost all questions are given numbered codes and the interviewer records only the response code on the questionnaire. Most of the codes are written directly in the box where the question appears. Where the list of codes is lengthy and applies to several questions, it is placed in a special box on the border of each page where it is needed or on the back of the preceding page (which will be visible while the

---

16. Years after the field work, photocopies of the questionnaire for use by analysts may be made if all the original questionnaires have been used up. In these cases the roster is usually reduced to fit on a regular sheet of paper, which hides its original, very important ability to facilitate the interviewer's accuracy.

Figure 3.3: Roster Arrangements

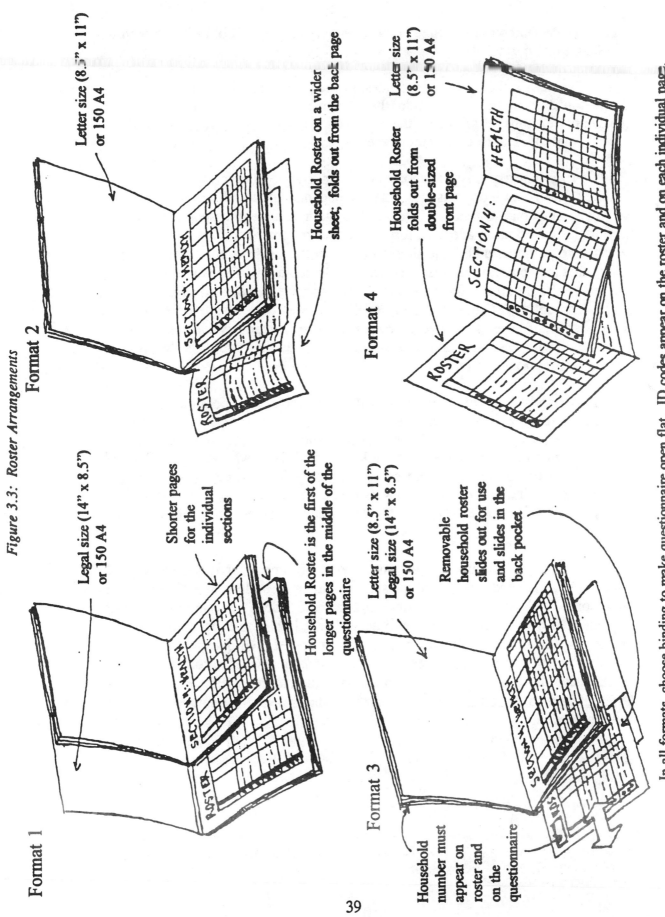

Format 1

Legal size (14" x 8.5")
or 150 A4

Shorter pages
for the
individual
sections

Household Roster is the first of the
longer pages in the middle of the
questionnaire

Format 2

Letter size (8.5" x 11")
or 150 A4

Household Roster on a wider
sheet; folds out from the back page

Format 3

Letter size (8.5" x 11")
Legal size (14" x 8.5")
or 150 A4

Removable
household roster
slides out for use
and slides in the
back pocket

Household
number must
appear on
roster and
on the
questionnaire

Format 4

Letter size
(8.5" x 11")
or 150 A4

Household Roster
folds out from
double-sized
front page

In all formats, choose binding to make questionnaire open flat. ID codes appear on the roster and on each individual page.
Lines on the roster must be aligned with the pages in the questionnaire.

39

interviewer is filling out the page in question). Examples of both these situations are shown in Figure 3.4.

Typically only a dozen or so questions require manual coding. Precoding allows the data to be entered into the computer straight from the completed questionnaire, thus eliminating the time-consuming and error-prone step of transcribing codes onto data entry sheets.

Precoding requires that choices be clear, simple, and mutually exclusive, that they exhaust all likely answers, that respondents will not all fall into the same category, and that categories will not contain too few respondents to be meaningful. Designing adequate response codes requires good knowledge of the phenomenon being studied and thorough field testing. A standard technique to ensure that the codes are mutually exclusive is to add a qualifier where more than one answer could apply, for example, "What was the *main* reason for dropping out of school?" Other standard qualifiers are first, last, or principal. Alternatively, spaces for several responses (i.e. several variables) can be designated, with an instruction to code all responses that apply, or the two or three most important of these.

A standard technique to ensure that codes include all possible answers is to add an "other (specify)" code to those questions where an explicit enumeration is impossible or inconvenient. In practice the detailed answers are almost never coded in the end and so analysis is done lumping all those who answered "other" into a single category. To increase slightly the chances that the information recorded in the "other (specify)" answers is coded, it can be helpful to record all such answers on a special page of the questionnaire where they can be found easily.

There are, of course, limits on the kind of material that can be covered even in well-designed, pre-coded questions. This may be less of a disadvantage than some believe. Most of the analysis of LSMS questionnaires uses sophisticated quantitative techniques into which it is difficult to incorporate the exploratory, qualitative information gathered in open-ended questions. So even if such questions are asked, the extent of their actual use would probably be low. If extensive information of an exploratory, qualitative nature is desired, a different data collection instrument or even another research technique altogether may be needed.

Figure 3.4: Illustration of Precoding and an Open-Ended List

SECTION 9. FARMING AND LIVESTOCK PART D. [EXPENDITURES ON AGRICULTURE INPUTS]

I would like to ask you about your expenditures on agriculture inputs over the past 12 months.

1. Did you purchase any seeds or young plants for crops cultivated in the last rabi and kharif seasons?

YES.....1
NO.....2 (> 6)

2 For which crops? LIST ALL CROPS BEFORE GOING TO 3-5 CROP	CROP CODE	3 How much in total did you spend for seeds and young plants? RUPEES	4 Where did you obtain them? PRIVATE DEALER...1 GOVT AGENCY......2 LANDLORD.........3 OTHER............4 (SPECIFY:____)	5 How did you pay for the seeds/young plants? CASH.........1 CREDIT.......2 CASH/CREDIT...3 ADVANCE BY LANDLORD.....4

CROPS

COTTON DESI.......01		CABBAGE..........65	
COTTON AMERICAN...02		CAULIFLOWER......66	
OTHER FIBRE CROPS..03		LADYFINGER (OKRA)..67	
WHEAT............11		GOURDS, SQUASH,	
RICE,FINE (BASMATI)..12		ZUCCINI.......68	
RICE, COARSE.....13		PEAS............69	
BARLEY...........14		OTHER VEGETABLE	
OTHER SMALL GRAINS..15		CROPS.........70	
CORN (MAIZE).....21		MANGO...........71	
SORGHUM..........22		GUAVA...........72	
MILLET...........23		BANANAS.........73	
OTHER FEED GRAINS..24		DATES...........74	
GRAM.............31		KINO............75	
MASH.............32		OTHER CITRUS....76	
MONG.............33		ALMONDS/WALNUTS..77	
RAWAN............34		APPLE...........78	
MASOOR...........35		APRICOT.........79	
OTHER PULSES AND		PEARS/PLUMS/PEACHES..80	
LEGUMES......36		MELON...........81	
CORN.............41		POMEGRANATE.....82	
SORGHUM..........42		GRAPES..........83	
MILLET...........43		PAPAYA..........84	
BEERSEEM/LUCERN		MULBERRY........85	
(CLOVER/ALFALFA)..44		PERSIMMON.......86	
MUSTARD-RAPESEED...45		OTHER FRUITS, NUTS,	
TURNIP...........46		BERRIES.......87	
OATS.............47		FIREWOOD........88	
OTHER FODDER CROPS..48		TOBACCO.........91	
MUSTARD-RAPESEED...51		CHILIES.........92	
SESAMUM..........52		TUMERIC.........93	
LINSEED..........53		GARLIC..........94	
SOYABEAN.........54		GINGER..........95	
GROUNDNUTS.......55		FENNELSEED......96	
SUNFLOWER........56		MEHNDI (HENNA)..97	
SAFFLOWER........57		OTHER SPICES,	
TARAMIRA.........58		DRUGS AND DYES...98	
OTHER OILSEEDS...59		SUGARCANE.......101	
PATATOES.........61		SUGARBEETS......102	
ONIONS...........62		ALL OTHER MONO-	
TOMATOES.........63		CULTURE CROPS...103	
EGGPLANT.........64			

41

VERBATIM QUESTIONS WITH SIMPLE ANSWERS. All questions are written out and are to be read verbatim by the interviewer. This is done to make sure that questions are asked in a uniform way, since different wordings may elicit different responses. For example, the answer a respondent gives to "Can you read?" or to "Can you read, say a newspaper or magazine?" might be somewhat different. Other changes may subtly change the time period referred to, as in the change from "Have you worked since you were married?" to "Did you work after you were married?" Scott and others (1988) report results from rigorous field experiments that compared schedules where the topic, but not exact wording, of a question was given with verbatim questionnaires. Use of the schedules produced 7 to 20 times as many errors as the equivalent verbatim questionnaire.

In wording questions, it is important to find terms that reflect the language as it is commonly spoken. Use of language that is too formal or academic will make the interview stilted and unnatural. For example, "Did you spend any time doing housework?" if necessary followed by probing "...such as cooking, mending, doing laundry, or cleaning..." is better than "Did you spend any time engaged in domestic labor? e.g., preparing food, repairing clothes, cleaning clothes, or cleaning house...." It is occasionally tricky to find terms that are simple, short, and yet concise, but that should always be the goal.

For most questions, the interviewer reads the question aloud and marks the code for the answer given by the respondent. For example, for the question, "Have you been ill in the last four weeks?" the interviewer would write down a 1 for yes or a 2 for no. For a few questions the response categories are part of the question, for example, "Is the school you attend public or private?" For a few questions where the responses may vary or be worded differently by different respondents, the interviewer will read the response categories. For example, in question 2 shown in Figure 3.5, after reading "Did you work as..." the interviewer will read the responses "permanent labor," "seasonal labor," and "casual labor." This last technique should be used as little as possible, because respondents may not listen to the full list before answering.

The answers to the questions must be kept simple. This means that additional filter questions are often used. Adding enough filter questions to ensure simple answers can make the number of questions and skips seem high. Attempts to shorten or simplify the questionnaire that result in complex answers are common, but should be avoided. For example, in the Ghana LSMS agricultural module, question 7 asks "Do you or the members of your household have the right to sell all or part of their land to someone else if they wish?" The pre-coded answers are "Yes," "No," "Only after consulting family members who are not household members," and "Only after consulting the chief or the village elders." It is not clear that the respondents would necessarily distinguish between the simple yes and the yes qualified by the need for consultation. Thus an alternate formulation might be better. The first question could be left the same, but only simple yes/no codes used. Then for those who answered, a second

Figure 3.5: Illustration of Case Conventions

```
SECTION 5.  WAGE EMPLOYMENT   PART A.
```

```
┌─────────────────────────────────────────────────────────┐
│ EMPLOYMENT IN AGRICULTURE (All persons 10 years and older)│
└─────────────────────────────────────────────────────────┘
```

```
EACH MEMBER OF THE HOUSEHOLD SHOULD ANSWER FOR HIMSELF/HERSELF.
IF NOT, WRITE ID CODE OF RESPONDENT BELOW.
```

IDENTIFICATION CODE	ID CODE OF RES-PONDENT FROM HOUSE-HOLD ROSTER	1 Over the past 12 months, that is, during the past rabi and Kharif season, did you work for payment in cash or kind on some other person's farm? YES......1 NO.......2 (> PART B)	2 Did you work as: Permanent labor?...1 Seasonal labor?...2 (> 14) Casual labor?...3 (> 14)	3 During the past 7 days, how many days did you spend working on someone else's farm? TOTAL DAYS	4 How many hours did you norm-ally work per day? NORMAL HOURS	5 How many days were spent working on someone else's farm over the past 12 months? (PROBE IF NECESSARY) DAYS
01						
02						
03						
04						
05						
06						

Note: the dotted lines indicate that the questionnaire
       page was truncated in this illustration

question could be asked, "Do you need to consult with anyone outside the household before selling the land?" The response codes would be "Yes" and "No." Then a third question would be asked for those who answered yes to the second: "Whom must you consult?" The response codes for this question would be for "Family member," "Village headman," etc. This formulation makes the questionnaire longer in terms of printed pages, but probably does not increase interview time since some sort of probing would probably have been used frequently. Most importantly, it makes the interpretation of the data much clearer.

SKIP CODES. Skip codes are used extensively in LSMS questionnaires. A skip code is an indication to the interviewer to proceed to the next appropriate question. An example is shown in Figure 3.1. In this case, if the answer to question 1 is "no," the interviewer skips question 2 and proceeds to question 3. If the answer to question 1 is "yes," the interviewer should proceed with question 2. In question 3, the same construction is used, but the instruction is to proceed to the next person. Where the skip applies only when a particular answer is given, the skip arrow is positioned in parentheses next to or below the individual response to which it applies, as was done in questions 1 and 3. Another kind of skip instruction is shown in question 6. The arrow is placed in a box below all the response codes, indicating that it applies regardless of which answer was given.

There are several advantages to extensive, explicit skip codes. Interviewers do not have to make decisions themselves, nor need they remember complicated rules printed in the manual but not on the questionnaire. This helps ensure that instructions will be followed uniformly. There is no danger that inapplicable questions will be asked, which would irritate the respondent, waste interview time, and confuse analysis. The "not applicable" code is seldom required on LSMS questionnaires because explicit skip codes are used.

It can be useful both in checking the logic of the questionnaire and in training interviewers to chart the flow of questions in a flow chart. Figure 3.6 is a flow chart of a simplified but typical health module. The proportions of people who answer yes at each branch are recorded, based on results from several LSMS surveys. The number of individuals that would be asked each set of questions is shown on the left, assuming a base of 10,000 individuals in the sample. The flow chart makes it easy to check that the skip patterns lead people through the module appropriately. For example, we can check that the question on health insurance is asked of all persons, not just of those who are ill. Putting the appropriate proportions on the branches makes it easy to check whether the effective sample size is large enough to support the planned analysis. For example, very few persons will answer the questions about hospitalization. Therefore asking more questions on that topic would not really result in more potential for analysis. When this kind of analysis is done for the questionnaire as a whole, it will give a better sense of likely interview time than the number of pages in the questionnaire, since many whole modules or sub-sections of them will be skipped by many individuals.

CASE CONVENTIONS. Everything that the interviewer is to read aloud is written in lower case letters. Answer codes that are not to be read aloud and everything that is an instruction to the interviewer is written in upper case

Figure 3.6: Flow Chart of Health Module

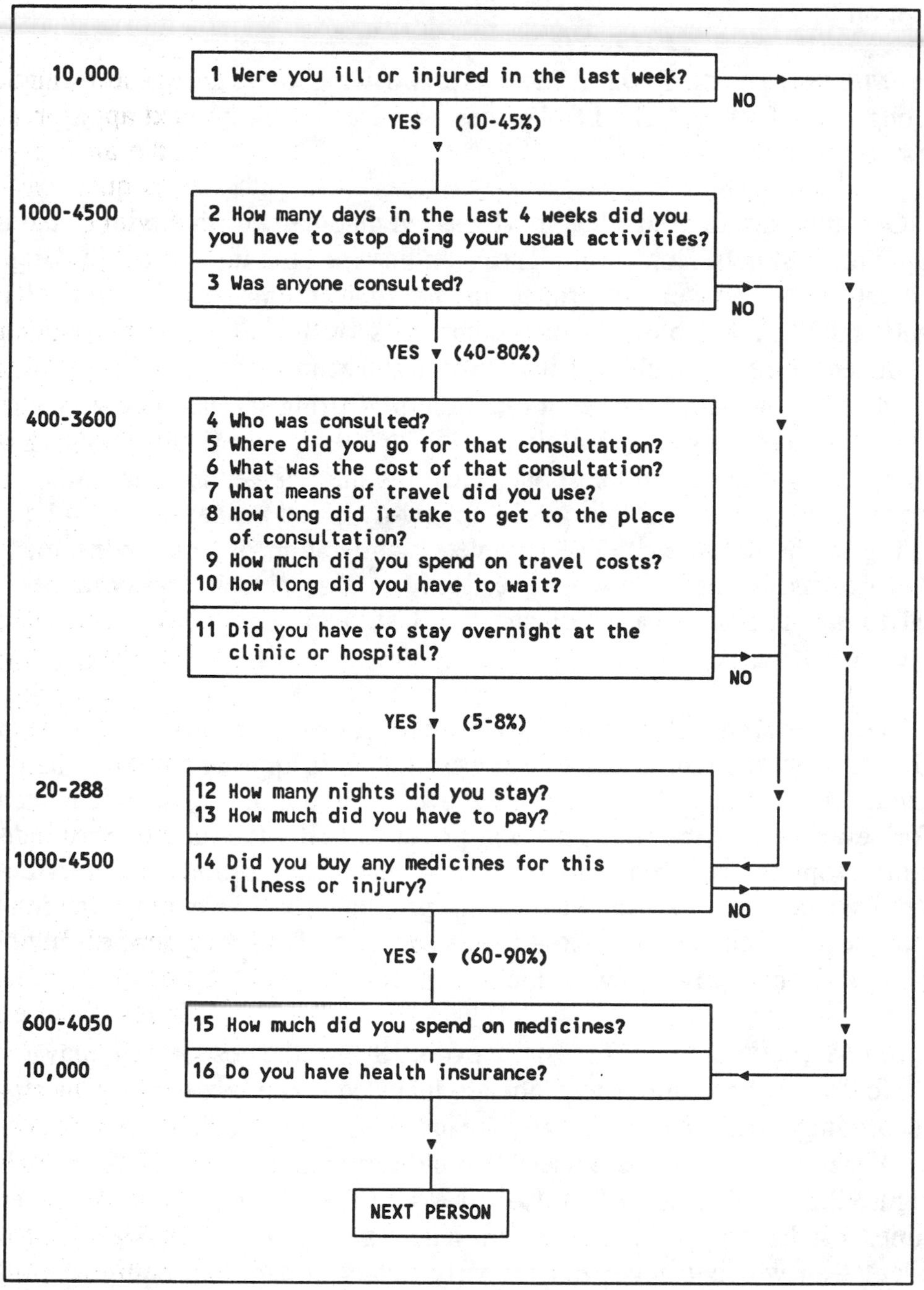

```
10,000        ┌─ 1 Were you ill or injured in the last week? ─┐──→ NO
                          YES │ (10-45%)

1000-4500     ┌─ 2 How many days in the last 4 weeks did you
              │     you have to stop doing your usual activities?
              ├─ 3 Was anyone consulted? ──→ NO
                          YES ▼ (40-80%)

400-3600      ┌─ 4 Who was consulted?
              │  5 Where did you go for that consultation?
              │  6 What was the cost of that consultation?
              │  7 What means of travel did you use?
              │  8 How long did it take to get to the place
              │     of consultation?
              │  9 How much did you spend on travel costs?
              │  10 How long did you have to wait?
              ├─ 11 Did you have to stay overnight at the
              │      clinic or hospital? ──→ NO
                          YES ▼ (5-8%)

20-288        ┌─ 12 How many nights did you stay?
              │  13 How much did you have to pay?
1000-4500     ├─ 14 Did you buy any medicines for this
              │      illness or injury? ──→ NO
                          YES ▼ (60-90%)

600-4050      ┌─ 15 How much did you spend on medicines?
10,000        ├─ 16 Do you have health insurance?

                          ▼
                    ┌─ NEXT PERSON ─┐
```

letters.[17] This makes it easy to include instructions on the questionnaire rather than to rely on the interviewers' memory of the manual or of instructions given orally during training. On the page shown in Figure 3.5, instructions to the

---

17. In languages that do not have an upper and lower case, some other way of distinguishing the instructions from the questions should be found. It may be possible to use italics, bold, a different font or size of letter, or a different color of ink.

interviewer are printed above the grid, in the first column, and below the question for question 5.

ENUMERATION OF LISTS. There are two ways of gathering information about long lists of items. The LSMS questionnaires use both, depending on the circumstances.

One approach is used when it is expected that many of the items in the list will apply to most households. In this case, a line for each item is put in the grid and the label for the item is printed in the first column of the grid. This approach is used in the consumption module, as shown in Figure 3.7. Although several dozen items are included, it is expected that most households will have consumed many of them. The first question is "During the last twelve months has your household consumed any [item]?" The interviewer first goes down the whole list asking this yes/no question. Then the interviewer returns to the first item that was consumed and asks all the follow-up questions for that item before proceeding to the next item. The complete enumeration of items consumed is done before asking the follow-up questions, so that respondents will not be tempted to say that they have not consumed something in order to avoid the follow-up questions.

The other approach is useful when it is expected that only a few of many possible items will pertain to any one household. This approach is often used in the agriculture modules. An example is shown in Figure 3.4. The grid contains lines for several crops, but these are not pre-identified. Rather, the respondent names the crops for which seeds or plants were purchased and the interviewer writes their codes into the grid. Codes are provided for 103 crops. Obviously it would not be efficient to ask about inputs for each of 103 crops when any one household will only grow a few of them.

PROBE QUESTIONS. Where it is expected that the respondent may omit useful information, indications to probe are included in the box for that question. Sample probing questions are usually included in the interviewer manual and occasionally in the questionnaire itself. An indication to probe occurs in question 5 of Figure 3.5. Probes are often used to ensure that all items in a respondent-determined list have been included. They may also be used to ensure that the respondent's answer is categorized properly. Such probes are common in the employment section, for example to determine correctly whether the respondent is unemployed, out of the labor force, or has a second job. Interviewers are also asked to probe for answers to "how much?" questions, such as are found throughout the consumption, agriculture, and small enterprise modules. Wherever probing is expected, the training of interviewers will be intense, so that they thoroughly understand what to probe for and how to do so without distorting information.

Figure 3.7: Illustration of a Closed-Ended List

SECTION 12. FOOD EXPENSES AND HOME PRODUCTION   PART A. FOOD EXPENSES

I would like now to ask about your household's food expenses, consumption of food produced at home and food received as gifts or payments in-kind (for example, payment for work on someone else's land)

1 During the past 12 months, has your household consumed any ..[FOOD].. that it purchased or acquired in-kind? PUT A CROSS IN THE APPROPRIATE BOX FOR EACH FOOD ITEM. IF THE ANSWER TO Q.1 IS YES, ASK Q.2-9.			2 Since my last visit, have you purchased any ..[FOOD]..? YES....1 NO.....2 (> 6)	3 How much in total did you purchase?		4 How much did you pay per (UNIT)?		5 Did you purchase the ..[FOOD].. on credit or "udhar"? YES...1 NO....2
	NO	YES		QUAN-TITY	UNIT OF PURCHASE	RUPEES	PAISA	
Wheat (grain)			301					
Wheat (flour or maida)			302					
Maize (flour or grain)			303					
Jawar/Bajra			304					
Fine rice (Basmati)			305					
Coarse rice			306					
Other grains/cereals			307					
Gram			308					
Dal			309					
Groundnuts			310					
Liquid Vegetable oils			311					
Ghee, Desi ghee			312					

Note: the dotted lines indicate that the questionnaire page was truncated in this illustration.

Because the interviewer probes for information, very few answers of "don't know" are expected and no code for "don't know" is placed on the questionnaire. In the exceptional case where sound interviewing techniques do not produce an answer, the interviewer is instructed (in the manual and in training) to write "d.k." in the space reserved for an answer code. This is then encoded in the data entry program with a special non-numeric code. The end result for analysis is much the same as merely having a "don't know" code for each question. However, the system discourages the interviewer from accepting "don't know" answers because they are handled differently and show up glaringly when the supervisor reviews the questionnaire.

47

RESPONDENT-CHOSEN UNITS. For many questions that involve payments or quantities, respondents are left to report their answers in whichever units they find convenient. Examples of this are found in Figure 3.8. In questions 13, 17, 19, and 21, the code of the time unit in which the respondent replies is placed in the box marked "time unit". The codes are provided in a box that runs above the grid.

Allowing the respondent to select the time unit means that transactions are expressed in the units in which they normally occur, which may differ from household to household or person to person. This avoids inaccuracies in conversion. For example, a person who is paid $510 per week can respond precisely if allowed to respond on a per-week basis. If the response must be in dollars per month, the figure might be rounded to $500 for ease of multiplication by the (approximately) four weeks per month. The annualized figure thus becomes $24,000 instead of the more accurate $26,520 that is reported when the respondent picks the unit and the analyst carries out the conversion.

Analysis is, of course, complicated by the need to convert observations in order to correctly annualize data. But since this is all handled by computer the issue is really trivial. The more important issue is to ensure that, where necessary, the questionnaire asks explicitly how many times per year the payments take place. For example, a worker who reports a daily wage rate may only be employed intermittently. To multiply the daily wage by the number of working days per year (which itself differs from country to country) is likely to overstate the worker's earnings significantly.

Another major application of flexible units is for the "quantities produced or consumed" data in the agricultural section. In Ghana, for example, 22 unit codes were used, as shown in Table 3.1. These create a more complex problem for the analyst who tries to convert quantities to a standard unit. Only about half of the units used in this example are standardized. Even some of those (minibag, maxibag) are local terms that need to be documented well for users of the data who are not familiar with farming in Ghana.[18]

RESPONDENT CODES. It is sometimes of interest to know who is answering a certain section of the questionnaire. This can be accomplished by leaving a space for the respondent code next to the beginning of the string of questions to which it pertains. The interviewer fills in the identification code of the person who actually responds to the question. An example of this is shown in Figure 3.5. The idea is that a proxy respondent may give less accurate information than the individual actually involved. For example, one household member may not

---

18. The conversion of quantities to standard units (e.g., bunches to kilos) is not required to calculate farm income, which was the purpose of the agriculture module in the Ghana LSMS. But as is common with such rich data sets, analysts are using the data for other purposes as well, for which it is of interest to convert to standard quantities.

Figure 3.8: Illustration of Respondent-Selected Units

SECTION 5. WAGE EMPLOYMENT   PART B.   EMPLOYMENT OUTSIDE AGRICULTURE (cont.)

TIME CODES

MINUTE....1 DAY....3 MONTH....5
HOUR....2 WEEK....4 YEAR....6

PRIMARY OFF-FARM EMPLOYMENT

know the exact salary of another. Some analysts may therefore wish to identify possible biases introduced by the proxy respondents or omit their responses from some analyses. Although not used in every section of every LSMS questionnaire, respondent codes could be of interest on several modules.[19]

SAMPLING AND SURVEY MANAGEMENT PAGE. Each questionnaire should include information on the sample and the management of the data collection process. The sampling information should include the serial number for the household, any codes required to describe the sampling strata, geographic location, whether rural or urban, etc., and whether the household interviewed was that originally selected in the sample or a replacement household (see Chapter 4 for a discussion of replacement households). Information such as an address, or approximate location with a sketch of where the dwelling is, or a phone number where possible, will aid in re-visits to the household. It is often convenient to put this on the cover page or the first page of the questionnaire.

Table 3.1: Units of Quantity

UNIT CODES	
POUNDS	*1
KILOGRAM	*2
TON	*3
MINIBAG	*4
MAXIBAG	*5
SHEET	6
BASKET	7
BOWL	8
AMERICAN TIN	*9
TREE	10
STICK	11
BUNDLE	12
BARREL	13
LITER	*14
GALLON	*15
BEER BOTTLE	*16
BUNCH	17
NUT	18
FRUIT	19
LOG	20
BOX	21
ALL	22

Note: Try to use unit code marked by (*) whenever possible.

The information on the data collection process should include the factors that may help in management of the survey or in ex-post facto methodological investigations. For example, the code numbers for the interviewer, anthropometrist, supervisor, and data entry operator who worked on that questionnaire should appear. Any information about whether the interview was completed or not and the number of callbacks made should be recorded. The language in which the interview was conducted should be noted. Some of this information can be recorded in the cover page for the household as a whole. In some cases, however, the answers may be specific to individuals. For example, some members of the household may speak the official language well enough to be interviewed in that language, while other members might need to be interviewed in a local language or through interpreters.

---

19. Wages and time-use information may be more accurately reported by the person affected than by another family member. Sensitive topics, such as those relating to contraceptive use or deliberately missing school, are more accurately answered by the individual than by someone else in the household. For the sections on household expenditures, farming, businesses, or use of credit it may be important to know who answered the questions on behalf of the whole household.

The date when the interview was conducted should be recorded as well. This is important not only in survey management, but may be used in important parts of the analysis as well. In economies with high inflation, for example, the monetary information will have to be inflated or deflated to reflect prices at a common date. This can only be done correctly when the date of interview is known.

CARDSTOCK COVERS. LSMS questionnaires are usually printed with cardstock covers. Where these have been omitted because of cost there have been problems with the front and back pages of the questionnaire coming loose. Since the front page usually carries the key household identifier information and the back page carries the household roster, any such loss is likely to render the rest of the questionnaire useless. The cardstock covers are well worth their cost.

IDENTIFYING SECTIONS. LSMS questionnaires are very bulky. The Nepal questionnaire, for example, has 70 pages. It is therefore useful to think of some ways to make it easy to find one's way around in them. A few ideas are listed here, but other ideas could be substituted. First, it is useful to have page numbers on the pages and a table of contents of the sections in the beginning or at the end. Second, some graphic techniques that are not expensive can be used to make it easier to tell where one is in the questionnaire. Some sections of the questionnaire can be printed on different colored paper or in different colored inks. Sheets of colored paper can be inserted between major portions of the questionnaire. It is also possible to print short, dark bars at the edge of each page, with the placement on the page being the same within modules but lower down (if on the vertical edge) or further to the right (if on the bottom edge) for each successive module. Using just one or a few of the techniques will be sufficient. The questionnaire should not become too rococo.

LEGIBILITY AND SPACING. There is an art to laying out the grids for a questionnaire. The lettering must be large enough to read, which is sometimes difficult to accomplish in the compact structure of the grid. Legibility is especially important, as interviews often take place in conditions with poor lighting — outdoors at dusk, or after dark in homes dimly lit with lanterns, oil lamps, or candles. The better print quality available now that laser printers are replacing dot matrix printers has helped, but poor legibility is an ongoing complaint among interviewers.

There must also be enough white space allowed in the layout of the questionnaire. Whenever the answer will be coded later, a generous space should be allowed to write out fully the information required — the person's name, the name of the school the respondent attends, the respondent's occupation, etc. In other places, judicious use of white space makes the questionnaire easier to read or less confusing than if every bit of every page were crammed with print.

SOFTWARE FOR QUESTIONNAIRE LAYOUT. Several widely available word processing and graphics software packages are now adequate for producing questionnaire page layouts.[20] Revisions between drafts can now be made much more simply and cheaply than in the days when graphic artists had to draw each page by hand. The computerized approach also simplifies translations, as the verbal parts can be overwritten in the local language, leaving the skip codes, response codes, and general format intact.

---

20. This was not true for the first LSMS surveys. For them, a special software called GRIDS was invented. The options available on the market have since superseded the use of GRIDS.

Chapter 4: Sampling

Key Messages

- LSMS samples are small in size, generally from 2,000 to 5,000 households, to balance sampling and non-sampling errors.

- LSMS samples are designed to represent the population of the country as a whole, as well as that of certain subgroups of the population, called "analytical domains."

- LSMS samples are drawn in two stages. In the first stage, a certain number of area units called *Primary Sampling Units* (or PSUs) are selected. In the second stage, a certain number of households, usually 16, are selected in each of the designated PSUs. Both stages are random selections.

- Two-stage sampling reduces the cost and effort of sampling and of field work compared with single-stage sampling, but at the cost of increasing the sampling error. This is a result of the so-called "cluster effect."

- The first stage of sampling requires developing a sample frame from census files. The second stage requires listing all households in the selected PSUs and then choosing a random sample of those households for the final sample.

- To derive unbiased estimates from the survey, the values observed in the sample may need to be weighted. To compute the needed raising factors and correct the sampling errors, all stages of sampling must be carefully recorded and made available to the survey analysts, both in written documents and in the survey data sets.

Many of those who work on survey implementation or who use the resulting data never learn the details of how sample designs are chosen and implemented. This chapter tries to dispel some of the mystery. Section A reviews the basics of sample design. It may be skipped by readers who know something about the subject. Section B explains the choices made in the usual LSMS sample design and the reasons for them. All readers should read this section. Section C provides a step-by-step guide on how to carry out the sampling. Readers who will not be involved in sampling may skip it or skim it.

A. Overview of Issues in Sample Design

The main objectives of an LSMS are understanding the determinants of household behavior and the overall distribution of welfare. The sample design should determine the number and location of the households to be observed in a

53

way that best achieves these goals within budgetary and organizational constraints. The following issues must be considered:

To reliably depict the overall situation of the population, the selected sample should contain a sufficient number of households, scattered as much as possible throughout the country. However, to reduce the costs, simplify management, and control the quality of the interviews, the sample size and its geographical dispersal must be kept within reasonable limits.

The population of the country may contain certain subgroups, such as urban and rural areas or other aggregates, that deserve to be studied separately. The sample of households should adequately represent each of these subgroups as well as the country as a whole.

Each household in the country should be given a chance to be selected in the sample. To simplify survey design and analysis, this chance should be similar for all households, or at least for all households within the same large domain.

Some insights into how to arbitrate among these objectives and constraints can be obtained from a quick review of four concepts: sampling error, non-sampling error, multi-stage sampling, and analytical domains.

SAMPLING ERROR. Sampling error is the error inherent in making inferences for a whole population from observing only some of its members (see Box 4.1). Sampling theory studies the behavior of sampling error for different design options. It is usually assumed that one of the variables to be observed is of particular interest, for instance, household income, unemployment, or infant mortality, and that the sample design should maximize the precision of the estimates of this variable, given cost constraints. Several good textbooks explore this complex issue and it does not need to be specified in detail here (see reference list in Annex II). It is important, however, to bear in mind two general conclusions of sampling theory.

First, the law of diminishing returns underlies the relationship between sample size and sampling error. Roughly speaking, and other things being equal, the sampling error is inversely proportional to the square root of the sample size. This means that, even with the best design, to reduce the error of a particular sample by half, the number of households visited must be quadrupled (See Box 4.2).

Second, the sample size needed for a given level of precision is almost independent of the total population. For instance, a 500-household sample would give essentially the same sampling precision whether it is extracted from a population of 10,000 or 1,000,000 households, or indeed, from an infinite population. Some people find it hard to believe that the sample size does not

Box 4.1: How Wrong Will Our Estimates Be?

Reports in the press of opinion polls often say something like, "Forty-two percent of those polled said they would vote for Candidate Jones; the margin for error on this poll is plus or minus two percent."

The reason for the margin for error is that in doing sample surveys we observe only some members of a population rather than the whole population. Any conclusions we draw from studying the members of the sample may be a little different that what we would learn if we could study the whole population.

It is desirable to know how far from the "truth" (what we would know if we studied the whole population) our estimates (what we do know from studying only the sample of the population) may be. Of course we cannot calculate this precisely, because to calculate it precisely would require knowing the "truth." Statistical theory, however, can help us establish boundaries on how large our errors might be, and therefore how much confidence we can put in our estimates.

Suppose we want to estimate the proportion of people who smoke, using data from a sample of the population. We want some predetermined level of certainty that our estimate is not too far from the true value of the proportion. We therefore calculate a range around our estimate of the proportion. This range is called the confidence interval. The formula used in calculating the confidence interval is

$$CI = \hat{p} \pm \hat{e} \cdot Z_{\alpha}$$

where $\hat{p}$ is the estimate from the sample, $\hat{e}$ is the estimate of the standard error, and z_{α} is a constant that depends on the degree of certainty, α, we want of the proportion. If we want to be 95 percent certain that the true value lies within the confidence interval, z_{α} would be 1.96. For 99 percent confidence, z_{α} would be 2.58.

Suppose that 28 percent of our sample smokes ($\hat{p} = 0.28$), we have an estimated standard error of 1.5 percent and we want to be 95 percent certain that the true value lies within our estimated interval. The interval in which we have 95 percent confidence that the true value lies would be from about 25 to 31 percent of population (that is, 28 $\pm$ 1.5 x 1.96).

Obviously, we want to have the smallest practical confidence interval. The confidence interval will be smaller, the smaller is the estimate of the standard error. The following boxes therefore discuss factors that influence the size of the standard error. To simplify the presentation, the following boxes discuss the true standard error, e, rather than our estimate of it, $\hat{e}$. But the intuition is the same for both.

depend very much on the size of the population; they feel the relationship should be more or less proportional. An intuitive grasp of this seemingly striking statistical fact can be obtained by noticing that, in order to test if the soup is salty enough, an army cook does not need to take a larger sip from the regimental pot

---

Box 4.2: Sampling Error and Sample Size: A Case of Diminishing Returns

For a simple illustration of the diminishing returns relationship between sample size and sampling errors, consider the case where a proportion (for instance, the proportion of households with pre-school children) is estimated from a *simple random sample* of n households, extracted from an infinite population. Let p be the value of the proportion in the population. The standard error is:

$$e = \sqrt{\frac{p(1-p)}{n}}$$

The table below gives the values of e for different sample sizes and p=50%:

Table B 4.2.1

Sample size (n):	100	200	500	1000	2000	5000	10000
Standard error (e):	5.00%	3.54%	2.24%	1.58%	1.12%	0.71%	0.50%

Notice that in order to reduce the error from 5.00% to 0.50% (a tenfold reduction), the sample must be increased a hundredfold, from 100 to 10,000 households. (See Cochran 1977, Chapter 3 for more information.)

---

than a housewife needs to take from the family saucepan (see Box 4.3). This does not *necessarily* means that the size of an LSMS sample is independent of the size of the country. Large countries generally require larger samples, not because they are large but because large countries tend to demand results for a larger number of internal subdivisions. India, for example, would probably require state-level data from any survey.

NON-SAMPLING ERRORS. Beside sampling errors, data from a household survey are vulnerable to other inaccuracies from causes as diverse as refusals, respondent fatigue, interviewer errors, or the lack of an adequate sample frame. These are collectively known as non-sampling errors. Non-sampling errors are harder to predict and quantify than sampling errors, but it is well accepted that good planning, management, and supervision of field operations are the most effective ways to keep them under control. Moreover, it is likely that management and supervision will be more difficult for larger samples than for smaller ones. Thus one would expect non-sampling error to increase with sample size.[21]

---

21. See UNNHSCP (1982) for a treatment of how to minimize non-sampling error.

MULTI-STAGE SAMPLING. Samplers usually do not have a single complete list of households from which to draw a random sample. Even if such a list were available, a sample taken from it would entail high travel costs because selected households would be spread thinly over the entire country.

Both of these problems can be diminished by using two or more stages in sampling. In the version of two-stage sampling generally used for LSMS surveys, a certain number of small area units are selected with Probability Proportional to Size (PPS), then a fixed number of households are taken from each selected area, giving to each household in the area the same chance of being chosen.[22]

The area units are usually the smallest recognizable geographic units in the national census. These are usually *census enumeration areas* (EAs), which are aggregates of 50 to 200 households. Less often, the first stage sampling has used administrative units such as wards, sectors, etc. Whatever their nature, these may be called *Primary Sampling Units*, or PSUs. However, in many countries

---

22. The size of an area is generally defined as the number of households in the area. Alternative size measures are the number of dwellings and the total population.

those PSUs that are exceptionally large have been divided into *segments*, one of which is selected per PSU, in order to economize on household listing. The final operational area units are then a mixture of PSUs and segments. To simplify the description it is convenient to continue using the word "PSU" for both PSUs and segments.

The two-stage procedure just described has several advantages. It provides an approximately self-weighted sample (i.e., each household has roughly the same chance of being selected), which simplifies analysis. It also reduces the travel time of the field teams relative to a single-stage sample, because the households to be visited are clumped together in the PSUs rather than spread out evenly over the whole country. An additional advantage of selecting a fixed number of households in each PSU at the second stage is that this makes it easy to distribute the workload among field teams.

A two-stage sample, however, will yield larger errors than a simple random sample with the same number of households because neighboring households tend to have similar characteristics. A sample of households drawn in two stages will therefore reflect less of a population's diversity than a simple random sample of the same size. The influence of two-stage sampling on the precision of the estimates is called the *cluster effect*. As would be expected, the cluster effect *grows* with the number of households selected in each PSU. In other words, for a fixed total sample size, a design with more PSUs and fewer households in each PSU will provide more precise estimates of sample statistics than a design with fewer PSUs and more households in each PSU (see Box 4.4).

The field teams will typically spend a large amount of time and thus incur substantial costs in travelling between PSUs. Surveying each PSU also entails certain costs that are independent of the number of households to be visited in each PSU, such as the listing operation explained below. It may therefore be tempting to try to reduce the cost of the survey by increasing the number of households in each PSU and reducing the total number of PSUs accordingly. However, the cluster effect indicates that this may often be a false economy.

ANALYTICAL DOMAINS. For political or policy reasons, some subgroups of the population are so important that the survey is expected to provide separate, reliable results for them. Typical examples include division into urban and rural locations and into major administrative units such as states, but the subgroups do not necessarily have to be geographical aggregates — for instance, the urban households whose head works for the public sector became an explicit field of interest in certain SDA surveys. The design will then have to ensure a minimum

If the sample of n households referred to in Box 4.1 is not selected by simple random sampling but in two stages (m households in each of c PSUs, with n=cm) and without stratification, the formula for the standard error should be corrected as follows:

$$e^2_{(corrected)} = e^2 \left[1 + \rho(m-1)\right]$$

The term in brackets is called the *design effect* (see Kish, 1965). It represents how much larger the squared standard error of a two-stage sample is when compared with the squared standard error of a simple random sample of the same size. ρ is the so-called *intra-cluster correlation coefficient* — a number that measures the tendency of households within the same PSU to behave alike in regards to the variable of interest (for the example in Box 4.1, this would be the tendency of households with pre-school children to be clumped in the same PSUs). ρ is almost always positive, normally ranging from 0 (no intra-cluster correlation) to 1 (when all households in the same PSU are exactly alike). For many variables of interest in LSMS surveys, ρ ranges from 0.01 to 0.10, but it can be 0.5 or larger for variables such as the access of the household to running water. Table B 4.4.1 below gives the design effects due to clustering for various values of ρ and m:

Table B 4.4.1

Number of households per PSU (m)	\multicolumn{7}{c}{Intra-cluster correlation (ρ)}
	0.00	0.01	0.02	0.05	0.10	0.20	0.50
	\multicolumn{7}{c}{Design Effect}
5	1.00	1.04	1.08	1.20	1.40	1.80	3.00
10	1.00	1.09	1.18	1.45	1.90	2.80	5.50
20	1.00	1.19	1.38	1.95	2.90	4.80	10.50
50	1.00	1.49	1.98	3.45	5.90	10.80	25.50

sample size within each of these subgroups, which can then be called analytical domains. For large domains this may occur automatically whereas in other cases it may be necessary to oversample certain analytical domains and to modify the expansion factors (also called "sampling weights") accordingly. The two stage sampling procedure is applied independently within each of those differently weighted domains.

Analysts would often also like to have sufficient sample sizes in smaller analytical groups, such as rural locations in the irrigated parts of a certain region. They may even want to carry the disaggregation further, for example, to study separately male- and female-headed households in rural irrigated areas. This ideal, however, cannot be fully achieved for all possible analytical domains because it would result in a prohibitively large total sample. Therefore, defining the most significant partitions for a sample entails establishing some priorities at the design stage. Often these will not be dictated by policy relevance alone, but also by local statistical folklore and geopolitical considerations.[23]

B. Sampling Practice in LSMS Surveys

THE BASIC SAMPLE DESIGN. The sample size for LSMS surveys has usually been small, in the range of 2,000-5,000 households (see Table 4.1). The samples are usually two-stage.[24] The Primary Sampling Units are area units selected with probability proportionate to size. The second-stage units are households, with a fixed number of households per PSU, normally about 16. When a partition into differently weighted domains has been defined, the two-stage sampling procedure is conducted within each of them; the number of differently weighted domains has generally been kept low, between one and four.

Decisions about the sample design for LSMS surveys have been made on a somewhat more qualitative (some would even say *ad hoc*) basis rather than through the application of quantitative sampling formulae for several reasons.

First, one of the overriding objectives of the LSMS was to create very high quality data sets. Thus, great weight has been given to minimizing non-sampling error. Because the questionnaire is complex and fieldwork requires extensive supervision, the consensus has been that non-sampling error could only be kept to the desired standard by using samples in the range of 2,000-5,000 households. As a result, survey planners decided to accept higher sampling error in exchange for lower non-sampling error.

Second, taking advantage of the wealth of information that LSMS surveys provide and addressing the complex behavioral questions that motivate the surveys

---

23. The partition of a sample into analytical domains is akin to the concept of "sample stratification." Sample stratification, however, is generally done to improve the overall precision of the sample, rather than to study each partition separately. A stratified design that seeks to reduce the overall error usually entails oversampling the parts of the population with the largest variance. In measuring welfare this would entail oversampling the richer parts of the population.

24. Procedures with more stages are possible and, indeed, are sometimes followed by statistical agencies. In three-stage sampling, for instance, instead of selecting small area units directly, some larger areas (such as provinces) are selected first; smaller areas are then chosen only within the first-stage areas so selected. The effect is that the small area units themselves (and not just the households) become clumped rather than being spread throughout the national territory. The most serious disadvantage of multi-stage sampling is that each additional sampling stage increases the sampling error, sometimes considerably. The one frequently quoted advantage of using more than two stages is that it reduces the amount of travel between survey localities. However, this does not apply to the LSMS because of the way field work is organized: the field teams return to a local headquarters between work in each locality. When they return to the field again it just as easy to go to any one of their assigned localities as to any other. Therefore, we do not recommend using more than two stages of sampling in LSMS surveys.

Table 4.1: Sample Design in Selected LSMS Surveys

Country	Year	Sample Size (HH)	Households per cluster	No. of Differently Weighted Analytical Domains	Partition Criteria
Côte d'Ivoire	1985-88	1600 (per year)	16	1	none
Peru	1986	5120	10 in Lima 16 elsewhere	25	Metro Lima, urban/rural in 12 locations
Ghana	1988	3200	16	1	none
Mauritania	1987	1488	16	4	Nouackchott, other cities, rural in river areas, other rural areas
Pakistan	1991	4800	16	4	Four provinces: Punjab, Sind, Balochistan and NWFP
Tanzania - Kagera Region	1992-93	816	16	3	Groups defined as a function of mortality rates and geographic location
Guinea-Conakry	1988	1728	8	1	None, but only in Conakry urban area
Mozambique	1991	1840	10	1	None, but only in Maputo/Matola urban area
Nicaragua	1993	4200	10	14	urban/rural in seven regions
Viet Nam	1992	4800	16	1	none
Nepal	1995	3300	12	4	Mountain, urban hills, rural hills, Terai

Note: Though the Guinea and Mozambique surveys were conducted by the Cornell University Food Security Program, their purpose and methodology are very similar to the World Bank surveys, which makes them interesting examples of LSMS field implementation.

requires sophisticated multivariate analytical techniques. Thus the precision of estimates of means from simple two- or three-way tables was not deemed of overwhelming importance. Moreover, in designing the LSMS it was judged of much greater analytical interest to have a large amount of information about a relatively small number of households rather than a little information about a larger sample.

Third, given the multiple purposes of an LSMS survey, it is hard to select one single variable for the purpose of minimizing sampling error.

HOUSEHOLDS AND DWELLINGS. The basic analytical unit of LSMS surveys is the *household*. Many surveys define the household as a group of people who share a roof and a cooking pot.[25] LSMS surveys often also require individuals to have been present for at least three of the past twelve months in order to be considered as household members (though heads of household and newborn infants are considered members even if they have not been present that long).

The second sampling stage almost always requires a field operation called "household listing." Enumerators visit each selected PSU to update the existing maps and prepare the list of all households currently living there. Households to be interviewed are to be selected from this list.

The practical implementation of this operation makes it difficult to preserve the above definition of a household, because that would entail time-consuming interviewing throughout each PSU. In practice, *dwellings* are listed instead of households. A dwelling is defined as "a group of rooms or a single room occupied or intended for occupancy as separate living quarters by a family or some other group of persons living together, or by a person living alone."[26] Besides the advantage of being shorter to complete, a listing of dwellings is more permanent than a listing of households.

Strictly speaking, therefore, the LSMS samples are samples of dwellings rather than of households, though the listing operation is still traditionally called "household-listing" rather than "dwelling-listing."[27] Some dwellings may be unoccupied and some may be occupied by two households or more, but the large majority of dwellings are occupied by one single household. (The average number of households per dwelling ranges from 0.9 to 1.1 in most countries.) If a dwelling with two households is selected in the sample, both are interviewed separately.

NON-RESPONSE AND HOUSEHOLD REPLACEMENT. Some households selected for the sample will not be interviewed because of one of the following reasons: the interviewer cannot locate the dwelling; the dwelling is uninhabited; the dwelling's residents are away from home and expected to remain so until after the end of the survey period in that area; or the residents refuse to be interviewed.

Non-responding households *cannot* be considered to be a random sample of all households. Non-response rates are always higher in urban than in rural areas and higher in rich households than in poor households. They also have a

---

25. For a discussion of the concept of household and its variants, and details on the operational definitions used by various UN agencies see UNNHSCP (1989).

26. Kish (1965).

27. The confusion in terms is further complicated by the fact that in regions without street addresses and house numbers, dwellings are usually identified by the name of the head of the household currently living there.

clear tendency to decrease as the survey proceeds and the field staff becomes more experienced and persuasive. Surprisingly enough, refusal does not seem to be related to the length of the questionnaire but to the unwillingness of certain people to be interviewed at all.[28]

There is a lot of controversy about what should be done about non-response. Some survey practitioners try to achieve the planned sample size by replacing the refusals with other households, whereas other specialists condemn these efforts as sterile and argue that the resulting sample of non-refusals will still be biased by definition. Neither replacing nor failing to replace non-responding households solves the essential problem of bias. Thus everybody agrees that all efforts should be made to keep non-responses to a minimum and that the choice of replacements, if any, should not be given to the interviewers lest a sample of "easy-to-interview" households results.

The solution adopted by LSMS surveys is pragmatic and is based on the principle that interviewers should not be "rewarded" by having to do less work in the case of a non-response. Non-responding households are replaced by other randomly selected households by means of an explicit procedure that is explained in the next section of this chapter. All the details of this process (including the codes of the replaced and the replacing household and the reasons for replacement) are properly documented, both in the questionnaires and in the computer files, to let each analyst decide individually whether or not to include the replacement households in the data sets being analyzed.

The survey managers should carefully monitor all replacements, especially those determined by refusal. Many surveys have demonstrated that refusals rates can be reduced to a minimum, since refusals often depend on the interviewers' attitudes and experience. There is empirical evidence that individual interviewers usually have very different refusal rates. It is useful to stress this to interviewers while monitoring the refusal rates for each interviewer.

Refusals and replacements have been relatively low in LSMS surveys. In the Mozambique survey, out of the 560 first households visited, only seven were not those originally selected and only three refused to be interviewed, a trifling number that is the more remarkable in a country at war. In Côte d'Ivoire, the non-response rate was 7.8 percent the first year, of which 1.4 percent was refusals. In Peru (1985) the non-response rate was 17.4 percent with a 1.4 percent refusal rate. The overall non-response rate during the first month of the Romania survey was 7 percent, though it reached 18 percent in some neighborhoods in Bucharest.

---

28. This is worth remembering when it is necessary to defend the riches of the LSMS questionnaire content against those who insist that it is unmanageably long.

C. Implementing a Sample Design

Determining the Basic Sample Design Parameters

As explained above, the decisions about the basic sample design parameters (the number of households in total, per PSU, and per analytical domain) are based on qualitative judgements based on past experience and estimates of cost and manageability. The decisions about the basic sample for an LSMS generally follows these steps:

(1)   A preliminary estimate of the total sample size is established. As explained above, the sample rarely exceeds about 5,000 households, but may be much smaller if a single analytical domain is required, or because of constraints on the budget or implementation capacity.

(2)   Using data from the most recent census, this sample is distributed in proportion to the total number of households in the major regions, urban and rural locations, etc. In other words, the option of using a constant sampling fraction throughout the country (i.e. a self-weighted national sample) is taken as a starting point.

(3)   If the sample seems insufficient for some particular analytical domains (fewer than, say, 300 to 400 households)[29], the sample size may be increased in these domains and decreased in other domains.

While implementing Step (2), parts of the population may be purposely excluded from the sample, because of their inaccessibility or for security reasons. This happened in Peru, where in 1985 three provinces were controlled by guerrillas and/or drug dealers, and in Pakistan, where the most remote parts of Balochistan were extremely hard to reach.[30] Likewise, the Mauritania survey

---

29. There is no rigorous, quantitative justification for using this particular number. Rather, a wide variety of analyses of different types on different variables have converged upon this as a reasonable ballpark figure. Analysts complain loudly when the numbers get much below this threshold, but are often reasonably content above it. For a variable with a proportion of forty percent (for example, the percent of households with pre-school aged children), ignoring the finite population correction, assuming a typical LSMS take of 16 households per cluster, and an intra-cluster correlation of .05, a 400 household sample gives a 95 percent confidence interval ranging from 33.65 to 46.35 percent. This underscores the need for caution in reporting results for very small subsets of the population.

30. The decision to exclude remote areas from the sample has to be considered carefully, though. Often these areas are very vast and tend to be frontier regions that are important to national politics (e.g. the Amazon basin in Brazil or the Chaco region in Paraguay), so that the survey may "look bad" in the eyes of policy makers if they are excluded from the sample. However, these areas tend to be also so scarcely populated that, if included, only a few clusters will be selected for the sample, and the extra cost of visiting them would be manageable.

excluded the nomadic population. The survey in these cases is explicitly designed to represent only the rest of the country.

Step (3) may have to be repeated a few times until a satisfactory partition is achieved. Given that the resources needed to conduct interviews can vary significantly across the territory (interviews are usually more expensive in the rural areas and in the most isolated parts of the country), it is useful and instructive to explore the alternative options with the aid of a spreadsheet to take into account their budgetary and logistical implications.

As a general guideline, we believe it is better to reduce the number of partitions imposed in this way to a minimum and to keep their sampling fractions as close as possible so that the total sample does not differ too much from a self-weighted national sample. While reasonable statisticians and econometricians hold varying opinions of the theoretical virtues of self-weighting, we are much swayed by more pragmatic issues. The more complicated the sample design, the more often the sampler will make mistakes in executing the sampling and the less often others will be able to detect them. There is also a long history of sampling weights being lost, incorrectly calculated, or omitted or misused in analysis. Self-weighted samples are much more robust to this kind of error than more complicated designs.

In a self-weighted sample, the proportions and averages obtained from the sample are unbiased estimates for the proportions and averages in the population. However, when adjustments are made in step (3), the sampling fractions will become different across analytical domains, and the sample will no longer be self-weighted. The households will need to be weighted differently to get unbiased estimates. Calling N_k the total number of households in the population of domain k and n_k the number of households sampled in domain k, the weight w_k to be applied to the values from that domain is

$$w_k = \frac{N_k}{n_k}$$

Note that w_k is the inverse of the selection probability of each household in domain k. As with all sampling information, the basic set of weights (also known as *expansion factors* or *raising factors*) resulting from this step of sample design should be carefully documented and made available to the survey analysts.

The number of PSUs to be sampled is determined by the total sample size and the number of households to be interviewed in each PSU. The latter depends on both theoretical and practical considerations. On the one hand, the number of households per PSU affects the precision of the sample, as explained above when discussing cluster effects. On the other hand, the number of households per PSU is a function of the length of the interviews, the number of interviewers in each team, and the time each team spends in the PSU. Typically, each field team visits 20 PSUs per year, spends two weeks in each PSU, and interviews 16 households in each, though in some LSMS surveys as few as 10 or as many as 24 households per PSU have been selected.

Implementation of the First Sampling Stage

THE SAMPLING FRAME. Implementation of the sample begins with the sample frame — the complete list or file of units from which the sample units are selected.[31] To develop a sample frame from census data, it is important to obtain a computer-readable list of all PSUs, with a measure of size such as the number of households, the number of dwellings or the population, recorded in each of them.[32] All statistical agencies must eventually process this information in order to obtain the classic census tabulations for larger geographic aggregates, but the preparation of the PSU list as a separate by-product is often forgotten. When the list is not available, the data must be compiled and put into a computer file as quickly as possible. This should not take more than a few weeks, and the list usually fits on one diskette; it does not require that all data from the census be entered or analyzed.

Though only the total number of households or dwellings in each PSU is really needed, the list will probably also include the total population of each PSU, broken down by sex. This information should be entered into a spreadsheet like the one shown in Figure 4.1. If the sample considers differently weighted domains, the procedure described here should be applied independently within each of them (i.e. the sample frame data should be entered in a separate spreadsheet for each domain). The spreadsheet contains one line for each PSU and columns for descriptive information such as the province, district (or whatever administrative hierarchies are used locally), PSU number, population, number of males, number of females, and number of households or dwellings.

---

31. For an extensive discussion of sample frames, see UN (1986).

32. At least minimally sufficient census information has been available in most LSMS surveys. One exception was the Conakry 1988 survey. There the last colonial census had recorded some 50,000 people in the city, which had grown to about 1 million by 1988. This situation was resolved with a special cartographic operation and a subsequent area sampling procedure that does not need to be further described because it is unlikely to be necessary in other countries. The current wave of LSMS surveys will benefit from the 1991-1993 wave of national censuses, which provide census data for most countries.

Figure 4.1: List of First Stage Sampling Units

	A	B	C	D	E	F	G
1	Pro-	Dis-	PSU	Popu-	N° of	N° of	N° of
2	vince	trict		lation	Males	Females	Hholds
3							
4	1	1	1	365	180	185	62
5	1	1	2	262	143	119	43
6	1	1	3	357	172	185	58
7	1	1	4	503	267	236	71
..	...	...	...	...	...	...	...

After all the data have been entered and before proceeding any further, a series of checks should be carried out to ensure that no PSUs have been omitted from the listing and that all the data are correct. These tests are relatively easy to implement within the spreadsheet, and may include the following: (i) The total population in each PSU should equal the number of males plus the number of females in the PSU. (ii) The masculinity rate (number of males as a percent of the number of females) in each PSU should be within reasonable limits (e.g., between 80 and 120 percent). (iii) The average household size in each PSU should be within reasonable limits (e.g., between 3 and 10 persons per household). (iv) The total number of PSUs and households, as well as the totals by sex in each administrative unit, should be consistent with the other information available from the statistical agency.

Also, the list should be scanned to make sure that the PSUs are not too small. Small PSUs may be too homogeneous (and some of them could even be too small to select the required number of households in the second stage). PSUs smaller than 30 households should be appended to some of the neighboring PSUs, which is facilitated by the fact that statistical agencies generally number the PSUs according to some geographical pattern, so that two PSUs with sequential codes will be neighbors. For example, when the sample frame was being developed for an LSMS being planned for Paraguay, almost all PSUs in urban areas were smaller than 10 households and an ad hoc computer program was written to create larger aggregates.

SELECTING PSUs. After the sample frame has been reviewed, the actual selection of the sample of PSUs to be visited by the survey can proceed. The method for making this random selection with PPS will be explained below. Here we assume that the *number of households* is used as a measure of PSU size. The same method would apply if some other reasonable measure of PSU size were used.

Another column must be added to the spreadsheet for the cumulative number of households. This column will contain the total number of households up to and including the corresponding PSU on each line, as in column "H" in

Figure 4.2. The last line in column H will contain the total number of households.[33]

Figure 4.2: Cumulative Totals in the List of First Stage Sampling Units

	A	B	C	D	E	F	G	H
1	Pro-	Dis-	PSU	Popu-	N° of	N° of	N° of	Cumulative
2	vince	trict		lation	Males	Females	Hholds	N° of Hhhs
3								
4	1	1	1	365	180	185	62	62
5	1	1	2	262	143	119	43	105
6	1	1	3	357	172	185	58	163
7	1	1	4	503	267	236	71	234
..	...	...	...	...	...	...	...	.....

The complete spreadsheet should be printed and kept for reference. Selecting PSUs with PPS can be done manually on the printout or automatically with the spreadsheet. For the sake of simplicity the manual procedure is described here.

First, divide the total number of households by the number of PSUs to be selected and round it to the nearest whole number. Call this number "SI" (the sampling interval).

$$SI = \frac{Number\ of\ households}{Number\ of\ PSUs\ to\ be\ selected}$$

For instance, if the number of households is 200,000, and 184 PSUs are to be selected, then SI = 200,000 / 184 = 1,087.

Second, using a table of random numbers or a scientific pocket calculator, obtain a random number between 1 and SI (if a calculator is used, obtain a random number between 0 and 1, multiply it by SI, add 1, and drop the decimals). Call this number "RS" (the random start). Assume, for instance, that RS turns out to be 127.

---

33. Column H can easily be calculated within the spreadsheet with a simple formula. Continuing with the example in Figure 3.1, the formula G4 + H3 would be entered in cell H4, and then copied all the way down column H.

68

Third, write a sequence of the 184 numbers obtained by starting with RS, and repeatedly adding SI. With the above values of RS and SI, this sequence would start like this:

$$127$$
$$127 + 1087 = 1214$$
$$1214 + 1087 = 2301$$
$$2301 + 1087 = 3388$$
$$\ldots \qquad \ldots$$

Fourth, starting with the first number in the sequence, scan the printout of the PSU list for the first PSU where the "Cumulative N° of Households" is equal to or larger than this number. This PSU is selected for the sample.

Continuing with the example above, the first number in the sequence is 127. Scanning the PSU list, the first and second PSUs should be skipped, because the respective cumulative numbers of households are 62 and 105, which are less than 127. However, the cumulative number of households for the third PSU is 163, which is greater than 127. PSU Number 3 in District 1 of Province 1 would therefore become the first PSU selected in the sample (see Figure 4.3).

Figure 4.3: Selecting the First Stage Sampling Units

	A	B	C	D	E	F	G	H
1	Pro-	Dis-	PSU	Popu-	N° of	N° of	N° of	Cumulative
2	vince	trict		lation	Males	Females	Hholds	N° of Hhs
3								
4	1	1	1	365	180	185	62	62
5	1	1	2	262	143	119	43	105
6	1	1	3	357	172	185	58	163 ←
7	1	1	4	503	267	236	71	234
..	...	...	...	...	...	...	...	....

Finally, repeat the above procedure for the remaining 183 numbers in the sequence and create a separate list of the province, district, and numbers of the PSUs thus selected.[34]

SORTING THE SAMPLE FRAME. The selection procedure described above will almost certainly result in a sample of households that conserves the overall characteristics of the sample frame. In other words, the proportion of urban households in the sample, the distribution of the sample by province, and so forth, will all be statistically similar to those in the general population. However, since the selection is random some slight deviations may occur. For instance, by

---

34. This method is known as "systematic sampling with PPS." Alternative methods for PPS selection are possible but seldom used in practice.

sheer bad luck the sample may contain a larger proportion of northern households than the sample frame.

There is, however, a simple way of making sure that one particular distributional criterion of the households is reproduced in the sample in the best possible way. All that is needed is to sort the PSUs in the sample frame according to that criterion (north to south, for instance) before the selection.[35] In many cases, the "natural" order of the sample frame — according to encoding of administrative units — will be adequate and no further sorting will be necessary.

SEGMENTING LARGE PSUS. The household listing operation becomes too burdensome in PSUs larger than 300 households. This problem is aggravated by the PPS procedure, which tends to bring disproportionately many of the larger PSUs into the sample. One possible solution is just to accept that the household listing operation will be harder and longer than usual in those cases, but if they are very large or if many of them are selected in the sample, it may become necessary to split them into smaller units, called *segments*. This need only be done for the large PSUs actually selected in the sample. Segmentation consists of dividing the area of the PSU into pieces, only one of which is selected in the sample. Segments should have clearly defined boundaries, and a rough estimate of the number of households in each segment should be made, either using recent maps or aerial photographs or by means of a "quick count" of dwellings in the field. The original PSU in the list is replaced by the segments (each with their size measures adding up to the original). Then listing only the segment that is selected need be done.

PLANNING THE FIELD WORK. To distribute the selected PSUs among field teams, their locations should first be plotted on a map of the country. They can then be grouped into regions of approximately equal size while trying to spread the workloads evenly and reduce travel time as much as possible. As a by-product of this process, the optimal locations of the teams' base stations are determined. Figure 4.4, for example, shows the location of the clusters surveyed in the 1988-89 Ghana LSMS survey, the regions covered by each field team, and their headquarters.

The next step is to establish the work schedule for each team, that is, to determine in advance when each PSU will be visited. In standard LSMS surveys household interviews are conducted throughout a 12-month period. To even out

---

35. Sorting of the sample frame prior to systematic selection is sometimes referred to as "implicit stratification." This method is simpler and more reliable than forcibly allocating the number of PSUs to be selected to certain categories. The latter approach is prone to subjective decisions that unnecessarily sacrifice the self-weighted character of the sample or its domains. In addition, all too often these decisions are undocumented or the documentation lost, so that the required corrective weights cannot be used.

70

the effects of seasonality, the order in which each team visits the PSUs assigned to it should be random.[36]

For the Nepal LSMS, this was done by giving a serial number to each of the 275 PSUs selected in the first sampling stage. The numbers 001 to 275 were given to the PSUs at random. After the 275 PSUs were distributed among the 12 field teams (unevenly in this case, given the differences in accessibility inside the country), a simple sort by PSU serial number produced a work schedule for each team.

Most programming languages and other software have built-in random number generators, but applying them to assign serial numbers to a group of objects in a random order (a problem technically known as "random permutation," or colloquially as "shuffling") is not as easy as it seems. A short algorithm to produce a random permutation of the first N integers is given in Basic in Figure 4.5. The algorithm can easily be implemented in other languages.

Implementation of the Second Sampling Stage

HOUSEHOLD LISTING. A list of all dwellings in each selected PSU is needed to determine which dwellings on the list will be visited in the survey. Usually this list will have to be created or updated for the survey, though in some cases it can be borrowed from a census or from another survey. The option of borrowing an existing list should be examined critically, however, to ensure that the existing lists are recent, complete, and have good addresses. In particular, demographic mobility makes it dangerous to use lists that will be more than one or two years old by the time of the actual field work. The standard for completeness is difficult to set, but under-enumeration in the census of five percent would be worrisome and the standard could well be stricter. The information on the list should make it easy to locate the households once they are selected. In areas with a good street address system, addresses may be sufficient. Alternately, grid codes on census maps may be used, or references to landmarks and the name of the household head.

---

36. It is sometimes argued that such a random arrangement is too expensive because it forces the teams to move back and forth across their territories during the year rather than visiting the PSUs in a more orderly fashion. The latter option, however, entails the danger of confusing time and space at the analytical stage. In other words, if all PSUs in an area are visited in the same months, it may be unclear if a certain constant condition is due to seasonality or to some geographic characteristic. An "orderly" arrangement of the PSUs is also unlikely to be more economic in any case because LSMS surveys are devised so that field teams come back to their headquarters between field visits — a feature that will be explained later, in Chapter 5.

Figure 4.4: Assignment of Work Areas, Ghana Living Standards Survey, 1988-89

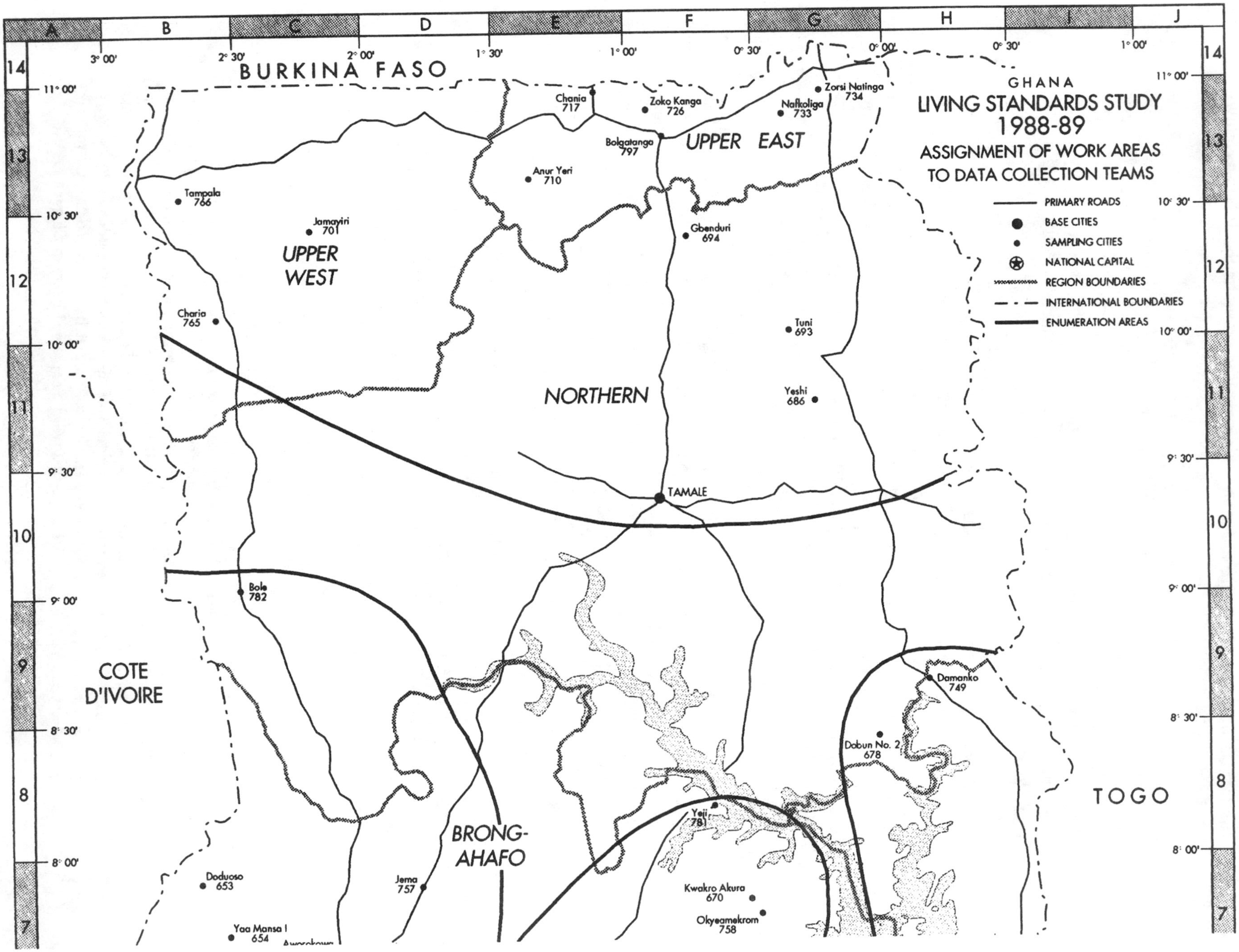
GHANA
LIVING STANDARDS STUDY
1988-89
ASSIGNMENT OF WORK AREAS
TO DATA COLLECTION TEAMS
PRIMARY ROADS
BASE CITIES
SAMPLING CITIES
NATIONAL CAPITAL
REGION BOUNDARIES
INTERNATIONAL BOUNDARIES
ENUMERATION AREAS
BURKINA FASO
COTE D'IVOIRE
TOGO
UPPER WEST
UPPER EAST
NORTHERN
BRONG-AHAFO
Chania 717
Zoko Kanga 726
Zorsi Natinga 734
Nafkoliga 733
Bolgatanga 797
Anur Yeri 710
Tampala 766
Jamayiri 701
Gbenduri 694
Charia 765
Tuni 693
Yeshi 686
TAMALE
Bole 782
Damanko 749
Dobun No. 2 678
Yeji 781
Doduoso 653
Jema 757
Kwakro Akura 670
Okyeamekrom 758
Yaa Mansa I 654
A B C D E F G H I J
14 13 12 11 10 9 8 7
3° 00'
2° 30'
2° 00'
1° 30'
1° 00'
0° 30'
0° 00'
0° 30'
1° 00'
11° 00'
10° 30'
10° 00'
9° 30'
9° 00'
8° 30'
8° 00'

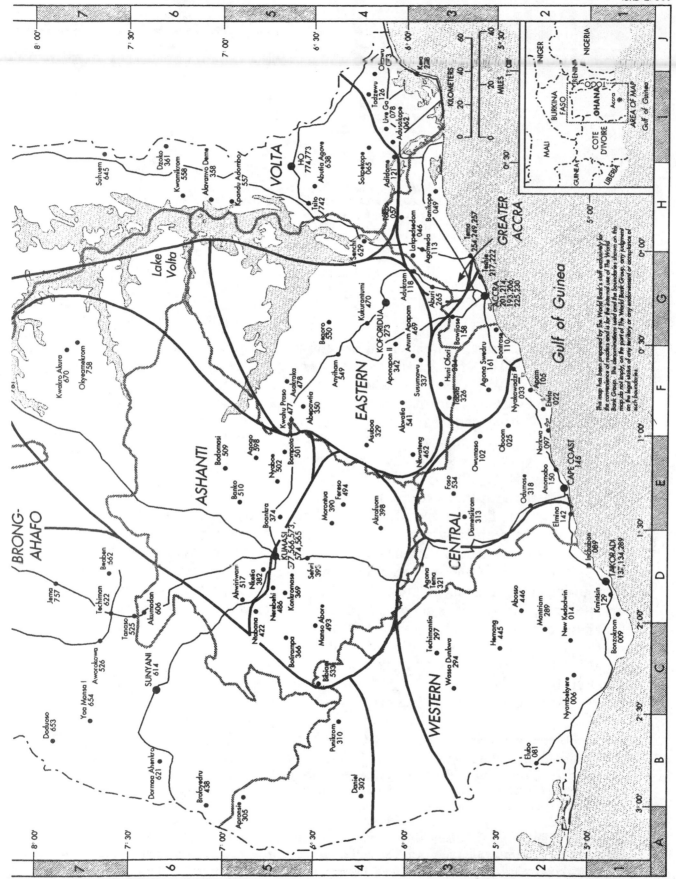

IBRD 27533

NOVEMBER 1995

Figure 4.5: An Algorithm to Produce a Random Permutation of the Integers 1 to N

```
                    randomize timer
                    input N
                    dim P(N)
                    for I=1 to N
                      P(I)=I
                      K=1+int(I*rnd))
                      swap P(I),P(K)
                    next
```

The statement "dim P(N)" initializes an array P with N elements. In the subsequent "for ... next" loop, the array elements are successively given the values 1, 2, 3, .., I, .., N. The element I is interchanged with one of the elements already present in the array (K), selected at random. The initial values are given in the "P(I)=I" statement and the interchange is done with the "swap P(I),P(K)" statement". The statement "K=1+int(I*rnd)" produces a random integer K, from 1 to I ("rnd" generates a random real number between 0 and 1 and "int" takes the integer part of a number).

Household listing can be carried out either as a separate field operation conducted in all PSUs before the survey starts or by the survey teams themselves when they first arrive in each PSU. The first option is more expensive but more reliable. The expense is incurred because each locality must be visited twice, once during the listing and then again during the survey. It may also entail some difficulty in locating the selected dwellings during the survey because of the time that will pass between the listing and the survey itself.

Listing as a separate exercise is more reliable than listing as part of field work because staff that are specifically trained and devoted to listing are less likely to bias the sample by excluding the dwellings that are harder to reach. (These dwellings are usually inhabited by poorer households who have arrived in the area recently). The survey teams, working under pressure to start interviewing quickly, are more prone to make mistakes in this regard. Also, with separate listing the dwellings to be surveyed can be randomly selected from lists in a single central location using reliable and uniform procedures.

The two most important characteristics of the list are that all dwellings in each PSU be included on it and that it allows the selected dwellings to be located easily.[37] Some practical guidelines can help attain these objectives:

---

37. The importance of listing procedures is underscored by the experience of the Côte d'Ivoire LSMS surveys. The mean household size observed in the survey dropped from 8.31 to 6.33 persons between 1985 and 1988. Close investigation of this striking phenomenon suggests that it was probably caused by a change in the listing method (see Coulombe and Demery, 1993 and Demery and Grootaert, 1993.) In 1985 and 1986 shortcut procedures were used, rather than the recommended full listing of the households in reasonably sized PSUs. The implications for policy analysis of the apparently inaccurate sampling in the early years were considerable. Demery and Grootaert, 1993, calculated weights to try to correct for the change in sampling procedures. They

- Field work should always start with a cartographic reconnaissance. The maps do not need to be very precise in terms of scale or the locations of the dwellings, but they should show the PSU boundaries and the landmarks used to split it into smaller areas. This helps to organize the daily work of the different enumerators.

- Each enumerator should scan the assigned area in an orderly fashion, striving to keep neighboring dwellings close to each other in the list.

- As a rule of thumb, the time needed to list a PSU can be estimated from a standard daily yield of 80 dwellings per enumerator in urban areas to 50 in rural areas.

- The lists should reflect the proper concepts of dwellings and households. Enumerators should be trained to tell the difference between the two.

- Dwellings should be clearly listed with appropriate addresses so that interviewers can find them easily during the survey. Designers should use some imagination to achieve this goal where street names and house numbers are not well established. In many surveys dwellings are numbered as a part of the listing operation, either by affixing a numbered sticker to the outside of the home or by painting a number on the wall or door. At the time this is being written (in fall 1995) the possibility of using Global Positioning Systems (GPSs) to support field work of future LSMSs is being considered. GPSs are battery-operated devices the size of a pocket calculator, currently commercially available for about $500, that use satellite signals to pinpoint the user's position with remarkable accuracy (within 10 meters or so in the three dimensions: latitude, longitude, and altitude). Enumerators could use GPSs to record the dwelling locations during the listing operation; interviewers would use them later to locate those selected for the sample.

- The complete list should always be recorded in a standard form with one line per dwelling. The list can be several pages long, depending on the size of the PSU and the number of enumerators engaged in the operation. Though the precise layout of such a form depends on local conditions, a typical list form is shown in Figure 4.6.

---

then calculated mean consumption, poverty, and a series of other important indicators using the weighted and unweighted data and found substantial differences. For example, the head count estimate of poverty in 1986 fell by 14 percent when corrective weights were applied. The bias differed widely among socioeconomic groups and regions. The time series analysis of poverty was also affected. The unweighted data apparently underestimated the increase in poverty between 1985 and 1987.

Figure 4.6: Typical Listing Form

Region: _____ Province: _____ Locality: _____ PSU Code: [ ]

Date of the listing: _____ Enumerator: _____ Page: [/]

| Serial Number | Address of the dwelling | Head of the household | Household size | | |
			M	F	total
01					
02					
..	...	...	...	...	...
nn					

• Supervision of the listing operation is crucial. Listers have an obvious incentive not to be too diligent in locating hard-to-find or remote dwellings. Since there is no criterion to tell how diligent they are being that can be easily monitored in the office, the field supervision will be key. Supervisory staff (or other listers) must re-visit a subset of listed areas, especially the difficult parts of them, to verify the listing.[38] An option that might be feasible in some settings is to use lists from other sources to help in this process. For example, if the PSUs can be identified with electoral areas, voting lists might be used. Although not every resident of the PSU will be on the voting list, any address on the voting list should be listed in the PSU listing.

Columns may be added to this model for key landmarks, the occupations of the head of the household, or whatever other information could help in finding the dwelling. It may also be useful to have the enumerators fill in separate lines for buildings that are not dwellings, such as shops and offices; in that case, a special check column should be added so that the real dwellings can be told from the other buildings. However, only essential information needed to identify the dwelling should be recorded. Including too much data slows the field process and risks shifting the enumerators' interest from listing to interviewing.

So far this discussion has assumed that the maps from the most recent census are available, so that the listing focusses on updating the listing of dwellings within well defined boundaries. In fact, it is often the case that some, or even all, of the maps have been lost in the intervening years.[39] In such cases,

---

38. It can be especially useful to do this around dusk, when lights or smoke from cooking fires may help locate dwellings. Carrying binoculars may be useful for finding dwellings across ravines, or down roads marked no trespassing.

39. The sampling chapter in Delaine and others (1992) treats the allied problem of what to do when the boundaries were poorly defined in the original maps.

76

it is sometimes possible to reconstruct the maps. This would happen, for example, when only the occasional map has been lost and other maps for the contiguous sampling units still exist.

Another means of reconstructing the maps may be possible when the sampling units correspond to some administrative unit that the populace or officials will recognize. This is often the case, especially in rural areas. For example, a sampling unit might correspond to a ward or village. In this case there is a special detail to watch for. Say that PSU 348 was labeled Alama, which is the name of the ward that it corresponds to. It would seem a straightforward matter to send listers to the ward of Alama and have them establish the boundaries of the ward and start listing. But Alama may have grown a good deal in the several years since the census and the area subdivided into new wards. The central area will still be called Alama, but the new wards will have other names, say Bendicion, Caceres, Durango, and Esperanza. In this case if the lister goes to Alama and asks where its boundaries are, he or she will be told about the new boundaries that cover only a fraction of the area of the original Alama. All the area covered by Bendicion, Caceres, Durango, and Esperanza would be omitted and would not be listed. The population of these areas would effectively be excluded from the sample. The solution to these problems lies in trying to verify from the appropriate authorities (the ministry of local government, ward officials, etc.) whether the boundaries and names have been constant since the last mapping. This should be done both by the statistical agency's central office for the country as a whole and verified by individual listers.

ADJUSTING FOR DIFFERENCES IN PSU SIZE. Differences are sure to be found between the "census" size of each PSU (the size that was used for PPS selection in the first sampling stage) and the "observed" size (from the listing operation). For instance, the listing operation of the Nepal LSMS — conducted in mid-1994, two years after the 1992 census — showed that in 153 of the 275 selected clusters the "census" and "observed" cluster size differed by more than ten percent. The minimum and maximum values of the ratio of "census" to "observed" size were 0.23 and 3.84. The mean value of the ratio was 1.06.

These differences are partly due to imperfections in the census and partly due to demographic mobility. Whatever the reason, the differences alter the self-weighted character of the sample in each analytical domain, which makes it necessary to correct the sampling weights in order to obtain unbiased point estimates from the survey. Assuming for simplicity that the number of households was used as a measure of PSU size in the first sampling stage, and calling C_i and O_i the census and observed number of households in PSU i (belonging to weighted domain k) the expansion factor w_i for the households in that PSU should be

$$w_i = w_k \frac{O_i}{C_i}$$

where $w_k = N_k/n_k$ is the basic sampling weight of domain k, defined before (see Section *Determining the Basic Sample Design Parameters*). The formula would be slightly different if some other measure of size (such as the population or the number of dwellings) had been used in the first sampling stage.

It goes without saying that the complete list of weights w_i for all PSUs (and better still, the list of all C_i's and O_i's) should be carefully kept and made available to analysts as a part of the survey documentation and data sets.

SELECTING DWELLINGS. The dwellings to be visited are selected by systematic sampling from the PSU listings. A few extra dwellings are also selected to be used if replacements are needed in the field.

The selection procedure, though generally well known to statistical officers everywhere, is illustrated below in Figure 4.7. This example assumes that 16 dwellings are to be interviewed and that 4 extra dwellings are to be selected in each PSU as replacements. The exercise is to select those 20 dwellings, based on information contained on a typical listing form such as that shown in Figure 4.6.

First, count the total number of dwellings in the PSU and record it in the space on top of the form. Assume, for example, that there are 86 dwellings in the PSU.

Second, divide the total number of dwellings by the number of dwellings to be selected and keep the first decimal place. The result is called the sampling interval (SI) and is also recorded on top of the form. In this example, if the number of dwellings to be selected is 20, SI would be 4.3 (because 86 / 20 = 4.3).

Third, select a one-decimal random number less than the sampling interval (in the example, this would be a number from 0.0 to 4.2; it can be obtained by selecting a random integer from 00 to 42 and inserting a decimal point before the last digit). Add 1 to that random number. The result is called the "random start" (RS) and is also recorded on top of the form. Assume, for instance, that RS turns out to be 3.2. Write the 20 numbers obtained by starting with RS and repeatedly adding SI. With the above values of RS and SI, the 20 numbers would be:

```
           3.2       20.4 + 4.3 = 24.7      41.9 + 4.3 = 46.2      63.4 + 4.3 = 67.7
 3.2 + 4.3 = 7.5      24.7 + 4.3 = 29.0      46.2 + 4.3 = 50.5      67.7 + 4.3 = 72.0
 7.5 + 4.3 = 11.8     29.0 + 4.3 = 33.3      50.5 + 4.3 = 54.8      72.0 + 4.3 = 76.3
11.8 + 4.3 = 16.1     33.3 + 4.3 = 37.6      54.8 + 4.3 = 59.1      76.3 + 4.3 = 80.6
16.1 + 4.3 = 20.4     37.6 + 4.3 = 41.9      59.1 + 4.3 = 63.4      80.6 + 4.3 = 84.9
```

Finally, take the integer part of each number. The 20 numbers obtained in this way (3, 7, 11, 16, 20, 24, 29, 33, 37, 41, 46, 50, 54, 59, 63, 67, 72, 76, 80 and 84), are the sequence numbers of the dwellings to be visited in the survey. The corresponding lines in the listing should be transferred to another form, called the *List of Selected Dwellings* (see Figure 4.7).

The households to be visited during the survey are those listed on the sixteen unshaded lines in the form. The dwellings on the shades lines are kept as reserve for possible replacements.

Both the full listing form with all dwellings and the list of selected dwellings will be needed by the field team responsible for the PSU during the survey (the former will help them locate the selected dwellings in the field, by referring to their neighbors). As this operational requirement entails the risk of loosing these documents, it is highly recommended to provide the field teams with photocopies and to file the original lists securely for at least five to 10 years. The lists constitute a precious material for central supervision and may even be required long after the end of the original project for panel or follow-up surveys, or even as base material for different surveys conducted by the statistical agency.

REPLACING HOUSEHOLDS. The above selection procedure implicitly assumes that it may be impossible to interview the households in some of the selected dwellings and that a standard procedure for replacing them has to be implemented. The most frequent reasons for replacement are:

The dwelling is unoccupied and is likely to remain unoccupied for the full survey period.

The dwelling has disappeared or is not being used for housing.

The dwelling cannot be located because the information in the listing is bad or insufficient (for example, illegible names or addresses).

The household refuses to be interviewed.

Figure 4.7: List of Selected Dwellings

Region: _____ Province: _____ Locality: _____ PSU Code: [ ]

Total No. of Dwellings: _____ Random start: _____ Interval: _____

Serial Number in the sample	Page and in the list	Serial Number	Address of dwelling	Head of the household	Household size		
					men	women	total
01							
02							
03							
04							
05							
06							
07							
08							
09							
10							
11							
12							
13							
14							
15							
16							
17							
18							
19							
20							

These cases should be carefully studied by the team supervisor. Only when the supervisor is convinced that the interview is impossible should the dwelling be replaced with the one on the nearest shaded line in the form.[40]

---

40. Notice that the shaded lines in the form are evenly interspaced between the unshaded lines. The idea is to replace households by near neighbors, which are likely to have similar socioeconomic characteristics. Shading every fifth line allows for replacement of up to 4 out of the 16 dwellings selected (a 25 percent non-response rate). A smaller proportion of replacements could be insufficient in certain worst-case PSUs; shading a much larger proportion of lines could

If the dwelling is occupied by a household different from the one recorded during the listing operation, the new household is interviewed without more ado. As said before, the LSMS samples are actually samples of dwellings, and such cases should not be counted as non-responses.

Selecting Random Persons in a Household

To reduce interview time, the LSMS questionnaire is sometimes designed so that certain modules are applied to one randomly selected person in the household.[41] The Côte d'Ivoire LSMS, for instance, collected fertility information from one woman 15 years or older.

As opposed to the other random selections described so far, which are most reliably carried out at central offices, the choice of a person at random in each household must be performed by the interviewer in the field. A simple procedure must be devised for this that gives each eligible person the same chance of selection and is verifiable so that the work of the interviewer can be tested for accuracy (the latter precludes the use of dice or other "truly random" methods).

Instead of the traditional Kish tables (Kish, 1965), LSMS surveys have opted for an original, alternative method.[42] As explained in the chapter on questionnaire design, each household member is assigned an identification code, generally from 01 to 20, in the household roster of the questionnaire. An adhesive label with a different random permutation of these numbers is affixed to each questionnaire. To select the person, the interviewer scans the list of identification codes on the label until the code of an individual who meets the defined eligibility criteria is reached. Figure 4.8 shows one of these labels.

Figure 4.8: Sticker Used for Selecting a
Random Individual Within the Household

```
┌──────────────────────────────────────┐
│  03 06 07 08 11 12 10 17 04 02        │
│                                        │
│  16 15 05 18 19 01 13 20 09 14        │
└──────────────────────────────────────┘
```

---

be interpreted by some field supervisors as an invitation to replace with abandon.

41. This section has been adapted from Ainsworth and Muñoz (1986).

42. Kish tables do not always give exactly the same chance of selection to every eligible individual. A more serious disadvantage of Kish tables is that they require the eligible individuals to be given a serial number prior to the selection, in addition to their standard ID codes. The co-existence of two different numbering systems for the same person may confuse the interviewer, and is avoided in the LSMS method.

The procedure is simple but requires careful training of the interviewers. They should scan the list of ID codes one line after the other, always from left to right, crossing out all the numbers that are rejected and circling the number of the first person who qualifies. This was not made clear at the beginning in Côte d'Ivoire, where at least one of the interviewers always searched for code 02 (usually the head's wife), and circled it without considering other women's IDs.

The process is verifiable by the supervisor, who can repeat the procedure with the label stuck to each questionnaire. It can also be checked by the data entry program.

The labels for all questionnaires in a survey can be quickly generated with a personal computer. A complete program is not given here because it needs to be adapted to specific circumstances as well as to the number of ID codes needed. The production of a different random permutation for each sticker is done with the algorithm presented in Figure 4.5.

Chapter 5: Field Operations

Key Messages

- LSMS field operations are conducted by independent teams. Each team is headed by a supervisor and composed of interviewers, a data entry operator, and a driver. An anthropometrist may also be included to record height and weight data and help complete the community-level questionnaires.

- Each team works throughout one year, visiting two PSUs per month. Each interviewer visits eight households in each PSU. Each household questionnaire is completed in two rounds, with visits two weeks apart.

- Data from the questionnaires are entered into a computer between the two rounds. If errors are detected, they are corrected immediately by actually re-visiting the households.

- The supervisor controls the quality of the team's field work through a variety of means that includes check-up interviews in some of the households.

- Central supervision of the field teams is performed by the survey core staff, composed of the survey manager, the field manager, and the data manager.

The field operations for LSMS surveys face two major challenges: to collect high-quality data and to make the information available for analysis quickly. These goals have often been realized, thanks largely to the procedures developed for field work. Since the first two LSMS surveys were conducted in 1985, field operations have evolved in response to changing technologies and to differing conditions in specific countries. Certain basic features, however, have remained relatively stable. Section A of this chapter describes recommended LSMS field procedures. It is of interest to all readers. Section B describes how to prepare for the field work. It will be of interest to those involved in planning the field work for a survey; others may skip or skim the section.

A. Standard LSMS Organization of Field Work

Four-Week Interview Cycle

LSMS field operations are organized on the basis of four-week cycles, which are spread over a 12-month period. In each four-week cycle, the field team completes the interviews for the sample households in two of the sample clusters (localities). The data entry operator works on the computer installed in the team base office, while the rest of the team travels between the office and the two locations.

The household questionnaire is divided into two parts, or "rounds," which are approximately equal in interview time. In the first week of the cycle, the first round of interviewing is completed in locality A. During the second week, the first round of interviewing is completed in locality B. The data from the first round of the household interviews in locality A are entered into the computer during the second week. Many common errors can be detected at this stage, as will be described in Chapter 6. During the third week, the interviewers return to locality A to carry out the second round of interviews. They can also correct any errors found in the first round of data. The data entry operator, meanwhile, enters the data from the interviews in locality B. During the fourth week of the cycle, the interviewers return to location B. They complete the second round of interviews and make any corrections needed on the first round. The week-by-week activities of the team members are summarized in Figure 5.1.

During the first visit to the household, the interviewer fills in the roster section and tries to schedule interviews with all of the people who should be respondents for the other modules in the questionnaire. For the sections that pertain to individuals, such as health, education, employment, and so forth, the interviewer tries to interview in person each household member who is 7 years or older. The adults who are the most responsible for young children respond on their behalf. Usually the interviewer will try to go through the roster in all households in the first day or two in the locality. On these first visits, some of the mini-interviews may be done if it happens to be convenient to the respondents. But more often a series of mini-interviews will be set up during the remainder of the week. For sections of the questionnaire that pertain to part or all of the household, such as household purchases, farming activities, and housing quality, the person best informed is determined during the round one interview. Then an appointment is made to interview that person in round two.

In each mini-interview the interviewer will go through all pertinent modules in the order they appear in the questionnaire. Thus the first week's interview with the woman of the house would cover her health, education, labor activities, etc. Then, if she had a child under the age of 7, the interview would proceed with the appropriate modules for health, education, child health, etc. with the mother responding for the child. Then, possibly at a different time or on a different day in the first week, the interview with a teenage member of the household would take place. In the second week in the locality, the woman of the household might be interviewed again for the consumption modules.

This practice raises data quality in several ways. First, since the person best qualified to answer each part of the questionnaire is interviewed, inaccurate responses are avoided. Second, the whole survey, which can take three or more

Figure 5.1: Weekly Activities of the Field Members[43]

Week	Locality	Team members			
		Supervisor	Interviewers	Anthropometrist	Data entry operator
1	A	1 Introduces the team to local authorities 2 Selects households or locates households selected previously 3 Contacts selected households and determines replacements if needed 4 Observes one interview per interviewer 5 Verifies that questionnaires are complete and encodes items if needed 6 Re-interviews randomly selected households 7 Collects community-level data 8 Gives completed questionnaires to data entry operator 9 Reviews printouts of round two from previous locality	Conduct round one in all households	Weighs and measures individuals in all households	Corrects inconsistencies and enters round two data from previous locality
2	B	1 to 8 (same as week 1) 9 Reviews printouts of round one, locality A	Conduct round one in all households	Weighs and measures individuals in all households	Enters round one data for locality A
3	A	1 to 8 (same as week 1) 9 Reviews printouts of round one, locality B	Conduct round two in all households Correct round one errors detected by data entry program	Weighs and measures selected individuals	Enters round one data for locality B
4	B	1 to 8 (same as week 1) 9 Reviews printouts of round two, locality A	Conduct round two in all households Correct round one errors detected by data entry program	Weighs and measures selected individuals	Corrects inconsistencies and enters round two data for locality A

hours in each household, is broken into a series of more manageable mini-interviews that usually run no more than 30 minutes. Respondent fatigue is thus minimized. Third, since the mini-interviews are scheduled according to the respondents' convenience (within the week in the locality), the refusal rate is also minimized. Fourth, the period between the two interviews bounds the recall period for many of the questions on consumption, which minimizes one kind of recall error.

---

43. Adapted from Ainsworth and Munoz (1986).

The actual length of the interview varies widely from one household to another and between countries. The difference between countries depends on the length of the questionnaires used. Within countries, interview time varies depending on the number of people in the household and the number of different household activities. For instance, the agriculture module is only given to farmers and the module on household enterprises only applies to the self-employed; likewise, the health section can take a few seconds or several minutes, depending on whether the respondent has been sick recently. However, given that interviewers generally need to visit each household several times, it is more useful to evaluate interview time (and consequently interviewer productivity) in terms of "households per week" or "households per day" rather in "hours per household." With the standard LSMS setup, interviewers are expected to complete eight half-interviews per week — an average of two half-interviews per day. (The term "half-interview" refers to the splitting of the questionnaire into two rounds of approximately equal length).

The LSMS field organization offers several powerful advantages. First and perhaps most important, it raises data quality. The concurrent data entry makes it possible to correct mistakes while interviewers are still in the field. Spreading the interviews over a full year also makes it possible to use a small number of field teams. With a small number of teams, training can be centralized. This helps ensure that all field staff receive the same instructions. Each interviewer conducts many interviews and thus becomes more adept than in surveys that rely on larger teams. Using a small number of teams also makes their close supervision by the central office possible. Perhaps more important, it makes management easier. It is difficult to imagine that the quality would remain as high with hundreds of teams as with a handful.

Second, the concurrent data entry also makes the whole data set available for analysis just days or weeks after the final interview. Thus the goal of the timely availability of the data is accomplished. Third, the year-round field work ensures that estimates derived from the whole data set will not be subject to seasonal biases, an analytic/measurement advantage. Fourth, since each team must be equipped with a vehicle and computer, having fewer teams lowers overhead costs.

There are a few disadvantages to the LSMS field organization. For one thing, the field workers need to be highly competent. Often they command high salaries partly because of their high skill level and partly because of the hardship of continuous travel. For statistical agencies with permanent interviewers who work on a series of surveys that have a short field work period, the LSMS teams may seem outside the mainstream and the wage differentials may be difficult to accept. Also, frustration is often expressed that the lead time between the decision to carry out the survey and the availability of data is extended by the long period of field work. Although LSMS surveys are usually able to produce preliminary results after the first six months of field work, the delay is sometimes of real concern. However, given the usual record of long lags between the end of interviewing and the availability of data, the total lead time for LSMS surveys remains better than the average for national household surveys of similar complexity, even with the long period of field work.

Composition of Survey Staff

The key headquarters staff includes the survey manager, data manager, and field manager. These are the minimum requirements. In most countries this base structure must be strengthened by appointing a deputy data manager and a deputy field manager, and sometimes it is useful to employ a secretary and a bookkeeper. The need for a bookkeeper will be greater where financing is being provided by more than one agency or where substantial procurement will take place.

The LSMS core staff should be organized to work together *as a team*, with the survey manager being the only head during the entire preparation stage instead of having individuals respond to separate divisions in the data collection agency. This is especially important — and sometimes hard to achieve — in large national statistical agencies that are organized under the traditional departmental structure with a census department, a household survey department, a data processing department, and so forth. If the LSMS is designed as a permanent effort, rather than a one-shot exercise, the statistical agency may decide on a different managerial structure once the survey has become a routine activity.

In cases where rather than having the core team report to a single head of the LSMS survey, each person reports to the head of department (for example, the data manager to the head of the data processing department, the field manager to the head of the surveys department, etc.) it is exceedingly difficult to ensure that the numerous details all get done in time to dovetail with each other. And often tasks fall between the cracks altogether. The most recent case of this in LSMS experience is in Tunisia. Although they had planned to use full LSMS field work techniques, in fact at the time of this writing, the survey has been in the field for two months and the computers are still stuck in customs, the data entry program is not finished and data entry operators have not been trained. This probably has multiple causes, including a lack of conviction that concurrent data entry is worthwhile, but clearly the fact that arrangements for field work and data management were not coordinated by a single team was critical to the failure to realize the original plan.

Each of the LSMS field teams is headed by a supervisor and usually includes two interviewers, a driver with a car, and a data entry operator. This standard setup has been used in Côte d'Ivoire, Peru, Ghana, Mauritania, and Tanzania and elsewhere. In some countries local conditions have dictated changes in the composition of the field teams:

If the survey is to collect weight and height data for the household members then a specialized technician — the anthropometrist — may be included in the team.[44]

When a team has to work mainly in large urban areas, a third interviewer may sometimes be added. This allows for additional interviews to take place at a low marginal cost.[45]

Cultural constraints in certain countries may require that an adult must be interviewed by someone of the same sex. This was the case in the Pakistan LSMS. Since it would likewise not have been appropriate for a female to travel alone with several men, each team had two female and two male interviewers. The female interviewers also served as anthropometrists.

Duties of Survey Team Members

SURVEY MANAGER. The survey manager should have decision making authority. This person coordinates the questionnaire's design, maintains communication with the technical assistance suppliers and data users, sets up the activities leading up to the survey in liaison with the existing statistical structures, and manages the implementation of the survey itself, and ensures that data documentation and dissemination procedures are put in place.

---

44. The LSMS's practice of using a special team member for anthropometry rather than assigning this task to the interviewers developed in part for reasons specific to the first countries where the surveys were done and that may be not persuasive in other countries. If anthropometry is assigned to the interviewers, then the logistics of whether to have one set of equipment or two, how to avoid carrying it around more than necessary, how to arrange adequate training and the like, need to be worked out but should not be insurmountable. Also, since the anthropometrists often provide a good deal of assistance to the supervisors in helping administer the community and price questionnaires, their elimination may have repercussions for the total work load of the supervisors which would need to be considered.

45. The only additional cost is the third person's salary and travel expenses. No extra supervisors, data entry operators, cars, or computers are needed. One obvious disadvantage of the larger team is that supervision is somewhat diluted. The cost/benefit tradeoff of increasing the size of the interview team is, however, also affected by the sample design and cluster size. Normally all team members need to work in the same location, where households will tend to be similar. Thus the marginal value in the accuracy of the estimates gained from adding an interviewer to an existing team and location will be lower than from using the extra interviewer in a different location. For instance, three teams of two interviewers working in three clusters would provide more accurate estimates than two teams of three interviewers working in two clusters. However, in big cities it is possible to have the three interviewers work in different clusters and still be within reach of the team supervisor. This requires selecting more clusters in the first sampling stage and fewer households per cluster in the second. Alternately, the number of days spent in each cluster might be reduced.

DATA MANAGER. The data manager designs and develops the data entry program and has input into the data entry aspects of the questionnaire design. This person writes the data entry manuals, selects and trains the data entry operators, prepares the data bases for analysis, and helps prepare tabulations and graphs for the first statistical abstract.

FIELD MANAGER. The field manager designs and supervises the sampling procedures and the household listing operation, and is responsible for preparing the pilot survey and the field test. This person also designs the field operational procedures and the field manuals and is responsible for selecting and training the field staff. When the survey is fielded, this person implements the central supervision of the teams. This includes reviewing the various written supervision instruments described below and occasionally conducting the same kind of observation and double-checking of interviews as the field supervisors.

SUPERVISOR. As the primary person responsible for the quality of information collected in the field, the supervisor is the most important member of the field team. The supervisor's main responsibilities include:

- OVERALL FIELD SUPERVISION, COORDINATION, AND MONITORING OF DATA COLLECTION ACTIVITIES. An important part of this task is coordinating the work of the anthropometrist and interviewer in each household and of the male and female interviewers when staff of both genders are needed. This is particularly important when an exchange of questionnaires between them becomes necessary. In addition, the supervisor may on occasion have to assist the interviewers in locating households and ensuring their willingness to respond to the survey. If necessary, supervisors will select replacement households in line with criteria determined for the survey as a whole by the central managers.

- PUBLIC RELATIONS. The supervisor should establish contact with local authorities in each area visited by the survey, and deliver letters of introduction, specially prepared brochures, and any other materials and information that might be necessary to ensure their cooperation.

- PREPARATION OF THE QUESTIONNAIRES. The supervisor must copy the household number and the name of the household head onto each questionnaire before giving it to the interviewers.

- COMPLETING THE COMMUNITY-LEVEL QUESTIONNAIRES. When the task cannot be delegated to the anthropometrist, the supervisor must complete the community, price, and facility questionnaires. For the community questionnaire, part of the information is derived by observing the place and recording aspects actually experienced by the teams (e.g. the condition of the roads or the distance to the nearest large city). Other data must be obtained from knowledgeable people in the locality, such as mayors, village elders, police chiefs, and so forth, For this part of the questionnaire, the supervisor has a great deal of discretion over whom to choose as respondent.[46]

For the part of the community questionnaire or the facility questionnaires pertaining to local schools and health facilities, the supervisor must identify which schools and clinics to include and then interview the headmaster and clinic administrator or their delegates.

For the price questionnaire, the supervisor determines which markets or shops to visit and fills out the price questionnaire. The supervisor explains to the vendor the purpose of the survey and gathers price information in an interview. The interviewer does not bargain for the goods.[47] Most food and some non-food items are weighed as well. The full instructions for the price questionnaire used in the Kagera Health and Development survey are given in Annex IV.

- MONITORING, REVIEW, AND EVALUATION OF THE QUALITY OF FIELD INTERVIEWS. The supervisor is expected to routinely observe interviews without advance notice to the interviewer. The supervisor should give immediate feedback based on established criteria for evaluating interviewers. The supervisor uses the "Interviewer Evaluation" form provided for this purpose. (Examples of this form and information on how it is designed are provided below).

- QUALITY CONTROL OF COMPLETED QUESTIONNAIRES. Once data are collected for each round of the survey, the supervisor should check that the interviewer's writing is legible, skip patterns were followed, and the instructions in the questionnaire were followed. The "Questionnaire Verification" form is used to record the information from the quality check. (See below for more details on the design of the form.)

---

46. In contrast the SDA community survey handbook (Wold, 1995), recommends using group interviews where the group is meant to include representatives of different sub-groups within the community (men and women, poor and better-off, different ethnic groups). Two interviewers are used in such cases, one to lead the discussion and another to record the results.

47. Since it is generally true that outsiders will have to pay higher prices than local residents where bargaining is the norm, the question arises as to whether this procedure for gathering data results in accurate prices. The reader must remember, however, that in the small towns and villages where the procedure is most often used, the news of the survey team's arrival will probably have already spread and been commented on. Thus the social context of the transaction is different than if someone from the capital city arrived and just wanted to buy some food for his own consumption. The SDA community survey handbook (Wold, 1995), nonetheless recommends using one of three alternate procedures: hire local residents to conduct the price survey, interview a community group, or gather price information on the household questionnaires.

- CHECK-UP INTERVIEWS. The supervisor should also revisit randomly selected households in each location to verify that the interviewers have visited the household and to cross-check some of the information provided by the household. The results are recorded on the "Check-up Interview" form (see below).

- CHECKING THE DATA ENTRY PRINTOUTS. The supervisor should compare the printout with the data on the questionnaire and should check errors in data that were detected by the data entry program. Either the supervisor or one of the interviewers should revisit the household, if possible, to correct the errors.

- MANAGEMENT OF PERSONNEL, EQUIPMENT, AND VEHICLES. The supervisor is responsible for managing the team's support staff (i.e., the data entry operator and the driver). The supervisor should ensure that the staff work efficiently to provide efficient and trouble-free data collection and be responsible for the proper handling and care of computer equipment and vehicles. In certain cases the supervisor may be also be responsible for managing the team's finances, including the monthly payroll of salaries and bonuses.

- EXCHANGE OF INFORMATION BETWEEN CENTRAL SURVEY STAFF AND FIELD TEAMS. As the main channel of communication, the supervisor sees to it that any advice or instructions from the central management staff is relayed to and followed by the field team and that the central staff is regularly informed of the progress of data collection.

In order to manage the field work effectively, the supervisor must have a thorough understanding of the tasks required of each member of the team. The supervisor should be able to respond to specific interviewing problems that may arise in the field and may on occasion need to perform interviews personally if any of the team's regular interviewers falls ill or becomes otherwise unavailable.

INTERVIEWERS. The interviewer's main responsibilities include:

- ESTABLISHING CONTACT WITH THE HOUSEHOLDS. With the help of the supervisor, the interviewer must first introduce him or herself to each household and explain the survey's objectives and methodology in simple terms. The interviewer should explain that the household was selected at random, along with many other households in the country, to help planners understand the people's living conditions. It should then be made clear that the survey is not concerned in any way with taxes and that all information will be kept confidential.

- SELECTING INDIVIDUAL RESPONDENTS. The interviewer should complete the family roster, determine who the members of the household are, and agree upon a convenient schedule for interviewing individual household members. The interviewer should try by all means to interview each adult member personally, if possible in private. This may require visiting the household several times during the survey period or going to the farm or place of business of the respondent.[48]

- CONDUCTING THE INTERVIEWS. The interviewer should conduct the interview in accordance with good survey practice. For example, they should be polite but exhibit a neutral attitude toward whatever answers the respondent gives. They should respect the wording on verbatim questions and follow the flow dictated by the skip pattern, without any variation.

- PROBING. Probing for responses may be necessary, either because of explicit instructions in the questionnaire (such as when looking for secondary activities or establishing the list of crops grown by a farmer), or in order to help respondents when they cannot answer exactly. The latter may be necessary, for instance, to obtain approximate amounts spent on certain budget items or to record approximate birthdates. As said before in the chapter on questionnaire design, approximate answers are always preferable to "don't knows." For the recording of dates, interviewers are usually provided with a calendar of events (see Figure 5.2).

ANTHROPOMETRISTS. The anthropometrist is responsible for measuring the height and weight of designated individuals. In the most ambitious LSMS surveys, all individuals will have their weight and height measured. In other countries some subset, often children under the age of five or children and their mothers, will be measured.

On the first trip to the cluster the anthropometrist tries to weigh and measure everyone for whom anthropometric data are to be gathered. The heights, weights, and ages are input with the rest of the data. The data entry program will flag observations whose combination of height, weight, and age is unusual (more than three standard deviations from the established norms).[49] The program will

---

48. In marketing research surveys, where usually just one person is selected to answer a few questions in each household, it is generally accepted that at least three attempts to personally interview that person should be made, *at different dates and times*, before abandoning the household or accepting a proxy response. LSMS interviewers, who generally have to spend two weeks in each locality, should be still more enterprising in getting their person.

49. The norms used in the data entry program are based on those used by the World Health Organization.

Figure 5.2: A Calendar of Events

A calendar of events is a list of important milestones likely to be commonly remembered. Calendars are typically done in two formats. One gives a great deal of detail for the five years preceding the survey. It is used to place accurately the month of birth of young children. Accurate measurement of their ages is required to accurately judge their nutritional status. A hypothetical example of such a calendar is shown here. Further guidelines for constructing and using such calendars are given in UNNHSCP (1986b). Less detailed calendars covering longer time periods can be used to establish the age of adults. The calendar used in the Kagera Health and Development Survey is shown in Annex V.

Annual Events	January	February	March	April	May	June	July	August	September	October	November	December
	New Year's	School begins	Indepen-dence Day	Lent/ Easter	Labor Day	Rainy season begins	mid-term school holiday	National Hero's day	National soccer tourney	Harvest begins	Harvest Festival	School holiday begins
1986						World Soccer Cup						National elections
1987			Earth-quake in the north									
1988		Winter Olympics				Summer Olympics				Pepe wins feather-weight crown		
1989				National Census								
1990		Great riots of 1990	Martial law announced			World Soccer Cup	Curfew lifted					
1991			Carmen wins Miss Universe contest					The big flood				
1992		Winter Olympics				Summer Olympics						National Elections
1993									Sugar scandal			
1994		Winter Olympics				World Soccer Cup						

also randomly select a portion of individuals in each household (usually 20 percent) to be remeasured as a check for measurement error.

During the second visit to the cluster, the anthropometrist will weigh and measure anyone missed the first time and will remeasure the individuals indicated by the data entry program. For individuals measured twice, the measurements are compared by the data entry program. Significant differences are flagged so that the anthropometrist and supervisor will be alerted that there may be a problem in the quality of measurements.

The anthropometrist may also be assigned to help collect information for the price, community, or facility questionnaires.

DRIVER. The driver not only provides transportation from the regional base to the location itself, but will help ferry team members to the various households, farms, and markets they may need to visit. When these are spread out and the supervisor, both interviewers, and the anthropometrist all need to visit two or more places in one day, the driver will be kept very busy.

DATA ENTRY OPERATOR. The data entry operator enters the data from each round of the interviews on the week following data collection. This person revises all errors and inconsistencies flagged by the data entry program, corrects *those that are an outcome of his or her own mistakes or omissions*, and produces printouts with the rest of the errors so that they can be reviewed by the supervisor in time for corrections to be made in the field.

Team logistics

A sufficient initial stock and a steady supply of survey materials and inputs should be ensured for all field teams throughout the whole survey period. The list of materials includes obvious items such as questionnaires, pencils, and erasers, less obvious ones such as diskettes, clipboards, and briefcases, and a myriad of country-specific items ranging from raincoats to camping stoves.

The elements that have proven hardest to manage in all countries are fuel, oil, and everything related to car maintenance. Probably the best solution is to provide a cash revolving fund and make the supervisor accountable for it. This may be hard to do in the more bureaucratic statistical agencies.

Complexity of LSMS Field Operations

One of the main reasons why countries considering whether to do an LSMS survey decide not to do so, is that the field work seems too intimidating. Reading this chapter might even reinforce the impression that the field work is difficult because there are so many details to get right. The intent is, of course, different. All surveys require getting myriads of details right, and at the right

94

time. We hope that by providing guidelines and examples here we can make it easier to plan for and carry out a survey.

The reader should further note that while some aspects of LSMS field work procedures are new, many others are not. The LSMS surveys have, however, been unusually vigorous in implementing quality control procedures. For example, the job description of survey supervisors in all sorts of surveys around the world includes the notion of check-up interviews. But in practice this is done far too little — the ratio of interviewers to supervisors is too high, the distances involved too great, access to vehicles too limited, and the importance of the task deemed too low. The LSMS surveys, in contrast, have low interviewer to supervisor ratios, supervisors that travel with the interviewers, a set standard for the number of interviewers that must be checked, forms to note results from the checks for feedback to the interviewer, and a mechanism to verify that the check-up interviews are in fact done.

There is no denying that LSMS surveys are complex and demanding. But the difference between what LSMS surveys require and what *should* be done to guarantee high quality data from other surveys is not so large. Indeed, often it is less than the difference between what *should* be done for the other surveys and what *is* done. Thus the reluctance to undertake an LSMS may not be due solely to its inherent complexity, but partly to its adherence to high standards.

Alternatives to LSMS Standard Field Procedures and Their Implications

Most countries that have implemented LSMS surveys have not traditionally used the mobile field team organization for field work. Indeed, many countries considering an LSMS are reluctant to undertake such major changes in their procedures. This section therefore discusses the implications of common alternative systems of field work.

SHORT, INTENSE PERIOD OF FIELD WORK. In the traditional setup used by many statistical agencies, the interviews are conducted during a shorter period (usually one to three months), rather than spread throughout a year. This requires using a large number of interviewers for each survey. In some cases the interviewer staff is permanently employed, and their time allocated to a series of different surveys during the year. In other cases, the permanent staff is very small and new, temporary interviewers are recruited for each survey.

Besides the fact of it being familiar to statistical agencies, this organizational setup presents certain advantages, especially for conducting single-purpose surveys with simple questionnaires. It can reduce the period during which the survey is in the field and provides a massive number of completed questionnaires in a short period of time. Also, in circumstances of high inflation, concentrating all interviews in a short period may be the only way of obtaining expenditure data that are comparable across households.

95

This system of data collection also has some serious disadvantages, which are especially worrisome in the case of complex surveys such as the LSMS.

First, it is very difficult to provide uniform training of good quality to a large number of field operators. Training in such cases often must be done in batches, which entails the risk of giving different instructions to different interviewers. Sometimes, the same trainers go to different regions to provide training to different groups of interviewers. Often this is not practical, so central trainers train other persons who then provide training to local groups of interviewers, which makes uniformity even more difficult to achieve. These problems will be especially acute when temporary interviewers are used. Furthermore, the interviewers never get very experienced with the questionnaire. In the typical LSMS set-up, each interviewer would be responsible for interviewing 320 households. In contrast, in one recent survey with purposes similar to the LSMS', the number of interviewers used was so large that on average each conducted only twelve interviews, fewer than an LSMS interviewer would do in the first two weeks in the field.

Second, it is also hard to implement effective procedures for supervising the interviewers. Even when this is done, problems can be detected, but seldom corrected opportunely. Moreover, this approach is often (though not necessarily) associated with high ratios of interviewers to supervisors, say five or ten to one, which compounds the difficulties in providing adequate supervision.

Third, this scheme makes it almost impossible to integrate coding, data entry, and data editing with field operations. These are designed as independent, ex-post facto activities, either with classic batch techniques (i.e., straight data entry followed by a series of editing programs) or with programs that check the quality of the data as they are entered. This serious disadvantage of short, intensive surveys is shared by other departures from the standard LSMS setup, and is explored in more detail below.

USE OF A MASTER SAMPLE. The so called *master sample* is the other common method of organizing field work. A master sample is a large number of clusters (usually several hundred), which are selected by the statistical agency at one moment (generally just after the census) and for which updated household listings are maintained, in order to select from that pool of households those to be interviewed in each survey. Often, arrangements are made for a resident in or near each cluster to became the interviewer for all surveys for the years until the next census.

This setup has many appealing features for a country that expects to conduct a program of household surveys over several years, the most obvious being the economies of scale it provides to the survey sampling component. It is not necessary to select a new set of clusters for each survey, nor to conduct a household listing operation each time. Another advantage is that travelling costs are reduced, because each interviewer only has to move within the relatively small area of his or her own cluster. Finally, for continued surveys, the concept of a master sample lends itself easily to various strategies for gathering panel data.

For complex surveys such as the LSMS, however, the master sample presents certain inconveniences. The first very serious one is that it is virtually impossible to give to hundreds of interviewers the kind of intensive, uniform training that is required by the LSMS. Even in the unlikely event that gathering them all for one month (and finding enough trainers, etc.) were possible, that would entail travel and lodging costs large enough to annihilate the savings gained from their immobility during the survey done until the next census. Another inconvenience is the difficulty of maintaining effective supervision of the interviewers. The latter can only be done if supervisors are made to travel extensively, which would again erode the benefits of having static interviewers. Third, it can be difficult to arrange for concurrent data entry since the interviews are so dispersed.

It is sometimes mentioned as a benefit of master samples that interviewers will become familiar with the households to be interviewed, which may minimize non-response. This feature, however, is more of a disadvantage than an advantage because answers given to acquaintances are essentially unreliable.[50]

ONE-ROUND INTERVIEWS, WITH MOBILE DATA ENTRY. The Nepal LSMS (which began in June 1995) is faced with significant obstacles in implementing standard LSMS procedures. These are caused by difficult access to most parts of the country. The average time to reach each locality is expected to be about two days (each way), with cases of five days or more being not uncommon. In addition, most travel has to be done by foot, so that interviewers have to carry with them all the necessary equipment and survey materials. An added complication is that electricity is rarely available, except in Kathmandu and a few other cities.

Obviously, the standard LSMS setup of two visits to each household, two weeks apart, could not be implemented under these conditions. Instead, the field teams visit each locality only once and spend there the necessary time to complete the questionnaires for all households. Instead of staying at a regional office, the data entry operator travels with the rest of the team and enters the data from the questionnaires onto a portable computer while the team is still in the locality.

Though the localities to be visited by each team in the year were arranged at random, the teams will not always go back to their regional headquarters in

---

50. In market research surveys interviewers are indeed instructed never to interview persons they know beforehand if they happen to be selected in the sample.

between localities. If two localities that have to be visited serially happen also to be close to each other, the team may proceed directly from one to the next.

Using the mobile interview teams required solving two further problems. The first is ensuring a good level of central supervision of the field teams. This will require spending greater time and money to get to the remote areas than would be necessary elsewhere. It will also require finding the field team's exact location once the central staff get to approximately the right location. Since the field teams do not report to the base office on such a regular schedule as in the standard set up, this may require some extra trekking or detective work.

The second problem was how to operate the data entry computer without access to electricity, sometimes for weeks at a time. The option selected was to provide each team with a set of solar panels, high-performance batteries, and other electric equipment. In addition to the electric paraphernalia, the teams have to transport the computer itself, the printer and a sufficient supply of paper, diskettes, and so forth. The advantage is that this will allow proven field and data entry procedures to be used with only minor modification. The modifications that are being made relate mostly to reducing the amount of paper used in the supervision and data management process, in order to reduce the weight that has to be carried around. The main disadvantages of this approach to mobile data entry are the risk of something going wrong with such an elaborate setup and the weight the teams will have to carry. As this manual is going to press (in fall 1995), no major problems had been detected.

ENHANCING AN EXISTING SURVEY BASED ON LSMS EXPERIENCE. In some countries, the lessons from LSMS experience are being used to enhance an existing survey rather than to start a completely new survey. In this subsection we make some general observations about issues that occur in the enhancement process. Then we describe the enhancements carried out or planned in Indonesia and Bangladesh.

An enhancement program can involve either one or several aspects of a survey: the questionnaire, the sample, the field work techniques, and/or the data management. Conceptually it is very straightforward to add modules to an existing survey to move it toward the integrated content of an LSMS. However, as the total complexity and length of the questionnaire grows and begins to approach that of the full LSMS, it will become increasingly important to ensure that the quality control mechanisms are able to cope with the new requirements. This will probably involve adopting some or all of the LSMS field work and data management techniques.

It is also straightforward to think about enhancing the field work and data management techniques independently of the questionnaire. Enhancements of the field work and data management will, however, generally require more management commitment to implement than those that pertain only to the questionnaire. The field work involves a much larger number of people and more fundamental administrative and management systems than the design of the questionnaire. Thus the consensus that enhancement is necessary and beneficial will need to be held by a wider group of people. Some of these may initially feel threatened by the closer quality control or change in job description that may be implied.

Enhancement programs are often harder to carry out than entirely new surveys. Sometimes the opposition to changing procedures is greater for an established product than for an "experimental" survey. Enhancement programs may require significant creativity and managerial oversight to blend the old procedures with the new in an appropriate way. There is also a tendency to provide inadequate financing and supervision for enhancement programs, since they do not lead to a "new" product.

In Indonesia, the SUSENAS survey was to be reformed in 1991 (for a fuller discussion of the reforms, see World Bank, 1993). The SUSENAS questionnaires have had a core and a rotating module design for many years. The core is administered annually and the rotating modules are alternated. The field work is organized along a master sample principle, with a very large permanent field staff (on the order of 2000 interviewers). Before the reform, the sample was representative at the province level, with about 64,000 households in the sample.

One element of the reform plan was to refine the way the core and rotating modules fit together. In particular it was desired to include a measure of consumption in the core rather than as one of the periodic rotating modules. Other indicators that it was desired to measure annually, or that were needed for the analysis of the information in the various core modules, were also moved to the core. The second element of the reform was to produce results representative at the district level, for which about 200,000 households would be interviewed.

The increase in sample size was achieved by reallocating the time of the permanent interview force away from other tasks to spend more time on the SUSENAS. Their annual quota of interviews for the SUSENAS moved from an average of about 30, to an average of about 100. Fundamental changes in the field work, supervision, and data entry techniques were not contemplated. Thus it was necessary to devise a consumption module that would not radically shift the balance between the core and rotating modules in the overall burden of field work.

To achieve the goal of collecting more useful information without having to revamp field work procedures, a carefully controlled experiment using alternate formulations of the consumption modules was carried out on samples large enough to be statistically meaningful. The statistical comparisons of the resulting measures of consumption suggested that a relatively short consumption module could be used to gather information of acceptable quality.

There are several features to note from the Indonesia experience. First, the scientific rigor of the experiments that preceded the reformulation of the questionnaire was unusually high. This reflected a very strong management commitment to the reform process. Second, because the field work and data management procedures were not fundamentally changed, there were relatively few technical or political difficulties in implementing the reform program, which proceeded rather smoothly.

In Bangladesh, the starting point in 1995 was the Household Expenditure Survey (HES), a classic household budget survey that had been in existence for almost two decades. The questionnaire content was standard for a budget survey. A master sample approach was used, with interviewers coming from the approximately 400 *thana* (county) level offices. A detailed daily diary system for recording household expenditures was followed. Data entry was ex post facto and centralized, with data editing in the traditional sense. The enhancement plan was as follows: In terms of survey content, a new community module and a module on education were to be added to the questionnaire used in previous HES rounds. An LSMS-type data entry program was to be developed and data entry was to be carried out at a regional level (26 offices nationwide). Apart from the LSMS-type components, core interviewer training and supervision procedures were to remain unchanged.

Recognizing the long tradition of household surveys in Bangladesh, a central objective of the enhancement program was to emphasize ownership by the Bureau of Statistics. Accordingly, management of the surveys and design of the new questionnaires remained largely the responsibility of the Bureau of Statistics and local experts, with technical expertise provided as necessary by expatriate consultants. This objective also dictated to an extent the desire to limit changes so as to keep them manageable.

At the time of this writing, the enhanced survey has only been in the field for a month, so it is too early to judge the overall success of the program. Some early lessons from the program are, however, worth highlighting.

The development of new questionnaires proved to be more time consuming than expected, largely because of the lack of familiarity of the design team with rigorous questionnaire design aimed at ensuring consistency and ease of interviewing. Somewhat late in the planning process, it was also realized that a Demographic and Health Survey and a labor force survey were planned for the same year in the same clusters. In order to link the data files, it was therefore decided to interview the same households for all three surveys, yielding a richer data base than would the HES. However, since each survey had separate managements, the capacity for coordination was limited and the fine tuning of questionnaires to simplify matching at the individual level or to avoid unnecessary overlap in content was not possible. The coordination mechanism used was an identical system of household identifiers across all three surveys. Also, to allow capacity building and to limit the changes being made in field procedures in this first contact with LSMS-type techniques, it was also decided to focus only on the HES in terms of the quality control mechanisms of the field work, data entry, and data cleaning processes.

The enhancements of the data entry program and survey logistics were not easy to achieve. Despite detailed plans to the contrary, implementation remained a serious problems. Particular difficulties were experienced with finalizing the data entry program, ensuring that the data entry operators were sufficiently trained, and the rest of the field staff sufficiently aware of the new method of interacting with the data entry process. Within the first month of field work, steps were taken to overcome these difficulties. New regional managers were appointed, further functions were added to the data entry program to make it more user friendly and self-instructing, and more training was arranged for data entry operators. These remedial measures appear to be working. However, it is clear that the level of management effort involved was underestimated by the Bureau of Statistics, both to organize the new procedures and to fit the existing survey management processes.

An important lesson from this experience so far is that the requirements for successful implementation of an enhancement program can be even more onerous than for the successful implementation of a new LSMS survey. Management must be interested and committed to the program; they must also see how it may or may not dovetail into existing procedures. A core team with adequate management and logistic support must be put in charge of the survey. Consultants should be used when needed for specific tasks, but cannot completely substitute for the core team. Finally, field staff (interviewers, supervisors, and data entry operators) must be adequately trained. They must know not only how to do their specific task, but the quality control principles for the survey as a whole, and how their roles fit into them.

THE EFFECTS OF IMPERFECT TRAINING AND SUPERVISION. Many of the variations from the prototype LSMS organization of field work make it difficult to achieve adequate training and supervision or concurrent data entry. We therefore discuss the implications of these in turn.

A lively illustration of the importance of interviewer training and supervision can be obtained from market research. Market research surveys are more abundant than national surveys, occur in a much shorter time frame (days or weeks instead of months), involve smaller budgets (thousands vs. millions of dollars), and are subject to more immediate empirical, even painful, sanctions.

Years ago in Chile, a multi-national company commissioned a market study to assist them in deciding the best package for a product they sold. Due to a restrictive schedule and budget and the sheer incompetence of the survey planners, this study was neither supervised nor did the interviewers receive any training. The data collected indicated a marked preference for a 2 kg. package as opposed to the 1 kg. package that was available at the time. Important strategic decisions were made, millions spent, and the product packaging was changed. But this item, a perishable food product, spent months on the shelf in its new packaging without selling.

An ex post facto evaluation showed that the culprit in this debacle was a lack of supervision and training. As it turned out, the photo cards accompanying the questionnaire had been applied incorrectly by certain interviewers, thus skewing the collected data. The pictures on the photo cards were smaller than the actual size packages, a fact that interviewers were supposed to indicate to the respondents. Proper training would have stressed this point. Supervision would have also detected the mistakes as they were being made and would have given the firm an opportunity to have corrected them immediately.

This and many other anecdotes have been incorporated into the annals of marketing lore, demonstrating that good supervision and training are an intrinsic part of the terms of reference of serious market research. Since LSMS surveys are so much more complex, the need for excellent interviewer training and supervision is all the greater.

THE EFFECTS OF NOT INTEGRATING DATA MANAGEMENT TO FIELD OPERATIONS. A common feature of the departures from the standard LSMS setup seen so far is that they make it difficult or impossible to integrate data entry and field operations. As explained before in this chapter, the standard LSMS uses dedicated data entry operators and computers in each field team and organizes data collection in two rounds to allow for the correction of inconsistencies by *re-interviewing the households* in the field. Under other organizational schemes, data entry may be forced to become a separate operation, usually performed in a single location (or perhaps in a few centers), after field work is completed and without actually re-visiting the households.

Even under these less than ideal circumstances, the use of data entry programs that can check the quality of the information while it is entered (sometimes referred to as "intelligent data entry programs") can improve the quality and timeliness of the survey data sets. At the very least, a good program should be able to detect many of the errors produced by the data entry operators themselves and ensure that the data sets are "formally correct"; that is, that there are no alphabetic codes in numeric fields, no out-of-format records, and so forth.

Furthermore, if the survey is conducted over a sufficiently long period, data entry can be organized as an ongoing activity, conducted in parallel to data collection and with a minimum delay from it. In this case, an intelligent data entry program may *indirectly* improve the quality of field work, by providing early warning on the most common interviewer errors and allowing for corrective measures to be taken while the survey is still in the field.

The Romania LSMS provides an example. There the survey used over 500 interviewers, each working in a different clusters throughout the year — the master sample strategy. Because of the obvious difficulties of properly selecting and providing uniform instructions to such a huge number of people, the first month of the survey (March 1994) was expected to be a field test of field operations and procedures, and the information collected was then to be excluded from the survey data sets. However, even performing the necessary assessments and defining the subsequent corrective actions would have been impossible if an intelligent data entry program had not been available as was fortunately the case. Data entry for the Romania LSMS was done in 50 regional offices during the month following data collection and the resulting household files were sent to Bucharest by modem for centralized tabulation and analysis. The printouts with errors and inconsistencies were reviewed locally by regional supervisors who, albeit unable to return to the households for corrections, could at least point them out opportunely to the interviewers so that the same mistakes were not repeated.

Thus, in Romania, decentralized, intelligent data entry both provided the momentum for quality control and ensured that the same criteria were applied consistently throughout the country. It is probably not an exaggeration to say that the data entry program became the de-facto survey supervisor during the hectic early days of the Romanian LSMS. While perhaps not an ideal system, the Romanian survey found a way to preserve many of the principles of LSMS field work within the very different framework of the master sample.

However, it should be borne in mind that only a real re-visit to the household of the standard LSMS can ensure that the data sets are not just internally consistent, but also *reflect the reality of the field*. It should be also pointed out that the quality assurances provided by intelligent data entry are complements, not alternatives, to the other supervision tools (interviewer evaluation, questionnaire verification, and check-up interviews) that are described in Section B of this chapter. These should be implemented and enforced, regardless of the options adopted for data entry.

B. Preparation for Field Work

This section discusses the main features of preparation for field work, other than designing the questionnaire or drawing the sample. Many of the data quality control mechanisms rely extensively on the preparation for the field work. Survey preparation is thus very important and should be given due time and attention. Often there is the temptation to skimp on preparation in order to move to the field too rapidly. This temptation should be avoided.

The survey's success relies on its staff. In this section we discuss some of the criteria that have proved successful in recruitment for LSMS surveys.

- THE SURVEY MANAGER should be a social scientist or statistician with a grasp of the goals to be achieved by the survey. Often this person will have a graduate degree in statistics, economics, or demography. At a minimum the survey manager should have a lower university degree. Since the supervisor will be expected to have a permanent dialogue with top levels of the statistical agency and the sectoral ministries, as well as to liaise with financing agencies, data users, and technical assistants, a certain seniority is desirable.

- THE DATA MANAGER can be a systems analyst or senior programmer with prior experience in statistical data management. However, as substantial LSMS-specific data management skills will have to be transferred to that person in any case, it is usually better (and easier) to look for an economist or statistician with knowledge of computer programming instead.

- THE FIELD MANAGER is usually a person from the statistical agency and should have substantial managerial skills, inside knowledge of the statistical agency, and experience in conducting household surveys in the country. All members of the core staff (not just the data manager) should be familiar enough with personal computers to use word processing software and spreadsheets.

- THE SUPERVISORS should have completed secondary education and — within the possibilities of the local labor markets — some advanced education, preferably in the social sciences or humanities. In several of the LSMS surveys former primary school teachers have proved to be excellent team supervisors. However, experience in managing people and resources and the ability to foster teamwork are more important than credentials.

- THE INTERVIEWERS should also have a good secondary education, but they do not need to have pursued further studies. In fact, that may be a disadvantage, as graduates tend to be more likely to abandon the survey halfway through if they are offered a better or more interesting job.

- THE ANTHROPOMETRISTS should also have obtained a school leaving qualification. However, it is not necessary, as tends to be assumed, for anthropometrists to be nurses or other people with clinical experience. Weighing and measuring children in the field is very different from weighing and measuring them in a clinic, and extensive training is needed whatever the recruits' professional background.

- Similarly, experience with computers is not an essential requisite for the DATA ENTRY OPERATORS, but it is helpful if they have keyboard skills. It is not difficult to learn to enter data and it is not necessary to understand how a program works in order to use it successfully. It is better, in fact, if the data entry operators are interested in the survey rather than in computers; that way, when they note incorrect answers, they are more likely to use the same terms as the questionnaire instead of explaining the error in computer terms.

In some countries it may also be desirable that team members, especially interviewers, be fluent in two or more languages. Moreover, it is best if the interviewers in each team have complementary language skills so that between them they can conduct all (or nearly all) the interviews themselves.[51] In the Peru 1985 survey, for instance, all field staff in the sierras were able to speak either Aymara or Quechua (or both) in addition to Spanish.

Unless specific cultural or religious conditions dictate, there seems to be no *a priori* reason for preferring male to female interviewers or vice versa. There is some anecdotal evidence, however, that households are less likely to refuse women interviewers. In the 1990 Peru (Lima only) survey, for example, only female interviewers were used. Prior experience there had shown that it was culturally more acceptable for female respondents to admit female interviewers to their homes when the men were absent. Moreover, the survey was carried out during a time of widespread terrorist activity and women were considered less threatening. Even when male interviewers are used, anecdotal reports from several countries suggest that females may find it easier to establish rapport for the modules on fertility and child mortality. However, a comparison of results from the Côte d'Ivoire LSMS (which used only male interviewers) and the Ivorian Fertility Survey (which used only female interviewers) found basically the same levels of fertility; the interviewer's gender was not shown to have any effect on the reported number of children ever born. (Answers might have been different for questions about sexual behavior or contraception).

Hiring good field workers is tricky. Obviously all team members must be diligent, organized, and responsible. They should be enthusiastic about the survey and good at establishing rapport with the community members to be

---

51. If interpreters are needed, they are usually other members of the household or community members acquainted with the respondent. Though both the presence of a third party and the fact that the interpreter is acquainted with the respondent violate some of the basic rules of interviewing, this may be the only possible option for some interviews. Interviewers should be aware — and be trained to avoid — a still more serious problem posed by a local interpreter, which is a tendency to answer for the respondent.

interviewed. Because it is often difficult to assess these characteristics in a short job interview, LSMS surveys hire more field staff than will be required, usually 15 to 25 percent more. All the hires are trained. The rules are made clear to the prospective interviewers from the very beginning: they will have to work hard, including Saturdays and Sundays, in rain and snow, and with unusual working hours. Anthropometrists must be willing to travel with heavy anthropometric equipment. During the training period the candidates' work characteristics and ability to establish rapport with interviewees is displayed and can be assessed more accurately.[52] Then, after the training period, a final selection is made.

Regular supervision that includes practical suggestions to practical problems can be helpful in maintaining morale and professional standards. As discussed in the section on the supervisor's duties, supervision abounds in LSMS surveys.

Training

As in all surveys, good training contributes greatly to the quality of the data collection effort. There are several types of training used for LSMS surveys.

- THE SURVEY MANAGER AND FIELD MANAGER are assumed to be professionals already knowledgeable about surveys in general. Thus, the only training they need is in the peculiarities of the LSMS survey. This training occurs on the job as they prepare the survey in collaboration with people familiar with the LSMS in other countries.

- For the DATA MANAGER, the training needs are usually more specific but are also accomplished on the job. About two to four weeks of close collaboration with people who have developed and applied integrated data management techniques for other complex surveys are usually required. Training is both theoretical and practical. The conceptual framework includes criteria for survey data consistency, error levels (range checks and consistency checks), design of a dictionary of variables, file management for data entry and analysis, and questionnaire design techniques for effective data management. The practical part of the training consists of translating the questionnaire structure into a set of linked data entry screens, graphically designing several of these screens, and defining the most important range and consistency checks. Thus during the training, part or all of the data entry program is prepared.

- SUPERVISORS. Some supervisors will be trained on the job, as they will take part in the project from the early stages of field testing and will

---

52. Training more recruits than needed also provides a pool of candidates from which to draw replacements if any member of the team must be replaced because of illness, poor performance, or resignation.

106

actively participate in preparations for the survey. However, some aspects of the job should be presented formally, through training sessions and in the supervisor manual. These include: LSMS objectives, sample design, contents and design of the survey, structure of the interviews, community questionnaires, structure of the management team, structure of the field teams, quality control criteria, coding, and household replacement criteria. One or two weeks should be allocated for this training.

- INTERVIEWERS AND DATA ENTRY OPERATORS. LSMS surveys normally allow four weeks to train interviewers and data entry operators. A general outline of these courses is shown in Figure 5.3 and detail for the first day of training is discussed in Box 5.1. The training period for LSMS surveys is much longer than for other surveys (which tend to average less than one week) for two reasons. First, LSMS surveys have made an unusual effort to reduce non-sampling errors and the training of all personnel is key to this process. Second, the LSMS questionnaires are far more complex than those of most other surveys, so more training is required to achieve a given level of understanding. The training must cover the basic structure of how to understand and use the questionnaire, but it must go much further. In order to probe effectively, the interviewers must thoroughly understand the economic concepts being

Figure 5.3: Interviewer and Data Entry Operator Training Program

Week	Data entry operators	Interviewers
1	Introduction to the survey. Introduction to personal computers and printers. Unpacking the computer. Diskette Management.	Introduction to the survey. General survey procedures. The questionnaire. Definition of a household. Theory of round 1 sections.
2	The data entry program. Presentation of round 1 data entry screens.	Field practice of round 1. Trainees must conduct at least two observed interviews (one urban and one rural).
3	Practice of round 1 (trainees enter questionnaires completed by interviewer trainees the previous week).	Interpretation of the data entry program error reports. Theory of round 2 sections.
4	Presentation of round 2 data entry screens. Practice of round 2 data entry screens (candidates enter questionnaires completed by interviewer trainees the previous week). Inter-record checks.	Field practice of round 2 (trainees re-visit households visited on the second week).

Box 5.1: Day 2 of a Typical Interviewer Training Session

The first day of training is usually taken up with introductions. There may be a formal opening ceremony with big shots and benedictions, after which the trainers, core survey staff, and interviewers are introduced. Finally, there may be an overview of the purposes of the survey, the role of the interviewer, and the structure of the questionnaire.

Detailed coverage of each module will usually begin on the second day. The roster is usually covered first. Though it is only one page long, and takes very little interview time, it usually receives a day or more of training time. The definition of a household is essential to the success of the survey but may be easily misunderstood, so it must be covered thoroughly. In addition, many of the features of the questionnaire and of good interview technique are introduced at this time.

Each trainer has an individual approach, although obviously certain specific information always needs to be covered. An example of one trainer's technique can be instructive. In this case the trainer begins by giving the definition of the household. On the chalkboard or flip chart, the trainer sketches a simple household with stick figures and balloons describing each member's name, age, relationship to other members, and so forth. An overhead projector displays a copy of the roster page for a household; this is printed on a transparent film so that it may be filled in with markers as the session proceeds. The trainer demonstrates filling in the questionnaire, explaining in the process how to read skip codes, showing that instructions to the interviewer are in capital letters and not to be read aloud, and so forth. The proper way to code answers is explained, as is the need for legible handwriting. The meaning of each question is explained, along with any factors that are important in achieving a correct answer. For example, the age variable is meant to record the number of complete years that a person has lived, so that someone who is 35 and 9 months old would have a recorded age of 35.

After the trainer has filled in the roster for the first person or two in the sample household, or even for the whole first household, the trainer then has interviewers take turns coming to the front of the room to fill in a line in further examples. Eventually, instead of having the examples sketched on the board, the instructor begins to play the role of various survey respondents so that the interviewers have to extract the information for the examples. To keep this section lively, the trainer may use a few props, such as hats, pieces of clothing, or objects, to help the interviewers imagine they are speaking with people of different genders, ages, and ethnic or economic backgrounds. As the interviewers catch on to the basic concepts, more complicated cases are introduced — heads of household living away from home, children in boarding schools, domestic servants, boarders, guests, and so forth. As a change of pace from the examples, a more formal presentation is made on how to use the calendar of events to place ages. Calendar use is then included into the examples. By the end of the afternoon, the class breaks into pairs and the interviewers request information and fill out rosters for each other. The results of this trial run are discussed at the beginning of the third day.

Going into this kind of detail for every section of the questionnaire and providing interviewers the opportunity to practice administering each section and to receive feedback requires a great deal of time. This explains why the whole training takes four weeks.

There are several other things to note about training. First, it requires considerable preparation on the part of the instructor, who must have concocted numerous examples that illustrate all possible complications. The instructor should have thought out in what order to present material and have made up checklists that can be used to verify that all the concepts implicit in the presentation, such as skip patterns and probing, have been introduced. Second, the training is very interactive, with interviewers going to the board, interviewing the trainer in front of the others, carrying out practice interviews with each other, and doing other exercises. This is only possible if the group is kept small — to 20 or 30 people. Third, the training will be enriched by use of as much audiovisual equipment as is practical in the setting. This will require foresight in gathering the materials required and doing a technical rehearsal far enough in advance of the training to solve any problems that result.

measured, especially in the labor activities, household enterprise, agriculture and consumption modules.

- ANTHROPOMETRISTS. Anthropometrists should be trained at the same time as interviewers and data entry operators. It is tempting to assume that anthropometric training can be done in a few hours or days, because measuring and weighing people seems to be such an easy thing. It is not. Anthropometric training requires about two weeks (see UNNHSCP, 1986a) and it is best done at the same time as interviewer and data entry operator training. It does not need to be coordinated so closely with the training of the rest of the staff, but it can benefit from sharing some common sessions on the survey's general objectives and methodology. Of course, additional, specific training will be required if the anthropometrist are to assist in completing the community, price, or facility questionnaires.

Notice that the training programs for data entry operators and interviewers are coordinated. When fine tuning the training program for a specific LSMS, a common session for both interviewers and operators may be useful. This reflects the importance of doing the actual required tasks as part of the training and the fact that the work of all staff will be coordinated once the survey is fielded.

In order to ensure that uniform criteria and instructions are conveyed, most LSMS surveys strive for centralized training. This is also a reason to keep the number of teams small. In Côte d'Ivoire, Peru, Ghana, and Mauritania, for instance, all the interviewers could sit in one room. This becomes difficult with more than 10 teams, as in Pakistan or Viet Nam, and parallel training sessions are needed. This entails close coordination and monitoring of the different lecturers. In more extreme situations such as the Romania survey, which employs over 500 interviewers, decentralized training is the only possible option. In these cases training must be done in two steps: A group of trainers is trained first, so that they can later train others in different locations. All these factors should be carefully considered when planning a course of training because of the need for suitable rooms, audiovisual equipment, and so forth. Other logistical arrangements for training include lodging and transportation for the trainees who come from outside.

The training plan should emphasize practice interviews with households. Indeed, in the plan shown in Figure 5.3, half of the time is taken up actually in the field. This is the only way to discover whether interviewers are really understanding what they are meant to learn. Not even practice interviews with each other will be as useful. Moreover, the interviewers will at first be rather shy with households and need time to get over that before the survey starts. Parts of the practice interviews should be observed by trainers, their assistants, or supervisors, to help detect where the interviewers are having problems.

109

When planning the training, it is therefore important to select two localities, one urban and one rural, that are close to the training quarters. The survey planners and team supervisors should visit those places well in advance and select (not necessarily at random) households willing to cooperate with the survey in both places so that team members can interview them during their training.

Depending on the number of field staff to be trained, the experience and skills of the core staff, and language constraints, the training may be conducted by the core staff, international technical assistants, or a combination of the two. In Côte d'Ivoire and Ghana, training was done primarily by consultants and in Peru primarily by the local core staff, with consultants acting as advisors on the side. In Pakistan, where fifteen teams of six people (mostly non-English speakers) had to be trained, a small team of local consultants was trained in the afternoon by foreign experts in English; the next morning, each of these consultants in turn trained a group of field staff in Urdu.

The data entry program should be close to its final form at the moment of training, though fine-tuning and debugging are almost always necessary during the training period because the data from the actual questionnaires completed by the trainees reveals situations that were not foreseen during program development.

The importance of interviewer training can hardly be overstressed. In one recent LSMS survey, one interview team decided that collecting data on wages in kind and consumption in kind was double counting, so it stopped collecting either! This team apparently understood neither the role of the questions in analysis (that analysts wanted to be able to measure both the total value of income and the total value of consumption and knew how to avoid double counting) and the role of the interviewers (to administer the questionnaires as designed).[53]

Manuals

The main written materials used for training supervisors, interviewers, anthropometrists, and data entry operators are the questionnaires and the field manuals. Manuals are usually reproduced by photocopying.[54] It is recommended to reproduce many more manuals than needed for training, at least a few hundred copies of each, because apart from their obvious use as a support for field operations the manuals are also valuable tools for the survey analysts.

---

53. Both the data entry program and good supervision from the central office should help to detect such mistakes early in the survey and correct them before data collection gets very far.

54. Because of print shop delays, it often happens that household questionnaires cannot be printed in time for the training. In those cases a few questionnaires may have to be made by photocopying as well.

The basic contents of each kind of manual is described in the following paragraphs. An idea of their detail and clarity is provided in Annex IV, which reproduces a section from the interviewer manual for the Kagera Health and Development Survey.

- SUPERVISOR MANUAL. This manual should start by making explicit the objectives, methodology, and organization of the survey. It should then specify the supervisor's responsibilities, duties, and the way the supervisor should be connected to the survey's core management team and to the statistical agency's regular organization.

  Another chapter of the manual should be devoted to the procedures to be carried out in each cluster, including completing the community, price, and facilities questionnaires and the public relations tasks needed to ensure cooperation from the local authorities and the selected households. The difficulties in locating the selected households and ways to deal with refusals and other forms of non-response (as well as selection and documentation of replacements) should also be made clear.

  Sections in the supervisory manual should address the relationship of the supervisor and the interviewers, including procedures for preparing questionnaires for both survey rounds, and the use of the supervision forms for interviewer evaluation, questionnaire verification, and check-up interviews. The latter should include detailed instructions on dealing with problems that might be found. If the survey collects anthropometric data, the manual should also indicate how the supervisor is to manage the anthropometrist's work and its relation to the interviewers' work.

  The manual should also specify procedures for coding the open questions in the questionnaires, including the complete code lists to be used for occupations, activities, and geographic locations.

  An important part of the supervisor manual should be devoted to data entry. It should explain how and when the questionnaires are to be given to the data entry operator and how to interpret the data entry printouts along with the rest of the inconsistencies signaled by the operator on the questionnaires. The manual should also explain how the data entry diskettes are to be sent to the survey core management team.

- INTERVIEWER MANUAL. The fundamental objectives of the interviewer manual are to provide concepts and definitions, to define field procedures, and to ensure uniform criteria in the few parts of the questionnaire that are not self-explanatory. The manual should include general sections on the survey's objectives and methodology, the attitudes and behavior expected from the interviewer, the relationship between the interviewer and the supervisor, the structure of the questionnaire, the conventions used in the

111

questionnaire's design and interpretation of the data entry program outputs, and specific sections on each module of the questionnaire. Some of the documents used in other LSMS surveys are available from the LSMS division of the World Bank and can be used as guidelines.

In many other surveys the interviewer manual contains a list of all questions in the questionnaire, with detailed instructions on how to ask and record the answers to every single one (for instance, "Question 4 (Gender). Record the gender of the respondent, using code '1' for male and '2' for female", and so forth). Such an exhaustive approach would have been both tedious and useless for LSMS surveys, given the length of the questionnaires and the fact that they are pre-coded and have explicit skip patterns. Instead, the LSMS manuals should focus on clarifying economic concepts such as the difference between wage earning and self-employment, the treatment of sharecropping, etc.

- DATA ENTRY OPERATOR MANUAL. This manual should explain in great detail the role of the operator in the field operational setup and how outputs of the program (e.g., on-line messages and printouts) are to be transferred from the operator to the team supervisor. Contrary to what might be expected, this manual needs to make very little reference to the computer or the data entry program. The use of the latter should be intuitive enough not to need further explanation.

- ANTHROPOMETRIST MANUAL. This manual is not country-specific and generally can be based on existing material (such as United Nations, 1986). If the anthropometrist is made responsible for completing the community, price, and facilities questionnaires, a separate manual should be prepared for these tasks.

Developing Supervision Forms

Three of the tasks of the team supervisors should be supported by written documents, known as *supervision forms*. These are (1) interviewer evaluation, (2) questionnaire verification, and (3) check-up interviews. The forms are intended to give these tasks formal definition, as opposed to loosely defined responsibilities left to the supervisor's personal initiative, and to make it possible to supervise the supervisors themselves (e.g, make supervision tasks verifiable by the survey core staff). Guidelines for the design of these forms are given below, with examples taken from the Pakistan Integrated Household Survey.

INTERVIEWER EVALUATION. The purpose of interviewer evaluation is to monitor the performance and attitudes of the interviewers. At least once a week (more often for weak interviewers), the supervisor should sit in on interviews conducted by each of the interviewers in order to observe that they are administering the questionnaire correctly.

The supervisor witnesses an interviewer strictly as an observer and should not talk to the interviewer or the respondent. The interviewer should be informed that he or she is not allowed to ask for advice during the interview and that the interviewer must behave as though the supervisor were not present. The interviewer evaluation form allows the supervisor to make notes on any questions or concepts that the interviewer may have difficulty asking or understanding. It should be filled in on the spot before the details of the interview are forgotten.

The main points to consider when designing the interviewer evaluation form are well illustrated in the form used in the Pakistan LSMS, shown in Figure 5.4.

Interviewer evaluations also offer the chance to spot weaknesses in the questionnaire and suggest improvements for future versions. The form might also contain space for making note of problems or difficulties in the interviewing process, particularly with respect to inappropriately worded questions, concepts that are unclear to the respondent, or questions that are not answered because they are too personal or too sensitive.

QUESTIONNAIRE VERIFICATION. The purpose of this operation is to ensure that the questionnaire is completely filled out; that is, that everyone who should have been interviewed has replied and that every section is complete. Verification should be done the day after the questionnaire is completed, before the supervisor leaves the area and before the questionnaires are given to the data entry operator.

A Questionnaire verification form should be designed to assist the supervisor in this task. It should be filled out for all questionnaires after each round of the survey. If problems are found in the questionnaire, it should be returned to the interviewer with instructions to correct them immediately before leaving the area. The supervisor must keep the verification forms for each questionnaire until the end of the second round. After data for the second round have been entered, the forms will be kept at the field office with the questionnaires.

Questionnaire verification is not supposed to replace exhaustive quality controls to be performed later by the data entry program, but rather serves as an early warning of major omissions that could be amended by sending the interviewer back to the household before the team leaves the area.

Figure 5.4: Interviewer Evaluation Form

INTERVIEWER:_____

E V A L U A T I O N C R I T E R I A	RATING	
	Satisfactory	Unsatisfactory
A. Comportment of the Interview		
1. Did the interviewer greet everyone before beginning the interview?		
2. Did the interviewer introduce himself or herself and explain that he or she is working for the Federal Bureau of Statistics?		
3. Did the interviewer explain the objectives of the survey properly, how the household was chosen, and that the interview would be completely confidential?		
4. Was the interviewer polite and patient with the respondents during the interview ?		
5. Did the interviewer thank everyone at the end ?		
B. Interview of Respondents		
1. Did the interviewer ask the questions as they appear in the questionnaire ?		
2. Did the interviewer try to interview the appropriate person in each section of the questionnaire?		
3. Did the interviewer accept "I don't know" as an answer without probing ?		
C. Time Spent on the Interview		
1. Did the interviewer avoid long discussion of the question with the respondents while still being patient and polite ?		
2. If the interviewer received irrelevant or complicated answers, did he or she break in too suddenly ?		
3. Did the interviewer rush through the interview, thereby encouraging respondents to answer questions quickly ?		
D. Impartiality		
1. Did the interviewer maintain a neutral attitude toward the questions and answers during the interview ?		
2. Did the interviewer volunteer an opinion ?		
3. Did the interviewer appear surprised or shocked or disapproving about any of the answers ?		
4. Did the interviewer suggest answers when asking the questions?		

SUPERVISOR _____   DATE

Figure 5.5 shows the first page of the questionnaire verification form used for the Pakistan LSMS. The full form has four pages and is shown in Annex VI. Typical items to be considered in questionnaire verification are:

- MANDATORY SECTIONS. Some sections, such as housing and the inventory of durable goods, should be present in all questionnaires. Other sections, like farming, should *almost* always be present in certain locations but not in others.

- COMPLETENESS OF INDIVIDUAL SECTIONS. Depending on age, sex, or some other characteristic, certain sections of the questionnaire may or may not have to be completed. For instance, all women 15 to 49 years old, but no men, should answer the fertility section.

- COMPLETENESS OF LISTS. If the exhaustive approach is used to scan item lists in certain sections of the questionnaire (see Chapter 3), then all Yes/No questions should be completed, and a series of answers should follow each item marked "Yes."

- FILTER QUESTIONS AND OTHER MAJOR SKIPS. Some questionnaire sections are headed by "filter" questions, which indicate if the section is applicable or not to a particular household. The questionnaire should be consistent about the structure and use of skip patterns.

CHECK-UP INTERVIEWS. The purpose of the check-up interview is to confirm that the interviewer is indeed interviewing completely and accurately. The check-up interviews convey the importance of accuracy and completeness to the interviewer. This reinforcement is important in maintaining high standards, even among diligent interviewers. The check-up interview may also reveal any unsatisfactory interviewers so that corrective action may be taken. These random revisits tend to be ignored or neglected by official statistical agencies throughout the world. However, they are the best way to ensure effective interviews and are a standard procedure in all serious marketing research surveys.

It is generally considered acceptable to conduct check-up interviews in 15 to 25 percent of the households. The check-up interviews should not take longer than 15 minutes. It should be kept in mind that a difference in a response from the re-interview and a response from the original interview does not necessarily mean that the interviewer is not doing a careful job. Respondents may provide different information at different times and sometimes the respondents contacted by the interviewer and the supervisor may not be the same. However, numerous differences indicate the need to follow up with the interviewer regarding possible causes.

Figure 5.5: Page One of Pakistan Questionnaire Verification Form

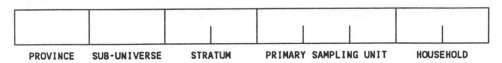

| | | | PROVINCE | SUB-UNIVERSE | STRATUM | PRIMARY SAMPLING UNIT | HOUSEHOLD |

Sec-tion	Ques-tion	Round One Check	RESULT Satis-factory	RESULT To be redone	Notes / Remarks
1A	2-5	These questions must be completed for all names in Q.1			
1A	9	All persons were correctly classified as members of the household.			
1A	A-B	A cross was written in column A for all members of the household (code 1 in Q.9) and the age in years was copied from Q.5 to column B.			
2		This section was completed.			
3A		A line is filled in for each household member 5 years or older.			
4A 4B		A line is filled in for each household child 5 years or under.			
4C		A line is filled in for all household members.			
5A		A line is filled in for each household member 10 years or older.			
5B		A line is filled in for each household member 10 years or older.			
6A	1	If the answer is 1 (YES), a line is filled in for each household member 10 years and older. The ID code of the best-informed person is to be transferred to the second page (Summary of survey results).			
6B	1	If the answer is 1 (YES), Q.1-5 for First, Second or Third Enterprise should be filled in. Industry codes of all enterprises must be filled in, and ID codes of best-informed persons must be transferred to the second page (Summary of survey results).			
6C		A line is filled in for each female member 10 years or older.			
M7A		This section is completed.			
M7B	1	If the answer is 1 (YES), then Q.2-43 must be filled up.			
M7C	1	If the answer is 1 (YES), then Q.2-16 must be filled up.			
M7D	1	If the answer is 1 (YES), then Q.2-12 must be filled up.			
M7E	1	If the answer is 1 (YES), then Q.2-28 must be filled up.			

In LSMS surveys, supervisors fill out a check-up interview form to document the results of the re-interview. This ensures that the double-checking is thorough and impartial. It also allows the headquarters staff to effectively supervise the supervisors. Figure 5.6 shows the check-up interview form initially used for the Pakistan LSMS. The most important things to control for in the check-up interview form are the questions for which certain answers may represent substantial differences in interview time later. For instance, the simple omission of a person from the roster means that this person does not need to be looked for and interviewed later. "Rounding up" a woman's age a little bit may make her ineligible to answer the fertility section, and so forth. Other typical omissions are not probing hard enough for secondary activities (especially when the person is self-employed) or not probing for the complete list of crops grown. More subtle omissions are not considering an illness serious enough to be reported in the health section, nor the purchase of small amounts worth the inclusion of certain items in the list of expenditures. Apart from those, the check-up interview form may include certain observational records (like some the building materials in the housing section) and other questions that are deemed unlikely to change between the interview and the check-up interview.

Interviewers should be made aware that some check-up interviews will take place, though of course they should never know in advance the households where these will be conducted. In marketing research surveys, which are always brief field operations, it is also considered that the contents of the check-up interview (that is, the questions that will be re-asked) should be kept secret from the interviewers. In LSMS surveys this is impossible, given that they are conducted over a much longer period of time, but it is possible to modify parts of the check-up interview a few times during the period of field operations.

The check-up interview forms are also instrumental tools for centrally supervising the field teams. Occasionally, the survey field manager should join each team, select a few of these forms, and take them back to the same households for another check. There do not need to be very many of these double checks, but they should be random and unexpected.[55]

---

55. This should be done even though it often causes the interviewees considerable irritation. In fact, this reaction confirms the original interview and the supervisor's visit. As far as the super-supervisor is concerned, the ideal response to a knock on the target household's door is for the household member to snap, "Oh no, not the people from the household survey again! This is the *third* time you've been around pestering us!" At this point the super-supervisor should apologize profusely and beat a hasty retreat.

Figure 5.6: Check-up Interview Form

PROVINCE	SUB-UNIVERSE	STRATUM	PRIMARY SAMPLING UNIT	HOUSEHOLD

SEC-TION	QUESTIONS	RESULT		COMMENTS
		SATIS-FACTORY	UNSATIS-FACTORY	
2	a) What type of dwelling unit does the household reside in? b) Does the household rent or own the unit?			
3	a) Which members of the household have attended school? How much schooling have they completed?			
4	a) Has anyone in the household been ill recently?			
5	a) Is any member of the household an agriculture laborer? Are they permanent workers, seasonal workers, or casual workers? b) Was any member an employee outside the agriculture sector? What were their occupations? Which industries were they employed in?			
6	a) Does any member of the household work on his/her own account or operate a business? Which member(s)? What type of work do they do?			
7	a) What do you cook your meals on (i.e. open fire, stove, etc.)? b) How do you heat you dwelling during cold months?			
9	a) How much total land is owned by your household? How much land is owned close to the village? How much land is owned far away from the village? b) Which crops did you grow during the last completed rabi and kharif seasons? (probe) If wheat or rice was grown, how many acres of each did you harvest? c) What kinds of agriculture machinery do you own?			
12	a) What kinds of foodstuffs has your household purchased during the past two weeks? Were some of these purchases on udhar or credit?			
13	a) How many children has your wife had? How many boys? How many girls?			
15	a) Do you currently have any loans outstanding? Who did you borrow from?			

SUPERVISOR: _____ DATE

118

As explained in the chapter on sampling, the task assignment of each team should be done concurrently with the first stage of sample selection. The clusters are distributed among the field teams and the order in which each team will visit the clusters assigned to it is decided at random. The schedule of each team should then be made explicit, to indicate what each team will be supposed to be doing each week of the survey year.

With the standard LSMS setup explained in Section A, the 20 clusters assigned to each team will have to be grouped into 10 "pairs." As four weeks are needed to visit each pair, each team will devote 40 weeks to field work during the survey year.

The remaining 12 weeks of the year should be scheduled for things such as:

REST. The schedule should consider several rest periods because field work is very intensive and the staff is not supposed to have much free time during the 40 weeks of work. The field staff are either working in a cluster or travelling in between the clusters and the team base station. Weekends are rarely devoted to rest because in most places these are the best days for finding respondents at home.

CATCHING UP. Bad roads, material breakdowns, natural disasters, and various other situations may make it difficult for some teams to keep their work deadlines. It is necessary to allow some slack time in the calendar for catching up with these contingencies.

PROJECT EVALUATION. After the first month of field operations — and perhaps also at other key points of the calendar — it is advisable to bring the teams back to the central survey headquarters to discuss and solve the problems found so far.

RETRAINING. If the survey is to be conducted for more than one year, it will be necessary to bring the teams back to the central office at the end of the first year for training in the new procedures for the second year. New material can include changes in the questionnaires, procedures for re-visiting certain households if the second year contains a panel component, and so forth.

Figure 5.7 shows an idealized schedule of field work for the first year of an LSMS survey with 100 PSUs, numbered randomly[56] from 001 to 100. These are assigned to five teams, sorted by PSU within each team and grouped in pairs. For instance, Team 1 will visit the PSUs numbers 009, 011, 013, 015, etc. The teams first go to the field for four weeks to interview one pair of PSUs each (for Team 1, this is composed of PSUs 009 and 011). They then come back to the central office to evaluate the experience during weeks 5 and 6. Over the next 10 weeks (weeks 7 to 16), each team will interview two more pairs; the last two weeks are devoted to rest or, if necessary, to catch up on contingencies. This is repeated three more times. At the end of the year, after each team interviews its last pair of PSUs, everybody comes back to the central offices to be trained in the second year's procedures.

Figure 5.7: Schedule for Field Work

Weeks	Team 1	Team 2	Team 3	Team 4	Team 5
1- 4	009,011	001,019	003,004	006,012	002,010
5- 6	Evaluation of first month				
7-10	013,015	032,045	005,007	020,021	016,022
11-14	017,027	047,048	008,014	026,029	024,025
15-16	Catch-up and rest				
17-20	028,031	049,050	018,023	035,041	034,037
21-24	036,039	055,056	030,033	044,052	038,040
25-26	Catch-up and rest				
27-30	057,060	058,063	043,046	064,066	042,051
31-34	062,070	065,074	053,059	069,073	054,061
35-38	075,079	080,081	067,071	076,082	068,077
39	Catch-up and rest				
40	Important national holiday				
41-44	083,092	085,089	072,084	087,091	078,088
45-46	Catch-up and rest				
47-50	096,099	093,100	086,097	095,098	090,094
51-52	Rest (and training for second year)				

56. The numbers shown in Figure 5.6 represent the order in which the actual PSUs were drawn, not the geographic codes for the PSUs. The numbers seem to indicate that time and space will be correlated in the field, but it is not true.

Putting catch-up and rest periods together tends to reduce the time taken for minor contingencies. With the incentive of being able to take the full two weeks as leave rather than working to catch up, the field staff exhibit considerable diligence in overcoming minor contingencies and sticking to the schedule. This basic schedule can be elaborated by staggering the catch-up and rest periods for the different teams. This helps to avoid any bias that might be caused by seasonal factors. Since the work is already well spread out through the year, this has seldom been done in practice.

Designing the actual schedule is very country-specific, as it is usually developed around national holidays and other significant dates, with the goal of either excluding or including them in the work period. In Muslim countries, for instance, the Ramadan month is particularly interesting to observe because of the differences in the household consumption patterns; Ramadan, however, is not a good month to train interviewers or to initiate the survey.

For some important holidays, especially those that last only a few days or a week, it may be unreasonable to expect field crews to work or respondents to be willing to be interviewed. Christmas in the United States is an example of such a holiday. In these cases, the schedule should be planned so that the holiday week comes between the four-week, two-PSU cycles. That will maintain the interval between interviews, which is important when there are recall periods bounded by the first interview. Such an adjustment is shown in Figure 5.7 for the holiday in week 40.

Ensuring Collaboration by Households

The most important way to ensure collaboration by the households is to use polite, diligent, well trained interviewers and to have them make several return visits to ensure that the household is contacted and a time convenient for the interview arranged. Some additional measures may be needed. There are no fixed prescriptions that will work everywhere, but experience from various countries should be observed and evaluated.

•   USE OF MASS MEDIA. In general, the use of mass media is a waste of money because the mass media reach many people whom the survey does not. However, if mass media coverage can be obtained free it can be useful. Even if it is limited to a short newspaper story or some radio or TV briefs at the start of the survey, it can boost the field teams' morale and self-confidence at this critical time. (Occasionally interviewers keep the old newspapers throughout the entire survey period, to show the households that they are official and serious.) Obtaining free publicity requires some imagination; for the Peru 1985 survey, the head of the National Statistical Institute took advantage of the monthly disclosure of the Consumer Price Index to publicize the survey. (The announcement of the CPI was understandably a major media event, given inflation levels at that time.)

- TARGETED PUBLICITY. This may include letters to the households and leaflets (preferably in color, with graphs or other illustrations) that explain the purpose of the survey and the sampling methodology in simple terms. In Ghana, the publicity was handled as follows: One to two weeks before the team arrived in an urban cluster for interviewing, the supervisor sent out letters to inform the heads of households of the team's arrival in the community and the date the team would possibly visit. The supervisor then visited the foremost local political figures (such as the members of the Revolutionary Defense Committee) and the heads of all selected households.

- MATERIAL INCENTIVES. Sometimes a gift or payment is given to the households in return for their collaboration. There is some controversy about the quality and quantity of the material incentives that should be used to foster the household's collaboration. LSMS surveys generally follow the practice standard in each statistical agency. Some consider incentives to be standard procedure for all surveys. This was the case in Romania, where the households interviewed for the earlier Family Budget Survey received a monthly cash payment (albeit a very modest one). The Romanian LSMS inherited that feature. Other statistical agencies are reluctant to even consider the idea of rewarding the households in any way, to prevent households from becoming increasingly demanding and affecting all the household surveys conducted in the country. This is the case in Jamaica. A relatively inexpensive alternative, likely to be cost-effective and be accepted in all countries, consists of giving away small presents for the interviewed households. These can include t-shirts, calendars, brief statistical brochures, and similar items. In Peru (1990 and 1991), for example, households were given copies of an attractive popular magazine published by the private survey firm that conducted the survey. Ideally, the giveaways should have little or no intrinsic value. This both ensures that they do not affect the household welfare measurement and reduces the accounting controls required.

- COMMUNITY LEVEL. Publicity and motivation at the local community level are especially important in rural areas. Local authorities should be contacted and convinced of the usefulness of the survey. In rural areas of Ghana, letters were sent to the local chief or regent. The weekend before the survey, the team paid a courtesy call to the chief/regent and other prominent members of the community to explain the objectives of the survey, to introduce the team members, and to discuss the survey schedule for the week. The supervisor often used the occasion to administer the community questionnaire. After this meeting the interviewers contacted the selected households to introduce themselves and to make appointments for interviews.

Piloting Field Procedures

Since the LSMS field procedures have worked well in several countries, the pilot test for field procedures is less to determine whether they can work in general than to fine tune the details of how they are implemented in the specific country. After the first four-week cycle of field work, all the teams convene in one place for a week or two. They discuss their experience and teams compare notes about problems and how they could be resolved. This has been done in most of the LSMS surveys conducted under the standard scheme presented Section A. Most problems found during the field test fall into three classes:

- REFINING LOGISTICS. In spite of all precautions, some problems regarding the supply of one survey material or other is always found, fuel for the cars being the most common. Sometimes this is due to excessive bureaucracy at the central level but often also to the supervisors' failure to understand the extent of their autonomy.

- DEBUGGING THE DATA ENTRY PROGRAM. A major subject of discussion is the working of the data entry program. Again, and as always is the case with software, no lab testing is ever able to show all the hidden features of the program that will be revealed when data from numerous real household are entered. More importantly, the need to program new consistency checks that were unforeseen by the survey data managers will become obvious after the first few weeks of field work.

- STATISTICAL QUALITY CONTROL OF THE DATA. Concurrent data entry makes it possible to conduct some preliminary statistical analysis of the data collected in the first month. From an analytical standpoint, the data from just one month has no statistical significance unless the total sample is exceptionally large, but it often can provide interesting insights into the quality of the field work. For instance, after the first month of the Mauritania survey, the frequency distribution of the last digit of the ages recorded in years showed too large a proportion of "zeroes" and "fives" (demographers always expect this to happen, but not to that extent). More interesting, the same phenomenon was observed in the last digit of weights (in tenths of a kilo) and heights (in tenths of a centimeter) that were recorded by the anthropometrists. The early detection of this problem allowed for corrective re-training, and also gave the data entry program credibility in the eyes of the field teams.

It may happen that the problems revealed in the four-week assessment are serious enough to make the data collected during the first four weeks unreliable. Though this has not been the case in the LSMS surveys conducted so far, it is a

123

real possibility and the survey planner should be prepared to deal with this contingency by excluding the first month from the data sets. This would entail either a smaller total sample or expanding the data collection process by an extra month.

In cases with more innovative features, the field procedures may be piloted before the actual interviewing starts. In Nepal, for example, a test of logistics was done to see how well it would work to have the data entry operator and computer travel with the field team. In Romania, because the survey involves 500 interviewers, it was impossible to bring them all to Bucharest for discussions. The first month of the survey (March 1994) was considered a *de facto* field test of the survey, with the explicit intention of excluding the collected 3,000 households from the data sets if too many implementation problems were found. This, in fact, proved to be the case.

Chapter 6. Data Management

Key Messages

- Integrated data entry and field work are key to the timeliness and the quality of data from LSMS surveys.

- The data management approach for the LSMS surveys has four primary features:
    - (1) precoded, verbatim questionnaires;
    - (2) error detection at the time of data entry;
    - (3) data entry that is concurrent with field work; and
    - (4) correction of suspected errors in the field.

- There must be substantial interaction between the data manager and the analysts during the drafting of the questionnaire and the definition of error checks.

- To ensure smooth field operations and credible data, the data entry program must be well developed and tested before field work starts. Sufficient time must be allowed for these procedures.

- Five kinds of checks should be made on the data as they are entered:
    - (1) range checks should be defined for every variable;
    - (2) checks should be possible between entered data and reference tables;
    - (3) skip checks should be defined for all skips, both within and between different units of observation;
    - (4) checks for consistency of answers to different questions should be made, both within and between different units of observation; and
    - (5) checks on typographical accuracy should be possible.

- Before distributing the data files to analysts the statistical office should check the *structural consistency* of the data files — that the files include all households and no redundancies, and that all files can be merged properly.

- When the full LSMS data management procedures have been used, ex post facto checks for *logical consistency* of the files — for missing values, outliers, etc. — will be redundant with the checks done at data entry. Any further treatment of these problems should be left to analysts, since there is no universally acceptable solution to these problems and their treatment is very difficult to document adequately but often critical to the interpretation of the analysis.

- The number of different levels of observation in LSMS surveys creates complexities in data management that are best handled by a file structure that:

  (1) assigns one record to each individual unit observed;
  (2) allows a variable number of records of each record type;
  (3) limits the number of variables in a record type to what can be contained on a data entry screen; and
  (4) uses a complete set of identifiers on each record.

Good data management is critical to ensure the timeliness and quality of the survey data. This chapter describes the problems to be addressed in managing LSMS data sets and the techniques that have been developed to deal with them. Sections A and B should be read by all readers and provide an overview of the LSMS data management philosophy and the requirements for the data management system. Section C describes the file structure used in the customized LSMS data entry program and is of interest to readers who will be involved in data management or choosing a data entry program.

A. An Overview of LSMS Data Management Philosophy

Objectives

Two principles guided the development of the LSMS data management system — timeliness and quality. The primary reason for this type of survey is to provide policymakers and analysts with information about household behavior and welfare; for the data to be useful, they must be recent.[57] The LSMS surveys also aspire to collect data of very high quality. The LSMS system speeds and simplifies analysis and gives the results credibility.

Approach Developed

In order to achieve the goals of timeliness and high quality, the LSMS approach uses four key features: (1) pre-coded, verbatim questionnaires with explicit skip patterns; (2) error detection in the data entry program; (3) data entry concurrent with field work; and (4) correction of errors in the field.

PRE-CODED VERBATIM QUESTIONNAIRES. As explained in the chapter on questionnaire development, nearly all questions on the LSMS questionnaires are pre-coded or require numeric answers and the remaining few questions are coded in the field, as explained in the chapter on questionnaire design. This eliminates

---

57. Before the LSMS model was developed, data from complex surveys (such as agricultural surveys, nutrition surveys or household expenditure surveys) could take two to five years from the completion of field work to the availability of data for analysis. While general survey practice has improved somewhat since then, the problem has not disappeared by any means.

the coding step in the data management process, which often took months or years in other surveys and which introduces the possibility of errors.

ERROR DETECTION AT THE TIME OF DATA ENTRY. The data are subjected to extensive checks on their validity and consistency at the time they are recorded, as will be explained in detail later in this chapter.

CONCURRENT DATA ENTRY. LSMS surveys enter data concurrently with the field work. As explained in the chapter on field work, this eliminates a long inactive period. Completed questionnaires are not stored unattended while field work progresses. Instead, the time-consuming task of data entry is carried out simultaneously with field interviews. The system of concurrent data entry detects errors quickly and allows interviewers to revisit the household to try to correct apparent errors.

CORRECTION OF SUSPECTED ERRORS IN THE FIELD. Suspect data in the first half of the questionnaire that are flagged by the data entry program can be checked or corrected during the second interview. For data gathered during the second interview, the opportunity to correct any errors is not guaranteed. However, in urban areas, and occasionally in rural areas, there is no great difficulty in visiting a household a third time if this is required to correct errors from the second interview.

Correcting the errors in the field greatly speeds the process of data editing and correction, since only a single, quick, and conclusive iteration is needed. It also increases dramatically the level of certainty that the appropriate correction is being made.[58] Even when such revisits are not possible, concurrent data entry improves the field work because it provides immediate feedback on common errors and problems. Thus, corrective measures can be taken early on rather than having errors replicated throughout the whole survey.

Implications for Survey Planning

The use of LSMS data management procedures has some implications for other parts of survey planning, as follows:

INTEGRATION OF DATA MANAGEMENT AND QUESTIONNAIRE DESIGN. Data management should be integrated into questionnaire design. The data manager should be consulted on each major draft of the questionnaire, since he or she will have an especially sharp eye for flaws in the definition of units of observation, skip patterns, etc. Likewise, the analysts who have helped to write the questions should help the data manager determine appropriate range and consistency checks.

---

58. With ex-post facto data entry, the best that can be achieved is internal consistency of the data sets. There is no guarantee that they truly reflect the reality found in the households.

SKILLS REQUIRED OF THE DATA MANAGER. The data manager's role is much more creative in this system of data management than in the old fashioned system where a programmer waited to be told what to program. In this system the data manager needs to be creative and adept at taking initiative. He or she should have sufficient statistical or economic training to determine the content of the data quality checks independently. The basic programming skills required to be able to learn techniques for LSMS data management are familiarity with the standard DOS commands and a programming language. The specific skills of using a particular data entry software are usually part of the on-the-job training for the LSMS survey. In other words, the data manager does not need to be a professional programmer — indeed experience suggests that it may be better if he or she is not too much enamored with computers per se.

TIMETABLE. The data entry program for questionnaires entered in the field must be carefully developed, tested, and corrected before field operations begin. A data entry program that does not work well damages its credibility and usefulness as a supervisory tool.

LSMS surveys have usually allowed six to eight weeks for the complete preparation and testing of the data entry program and another two weeks between the training of the data entry operators and interviewers and the commencement of field work. Regrettably, this entire period is often absorbed by the program for the household questionnaire. Programs for the community, price, and facility questionnaires have not been designed or tested as well in advance of the field operations, with noticeable consequences for the resulting quality of data.

B. Requirements for the Data Management System

The minimum requirement for a satisfactory data management system is that its output be a useful, high-quality data set. This section describes the requirements for achieving this goal.

Ease of Analysis of Resulting Data Files

The structure of the final files must facilitate analysis by commonly used statistical software. As the LSMS questionnaire contains so many units of observation, achieving this objective is not a trivial matter. Contrast, for example, the complexity in use resulting from alternate file structures for the demographic data on the household roster. One possibility is to have one record for each person in the roster, with one field for age and one field for sex. Another possibility is to have the whole roster in one single record, with separate fields for the age of person 1, the age of person 2, the sex of person 1, the sex of person 2, etc. Creating a table of sex by age requires a single program statement in the first case, whereas in the second case it requires previously combining the information from each of the sex variables and each of the age variables. The second approach will also have to allow a number of variables for each personal characteristic (sex, age, education, etc.) equal to the largest likely household size, say 20 or 25 persons, even though the average size is much smaller. Even worse structures are possible — in one recent survey, the structure created two variables for sex for each person: male yes/no and female yes/no. This meant yet another step of aggregation was required before substantive analysis was possible. It also introduced the possibility that individuals could be coded as both male and female or neither male nor female.

One of the principal challenges of managing LSMS data is to produce files from complex questionnaires that are easy to use for analysis. The questionnaires' complexity is due to the numerous different levels of observation and their interrelationships, rather than to large file size.[59] In the number of levels of observation and their interrelations, LSMS surveys are among the most complex to be found anywhere. The household questionnaires typically have approximately two dozen levels of observation. The questionnaires for schools or health clinics may again have several levels of observation but the community and price questionnaires usually have many fewer, sometimes only one, units of observation. Box 6.1 shows the whole list of levels of observation in the Kagera Health and Development survey.

To avoid repeating the work of labeling variables in the statistical software during the analytical stage, the program used for data entry should define the file structures in the formats of common statistical software such as SAS, SPSS, and Stata, as well as in the .DBF format used by data base managers such as DBase, Clipper, and FoxPro. This can save several weeks of work, since LSMS questionnaires can have hundreds or even thousands of variables. Many of them are categorical variables, a few of which have lengthy code lists (like occupations, geographic locations, or consumption items) and many more of which have shorter code lists (type of school or clinic attended, places where credit available). These are all labeled in the data entry screens so it makes sense not to have to duplicate the work later.

The data should also not be cluttered with unnecessary codes for "not applicable." Because of the explicit patterns built into the LSMS questionnaire, blanks can be reliably interpreted as "not applicable." At the data entry stage, this means that time need not be taken up by filling in artificial "not applicable" codes such as 999. This also greatly simplifies analysis since the annoying 999s have to be excluded by hand from all averages, cross-tabulations, models, and so forth.

---

59. In terms of bulk, LSMS data sets are large but not extraordinarily so. The average LSMS survey gathers information from some 3,000 households. The data from each household can be stored in about 10 kilobytes (the range usually being between 5 and 20 kilobytes), so the entire survey may require around 30 megabytes of disk space, a figure that personal computers now available can handle quite easily. When not in active use, the data can be compressed for storage to about one eighth of its uncompressed size.

Household Questionnaire
Household
Individual member of household
Children living elsewhere
Children ever born to women in household
Dead household members
Dead non-resident relatives
Plot of land
Crop grown
Type of crop processing
Item of farm equipment
Livestock type
Livestock product
Business
Business input expenditure
Business asset
Item of fishing equipment
Fishing input expenditure
Dwelling or buildings
Durable goods owned
Home-produced crop consumption item
Purchased food consumption item
Household expenditure item

Community Questionnaire
Community
Credit and lending agencies
Primary schools
Secondary schools
Health service providers
Major crops grown
Type of agricultural labor

Health Facility Questionnaire
Facility
Type of personnel
Type of vehicle
Services offered
Vaccines
Contraceptive methods
Types of support received
Drug supply
Outpatient consultations by diagnostic category

Traditional Healers Questionnaire
Healer
Health conditions
Prescriptions and referrals

Primary School Questionnaire
School
Grade
Types of support received

Data Quality Checks During Data Entry

When they are entered, data should be subjected to five kinds of quality checks: range checks, checks against reference data, skip checks, consistency checks, and typographical checks. Each is discussed in turn in this section.

RANGE CHECKS. There should be a range check on every variable in the survey. Categorical variables should take on only defined values. For example, for a yes/no question, the only legal codes should be "1" (yes) and "2" (no). Any other value should be flagged as an error. Chronological variables should contain valid dates. For example, the date of February 29 would only be allowed in leap years. Numeric variables should be verified to lie within prescribed minimum and maximum values. For example, the age of each person should lie between 0 and 95 years (see Box 6.2 for a discussion of how to set the boundaries for the ranges on numeric variables).

An error flag, such as a beep and a flashing field on the screen, may be set off when an out-of-range value is entered. If the error is merely typographical, the data entry operator can correct it immediately. It should, however, be possible to override the flag if the value entered represents what is on the questionnaire. In that case a written error report should be generated so the supervisor and interviewer can verify the value during the second interview. The suspect datum may be stored in a special format that registers its questionable status, but this format should be such that the analyst can use the datum in analysis if he or she deems it appropriate.

REFERENCE TABLES. For the anthropometric module, the validity checks should be made by comparing the individual's height, weight, and age with the World Health Organization standard reference tables. Any value for the standard indicators (height-for-age, weight-for-age, and weight-for-height) that falls more than three standard deviations from the norm should be flagged as a possible error so that the measurement can be repeated.

A similar check using an outside body of data can be performed on food composition data, but so far the Romania survey is the only LSMS survey that has had such a check. The Romania survey verified that the monthly per capita energy intake for the household lay within reasonable ranges, and also checked that the per capita energy provided by each individual food did not exceed certain absolute maximums or certain fractions of the total energy intake.

Box 6.2: Setting Boundaries for Range Checks

Setting the boundaries for the range checks on some numeric variables is an art. Optimally, for example, the maximum permissible value for expenditures on a particular food item should be selected by referring to a previous household survey, choosing a value that includes 97 or 99 percent of the households beneath the bound, and then updating that value for inflation. Such a rigorous method of determining ranges can hardly be applied to all variables; setting up the ranges in practice may require some guesswork. In so doing, it is worth keeping in mind that the purpose of range checking is not to flag *absolutely* impossible values but to warn of *probably* erroneous values. The temptation to set up extremely wide ranges (like, for instance, $100 per week for caviar, just in case Mr. Rockefeller happens to be selected in the sample) should be avoided. Setting tighter ranges entails, of course, the risk of flagging a few "false positives," but human supervisors are there precisely to apply their judgement to these situations; the data entry program should allow the operator to enter an out-of-range value if it correctly reflects what is written on the questionnaire and is not due to a typographical error. These values should, however, be flagged so that the interviewer and supervisor can determine in the field whether they are correct.

131

SKIP CHECKS.   Skip checks verify whether the skip codes have been followed appropriately. For example, a simple skip check verifies that questions to be asked only of schoolchildren are not recorded for a child who answered "no" to an initial question on school enrollment. A more complicated check would verify that the right modules of the questionnaire have been filled in for each respondent. Depending on his or her age and sex, each member of the household is supposed to answer (or skip) specific sections of the questionnaire. For instance, children less than 5 years old should be measured in the anthropometric section but should not be asked the questions about occupation. Women aged 15-49 may be included in the fertility section, but men may not.

The data entry program should *not* actually follow the skip codes itself. For example, if a "no" answer is entered to the question "are you enrolled in school?" the fields to enter data about the kind of school attended, grade in school, and so on should still be presented to the data entry operator. If there are answers actually recorded on the questionnaire, they can then be entered and the program will flag an incorrect skip. The supervisor or interviewer can determine the nature of the mistake. It may well be that the "no" was supposed to be a "yes." If the data entry program had automatically skipped the following fields, the error would not have been detected or remedied.

All the skip codes in the questionnaire should be verified in the data entry program. This may involve hundreds of checks.

CONSISTENCY CHECKS.   Consistency checks verify that values from one question are consistent with values from another question. A simple check occurs when both values are from the same unit of observation, for example the date of birth and age of a given individual. More complicated consistency checks involve comparing information from two or more different units of observation. There are many complex consistency checks that are applicable in almost all LSMS surveys and so have become something of a de facto standard. For example:

DEMOGRAPHIC CONSISTENCY OF THE HOUSEHOLD.   The consistency between the ages and genders of all household members is checked with a view to the kinship relationships. For example, parents should be at least (say) 15 years older than their children, spouses should be of different sexes, etc.

CONSISTENCY OF OCCUPATIONS.   The presence or absence of certain sections should be consistent with the occupations declared individually by the household members. For instance, the farming section should be present if and only if some household members are reported as independent farmers in the labor section.

CONSISTENCY OF AGE AND OTHER INDIVIDUAL CHARACTERISTICS.   It is possible to check that the age of each person is consistent with personal characteristics such as marital status, relationship to the head of the household, grade of current enrollment (for children currently at school) or last grade obtained (for those who have dropped). For example, an 8 year old child should not be in a grade higher than 3.

EXPENDITURES. Several different consistency checks are possible. Only in a household where one or more of the individual records shows that a child is attending school should there be positive numbers in the household consumption record for items such as school books and schooling fees. Likewise, only households that have electrical service should report expenditures on electricity.

It is very important to be able to do both skip and consistency checks that involve more than one unit and level of observation at a time.[60] This criterion should be given heavy weight in choosing a software package for data entry because complex checks are numerous and tend to disclose the most important flaws in the field work, as well as those least likely for the interviewer or supervisor to find by a visual check of the questionnaire. A list of all the checks between units of observation that were included in the Romania survey is included in Annex VII.

Since the resolution of checks on different units of observation often requires going back to the household, or at minimum a thoughtful perusal of the questionnaire, a written report should be generated for the supervisor and interviewer to use in the process. An example is shown in Box 6.3.

There is no natural limit on the number of consistency checks that can exist. Well-written versions of the data entry program for a full LSMS survey may have several hundred of them. In general, the more checks that are defined, the higher will be the quality of the final data set. However, given that the time available to write the whole data entry program is always limited (usually to about two months), some expertise and good judgement are required to decide exactly which should be included.

CHECKING FOR TYPOGRAPHICAL ERRORS. In most LSMS surveys the data entry program can print out the values entered in a format similar to that of the questionnaire. This printout serves two purposes. It can be checked visually against the original questionnaire (this is the duty of the supervisor) and the values that raised flags on the range, skip, and consistency checks are printed

---

60. The level of observation is the kind of thing being observed — persons, plots of land, crops, household businesses. The units of observation are the different individuals within each set — person 1 or person 2, rice or corn. An example of a check between units of observation would be to check that the parents of a child are at least fourteen years older than the child. An example of a check between levels of observation would be to check that if the head of household is a farmer, the agricultural module has been filled out.

```
o |                                                                    | o
o |  Household 02024: PART 3:   Inter-record checks:                   | o
o |  ---- Error number 1:                                              | o
  |  Person No. 03 answered Part B but was not a household member      |
o |  in Wave 3                                                         | o
  |  ---- Error number 2:                                              |
o |  Person No. 09 is missing from the household roster                | o
o |  ---- Error number 3:                                              | o
  |  Child No. 14C reports different ages on Section 2 and the Yellow  |
o |                            Roster                                  | o
  |                                                                    |
o |  ---- Error number 4:                                              | o
  |  Child No. 33C is not on Section 2: Children residing elsewhere    |
o |                                                                    | o
  |  ---- Error number 5:                                              |
o |  Woman No. 02 must answer questions 3 to 15 on Section 9.          | o
  |                                                                    |
o |  ---- Error number 6:                                              | o
  |        INTER-WAVE CHECK:   SECTION 4, QUESTION 8:                  |
o |  Household reported 2 family businesses during Wave 3 but          | o
  |  only 1 during Wave 4.  Please verify whether the household        |
o |  had these business in the past 6 months during round two.        | o
  |                                                                    |
o |   6 errors detected in this Household                              | o
  |                                                                    |
```

This figure offers an example of the inter-record checks generated by the data entry program for the fourth wave of the Kagera Health and Development Survey.   Once the operator has completed the data entry process for a household, he or she then runs the inter-record checks, which produce listings like the one shown.   The operator can also look at the listing on the screen, since there is a possibility that some of the errors might have been typographical mistakes that the data entry operator can fix. Otherwise, the supervisor receives the listing along with the questionnaire, since these types of inconsistencies have to be corrected during the second visit to the household.

The KHDS inter-record checks are particularly interesting as the survey had a four-wave panel design, so *inter-wave* checks had to be programmed into the process as well as the standard inter-record checks.

within bold boxes so that they show up easily for the interviewer to correct in the household.   An example is shown in Box 6.4.[61]

---

61. Specialized pages to be used in interviews may also be printed. For example, the program prints a page for the anthropometrist to use as a questionnaire during the second interview. It has the same format as the original questionnaire page used in the first interview and lists the names of the individuals to be reweighed. (Individuals falling more than three standard deviations from the reference norms are flagged as being possible errors and 20 percent of individuals are randomly selected for remeasuring as a validity check.)

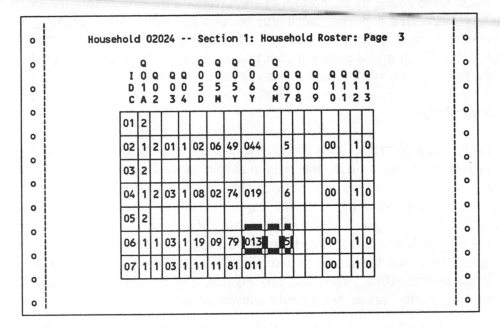

The figure shows a printout of a questionnaire page. The operator usually requests a complete printout of the whole questionnaire along with the inter-record checks, though he or she also has the option of selecting a single page as shown here. In this particular example, the page printed is the roster page of the Tanzania LSMS questionnaire. The format was specifically chosen to mimic as closely as possible the actual layout of the questionnaire.

The bold box surrounding the answers for individual number 06 to questions 6 and 7 denotes that an inconsistency was detected. How the error flag would appear on the data entry screen is shown in Box 6.7.

It must be admitted that the tedious job of visually checking the printout and the questionnaire is probably not done as rigorously as needed to fully substitute for double-blind data entry. Thus typographical errors that result in valid values may occur. These are probably most prevalent in the consumption or income sections, since the ranges for valid values are wide and relatively few consistency checks are possible. For example, an expenditure of either $14 or $41 would be valid for the monthly consumption of a staple food. The same mistake for age, however, might be caught by the consistency checks with marital status or family relations. For example, a married or widowed adult aged 41 whose age is mistakenly entered as 14 will show up with an error flag in the intra-record check on age and marital status. The impact of such errors in the consumption section is probably small, given the small fraction of the total that any one item contributes.

In Romania, an innovation helped detect typographical errors. Lines for check totals were added to the bottom of each page on the consumption module. The interviewer used a pocket calculator to total the value of expenditures on each page by hand and filled in the line. The resulting figure was entered with the raw data. Then an inter-record check was added in the data entry program to verify that the sum of the items entered equalled the check total.

After Data Entry

After data entry has been completed in the field, the central office has a few steps to perform. First, the data manager should gather the files with household data prepared by the various data entry operators throughout the country and verify that all households from each period are included without duplication. Though a good system of household identifiers should almost ensure that no households are duplicated, there is still room for human error, such as entering data from one household in two different computers or reading a diskette twice at the central office. The same process may also be necessary for the data from the community, price, and facility questionnaires.

Second, depending on the file structure used by the data entry program, numerous individual household-based files may have to be converted into the few larger thematic files that are useful in data analysis. This process is illustrated in Box 6.5.

Third, the files should be converted to the format of the software that will be used for analysis while producing the abstract. In fact, the files might be converted to additional formats in order to facilitate use by clients who use different software packages. A master version of the files should, however, always be maintained in ASCII, since it is the universal standard readable by all other software. The LSMS division, for example, distributes data sets in SAS, Stata, and ASCII formats. After the conversion it should be checked that the conversions between software were performed correctly, with the data assigned to the proper variables and the labels transferred correctly.

Fourth, the data manager should check the *structural consistency* of the files; that is, that the different thematic files with data from the household questionnaires can all be matched with each other, and that information from the household can be merged with information from the community and price questionnaires. Problems are most commonly found in merging information from the three questionnaires, so this aspect should be checked the most closely.

At this stage it is useful to compile basic univariate statistics for each variable. For qualitative variables (i.e., those that only have a small number of possible values like yes/no questions), frequencies should be produced. For quantitative variables, the minimum, maximum, and mean values should be reported. Then these results should be examined for rough plausibility. If, for

When data entry is integrated with field operations, the most natural unit for data management is the *household file* (the set of records of different types that pertain to one household), whereas at the analytical stage it is the *thematic file* (the set of all records of the same type generated by all households). An important step in the data management process is therefore to transform one form of file organization into the other. The record format structure used in the custom LSMS data entry program makes this process conceptually trivial, as will be illustrated below with a simple example. In practice this process may be complicated because of the large bulk of the data sets.

Consider a three-household LSMS survey with a three-section questionnaire: housing, roster, and budget. The housing page contains information on building materials for walls and roof; the roster contains the name, sex, and age of all household members; the budget page records the amounts spent by the household on various items. Such a questionnaire would generate three record types: 001 for Housing, 002 for Roster and 003 for Budget. Assuming that the three households are numbered 11111, 22222 and 33333, the data entry program would generate three files, as shown on Figure 6.5.A. Notice that each record is uniquely identified with a record type, a household number, and whatever extra identifiers are needed to distinguish individual records of the same type within a household. In this case, each person in the roster has a two-digit ID code, and each budgetary item has a three-digit item code (for instance, code "103" may mean "bread").

```
                Figure 6.5.A  The Household files

┌─ Household 11111 ──┐ ┌─ Household 22222 ──┐ ┌─ Household 33333 ──┐
│001 11111 1 2       │ │001 22222 1 1       │ │001 33333 1 1       │
│002 11111 01    JOE 1 37│ │002 22222 01    MOE 1 25│ │002 33333 01    SAM 1 40│
│002 11111 02  JANET 2 33│ │002 22222 02   MARY 2 23│ │002 33333 02 SANDRA 2 35│
│002 11111 03  JIMMY 1 12│ │003 22222 096 005500│ │002 33333 03  SAMMY 1 15│
│002 11111 04   JUDY 2 10│ │003 22222 103 000012│ │003 33333 015 000234│
│003 11111 103 000040│ │003 22222 199 000125│ │003 33333 103 000020│
│003 11111 217 002000│ │003 22222 205 001200│ │003 33333 201 000999│
│003 11111 260 000150│ └────────────────────┘ └────────────────────┘
└────────────────────┘
```

Box 6.5 continues on next page

example, the mean height for adults is reported as 15 meters, it is a sure flag that something has gone awry in the reading of the variable, since the plausible answer would be in the neighborhood of 1.5 meters.

A different aspect of data cleaning refers to checking for *logical consistency* in the observations. This refers to a hunt for and solution to blanks or missing data, invalid data, outliers, or inconsistencies between observations — the very things the data entry program and concurrent data entry were designed to detect and prevent. Thus to do this step centrally is redundant.

Box 6.5 (continued)

Records from all files should be first piled up together and then sorted by record type, household number, and any extra identifiers. This is easily done with any standard sorting program and is illustrated on Figure 6.5.B.

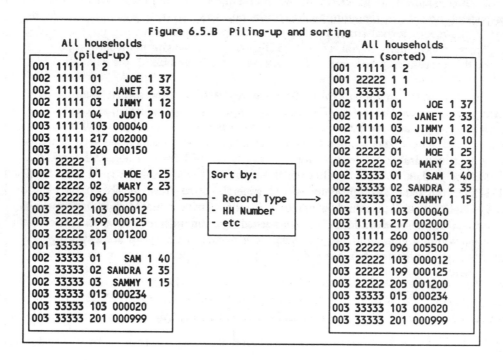

Figure 6.5.B Piling-up and sorting

Finally, the sorted file may be split into thematic files as shown in Figure 6.5.C. Each such file is a flat file, where records represent homogeneous statistical units and can be submitted to standard statistical software for separate analysis. The presence of household numbers in each record makes it possible to link these thematic files for more ambitious manipulation. The size of the thematic files should not exceed what would be easy to handle with the level of hardware and software expected of the final users.

```
                   Figure 6.5.C  Thematic files

       Theme 001              Theme 002                Theme 003
    ┌── Housing ──┐      ┌── Demographics ──┐       ┌── Budget ──┐
    │ 001 11111 1 2│      │ 002 11111 01    JOE 1 37│ │ 003 11111 103 000040│
    │ 001 22222 1 1│      │ 002 11111 02  JANET 2 33│ │ 003 11111 217 002000│
    │ 001 33333 1 1│      │ 002 11111 03  JIMMY 1 12│ │ 003 11111 260 000150│
    └─────────────┘      │ 002 11111 04   JUDY 2 10│ │ 003 22222 096 005500│
                          │ 002 22222 01    MOE 1 25│ │ 003 22222 103 000012│
                          │ 002 22222 02   MARY 2 23│ │ 003 22222 199 000125│
                          │ 002 33333 01    SAM 1 40│ │ 003 22222 205 001200│
                          │ 002 33333 02 SANDRA 2 35│ │ 003 33333 015 000234│
                          │ 002 33333 03  SAMMY 1 15│ │ 003 33333 103 000020│
                          └─────────────────────────┘ │ 003 33333 201 000999│
                                                       └─────────────────────┘
```

When the full LSMS field work and data management strategies have been adopted, the LSMS division has always recommended that any data cleaning with respect to logical consistency should be left to individual analysts. The files are thus ready for distribution to analysts at this stage.

One reason for recommending that checks for logical consistency be left to analysts is that no consensus exists as to how to identify or treat outliers and missing observations.[62] Since no procedure will satisfy all analysts, it has been deemed best to give them the raw data and let each analyst perform whatever cleaning he or she thinks best. Moreover, it is very important for analysts to know exactly what has been done so they can interpret their findings correctly. Since documenting data editing is very difficult, it may be preferable to leave it to the individual analyst.

Naturally one of the important analysts of the data will be the statistical institute itself. Thus, the recommendation that the data be made publicly available after checking only for structural consistency does not preclude further data cleaning with respect to logical consistency as part of the analysis process. The institute may wish to make public its corrections, e.g., imputations of alternate values for outliers or missing observations, along with its other computed variables, such as income or consumption aggregates. These computed variables should be labeled as such and distributed *in addition to* and not instead of the original data. The original data, free from adulterations, must be made available to outside analysts.

This small role of the central office in cleaning data is possible because so much of the data quality control has been moved to the decentralized data entry stage. Before the availability of personal computers made this possible, data entry and data editing had to be done separately after the field work was concluded. For certain simple surveys, ex post facto data editing might converge to a relatively "clean" data set after a few iterations, usually in a year or so. In complex surveys, however, implementing quality controls and the correction of the detected inconsistencies in batch operations becomes difficult. Editing a complex survey in this way could take several years, and in extreme cases the resulting data set — even if internally consistent — can be extremely unreliable because of the myriad of undocumented decisions that had to be made along the way. Now personal computers can perform powerful quality checks at the time of data entry, and data entry, data editing, and field work can be integrated into a single process. Thus the need for time-consuming and inaccurate ex post facto data editing has been eliminated.

---

62. Some analysts do nothing. Others spend a long time identifying these problem cases. Some analysts drop the problem observations. Others develop elaborate routines to impute some kind of correction.

Finally, and very importantly, the central office must add the variables containing the sampling weights and prepare adequate documentation to accompany the data sets. This is treated in detail in Section B of Chapter 7.

C. File Structure Used in LSMS Data Entry Program

A custom data entry program was developed for the first LSMS surveys and has been used since then in most of the surveys assisted by the LSMS division of the World Bank (see Box 6.6). The file structure it uses is described here. Experience has proved this structure to be satisfactory. It handles well the complexities that arise from having so many different levels of observation and addresses the perennial goals of limiting errors by data entry operators, minimizing storage requirements, and interfacing well with statistical software at the analytic phase.

In describing the structure two terms must be defined: the record type and the record. Imagine a matrix of information like the grids on the questionnaire. The columns are the questions or variables. The rows are the different individuals (or plots of land or businesses or whatever) to which the questions pertain. The variables may be divided into smaller, more manageable subsets which are referred to as record types (such as employment, health, and so forth). The information pertaining to any row — an individual, for example — is a record.

Correspondence Between Records and Individual Units Observed

The data structure maintains a one-to-one correspondence between the individual unit within each level of observation and the records in the computer files. For example, to manage the data listed on the household roster, a record type would be defined for the variables on the roster and the data corresponding to each individual would be stored in a separate record of that type. Similarly, in the consumption module a record type would correspond to food items and the data corresponding to each individual item would be stored in separate records of that type.

Variable Number of Records

The number of records in each record type is allowed to vary. This economizes the storage space required, since the files need not allow every case to be the largest possible. For example, the number of bytes necessary to enter the roster data for every person in one particular household will be determined by that household's size (with an average of about 5 persons per household), rather than be a fixed number that has to allow for the largest conceivable household (which might be 20 or 25 persons).

140

Box 6.6: An Evaluation of Data Entry Packages' Suitability for the LSMS

When the first LSMS surveys were undertaken there was little data entry software available that could take into account both the complexities of the LSMS questionnaire and the integration of data entry with the field work. A customized data entry package was developed and has been used for most of the LSMS surveys that have been implemented, especially for those that have integrated data management and field work.

The number and sophistication of commercially available data entry packages on the market and in use in statistical agencies has grown markedly since the first LSMS. In an effort to identify other data entry options for the LSMS, an independent software testing firm (National Software Testing Laboratories) was contracted by the World Bank to evaluate six data entry packages and one data base package to determine their adequacy for use with an LSMS. The software packages evaluated were:

Package	Developer
IMPS 3.1	U.S. Bureau of the Census
BLAISE III 1.0	Central Bureau of Statistics of the Netherlands
ISSA 2.28	Macro International
Rode/PC 3.09	DXP/IDES
EPI-INFO 60	U.S. Centers for Disease Control
SPSS/DE 5.02	SPSS Inc.
Paradox 4.5 (for DOS)	Borland Corporation

Based on the evaluation criteria presented in this chapter, IMPS was the only software package that was found to meet all of the requirements of the LSMS data entry process. Practical experience using it for LSMS surveys has been limited. The Romania team started to use IMPS since they were already familiar with it, but determined that it was difficult to do all of the data quality checks they wanted and thus switched to the custom program. In Ecuador, the statistical agency used IMPS and found it satisfactory in their LSMS survey.

Blaise III 1.0 was unable to generate reports and had no method for forcing out-of-range values and ISSA 2.28 could only handle 940 variables, well below the needs of the LSMS. Note that at the time of the evaluation in fall 1994, new versions of both Blaise and ISSA were being developed which would deal with the constraints listed above. The other packages had a variety of limitations which made them unsuitable for use with an LSMS survey.

It should be kept in mind that software developments are occurring rapidly and that there may well be other packages available now or in the near future that will meet the needs of the LSMS data entry process. If reviewing software options, the requirements listed in this chapter should be used. If the proposed software cannot function as outlined here, then a different option should be selected.

This structure can also be generalized to situations of higher complexity. So far we have considered the case of a single household, which might have from one to 25 members. A more extreme situation can be found in the fertility section, where data are sometimes collected for every child ever born to each woman older than 15. The questionnaire may include space for 5 such women and 15 children for each of them. The recommended approach uses just one record for each child *actually recorded in the household* (usually a reasonably small number), whereas the alternative approach might require keeping space for 75 children in *all* households. One can even imagine that the questionnaire might include information on each of several illnesses for each child of each woman, thus adding another factor to the total number of cases.

Limiting the Length of a Record Type

It can help to eliminate data entry errors to have a record type contain the same amount of information as each screen presented to the data entry operator. In some cases, this can be much less information than what would be conceptually acceptable to group together for each observation.

Consider the health module, which may be laid out across three or four physical pages of the questionnaire. Conceptually, the information on each person in the health section could be treated as one record type. But that amount of information is often difficult to fit into an easy-to-read layout on a single computer screen (see Box 6.7). Moreover, using a single screen would require the data entry operators to flip back and forth through the questionnaire as they entered all the information for the first individual, then for the second, etc. In this case the data entry screen (and thus the record type) would better correspond to a string of questions on a single physical page of the questionnaire. That way the data entry operators can fill in one screen for each individual and then turn to the next page of the questionnaire.

Identifiers

It is essential that each statistical unit have a unique identification code. In the LSMS data entry program, each unit of observation is assigned a code in three or more parts. The first part is the "record type," which appears at the beginning of each record. It tells whether the information is, for example, from the cover page, the third page of the health module, or for food expenditures. The record type is followed — *in all records* — by the household number. In most record types, a third identifier will be necessary to distinguish between separate units within the household, for instance, the person's ID or the code of the expenditure item. In a few cases there will be only one unit for the level of observation and thus the third identifier is unnecessary. For example, housing characteristics are usually gathered for only one home per household. In a few cases there may be an additional fourth code. For example, the third identifier might be the household enterprise, and the fourth code would apply to each piece of equipment owned for each enterprise.

Box 6.7: A Sample Data Entry Screen

```
HHOLD: 02024          SECTION 1: HOUSEHOLD ROSTER: (Record Type 002)    ID CODE: 06

 1A STILL LIVING HERE?:        1 <YES
 2 SEX:                        1 <MALE
 3 REL. TO HEAD:              03 <SON/DAUGHTER
 4 CAN TELL DATE...?:          1 <YES
 5 DATE OF BIRTH         DAY:19  MONTH:09   YEAR:79
 6 HOW OLD IS..?         YRS:013 MTHS: __
 7 MARITAL STATUS:             5 <WIDOW/WIDOWER
 8 PARTNER LIVES HERE?:        _
 9 ID CODE OF PARTNER:
10 No. OF MTHS AWAY:          00
11 WILL BE RESIDING HERE?:
12 HOUSEHOLD MEMBER?:          1 <YES
13 MTHS AWAY IN LAST 6M?:      0
```

This box shows a the data entry screen used for the KHDS family roster data. The fields that are underlined correspond to actual data entry fields. In practice, depending on the hardware used, these fields can appear in different colors or reverse video or in any other format to catch the operator's eye.

The rest of the screen contains the names of the variables and the meaning of recorded values for qualitative variables. For example, in variable "SEX", code 01 means "MALE". There are also comments on the screen for the data entry operator such as the title on top "SECTION 1: HOUSEHOLD ROSTER: (Record Type 002)". Notice that the data entry program repeats the household number in the upper left-hand corner of every screen, even if the operator only has to enter it once when beginning each questionnaire. The identification code for the person number is in the upper right corner.

On this screen there are two variables presenting an inconsistency. The age of the person is 13 years old and his marital status is widowed. On an actual computer screen the age and marital status fields would be blinking to flag the inconsistency.

Though the techniques are easy to learn, designing a data entry screen takes more skill than one might think. Here the designer decided to include the question number as part of the label for each variable, to make it easier for the operator to link each field with its corresponding box in the questionnaire. The screen size is a limiting factor since it only has 80 columns and 25 lines. This screen is simple enough, but when there are more than 20 variables, it cannot be laid out as one variable per line. It takes practice and creativity to fit all the variables into some sort of logical order without overcrowding the space available and to abbreviate the labels in such a way that they are understood by the operators as well as by the survey users at the analytical stage. This is particularly true given that the variable labels defined for data entry are usually borrowed by the statistical software. A good designer can fit up to 50 variables on a screen without making it look overcrowded, but that takes practice.

Transformation

Once data entry is completed, the structure of the files should be transformed from that appropriate for data entry to that appropriate for analysis. This process is illustrated in Box 6.5.

Chapter 7: Beginning Data Analysis

Key Messages

- Data from LSMS surveys support a wide range of analysis on many topics, with methods ranging from simple descriptions to complex behavioral models.

- Achieving full use of data from an LSMS survey requires that analysis be considered from the beginning. Identifying the uses to which the data will be put is a key part of planning, and many parties should be involved in analysis and planning for it.

- Plans should be made early on about how to promote use of the data through making them widely available, commissioning studies, holding workshops, or whatever other method is appropriate for the specific country.

- Adequate documentation must be prepared as a matter of course so that analysts can effectively make use of the data sets.

- The basic abstract should present a limited number of tables that are analytically interesting. They should be clearly presented and may be supplemented by graphs.

- More analytically complex studies can be done on a number of topics. Examples include an analysis of poverty (how many poor there are, what they are like, and the reasons for their poverty); social services (access to services, use, quality, and the effect of changes in prices and quality on use); the impact of social programs; determinants of household behavior (what affects decisions about labor supply, school enrollment, fertility, participation in transfer schemes); and other such studies.

The payoff to conducting surveys is in the analysis of the data they produce. Analysis will improve understanding of household welfare and augment the government's ability to make good policy decisions. This chapter is concerned with how to start the policy analysis process.

Section A highlights activities that may accompany the survey project in order to promote data use by many analysts. Section B describes the requirements for the documentation and dissemination of data sets. Section C gives some guidelines for producing a basic abstract from the survey. Section D outlines more sophisticated work. All readers of this manual should at least skim this whole chapter. It is supplemented by Annex X, which outlines how to construct some of the basic aggregates from the survey.

A. Policies and Project Components to Promote Data Use

LSMS are so rich in information that exploiting their full potential requires much more than a simple abstract.[63] It is thus important to facilitate data analysis as much as possible, beginning with the design of the survey itself. Box 7.1 summarizes the roles often played by different actors in data analysis.

In recent years LSMS survey projects have increasingly included activities to promote data use. The scope of what is included varies widely from country to country, depending on the funding available, the enthusiasm of project designers, and the expectations of how much analysis might occur in the absence of any specific activities to support data use. To date, we have not evaluated experience systematically enough to provide recipes for what is "enough" or what "works."[64] In this section we list some of the initiatives that have been tried, that might be tried, or that seem promising. These are presented to help the survey planner get started on a brainstorming process that will lead to actions appropriate for his or her own country:

- Hold a seminar or workshop to publicize the abstract as soon as it is available. At this workshop, advertise the availability of the data and make copies and documentation of the data available on diskettes. Have some remarks or presentations designed to get people thinking about what further analysis might be possible.

- Hold a second workshop six months or a year after the data are available to present all the analysis done during that time. This could be a simple workshop. Alternately, some papers could be commissioned for it or a competition could award prizes for the best papers.

- Provide funds for specific offices in the government (e.g., planning, health, agriculture, and so on) to commission analyses. These could be for topics identified at the time the survey is designed. Alternately, a dollar allocation could be made initially and the agenda left open.

- Identify a few key policy issues and ensure that high-quality analysis of these takes place promptly and is discussed with policymakers.

- Ensure that any international agencies engaged in policy dialogue are aware of the data's existence. Often these agencies have studies planned that would benefit from the data.

---

63. The abstract is, of course, very important and is discussed in Section C.

64. A qualitative evaluation should be available by 1996.

Since LSMS surveys are rich in analytic potential, many different actors should have a role in their analysis. This box describes the typical sharing of roles, though of course they may differ in different countries.

Central Statistical Agency. The central statistical agency has two main roles in data analysis. First, it will usually produce a basic abstract. Second, it will supply data sets and their documentation to other users. In a few countries, the statistical agency may also take on other data analysis functions. It may, for example, conduct is own program of analysis driven by sectoral or policy questions. In general, however, such analysis requires not only statistical infrastructure, but detailed sectoral knowledge and, sometimes, complementary data that are usually found int he sectoral ministries or research institutions rather than the central statistical agency.

Planning Agency. The planning agency is often the agency responsible for conducting or contracting out studies of interest to several sectors of government. Defining a poverty line, studying the amount of poverty, and identifying characteristics of the poor are common examples of such work. Studying the incidence of government subsidies across different socioeconomic groups and other targeting questions are additional examples. The planning agency may also take an active role in promoting analysis on a variety of topics by other agencies.

Sectoral Ministries. Sectoral ministries (e.g. of Health, Education, Agriculture, etc.) may separately use the LSMS data to look at the coverage of services they provide. They may be interested in analyses of how changes in the accessibility, quality, or pricing of their services would affect their use and the revenues from user fees. They may be interested in knowing what parts of households behavior or government action most affect the outcomes or indicators that their ministries are most interested in. For example, what are the determinants of child malnutrition or of school enrollment? The sectoral ministries may have the analysis performed by their own staff members. More often, they will find it convenient to contract out the analysis to persons or agencies more specialized in quantitative statistical analysis.

Universities and Private Research Institutes. Since universities and private research institutes encompass a wide range of disciplines and interests, it is difficult to generalize about what they may do. They may do any of the above kinds of analysis on any sectoral topic. They are probably the most likely to do analysis that not only describes the current situation but also analyzes how it came about or could be hanged.

International Development Agencies. International development agencies may conduct, fund, or use the results from all of the types of analysis listed above, since they require a solid empirical foundation for their policy advice and project evaluations.

- Provide training through in-service courses in-country. This might include training in any of four areas: (1) lessons in a common statistical software package (e.g., how to run a table or regression); (2) training in statistics (e.g., tests for significant differences in tables, regression analysis); (3) workshops in how to present the results of statistical analysis simply and clearly; and (4) seminars in special topics of analytic interest (e.g., how to draw a poverty line or conduct incidence analysis). The balance among the four and the level of sophistication of each will depend on the prevailing analytic skills in the target audience(s). The courses might be offered to staff in the planning and statistics agencies, staff in line ministries, or university researchers. Such seminars cannot replace sound university and post-graduate training in the social sciences, but they can help polish skills that may have been neglected due to the lack of an opportunity to apply them.

- Ensure that key offices in government have adequate hardware and software to conduct data analysis.

- Provide technical assistance to planning and evaluation offices in key government agencies.

- Sponsor a peer-reviewed working paper series on quantitative policy analysis.

- Put the data sets into the data banks of principal universities and/or make them available through the Internet.

- Contact the professors of quantitative methods courses in universities and encourage them to use the data sets in their classroom exercises.

- Advertise the availability of the abstract and of the data in places where local graduate students studying overseas will find out about them, perhaps through alumni newsletters or mailing lists held by the principal sources of overseas scholarship funds.

- Provide graduate scholarships in local universities for students who concentrate on quantitative policy analysis. Require them to work in appropriate government offices during or after their studies.

- Translate the questionnaires and documentation into English or other international languages so that researchers from around the world can have effective access to the data.

B. Documentation and Dissemination of Data Sets

If more than one agency (or indeed, if more than one person) is intended to use the data, a system of documentation and dissemination is required. Good support for data dissemination includes five things: (1) an open data access policy; (2) good basic documentation; (3) organized files of the unit record data files, (also known as "raw data"); (4) a filing system that guarantees that the data and important records will be permanently available; and (5) clear assignment of service standards and responsibilities for handling data documentation and dissemination.

Data Use Policy

In simple terms, data users should have early, unrestricted access to the survey unit record data files.[65] This should be formally recorded in a document that explicitly states the policy and is signed by someone in authority — at least the head of the statistical agency and possibly the minister of planning or finance. An example of such a document is provided in Box 7.2.

Obvious though it may be that collecting data is only useful if the data are used and that increasing the number of users means more use, statistical agencies may still be reluctant to distribute the unit record data. Some common arguments and their counter-arguments follow:

QUALITY CONTROL. The argument may be that the data need to be edited at the central level to ensure quality. As explained in Chapter 6, if the data entry program is prepared carefully and data entry is properly integrated with field operations, no further editing is needed or desirable at the central level. If the statistical agency wishes to add constructed variables (such as income and consumption aggregates) to the public use files, these will take time to prepare. The agency should set a performance standard of providing these supplemental files within a reasonable time, such as six months, of the end of field work, and the project budget should ensure that the resources to actually do the work in a timely fashion are made available.

SENSITIVITY. Sometimes the data reveal facts about the living standards in a country that the government may be reluctant to publish widely. The political repercussions can indeed be sensitive in some settings, but before data access is restricted, some factors should be considered. First, for those households suffering deprivations, the survey's showing that deprivation exists will not be surprising. Second, good data will make it difficult for people to exaggerate the extent of deprivation and, indeed, will sometimes reveal it to be less than popularly thought. Third, analysis of the survey data may help the government make better policy decisions about how to minimize poverty. Fourth, the

---

65. In many surveys assisted by the World Bank, the data access policies have been more restrictive. The data are usually owned by the host country and the World Bank has the unlimited right to use the data for internal purposes. The World Bank may sometimes release the data to third-party users only with written authorization from the host government. In some cases this permission is freely and promptly given, while in others it may be a slow process to get permission and in still others permission for distribution to third parties is only rarely granted. In the last few years, data access policies are becoming noticeably more open. A widespread consensus now exists that the World Bank should not assist with surveys unless the unit record data will be widely available to many users, especially to local government agencies, but also including national and international academics and international development institutions.

Box 7.2: *Prototype Data Access Policy*

A data access agreement should contain the points shown here in boldface type. The policy should be publicly known; one of the best ways to accomplish this is to include the agreement in the abstract published from the data.

Intended users. The data from the ....[Country X]....Living Standards Survey are intended for use by all researchers in government agencies, universities, and private research institutes, international development organizations, and other similar institutions. Researchers are requested to give due recognition of the source of the data in all publications and to provide copies of all publications arising from the analysis of the data to the libraries at the .....[statistical agency, planning agency, international agencies, and university library].

Procedures for obtaining data. Requests for access to the data should be accompanied by a one to two- page outline of the proposed analysis. This will be kept on file so that other interested researchers may contact the analyst about the outcome of the work. Requests should be submitted to ....[name, title, address and phone number, fax number, and internet ID].

Performance standards. The ....[agency implementing survey].... will normally have the data available for public use not later than six months after field work has been completed.   The request for data sets and basic documentation will normally be processed within three weeks of receipt. [A small fee consonant with the costs of staff time and supplies used in copying data and documents may be charged.] The data sets will be made available in ASCII and ....[any other].... format.

government may be able to broaden the social policy dialogue in a way that is politically positive. Analysis of the survey may help all parties to understand the constraints on action and thus aid in forming reasonable expectations and a consensus on policies to reduce poverty.

ANALYSIS WILL BE PROVIDED BY THE STATISTICAL INSTITUTE. Sometimes the data collection agency suggests that it will be able to provide the users with the tables they need, as opposed to the unit record data that would allow them to conduct the analyses themselves. It may be a desirable *additional* service if the statistical agency will perform analyses for users not able to do so themselves, but it does not replace dissemination of the complete data sets. Modern statistical modelling requires a continuous interaction between the analyst and the data; it cannot be reduced to the scrutiny of a set of predetermined tabulations produced by intermediaries. This is especially true for surveys and analyses as complex as the LSMS.

CONFIDENTIALITY. It is sometimes argued that releasing the unit record data violates the confidentiality of the responses made by each household. However, since the unit record data files need not contain any identification of the households other than a numeric identification code used to match sub-files to one another, this argument carries little weight.[66]

Sometimes the reasons above are given as pretexts to hide a simple and painful truth: statistical agencies may not have the data sets and documentation sufficiently well organized to feel confident about offering public access to them. The solution to this problem is to ensure that building this capacity is included in the design of the project.

Basic Documentation

The importance of adequate documentation can hardly be over-stated.[67] No reliance should be placed on individuals' memories or personal files. Not only are these haphazard, but it is inevitable that with time the staff will move into other positions or out of the institution altogether. The LSMS division of the World Bank, through its own experience and in its dealings with statistical agencies around the world, has seen crucial documents and even whole years' worth of data lost.

Each data user should easily be able to obtain three documents: the questionnaire, a summary basic information document, and the abstract. These should be sufficient to fill two needs: to allow the potential analyst to determine whether the data suits his or her needs, and to provide those who do decide to use the data to make full, appropriate, and easy use of them. The user should also be able to obtain, as needed, other documents such as the sampling plans and manuals for field staff.

The summary basic information document should include the following:

QUESTIONNAIRE. A synopsis of the questionnaire may be included. It can be very short, since the questionnaires themselves should be made available to all users.

SAMPLE. A concise but complete description of the sample design and its implementation should be given. The description of the design should include the sample size and cluster size, the number of strata used and any implicit stratification, the number of stages used in the sample, the number of sampling units at each stage, and the probability of selection at each stage. The description of the implementation should cover any deviations from the original design, especially those involving the level and sources of non-response and the number

---

66. Sometimes, and especially for panel surveys, records that include the names or addresses of the households may be kept. There is no need for these to be given to data analysts.

67. Even if there are restrictions on access to the data, the documentation is important and should be completed for qualified users.

of replacement households selected. The data files themselves must contain the sampling variables, especially the sampling weights (raising factors) that should be applied to the raw data to obtain an unbiased estimate of the population means, and strata and cluster codes that should be used in adjusting sampling errors for sample design features.

FIELD WORK. This section should describe the basic field procedures and quality control techniques. Anything (good or bad) that would influence the interpretation or credibility of the data set as a whole or of particular variables should be explained.

GUIDELINES FOR USING THE DATA. Full information on how to link the various parts of the survey must be clearly stated. The linkages may be between different parts of the household questionnaire; between the household, price, community, and facility questionnaires; between years of the panel; or between survey data and other external data sets. The codes for any items not pre-coded in the questionnaire should be made available in the text or appendices of the document. For items with very detailed coding, such as industrial or occupation codes, it is useful to include the codes at the one or two-digit level of aggregation and to steer the reader to the full code books.

Any problems encountered in the data and the solutions taken should be specified. Some illustrations are useful here. Occasionally a particular subset of the data is deemed too flawed to use. It is important to state clearly why the raw data are not available or to inform the user of precautions to be observed in using those variables. For example, the anthropometric data from the 1988 Jamaica LSMS survey had some observations recorded in English measurements and some in metric and it was impossible to distinguish with surety which was which. Sometimes flaws have been fixed, for example, sometimes the identity or location codes of certain questionnaires have been corrected ex post facto, or occasionally responses to "other (specify)" responses have been coded.

DOCUMENTATION OF CONSTRUCTED DATA SETS. Often the survey institute will make available some constructed variables in the public use files. The most common and useful of these are price indices, aggregates of household consumption or income, as well as adjustments to these to account for variation in prices over time and space. Z scores for anthropometric variables are sometimes also provided. Each of the constructed variables should have a clear explanation of how it was constructed so that the user can determine whether it suits his or her specific analytic purpose and how to interpret it. It is desirable but not essential to also include (in the appendices or electronic files) the programs that were used to construct the variables in question. Constructed data files should be distributed in addition to, *not* instead of, the raw data used in their construction.

DESCRIPTION OF FILES. The contents and names of the data files should be mapped to the corresponding sections in the questionnaire and the system of variable names and labels sketched. It is helpful to include the size of the files as well.

REFERENCES TO OTHER DOCUMENTS. At minimum a list of ancillary documents should be included. References to other analyses done with the same or similar data sets may also be useful, though these may be difficult to organize.

In addition to the summary documentation, the documents from which the summary draws should be made available to users who desire more detail on certain aspects of the survey. Most important among these documents will be the documents on sampling, the full code books, and the manuals for supervisors, interviewers, anthropometrists, and data entry operators.

It is useful if the documentation can be produced in both the national language and a language used by those in development agencies and international academia. Obviously, producing these documents in the local language will encourage local use and is natural if the survey agency is producing them. Translating them into English or another international language can be a low-cost way for the project to encourage analysis by other researchers.

Unit Record Data Files

The unit record data should be made available in some reasonably user-friendly way. This normally consists of a series of files for each section of the questionnaire that contain all the records for each household (e.g., the thematic files explained in Chapter 6).[68] The files should always be made available in ASCII; it may also be easy and useful to distribute them already translated into formats for the most commonly used statistical packages. The location of the variables in the raw data files should be clearly documented, ideally in a computer-readable form. If the statistical institute has taken the trouble to give detailed descriptive labels to variable names and codes, it will be performing a useful service by making these available in formats useful in the various statistical softwares.

---

68. A single file is usually not convenient, given the hierarchical nature of the data structure. It may also be too large for some users. Though those adept with computers can usually digest a single file, many local analysts have computers and software that are somewhat less than state of the art. They often do not have manuals (or cannot read them fluently because they are available only in English) and may be relatively inexperienced in handling data files.

It is important to store the various paper and electronic documents appropriately. Though it cannot be prescribed how exactly to do this, certain aspects are required for safe storage.

INVENTORY CONTROL. It is essential that master copies of all the important files be kept in a separate archive and be used only to make new copies. In this way there is no danger of the final copy being given away or damaged. It is convenient to have multiple spare copies of the most commonly used documents available for immediate dissemination.

SECURITY. To ensure that the data are not lost or corrupted, the agency in charge of the data should maintain a master and a backup copy of the data files. The master data set should include all the necessary files, but no redundant or outdated files.[69] The backup copy of the data set should only contain the files in the master data file. Only those who are responsible for them should have access to the master files. This is most easily accomplished by storing the files with a password required for write access. Reasonable safeguards against loss of the backup should be taken. This might mean putting copies into a fire-proof safe or depositing backups in a separate building (such as a regional office of the statistical agency, the records center of the planning agency, or a university library). Both the master file and backup copies should occasionally be re-written to reduce the chance of media failure.

INSTITUTIONAL MEMORY. More than one person should be familiar with the filing system and passwords so that if the primary person responsible is absent on holiday or sick leave or quits, the documentation is not lost.

Setting Service Standards Assignment of Responsibilities for Data Documentation and Dissemination

It is important to think through the tasks that will be required to document a data set and to support its dissemination for several years after the survey. For institutes that have traditionally focused only on publishing standard abstracts, this may require some innovative thinking.

First, the agency will have to think about what product or service it will offer and how. For example, it may determine that it will offer to individual researchers paper copies of descriptive documents and electronic data files in

---

69. Often a particular data set will go through many versions before it has been correctly compiled. Over the life of the data files, there may be problems with recording all the changes, but confusion can be reduced by keeping only the correct files in the master data set. To ensure that the history of all changes is not lost, the person in charge of archiving the data files may also want to keep copies of all versions; these should be kept separate from the master files.

ASCII. This will require that it set aside enough staff time and develop procedures agile enough to handle the anticipated number of requests within a reasonable response time. The agency could instead or additionally place all the information on the Internet or in public use accounts at universities. This would take slightly more preparation time initially, but if many users have access to those services, lower the number of individual requests for the data that the agency would have to cope with.

Then, responsibilities for carrying out the different functions for data documentation and dissemination must be clearly assigned. Otherwise there is a tendency for things to fall through the cracks. Writing the Basic Information document, for example, will require input from several people — especially the sampler, the data manager and the analysts, but none might think it principally their duty. Likewise, the archival function has a tendency to be split between a secretary for the paper records and the data manager for the electronic records, a recipe that leads easily to gaps. And who must do each part of servicing a request for data must be specified — who, if anyone, need grant permission, who assembled the information to send, who keeps whatever files are required.

It would appear that the lack of clearly assigned responsibilities for data dissemination may impede data access as much as poor policies. In the short run, it should be the survey manager who is responsible for organizing the documentation and beginning the data dissemination function. In the medium and longer run, that individual may be assigned to other activities, so a more permanent assignment of responsibilities should be made. Note that it is not a good idea to set up a system where someone at the top of the statistical agency's has to respond to each request for data. These people are too busy, and if they must act on each individual request, potential analysts will likely get very bad service. Rather authority should be placed closer to the working level.

C. The Abstract

The abstract is not only the first product of an LSMS survey, it is usually the most widely read. This section discusses its contents, its format, and the process required to produce it.

CONTENT. The abstract should present a carefully selected set of tables. The tables should include the basic description of the different facets of living standards. For example, employment status, housing conditions, literacy and enrollment, nutritional status, incidence of ill health and use of health care services, and availability of basic infrastructure such as transportation, water, and electricity, should be included.

Abstracts should present the frequencies or means of the select set of indicators of living standards. They should also tabulate these for selected socio-economic groups. For example, they might present literacy or employment rates by rural/urban area, by gender, and by age. The tabulations should show the contrasts that are most important to the country and topic at hand. For example, gender or regional differences in school enrollment may be very large in some countries and very small in others. Where they are small, it is less necessary to report them.

More ambitious abstracts will also present cross-tabulations by welfare groups such as quintile of consumption.[70] The most ambitious abstracts will include tabulations by categories of poor or non-poor.[71] If poverty lines are used in defining socioeconomic groups, the same tabulations should be presented by quintile or decile.[72] The quintiles or deciles present more information about the full distribution of welfare and their definition is less controversial than that of a poverty line. The calculation of welfare measures and poverty lines requires a high level of programming complexity and analytic decision-making. If available, such tables are always interesting and useful additions to the abstract. But if their calculation will greatly slow down the abstract's production or generate too much controversy over methods, it may be best to leave them out of the basic abstract and produce separate, later reports on poverty.

Many abstracts err on the side of including too many tables, a large number of which are of little analytic interest. At best, an overly thick volume may make it difficult for the user to find the items of interest to him or her and thus discourage use of the whole abstract. Worse, the mechanical tabulation of many variables by many others often results in tables with so few observations in each cell that conclusions are likely to be misleading. This is often not apparent given the format of the tables.

Annex VIII shows the table of contents for the statistical abstract of the 1991 Pakistan Integrated Household Survey. It is an excellent basic abstract. It presents information broken down by one or two factors for each variable — region, rural/urban, age, sex, and education as appropriate. Annex IX gives the table of contents from the 1993 Jamaica Survey of Living Conditions. It is more ambitious and it presents most tables disaggregated by quintile as well as by rural/urban area, parish, and, where appropriate, age and sex. It presents some longitudinal tables. It also produces many more tables, with the list having grown over the years in response to readers' comments on the abstracts from the five previous surveys. Thus, while the number of tables is higher than often recommended, they are analytically useful rather than merely mechanical.

---

70. Annex X provides guidance on how to calculate these.

71. Ravallion (1992) provides recommendations on how to draw a poverty line.

72. These divide the population into five or 10 equal-sized groups on the basis of a welfare indicator. For analysis of LSMS data, this is most often per-capita household consumption.

It is useful to include a basic description of the survey in addition to the tables. This should include survey content, the sample plan and its implementation, and the field work techniques used. Sometimes the full questionnaire and basic information document are bound right into the abstract as appendices. At minimum, reference should be made to where to obtain them. The policy on data access might be stated in the abstract.

It is often useful to include in the abstract some data from sources other than the survey. Comparisons of indicators obtained from other sources may be of interest — for example, comparing the age structure to that of the census or the mean per capita consumption figure from the survey to that from national accounts. When such comparisons accord well, it lends confidence to other analysis. When there are large discrepancies, it is important to note which technical factors might explain the differences. It may also be useful to add background information. For example, in a table on the incidence of a government program, it might be useful to note the cost of the program. This enhances the policy impact of the abstract, but usually requires an inter-agency team to help write since the statistical agency cannot be expected to be well-versed on many sectoral programs.

In addition to the basic abstract suitable for use by policymakers and data analysts, it can be useful to produce information in some other formats. In Nicaragua, for example, the statistical institute produced a very short abstract in cartoon form for distribution in primary schools (see Figure 7.1).

FORMAT. Producing a well-formatted table is an art. It is often learned by first producing confusing or cumbersome tables and then gradually refining them. Studying existing abstracts to see which best conveys information is useful (see Box 7.3 for an example). Here we give some principles that help produce clear tables.

- Row and column headers should be clear. They should use normal language rather than computer variable names. If they contain scales, the high and low ends should be indicated. For example, rather than labeling quintiles as 1,2,3,4, and 5, they might be labeled as 1(poorest), 2, 3, 4, 5 (richest).

- Detailed notes at the bottom of the table will often be required to supplement the short labels possible on row and column headers. These notes should provide complete definitions of the concepts covered. For example, a table might be titled "Employment Status by Age Group" and have columns labeled employed, unemployed, out of the labor force, and so forth. In that case the definition of employment used should be included at the bottom of the table, for example, "worked one hour or more for pay during the week preceding the interview." Many of these definitions vary slightly from survey to survey, so it is important to be clear.

Figure 7.1: Illustration of an Abstract for Primary Schools

FORMAS DE ELIMINACION Y DISPOSICION
DE LA BASURA

LA TIRAN 19%   LA QUEMAN 40%

41%

Source: Nicaragua Instituto Nacional de Estadísticas y Censos (1994)

The difference between good and bad table formats can be seen in Tables A, B, and C in this box. All are on the same topic from the Jamaica Survey of Living Conditions. The first two were included in the 1988 abstract, the latter from the 1992 abstract. (The 1988 tables were formatted by one of the authors of this volume, so it is fair game to criticize them here. The 1992 table was produced by the joint efforts of the Statistical and Planning Institutes of Jamaica.)

The 1992 table is much better than the 1988 tables. Note that by transposing the rows and columns, the later table can combine the two earlier tables into one single table, include what would have been two more tables, and still be easier to read. The 1992 table also has much better labeling. The title makes it clear that the group included is only those ill or injured who sought health care during the four-week reference period. The column headers make it explicit whether the care was sought in the private or public sector. To interpret the 1988 table, the reader had to know that doctor's office meant private sector and health centers meant public centers, and the distinction was not made at all for hospitals. The 1988 table neither indicated that the 1,2,3,4,5 in the column headers refer to quintiles of per capita household consumption nor which was wealthy and which was poor. The 1992 table does both. The later table also gives the number of observations in each row. From the percentages in the table, it is possible to calculate the number of observations in each cell. The later table could make explicit that the percentages in each three-column grouping sum to a hundred, but since the number of columns in each grouping is small it is fairly clear to the reader that they do, even though that feature has been omitted.

EXAMPLES OF BAD TABLES

Table A: Place of Consultation by Consumption Level

Place of Consultation	1	2	3	4	5	Jamaica
Hospital	22.0	34.8	25.6	31.2	14.1	25.0
Health Center	40.4	16.5	19.4	12.8	8.5	18.1
Doctor's Office	37.6	46.3	52.7	52.5	66.9	52.9
Pharmacy	0.0	0.0	2.3	0.7	1.7	2.1
Provider's Home	0.0	0.8	0.0	0.0	0.6	0.3
Patient's Home	0.0	0.0	0.0	1.4	2.9	1.0
Other	0.0	0.8	0.8	0.0	1.4	0.6

Table B: Place of Consultation by Area

Place of Consultation	Kingston Metropolitan Area	Other Towns	Rural	Jamaica
Hospital	32.2	33.8	19.9	25.0
Health Center	16.8	10.3	20.1	18.1
Doctor's Office	46.5	52.9	56.1	52.9
Pharmacy	1.0	1.5	2.7	2.1
Provider's Home	0.0	0.0	0.5	0.3
Patient's Home	2.5	1.5	0.3	1.0
Other	1.0	0.0	0.0	0.6

Box 7.3 continued on next page

159

Box 7.3 (continued)

EXAMPLE OF A GOOD TABLE

Table C: Use of Public/Private Sector By Ill/Injured Persons for Medical Care, Purchase of Medications and Hospitalization During the Four Week Reference Period By Area, Quintile, Sex, and Age

Classification	Source of care Percentage of those seeking medical care			Percentage purchasing medications			Percentage hospitalization (of those seeking medical care)		
	Public Sector	Private Sector	Both	Public Sector	Private Sector	Both	Public Sector	Private Sector	Both
Area									
KMA (N=321)	26.0	62.6	10.4	10.4	66.8	4.5	5.0	0.8	0.6
Other towns (N=345)	24.8	68.6	6.6	6.8	71.0	1.2	3.4	2.3	0.7
Rural areas (N=1,159)	27.4	63.7	8.9	9.8	52.1	2.7	5.5	0.8	0.3
Quintile									
Poorest (N=353)	46.3	48.8	4.9	13.9	45.1	0.8	9.0	1.6	0.0
2 (N=335)	41.8	48.4	9.8	14.5	45.4	4.0	5.3	2.6	0.7
3 (N=378)	28.8	65.9	5.4	9.4	57.4	2.0	3.0	0.0	0.5
4 (N=381)	27.1	65.4	7.5	7.0	60.3	1.9	5.6	0.9	0.5
5 (N=378)	12.3	78.1	9.6	4.0	73.7	3.1	4.4	0.9	0.4
Sex									
Male (N=834)	27.6	62.5	9.9	9.0	60.6	2.5	4.2	0.7	0.7
Female (N=990)	29.0	64.2	6.7	9.7	59.4	3.2	5.5	1.4	0.3
Age (years)									
0-9 (N=488)	36.0	55.4	8.6	8.6	57.8	1.9	5.0	0.7	1.0
10-19 (N=227)	34.5	63.2	2.3	11.3	59.4	1.0	3.8	2.2	0.0
20-29 (N=132)	26.0	63.7	10.3	14.8	59.5	2.5	7.1	1.3	0.0
30-39 (N=146)	22.4	69.6	8.0	3.9	63.5	0.0	9.1	1.9	2.2
40-49 (N=146)	18.1	71.4	10.5	12.6	61.7	4.9	9.6	0.0	0.0
50-59 (N=151)	20.8	70.0	9.2	4.8	69.8	3.7	0.8	1.1	0.0
60-64 (N=101)	32.8	58.8	8.4	4.2	54.6	2.0	2.6	0.0	0.0
65+ (N=433)	27.4	64.7	8.0	11.8	56.9	5.5	3.0	1.2	0.0
Jamaica (N=1,825)	28.5	63.4	8.1	8.9	58.5	2.4	5.1	1.1	0.4

- It must be clear what is tabulated. Is it the number of occurrences of each event? Is it a rate, percentage, or mean? If it is a rate or percentage, what is the divisor? If it is in monetary units, what is the currency, and what period or region's prices apply?

- Are the percentages based on the totals of the rows or of the columns? This can be made clear by including a row or column with the total percent.

- It should be clear whether the table pertains to the whole sample or to a subset of it. For example, in a table of mean receipt of remittances, it is critical to specify whether the average is across all households regardless of whether they do or do not receive remittances or only across the households that do receive remittances.

- Groupings should correspond to what is meaningful or common for the country and topic. For example, in the education module, enrollment or attendance rates should be shown for the sub-groups of children appropriate for different levels of schooling. This might mean primary, middle, and secondary. Some systems, however, do not differentiate between middle and secondary, so the exact age cut-offs will differ slightly among countries.

- Good tables indicate not only the percentages or means for each cell, but also the number of observations (N) in each cell. In some cases this can be done neatly within the cell itself. In other cases, it may produce a cluttered-looking table. Sometimes putting N on the row and column headers, or in separate rows and columns, will be neater and allow the interested analyst to calculate N for each cell.

- It is ideal, though admittedly rarely done, to present standard errors or confidence intervals or tests of significant differences between different cells. Even if not done for every table, it would be desirable for at least a few key tables, such as the levels of consumption, poverty or malnutrition among different socio-economic groups (see Table 7.1 for an example). The text should not discuss differences unless they are large and statistically significant.

Table 7.1: Sample Size, Mean, and Standard Error of Estimate of Per Capita Consumption, 1992 and 1993 Jamaica Survey of Living Conditions (SLC)

Area	SLC 92			SLC 93		
	No. of Households in Sample	Mean Consumption (1992 J$)	Standard Error (%)	No. of Households in Sample	Mean Consumption (1993 J$)	Standard Error (%)
KMA	1,001	22,653	3.6	647	30,766	4.4
Other Towns	841	18,032	3.0	384	23,523	6.3
Rural Areas	2,643	13,889	2.2	932	18,517	3.6
Jamaica	4,485	16,998	2.0	1,963	23,408	2.7

Note: KMA — Kingston Metropolitan Area.

Source: Statistical Institute of Jamaica (STATIN) and Planning Institute of Jamaica (PIOJ), 1995, Appendix II.4, p. 126.

- To the extent practical, it can help the reader to understand the tables if similar formats are used. For example, if a series of variables are being cross-tabulated by area (capital city, other urban area, rural areas), agro-climatic zone (coast, mountains, jungle), and sex (male, female), it can be useful to have these three sub-blocks appear in the same order down the rows of each table and have the columns always be specific to the new variable (or vice versa).

- Graphs may be used to enhance the presentation. Where they are used, it is important to ensure that the actual numbers behind them and their definitions are maintained. Sometimes this can be accomplished by thoroughly labeling the graph. More often the full table must be produced along with the graph. Tufte (1983) is a useful reference on how to use graphics effectively.

- It is not essential that much text be used to describe each table. Often such text is repetitive and boring, and writing it can slow the production of the abstract.

PROCESS. As should be clear from the above, producing an abstract is not a strictly mechanical exercise.

The most obvious requirements involve the computer programming. A good quality personal computer will be sufficient. For example, at the time of this writing, a 486DX with 8 megabytes of memory and 50 megaHertz speed would be considered desirable, but the earlier abstracts were written using much less sophisticated machines. There are several common statistical packages that will do the job, although some are slightly better at one or another aspect than others. An important selection criterion should be which is most commonly known in the country in question, since computer programming skills are often relatively scarce and jobs requiring them subject to high rates of turnover. A proficient programmer may be able to turn out the tables for an abstract in four to six weeks. More time will be required if the programmer is still learning the particular software package, or how to manipulate large and complex data sets efficiently. More time will also be required if it is not clear to analysts exactly how tables should be set up (which is often the case for the first abstract from a novel data set).

The production of the abstract requires significant analytic input. It obviously requires knowing which issues are most important. It also requires knowing many sector-specific details. For example, to a person outside the health sector it might seem natural to produce a table of vaccination rates for young children including all children under the age of 60 months. But health experts would not prepare the table this way because vaccinations should be spread over the first several months of a child's life. So health analysts generally look at rates for children from 11 (or 12) to 60 months. It is these rates that can be compared to a standard of 100 percent full coverage or the 80 percent goal for the decade. Thus it is important to have input from a range of sector specialists in writing the abstract.

The consultations as to what should be in an abstract, how to clean the data (see Box 7.4), what definitions should be used, and what interpretations can be drawn mirrors the process of questionnaire design. An initial list of tables, or set of actual tables, can be completed by a small team based on discussions held during questionnaire design and the review of relevant abstracts from similar surveys. Then that draft should be passed around to individuals knowledgeable about different topics. They should critique the draft with regard to i) whether some tables should be added or deleted; ii) whether the definitions, groupings, etc. are appropriate; and iii) whether the presentation is clear to them as potential users.

When the survey plan includes a full year of field work, it can be very useful to produce a preliminary abstract, based on the first six months of data, to be distributed to a limited number of experts. This allows ample time for the programmers to hone their skills and for full consultation among many potential users. Then the final abstract can be produced from the full data set quickly after the remaining field work is completed.

D. Examples of Further Analysis

The LSMS data sets allow exceptionally rich work beyond what might be included in an abstract. This section gives some examples of the kinds of uses to which data from surveys like the LSMS have been put. It is written as a "sample book" of common analyses based on data produced by LSMS surveys. The goal is neither to explain how to do the analysis nor to provide a connected discourse on poverty and household behavior. Rather, the examples are shown to spark the creativity of the survey planners in setting the agenda of analysis in each country.

This section sketches only a few of the major issues that can be addressed with LSMS data. A single example from a sector is presented here as an illustration, even when parallel questions in other sectors could be addressed as well. The emphasis is put on analysis with the most immediate policy implications. Much more analysis that could contribute to basic understanding of households is not covered here. Thus, the examples shown are by no means an exhaustive catalogue, either of potential or existing analyses. An excellent outline of analytic work to understand the effects of structural adjustment using data such as that produced by LSMS surveys is provided in Demery, Ferroni, and Grootaert (1993). Deaton (forthcoming) provides something of a textbook on the statistical issues in the policy analysis of household data for selected issues.

163

In doing the analysis for the abstract, the statistical institute is converted from its role of data producer to that of data analyst. In this guise, it will confront the problem of data cleaning at a more complex level than done for the minimum dissemination function. In particular it will face the problems of missing observations and outliers.

A missing value occurs when information that should have been filled in was not. For example, when a person who reports being ill and going to a doctor does not report how much the visit cost, how long he had to wait, etc.

An outlier can be an extreme but correct value (Mr. Rockefeller spending $100 a week on caviar) or it may be so unlikely that it is almost certainly a mistake (a poor subsistence farmer spending $100 a week on caviar). Occasionally other information from the household (that it is Mr. Rockefeller's) can help to determine that an extreme value is plausible. In many cases, however, it is very difficult to tell whether a value is correct or not. Even when outliers represent correct information, but unusual cases, they will have a large effect on statistics from the survey, raising the means and standard deviations noticeably.

Virtually every analyst will want to give some consideration about what to do about missing observations and outliers. Their decisions will, however, vary according to the analytic question being addressed, the statistic being employed, and the number of "problem cases" in the data. Let us consider three examples of problems and the common solutions for them.

Cross-tabulations of Qualitative Data. Consider a cross-tabulation of sex by primary school enrollment. Each variable in the table has two possible answers — male/female and yes/no. If all answers are present and in the correct range, the table will be have two columns and two rows. If the data quality mechanisms were not fully employed, there may be some cases where the information is missing or an answer other than 1 or 2 was recorded. Then the table produced would have spare rows or columns for missing values and invalid answers. Since these are nonsensical and do not add to understanding the issue being analyzed, the observations concerned are normally dropped from the analysis. The analyst should, however, note how often they occur. Invalid or missing answers in one or two percent of cases are not too disturbing. If they were to occur in 10 or 20 percent of cases, it would be a sign that something is seriously awry in the data set.

Minor Omissions in Aggregate Variables. Suppose the analyst is to compute total household expenditures and the problem is that a few households do not report the amount spent on kitchen matches. Some analysts would ignore the problem altogether, since kitchen matches would constitute an infinitesimal share of total household expenditures and cause little distortion in comparisons between households that reported expenditures on kitchen matches and those that did not. Other analysts might omit the households from the aggregate, and since there were few of them would not worry unduly about any bias or loss in degrees of freedom that might result.

Box continued on next page

Larger Omissions in Aggregate Variables. If the problem is that a few households did not report the value of expenditures on a staple food like rice or tortillas, then some solution must be found, since the item is likely to account for several percent of total household expenditure. Some analysts would drop those households from the data set. Other analysts would impute a value of expenditure for "similar" households. This might be done by using the average value observed for the other households in the same cluster. Or it might be the average value for households in the same region (perhaps rural area of the coastal zone) and same household size and same economic status (perhaps quintile of expenditure, where the expenditure variable includes all items save the staple in question). In either case the decisions will affect the analysis — the "corrected" data become more homogenous than the original data, the variances are lower, and the researcher has replaced some data with assumptions.

Treatment of problem data is an area of great controversy where reasonable professionals differ, often heatedly. It is therefore difficult to give firm guidelines on which solution to adopt. All analysts will, however, agree on four principles:

- Strict use of all quality control procedures in data management and data entry to minimize the problem as much as possible.

- Rigorous explanation of what procedures were used. This would include the number of cases treated, the decision rule used to determine that a case was a problem, and what was done. If the treatment consisted of imputations, then the full formula used in making the imputations should be given.

- Provision of the original raw data to all users (possibly in addition to "cleaned" data), so that the users can use other cleaning procedures if they prefer or if they deem the documentation of the cleaning procedures inadequate.

- Use of statistics that are relatively insensitive to outliers, where outliers are seriously problematic, e.g., the use of medians instead of means or of inter-quartile ranges instead of variances.

The Study of Poverty

POVERTY PROFILE. Poverty profiles show several dimensions of poverty. These include who is poor, where they are, how they earn their living, their access to and use of government services and subsidies, their living standards with regards to health, education, nutrition, and so forth. To cover the multiple dimensions of poverty, much of the information in a good abstract is used. Presented is part of a single table from the Ecuador Poverty Report, World Bank, 1995a (see Table 7.2). Some of the findings include:

- The education level of the head of household is very strongly associated with the level of poverty. The average poor household head in both urban

Table 7.2: Some Characteristics of the Poor in Ecuador, 1994

		Urban		Rural		Total	
		Poor	*Non-Poor*	*Poor*	*Non-Poor*	*Poor*	*Non-Poor*
Education							
Education of	National	5.2	9.1	3.2	4.7	4.0	7.5
household head	Costa	4.9	8.3	2.8	3.9	3.9	7.1
(years)	Sierra	5.8	10.5	3.4	5.1	4.1	8.0
	Oriente	5.9	8.8	4.5	7.4	4.6	7.8
Health							
Diseases treated	National	24.8	14.8	32.7	24.1	29.4	18.0
informally	Costa	27.3	19.0	45.3	33.7	36.4	22.6
	Sierra	19.7	9.6	21.4	19.4	20.8	13.7
	Oriente	26.3	10.7	20.1	14.4	20.4	13.2
Employment							
Informal sector	National	54.6	44.1	27.9	35.8	39.2	41.7
	Costa	54.6	44.1	19.6	24.8	37.6	41.6
	Sierra	56.3	41.3	35.1	42.6	42.3	41.9
	Oriente	54.9	40.8	25.7	41.1	27.3	40.9
Regulated	National	15.5	35.3	3.4	9.9	8.6	26.7
sector	Costa	11.8	31.1	1.1	3.1	6.6	24.4
	Sierra	22.1	41.3	5.4	12.6	11.1	29.2
	Oriente	8.7	40.0	6.4	26.8	6.5	31.0
Basic Services							
Sewerage	National	57.3	83.4	12.4	28.2	29.6	63.8
connection (%)	Costa	43.5	74.4	11.7	17.0	27.3	58.9
	Sierra	78.9	95.6	13.5	35.4	33.5	69.5
	Oriente	62.9	87.9	7.0	31.1	10.8	50.6
Electricity	National	97.8	99.5	62.0	75.8	75.8	91.1
supply (%)	Costa	97.9	99.4	55.5	63.3	76.4	89.6
	Sierra	97.7	99.7	69.8	84.3	78.4	93.0
	Oriente	93.6	96.5	36.3	74.4	40.1	81.9
Water from	National	61.2	78.8	18.3	23.0	34.8	59.3
public net (%)	Costa	48.9	67.1	6.1	9.1	27.2	51.4
	Sierra	79.9	94.5	27.9	34.0	43.8	68.2
	Oriente	85.3	92.5	12.1	23.2	17.0	47.2
Waste collection	National	59.7	76.7	1.1	5.6	23.5	51.5
(%)	Costa	52.2	68.9	1.3	6.8	26.6	52.1
	Sierra	70.5	87.7	0.9	3.9	22.2	51.3
	Oriente	59.9	84.9	1.8	21.5	5.7	43.3

Source: World Bank (1995a), Table 2a and 2b.

and rural Ecuador has not completed primary school, which lasts 6 years. In rural Ecuador, many of the poor households heads have barely completed the basic cycle of primary school (3 years). Not surprisingly, while literacy at the national level now stands at about 90 percent, more than one-third of the extremely poor in the rural Sierra cannot read or write. In contrast, the average schooling of the urban non-poor household head is well into secondary school, and even beyond the basic secondary school cycle (9 years) in the Sierra.

- A broad sectoral breakdown of the labor force reveals that informal activities play different roles for the urban and rural poor. The breakdown distinguishes between the informal, modern, public, and a narrowly defined farm sector. As expected, employment shares in the farm sector are negatively correlated, and in the public and modern sectors positively correlated with per capita expenditures, but the more interesting finding relates to the role of the informal sector. In the urban areas, the informal sector absorbs a higher share of the poor than the non-poor labor force, especially women. About 65 percent of the occupied poor women work in the informal sector, which is their predominant source of entry into the labor market. In the rural sector, the opposite is the case — informal sector activity is higher for the non-poor than for the poor. Rural off-farm employment plays an important role in supplementing agricultural income, and for the poor it has a high potential to become a road out of poverty. Using a broad definition of off-farm employment that includes both primary and secondary occupations, it appears that as much as half of the non-poor of working age have some employment in the off-farm sector.

- The link between poverty and basic services is not uniform but depends on area, region, and type of service. The rural non-poor are worse off than the urban poor in relation to water supply, hygiene facilities, garbage disposal, and electricity connection. However, services can have a different function in urban and rural areas, e.g., the threat from lack of hygiene facilities in rural areas is much lower than in the overcrowded urban centers, especially in the Costa, where the climate helps to breed diseases. Not all services distinguish the living conditions of the poor from the non-poor. Electricity in urban Ecuador now reaches nearly every household, independent of its status. In rural areas, however, there is a strong relationship between electricity connection and poverty — most markedly in the Sierra and the Oriente. Similarly, telephone service is not a distinguishing factor for the urban population but is for the rural population.

DETERMINANTS OF HOUSEHOLD WELFARE IN CÔTE D'IVOIRE, 1985. LSMS surveys are not only useful for measuring poverty, they can also be used to investigate the causes of poverty, which should provide useful information for designing policies to reduce it. An example of such a study is that of Glewwe (1990, 1991), which investigated the determinants of household expenditures using the 1985 Côte d'Ivoire LSMS survey. Using multiple regression methods, he investigated the impact of education levels, household assets, land owned, and local infrastructure on per capita household expenditures.[73] Separate regressions were run for urban and rural areas, some of the results of which are in Table 7.3. In urban areas education levels of both male and female household members had a positive impact on household expenditures. Several types of household assets (value of home, if owned, value of household business assets, and value of savings in financial institutions) also had a strong positive effect on household welfare. Once all these factors were accounted for, regional differences in household expenditure levels (measured by dummy variables for each region) were insignificant.

In rural areas of Côte d'Ivoire, the education of household members had very little effect on household expenditures, an anomaly which raises concern about the relevance of education for individuals employed in traditional occupations. As in urban areas, household assets were generally positively associated with welfare levels. Land ownership in rural areas also had a strong impact on household expenditure levels, and cocoa land appeared to have a substantially stronger impact than did coffee land. Infrastructure had substantial predictive power in rural areas — households located in villages that were nearer to both paved roads and public markets were relatively better off, as were households living in areas with higher wage levels.

These results have several policy implications. First, education of both men and women is an important determinant of household welfare in Côte d'Ivoire, especially in urban areas. Second, the result that education has very little relationship to household welfare in rural areas suggests that schools are performing poorly or that the skills learned have little relevance to employment prospects in rural Côte d'Ivoire. The higher impact of cocoa land, relative to coffee land, on household welfare suggests that coffee cultivation should not be subsidized or encouraged in any way. Finally, the impact of roads and distances to the market suggests that infrastructure improvements could have high returns in rural areas.

Understanding the Effects of the Economic Environment

CHANGES IN PRODUCER PRICES. One of the common discussions during the mid-1980s in Côte d'Ivoire concerned what should be the pricing policy for

---

73. One technical note. Although it may be more intuitively appealing to classify households as poor and non-poor based on their household expenditure levels, and then estimate a probit or logit regression of the determinants of poverty, this estimation technique ignores a large amount of information contained in the household expenditure variable and so is a very inefficient estimation method. It is more informative to use household expenditures directly as the dependent variable.

Table 7.3: Determinants of Household Expenditure Levels

	Urban	Rural
Education Level of Most Educated Male		
Elementary	0.3760 (5.3)	0.0406 (0.6)
Junior secondary	0.6202 (8.6)	0.0820 (0.9)
Senior secondary	0.7957 (9.6)	0.0561 (0.4)
University	0.9333 (9.4)	—
Education Level of Most Educated Female		
Elementary	0.1130 (1.7)	0.0740 (1.0)
Junior secondary	0.2418 (3.1)	0.2771 (2.2)
Senior secondary	0.3451 (3.4)	—
University	0.5208 (4.1)	—
Value of Selected Household Assets		
Home	0.0644 (5.3)	—
Business assets	0.0419 (3.3)	0.1655 (4.9)
Savings	0.0815 (4.7)	—
Hectares Agricultural Land		
Cocoa trees	—	0.1721 (4.3)
Coffee trees	—	0.0439 (1.3)
Distance to nearest		
Paved road	—	−0.0432 (−2.9)
Market	—	−0.0895 (−3.3)
Unskilled Wage (Males)	—	0.3764 (6.4)

Source: Glewwe (1990).

coffee and cocoa. The producer prices were maintained well below the international prices. The taxes raised from the policy were a major source of government revenue. Table 7.4 shows analysis performed by Deaton and Benjamin (1988) helps to understand one dimension of the possible effects of changes in the coffee and cocoa pricing policy. The first row of the table shows that 14 percent of persons living in farm households fall in the poorest decile and only 2.7 percent in the richest decile (based on per-capita household consumption). Thus farm households were poorer than average in 1985. The subset of farm households that produced cocoa and coffee were, on the other hand, slightly concentrated in the middle of the income distribution. The fifth row shows that cocoa sales were heavily concentrated in the sixth decile. Coffee sales were much less concentrated, but a larger share than proportional came from the middle deciles. This implies that if the cocoa or coffee prices were to have been increased, the gains would have been spread over the whole welfare

Table 7.4: Côte d'Ivoire 1985 — Distributional Characteristics of Coffee and Cocoa Farming

| | Percentages in countrywide deciles of population | | | | | | | | | | |
	Poorest 1	2	3	4	5	6	7	8	9	Richest 10	Total
Farm people	14.0	13.6	13.2	12.5	11.4	11.4	8.1	7.2	6.0	2.7	100
Cocoa people	9.5	9.8	13.0	13.9	12.3	13.6	9.9	8.6	5.7	3.7	100
Coffee people	9.0	11.5	13.9	14.1	12.4	13.0	9.2	8.1	6.0	3.1	100
Land cultivated	11.6	9.6	11.2	10.3	9.2	22.2	7.6	9.2	5.6	3.7	100
Cocoa sales	9.1	3.0	6.9	4.6	5.3	49.0	5.5	6.6	3.9	6.1	100
Coffee sales	7.8	6.5	8.7	12.7	13.8	9.2	12.4	16.1	9.2	3.6	100

Average rank of people in agricultural households → 40th percentile
Average rank of people in cocoa households → 45th percentile
Average rank of people in coffee households → 43rd percentile

Note: Each row adds up to 100 percent, so that, for example, the first row shows the distribution of people living in farm households across the deciles of population for the whole country, while the last shows the fraction of total coffee sales that accrue to people in each decile. Each person is accorded the household per capita total expenditure of the household to which he or she belongs, and each decile refers to 10 percent of people, not of households.

Source: Deaton and Benjamin (1988), Table 11, page 38.

distribution but slightly concentrated in the middle deciles. The change in income would have been neither greatly pro-poor nor pro-rich.

Of course, a more complete evaluation of the effects of such price changes would have had to take account of changes in behavior induced by the changes in income. For example, farmers might have used inputs more extensively and would have spent their income in ways that would have effects throughout the economy. Perhaps most importantly, the revenue to government would have declined significantly, so some policy of reducing expenditures or of raising revenue from an alternate source would necessarily have had to accompany an increase in coffee or cocoa prices.

CHANGES IN CONSUMER PRICES. It is similarly often important to understand the effect of consumer price changes on household welfare. Important changes can come about as a result of reforms in tax, subsidy, or trade policies. In Tunisia, the consumer prices of several staple goods have been fixed by the government and heavily subsidized for many years. Since 1990, the government has been incrementally changing the level of subsidies and the commodities that are subsidized in an attempt to improve the effectiveness and reduce the fiscal costs of the subsidy program. Table 7.5 shows some analysis done in the course of discussions between the Government of Tunisia and the World Bank to try to determine what policy changes should be adopted (see World Bank, 1995). The effect of various price changes on the caloric intake of expenditure quintiles was

170

Table 7.5: Tunisia — Estimated Nutritional Effects of Alternative Price Policies:

| | Expenditure Quintiles | | | | | |
| | Poorest | | | | Richest | |
	1	2	3	4	5	Average
Impact of Hypothetical Price Changes:						
(1) 50% subsidy cut						
Percent change in calories as share of total caloric intake	-30.1	-24.3	-22.2	-20.6	-15.3	-21.9
Resulting caloric intake	1483	1688	1813	1975	2549	1902
(2) Targeted cut						
Percent change in calories as share of total caloric intake	-19.5	-20.9	-22.6	-22.6	-22.5	-21.7
Resulting caloric intake	1708	1764	1803	1925	2332	1907
1993 levels (Kcal):	2122	2230	2330	2487	3009	2435
Subsidized goods as a share of total intake (1993)	58.9	49.4	47.4	42.4	28.4	45.3

Notes:
Scenario (1): Impact of cutting subsidies by 50 percent from 1993 levels on quantities consumed.
Scenario (2): Impact of eliminating subsidies on specific goods on quantities consumed.
　　　(sterilized milk, *gros pain*, bottled generic oil)
A negative number signals a loss in calorie intake.
Estimations omit introduction of new goods since 1993.
Recommended daily allowance: 2165 calories per capita (INS).

Source: World Bank (1995b), Tables 28 and 29.

simulated. The simulations take into account the changes in consumption shares of specific foodstuffs due to price changes (e.g., total price elasticities) holding all other factors constant. The estimated effect of a hypothetical policy of reducing subsidies across the board by 50 percent was that caloric intake might fall by 30 percent among the poorest quintile. Targeted subsidy cuts on specific goods, however, are predicted to lead to a much smaller reduction in caloric intake, of about 19 percent for the poorest group, although simulations reveal that the subsidy cuts under both scenarios would generate comparable fiscal savings for the Tunisian government. Not surprisingly, the government has adopted a strategy that includes targeted subsidy changes.

CHANGES IN THE WHOLE ECONOMY. Household welfare is obviously affected by the health of the economy as a whole. In Peru, the economy went through considerable upheaval in the late 1980s. GDP per capita fell by about a quarter. The price index (base of 1980=100) rose from 3,474 in 1985 to 40,216,592 in 1990. Net international reserves plummeted. Data from LSMS surveys in Lima in 1985 and 1990 have been analyzed by Glewwe and Hall (1992) to show how household welfare changed during this period.

Table 7.6: Changes in Welfare in Lima 1985 to 1990

	All Lima 1985–86		All Lima 1990		Percent Change in Expenditures since 1985
	Mean Expenditures	(Percent of Population)	Mean Expenditures	(Percent of Population)	
SEX					
Male	7,943.2	(86.6)	3,613.6	(85.4)	-54.5
Female	6,681.0	(13.4)	3,012.2	(14.6)	-54.9
EDUCATION LEVEL					
None	4,288.5	(2.8)	1,770.7	(3.5)	-58.7
Primary	5,677.6	(37.1)	2,324.4	32.6)	-59.1
Secondary General	7,145.7	35.4)	3,209.8	(44.1)	-55.1
Secondary Technical	7,087.5	(5.3)	3,798.2	(2.3)	-46.4
University	15,112.3	(15.5)	6,945.7	(12.9)	-54.0
Other Post-Secondary	7,634.3	(3.9)	4,665.0	(4.6)	-38.9
EMPLOYER OF HEAD					
Government	9,474.3	(19.1)	4,155.0	(14.6)	-56.1
Private	7,604.0	(35.2)	3,321.2	34.4)	-56.3
Private Home	3,931.5	(1.3)	1,782.4	(0.7)	-54.7
Self-Employed	7,126.7	(36.3)	3,466.2	(36.4)	-51.4
OCCUPATION OF HEAD					
Agriculture	6,430.0	(3.7)	3,189.4	(2.1)	-50.4
Sales/Services	7,532.4	27.8)	3,259.3	(30.3)	-56.7
Industry/Crafts	5,858.5	37.3)	2,793.3	(34.7)	-52.3
White Collar	11,307.8	(23.0)	5,195.3	(19.8)	-54.1
UNEMPLOYED	8,098.5	(2.9)	2,763.5	(5.1)	-65.9
RETIRED	7,495.9	(4.9)	3,733.3	(6.9)	-50.2
ALL LIMA	7,774.4	100	3,531.7	100	-54.6

Notes: Population percentages do not add to 100 due to missing information for 0.3 percent of observations in 1985-86 and 1.8 percent in 1990. The mean expenditure level for those with secondary technical training becomes 6,252.4 for All Lima, 1990, if one outlying value is included in the calculations. This would represent a -11.8 percent change in expenditures since 1985.

Source: Glewwe and Hall (1992), Table 5, p. 21.

Key findings of the analysis were that the welfare of the average household in Lima fell by slightly over half (see Table 7.6) and the welfare of the poorest dropped even more than the average. Poverty, defined as the inability to cover the household's basic nutritional requirements, increased from 0.5 percent to 17.3 percent of the population. Households headed by persons with little or no education experienced the greatest loss of welfare. Households headed by women were not hurt worse than other households.

Provision of Public Services

Several aspects of the provision of public services can be studied with household survey data.

Table 7.7: Access to Infrastructure in Rural Viet Nam

	South			North		
	Total	Non-Poor	Poor	Total	Non-Poor	Poor
Passable Road	58.0	58.1	57.9	76.8	88.5	69.4
Public Transport	61.2	61.1	61.3	47.2	54.3	42.7
Electricity/Generator	91.6	91.6	91.6	85.6	90.0	82.8
Pipe-Borne Water	7.5	9.3	5.8	3.6	5.6	2.3
Permanent Market	71.5	72.6	70.4	43.5	55.6	35.8
Post Office	46.8	43.4	50.3	27.7	28.9	26.9
Lower Secondary School	82.9	81.9	83.8	90.6	92.6	84.9
Upper Secondary School	10.6	12.3	8.9	9.3	9.4	9.3
Dispensary	55.6	60.0	51.3	19.7	20.0	19.6
Pharmacy	78.3	80.7	76.0	65.5	72.0	61.3
Clinic	92.2	90.1	94.2	93.9	97.1	91.9
Doctor	50.9	60.8	41.0	34.7	42.5	29.8
Physician	100.0	100.0	100.0	94.0	96.8	92.2
Nurse	94.4	95.2	93.7	88.4	88.8	88.2
Ag Extension Office	18.4	22.2	14.5	27.8	29.9	26.4
Ag Ext Agent Visited	72.1	68.9	75.3	71.3	75.8	68.3
Cooperative	8.7	8.9	8.4	90.6	94.2	88.3
Adult Literacy Program	81.9	81.0	82.8	85.3	86.9	84.3
Labor Exchange	93.0	92.7	93.4	97.4	97.1	97.6

Note: The poverty line used is calculated for seven different regions and separately for urban and rural areas in each region. The rational average poverty line is 1,117 thousand dong per person per year.

Source: World Bank (1994), Annex 3.1, Table 4 and 5, pp. 168-169.

WHO HAS ACCESS. The first question to address in thinking about service provision is, who has access to services? In addressing this issue the data from the community questionnaires can be especially helpful. Table 7.7 shows a subset of the information available for rural areas from the Viet Nam LSMS used in the poverty assessment (World Bank, 1994b). It shows that in general the poor have less access to services than the non-poor but that the differences are relatively small. Health facilities are more accessible in the south than the north, but agricultural services and literacy programs less so.

WHO USES SERVICES. The next question is, who uses public services? This can also be answered by household surveys if they include appropriate questions. Figure 7.2 shows results from the 1990 Indonesian SUSENAS as reported in World Bank (1993). Among those ill during the month preceding the field work, 67 percent of those in the richest decile sought health care, while 56 percent of those in the poorest decile sought care. More marked differences were shown in the places health care was sought. Among the poorest decile, 37

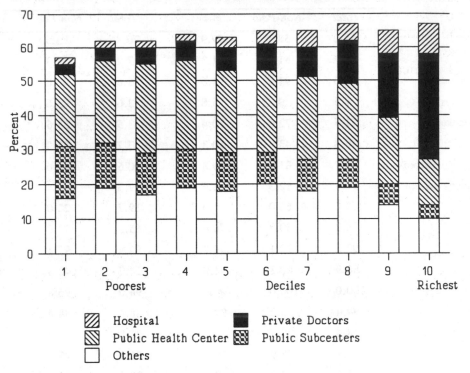

Figure 7.2: Indonesia – Percent of Those Ill in Last Month Who Sought Health Care, by Decile and Place Where Care Sought, According to 1990 SUSENAS

	Poorest				*Deciles*					*Richest*
	1	*2*	*3*	*4*	*5*	*6*	*7*	*8*	*9*	*10*
Hospital	2	2	2	2	3	4	5	5	7	9
Private Doctors	3	4	5	6	7	8	9	13	19	31
Public Health Center	21	24	26	26	24	24	24	22	19	13
Public Subcenters	15	13	12	11	11	9	9	8	6	4
Others	16	19	17	19	18	20	18	19	14	10
Total	57	62	62	64	63	65	65	67	65	67

Source: World Bank (1993), Figure 1.10, p. 18.

percent went to public health centers and sub-centers; only 3 percent of the ill sought care in private doctor's offices. In contrast, in the richest decile, only 17 percent of those ill sought care in the public health centers and sub-centers and 31 percent went to private doctors.

HOW IS THE VALUE OF THE SUBSIDY DISTRIBUTED? In order to complete the calculation of incidence, it is necessary to supplement information on the use of services from the household survey with information on the costs of providing services. This can come either from budget accounts or from special studies. When such information is available, it is possible to conduct analyses like that

174

shown in Table 7.8. The value of subsidies to education is greater than the value of subsidies to health and to household consumption of kerosene. The absolute value of the subsidy captured by the richest decile is two to four times greater than the absolute value of the subsidy captured by the poorest decile. However, the share of the subsidies in household expenditure is greater for the poor than the rich, indicating that these factors do help equalize the distribution of welfare.

WHAT IS THE QUALITY OF SERVICES? Data from the facility surveys that sometimes accompany LSMS surveys can describe the quality of services available. A very sophisticated facility survey was carried in conjunction with the 1989-II Jamaica Survey of Living Conditions. It surveyed all public and private hospitals, all public health centers, and a sample of private health centers. Information on staff, buildings, equipment, supplies, and finances was collected. A wealth of information was available and synthesized in Peabody *et al.* (1993). Among the interesting insights gained (see Figure 7.3), it turns out that public (urban and rural) facilities provide better perinatal diagnosis and counseling, immunization, and family planning than do private facilities. Private facilities, in contrast, are in better repair, better able to do laboratory testing, and have more equipment and supplies. In general differences in the quality indices between public urban and public rural facilities were small.

WHAT WOULD HAPPEN IF USER FEES WERE RAISED? An important policy question in several sectors is the impact of cost recovery on the use of services and on the revenues of the service providers. Both of these have been analyzed extensively using LSMS data, mostly for health but also for education. Figure 7.4 shows a simulation of how the use of health services for children might change in response to four alternative pricing policies. The simulation is done by Gertler and van der Gaag (1990) for the Sierra regions of Peru using the 1985

Table 7.8: Indonesia — The Distribution of Selected Subsidies

	Year	Poorest Decile	Richest Decile	National Average
Subsidy per capita in Rp. per month				
Education	1989	1161	2469	1520
Health	1989	113	313	213
Kerosene	1990	94	447	243
Subsidy as percentage of household expenditure				
Education	1989	13.18	4.04	6.57
Health	1989	1.00	.38	.70
Kerosene	1990	.84	.56	.82

Source: Drawn from World Bank (1993), Annex 2.2, Tables 3, 4, 8, 9, 13 and 14.

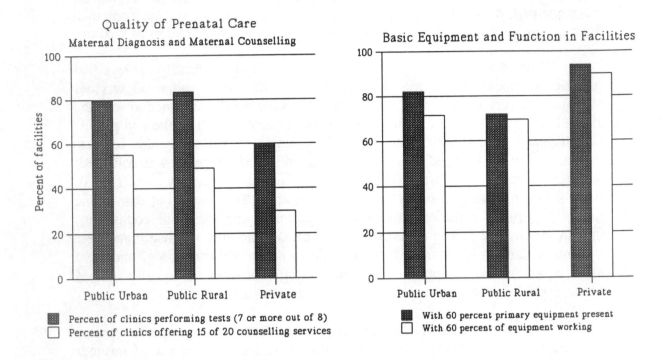

Figure 7.3: Selected Indicators of Quality of Health Facilities in Jamaica, According to the Expanded Health Module, 1989 Survey of Living Conditions

Note: The source did not give the tables with the exact numbers. These graphs are approximations of the originals based on visual inspection.
Source: Peabody *et al.* (1993), various figures.

LSMS data. The simulation is run twice, first showing what would happen if private doctors did not raise fees in response to a rise in fees for public sector health care and then showing what would happen if private doctors did raise their fees. In both cases, children would use less health care. In the first case, some of the ill would use less health care. Others would still use health care, but would switch from public clinics to private doctors. In the second simulation, the use of private doctors would actually fall.

Impact of Government Programs

Finally, it is of interest to know the impact of government programs. Impact evaluations often require special sampling or other data sets to complement household survey data. Three examples where the special design features were kept fairly simple follow.

**Figure 7.4: User Fee Simulations for Children's
Health Care in Sierra Regions of Peru, 1985**

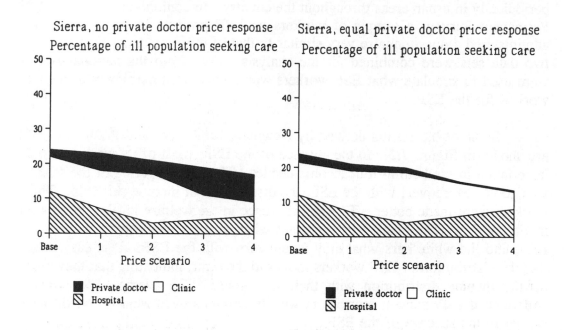

Sierra, no private doctor price response
Percentage of ill population seeking care

Sierra, equal private doctor price response
Percentage of ill population seeking care

Notes on price scenarios:

Base: All fees at 0 intis.

Scenario 1:   Hospital fees set at 7.5 intis.
Scenario 2:   Hospital fees set at 15 intis.
Scenario 3:   Hospital fees set at 15 intis and clinic fees at 7.5 intis.
Scenario 4:   Hospital fees set at 15 intis and clinic fees at 15 intis.

Note: The source did not give the tables with the exact numbers. These graphs are approximations of the originals based on visual inspection.
Source: Gertler and van der Gaag (1990), Figure 7-4, p. 113.

HOW MUCH DO WORKERS BENEFIT FROM PUBLIC WORKS SCHEMES?
Governments often fund public works schemes as part of their poverty alleviation efforts. The idea is that only the truly poor are willing to accept temporary jobs that require hard physical labor and pay low wages, so that the jobs will be self-targeting. It is important not only to evaluate whether the prospect of good targeting is true, but how much workers benefit. Often the workers on such schemes could not afford to be completely idle if the scheme did not exist. Instead they might be selling chewing gum on street corners or turning up each day at places where daily laborers are hired. The earnings from these other activities might be low, but they would bring in some income. Thus for the workers, the monetary benefit of a public works job is the difference between the wage it pays and whatever the workers could earn in their alternate activities.

In order to evaluate the benefits from the public works schemes financed by the Bolivian Emergency Social Fund (ESF), an extension of the Bolivian Permanent Survey was arranged. The Permanent Survey was carried out periodically in urban areas throughout the country. In conjunction with the 1988 Permanent Survey, a sample of workers on ESF projects in urban areas was administered a questionnaire very similar to that of the Permanent Survey. The two data sets were combined for the analysis. Data from the national survey were used to simulate what ESF workers would have been earning had they not worked for the ESF.

Some of the results derived by Newman, Jorgensen, and Pradhan (1992) are shown in Figure 7.5. In the absence of the ESF, most of its workers would have fallen in the bottom four income deciles. Thus the targeting of the scheme was good. Moreover, with the ESF, the distribution of income shifts up. Thus, workers were made better off. The difference in the welfare levels can be seen in Figure 7.5. The black bars represent what workers would earn without the ESF, and the white bars what they would earn with the ESF. It is easy to see that the distribution of ESF workers moves to the right, indicating that they move up the income distribution with their ESF jobs. The average ESF worker experienced a 45 percent increase in weekly earnings over what he would have earned in the absence of the ESF.

THE EFFECT OF GOVERNMENT TRANSFERS ON PRIVATE TRANSFERS. Private, non-market transfers occur almost everywhere in the world, but they are a particularly important part of economic life in developing countries. While 15 percent of individuals in the United States report receiving transfers, the same figure in developing countries is much higher — 19 to 47 percent (Cox and Jimenez, 1993). Policymakers need to consider these patterns in their decisionmaking. First, the appropriate size of the public safety net depends in part on the size of the private safety net already in place. Tight public budgets imply that spending must be concentrated where the private network helps least. Second, private transfers might respond to changes in government programs in ways that could dilute or perhaps reinforce program effectiveness. For example, an increase in publicly funded pension benefits may not benefit the elderly as much as expected if their children react by cutting their private support.

Household surveys are key to analyzing patterns for private, inter-household transfers of goods in-kind and cash. They can be used to explain how the patterns and amounts of private transfers are related to access to public transfers and other household characteristics. These functions can then be used to simulate what would happen if the amounts of those public transfers were to change. Researchers have used household data sets from several developing countries (Peru, Côte d'Ivoire, Ghana, the Philippines, Columbia, Poland, Kyrgyzstan, and Russia) to study the role of transfers.

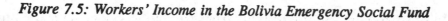

Figure 7.5: Workers' Income in the Bolivia Emergency Social Fund

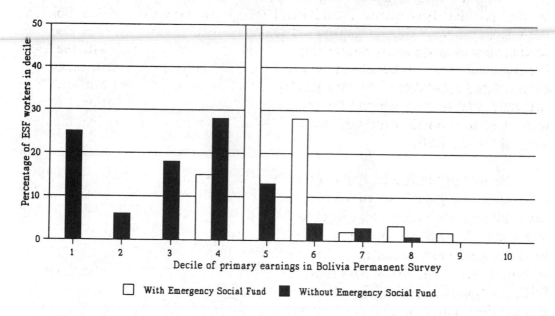

Note: The source did not give the table with the exact numbers. This graph is an approximation of the original based on visual inspection.
Source: Newman, Jorgensen, and Pradhan (1992), Figure 4.3, p. 61.

What are the results from recent research? Researchers have found that private transfers are directed toward those households that are also the recipients of government programs, such as the poor, the elderly, the infirm, those who lack access to formal credit (such as women and young people), and the unemployed. Moreover, private transfers are responsive to government policy, with important operational implications for the incidence of public transfers.

The evidence shows that public transfers can "crowd out" private ones. Cox and Jimenez (1993) estimate that, in Peru, an increase of 100 units in public pensions would be associated with a decline in private transfers by 17 *intis*, leaving a net gain of 83 *intis* for the older household (Figure 7.6a).

The "crowding out" results are most striking for the Philippines, a country with a minimal welfare state and widespread private transfers. For example, a 100-peso increase in public pensions to a retired household would cause private transfers to decline by an estimated 37 pesos (Figure 7.6b). But if employment insurance were instituted in the Philippines, reductions in private transfers would be so large that jobless households would only be slightly better off (Figure 7.6c). Thus, while public transfers would still benefit targeted households, such benefits would be smaller than those implied by analyses that ignore private transfer behavior.

Figure 7.6: Response of Private Transfers to Public Transfer Programs

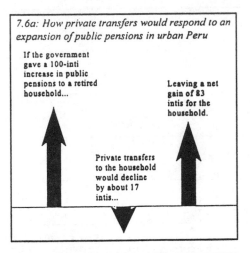

7.6a: How private transfers would respond to an expansion of public pensions in urban Peru

If the government gave a 100-inti increase in public pensions to a retired household...

Leaving a net gain of 83 intis for the household.

Private transfers to the household would decline by about 17 intis...

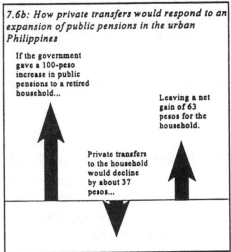

7.6b: How private transfers would respond to an expansion of public pensions in the urban Philippines

If the government gave a 100-peso increase in public pensions to a retired household...

Leaving a net gain of 63 pesos for the household.

Private transfers to the household would decline by about 37 pesos...

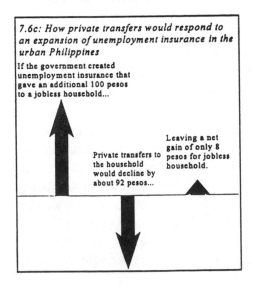

7.6c: How private transfers would respond to an expansion of unemployment insurance in the urban Philippines

If the government created unemployment insurance that gave an additional 100 pesos to a jobless household...

Leaving a net gain of only 8 pesos for jobless household.

Private transfers to the household would decline by about 92 pesos...

Source: Cox and Jimenez (1993)

HOW SCHOOLS CAN INCREASE LEARNING. The contribution of education to economic development is now widely accepted. Yet in many developing countries schools are very inefficient in teaching basic skills. Research on how schools can be improved is therefore a high priority. By supplementing the Ghana Living Standards Survey with detailed school questions and tests of cognitive achievement, a standard LSMS survey was augmented to examine the impact of school and teacher characteristics on school achievement. Results are reported in Glewwe and Jacoby (1992).

The major findings of the research on determinants of achievement in Ghanaian middle schools were: (1) Having blackboards available (which are not always found in Ghanaian schools) raises mathematics and (English) reading achievement; (2) Schools with classrooms that leak when it rains have lower mathematics and reading achievement; and (3) Increased availability of textbooks raises reading achievement. Not only does improved school quality lead to increased learning per year of schooling, but it also raises the number of years attended by the typical student.

To supplement the household data, cost information was gathered for blackboards, roof repairs, and text-books and benefit/cost ratios were calculated for each type of investment. Blackboards had the highest ratio, followed by repairing leaking roofs and providing additional textbooks. These investments would be more cost-effective than the commonly discussed options of building more schools or hiring more teachers.

If the government hopes to influence certain outcomes, such as whether parents will enroll their children in school, the nutritional status of children, or the number of children a woman bears, it must understand what factors influence household decisions. Thus much "basic" research is useful background to government policy. A great deal of analysis of this sort has been done using LSMS data.

THE DETERMINANTS OF FERTILITY AND CONTRACEPTIVE USE. The main advantage of using LSMS surveys for analysis of demographic behavior is the wealth of economic variables that can be linked to individuals and households. Demographic surveys, such as the World Fertility Survey and the Demographic and Health Surveys, collect vast amounts of information on demographic variables. They provide the basis for estimating very precise levels of fertility, mortality, nuptiality, contraceptive use, breast feeding, and so forth. However, greater demographic coverage is realized at the expense of not collecting other information on women, children, and households that would help to understand what motivates these demographic outcomes.

The LSMS surveys, on the other hand, typically collect information on a sub-set of these demographic variables (fertility, child mortality, contraceptive use) but can link them to a vast number of economic variables, measured in the household and community: household income, expenditure, wealth, and productive assets; education, training, and labor force participation of women, children, and all other household members; past and current investments in the schooling and health care of children; price, quality, and availability of health care and family planning services in the community; price, quality and availability of child schooling; and wage and price levels in the communities. The LSMS surveys also establish extensive links between different individuals within the household, making it possible to perform detailed analyses of household composition and issues such as child fostering.

LSMS surveys have been used to analyze many demographic issues, including:[74]

- What is the effect of female schooling, male schooling, and household income on fertility?

- What are the factors that induce couples to have fewer children and invest more in each child?

- How is the availability, quality, and price of family planning services affecting contraceptive use? What are the socioeconomic characteristics of

---

74. See for example: Ainsworth (1989, 1990, and 1992); Benefo and Schultz (1994); Montgomery and Kouamé (1995); Oliver (1995a,b); and Schafgans (1991).

users and non-users? Of those with access to family planning and those without?

- What are the economic factors affecting child mortality? How does the family's child mortality experience in turn affect fertility decisions?

Figure 7.7 and Table 7.9 illustrate some of the potential uses of LSMS data in analyzing fertility and contraceptive use. In Côte d'Ivoire, women in the highest consumption quintile have the lowest age-specific fertility rates, but those in the lowest consumption quintile have the next lowest current fertility (see Figure 7.7). On the other hand, current fertility is sharply lower among all women with secondary schooling and among women over 30 with primary schooling (not shown). This suggests that increasing incomes among the poorest Ivorian women will raise fertility unless levels of female schooling are also raised.

Contraceptive use is far more sensitive than is fertility to differentials in income and female schooling, however. In Ghana, for example, knowledge, ever use, and current use of a modern method of contraception increase with levels of female schooling and household income and decline with distance to a source of family planning, although distances of 4 miles or greater do not seem to have an effect on use (see Table 7.9). Multivariate analysis of current use of contraception revealed that: increased female education and household expenditure are strongly and independently associated with greater contraceptive use; reducing the distance to family planning facilities would have only a small effect on raising contraceptive use; but improving the availability of spermicides in public and private facilities would raise use by a larger amount.

THE DETERMINANTS OF LATE SCHOOL ENROLLMENT. In many developing countries children enroll in primary school at a relatively late age, such as 7, 8, or 9. From the point of view of learning and subsequent income, these delays appear to be wasteful. The data from the 1988-89 Ghana Living Standards Survey were used to examine several hypotheses concerning the determinants of late enrollment (see Glewwe and Jacoby 1992). Little support was found for the conjecture that credit constraints led to delayed enrollment and no support was found for the hypothesis that overcrowded schools led to rationing of school places to students. However, convincing evidence was found that indicated that malnutrition led to delayed enrollments. Stunted children (as measured by low height for age) were much more likely to enroll in high school at a late age than were otherwise identical well-nourished children. These findings indicate that nutrition interventions may lead to improved education outcomes.

This section has given a brief tour of the rich and varied policy analysis possible with data from LSMS surveys. It should be clear why an abstract is not enough to exploit the potential, and why mechanisms to disseminate data and to support many researchers should be planned from the outset.

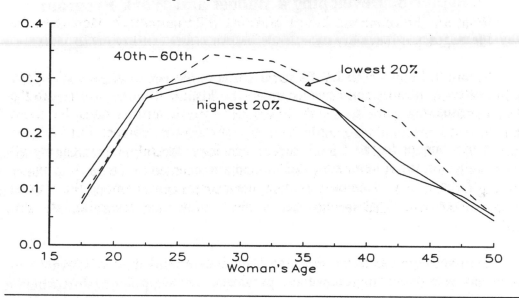

Figure 7.7: *Age-specific fertility rates by women's age and consumption percentile, Côte d'Ivoire, 1985-87*

Source: Montgomery and Kouamé (1995).

Table 7.9: *Percent of women who have heard of, ever used, or are currently using a modern method of contraception, Ghana, 1988-89*

Explanatory variable		Knowledge	Ever use	Current use
Women's education	None	66	10	2
	1-6 years	91	24	7
	7-10 years	95	45	10
	More than 10 years	98	55	16
Expenditure quartile (per adult)	Lowest	73	16	3
	Second	81	21	6
	Third	84	29	6
	Highest	90	40	9
Miles to the nearest source of family planning	None	92	39	11
	1-3 miles	89	29	6
	4-8 miles	72	17	3
	More than 8	72	18	4

Source: Oliver (1995a)

Chapter 8. Developing a Budget and Work Program

Key Messages

- Before designing an LSMS survey, it is important to assess the country's survey infrastructure and examine the history of previous surveys and censuses.

- The budget for an LSMS survey can vary depending on local factors: whether or not items provided in kind are included in the budget; the size of the staff and amount of equipment; and prices of items. The two design-related factors are size of the survey sample and length of the questionnaire.

- A prototype budget can help the planner determine that all relevant items are included in the budget and provides a starting point against which to measure costs. A prototype budget is provided in section B.

- The work program takes place in three phases. Planning often takes around a year. Field work takes another year, while writing an abstract, documenting the data sets, and starting dissemination of the data require at least another six months.

- Many preparatory tasks take place simultaneously. Effective scheduling requires knowledge of how long each activity takes and how the activities are interlinked.

This chapter is designed to help the survey planner set realistic work plans and budgets for an LSMS survey. It covers the planning and data collection phase. Only the most minimal set-up for data analysis is covered — the production of the abstract and documentation of data sets. Further time and money should usually be set aside for more analysis, but since the extent of these is so varied, they are not covered here. Section A addresses how to assess the existing capacity of the statistical institute. Section B provides a generic budget that includes all the major items required to carry out an LSMS survey. Section C presents a generic work program and guidelines to adjust it to the existing capacity of the institute.

Obviously the details of work program and budget will vary widely from country to country. The survey planner will need to adapt the generic information presented here to the specific circumstances at hand. This framework should be used to ascertain that all required elements have been included. The planner will need to consider how big a gap there is between the statistical agency's existing capacity and what is needed to carry out the LSMS survey. This should be done separately for each of the elements required for the survey, rather than on the basis of some sort of general average.

A. Assessing the Country's Statistical Capabilities

Before planning a project, it is necessary to know not only the desired end product but also the starting point. This section discusses how to assess existing statistical capacity, starting with the outputs of the statistical agency and then assessing the inputs it has available.

Assessing the Outputs of the Statistical Agency

This approach is based on the philosophy that "the proof is in the pudding." If an agency has successfully carried out complex surveys in the past, this is a promising indicator that it may be able to do so again. If an institute has never carried out a complex survey, it will probably need a larger infusion of outside resources and take a longer time to do an LSMS survey than an institute with extensive survey experience.

The first thing to examine is the record of surveys over the last five or 10 years and those planned in the next two or three years. The best finding would likely be an institute that has certain nationwide surveys it carries out regularly with resources from its normal budget (say, a census every 10 years, a household budget survey every five or 10 years, labor force surveys every six months, consumer price index every month, or similar surveys) and a diverse set of *ad hoc* surveys, which may be financed on a contract basis. The regular nationwide surveys imply some stability and permanent capacity, while the *ad hoc* surveys indicate flexibility and client orientation.

Next, one should find out about each of the surveys. Questions to verify are listed in Box 8.1. The motivation is to assess the complexity and quality of recent surveys. The assessment of outputs should include the analysis and dissemination record as well as the data collection itself.

As part of the verification process, the assessor should try to obtain written materials about the different surveys. This serves two purposes. First, if the agency cannot produce key documents (questionnaires, sample plans, or abstracts) for recent surveys, it is a telling sign that some aspect of its capacity is weak. In this case it is worth trying to determine why the documents are not available. If they were never produced, the survey implementation may be of poor quality. If they were produced but no copies are on file, there may be a lack of good management. If there are archival copies but no extras, it may indicate that operating funds (such as the photocopy budget) are scarce. If the documents are considered "secret," client orientation is extremely poor.

Second, it is much easier to assess quality from written documents, especially to distinguish between average and excellent. For example, it is a bad sign if a survey does not have an interviewer manual. But if it does have a manual, it is important to see the manual to judge how well it is done.

185

Box 8.1: *Assessing the Products of a Statistical Institute*

For each important survey that has been carried out over the previous three to five years, the assessor should try to determine answers to the following questions:

Questionnaire .

How many different units of observation does it use?
How coherent is the content?
How good is its formatting?
How long is the average interview?

Sample

How large was the sample?
How many strata and clusters were there?
Is the sample nationwide?

Field Work

What was the ratio of supervisors to interviewers?
How many re-interviews were conducted?
Were there any written supervision instruments?
What was the non-response rate due to refusals?
How good are the manuals?

Data Management

What kind of data quality assurance procedures were used?
How soon after the completion of field work were data available for analysis?
What kind of documentation is provided with the raw data to users?

Dissemination Record

What publications are available from the survey?
How much time elapsed between the field work and publication?
How sophisticated is the analysis and presentation?
Does the institute supply the unit record data to any users, or only to those who financed the survey?

The assessment of the statistical agency's capacity must also include an assessment of the inputs available in the institute. A list of questions to verify is produced in Box 8.2. The assessor should take particular interest in how the agency is budgeted (see Table 8.1). It will be possible to determine how much additional staff and equipment are needed based on what can be provided locally, and to arrange a financing plan for the total budget. Furthermore, knowing the existing capacity will help customize the work plan (discussed in Section C of this chapter).

```
Box 8.2:  Assessing the Inputs of a Statistical Institute

Personnel

How many people are on staff in relevant positions (field supervisors, interviewers,
data entry personnel, programmers, samplers)?
What is their level of formal education?
How much experience do they have?
What is the turnover rate (differentiated by type of job)?
Do the people who worked on previous complex surveys still work at the agency?
How much are staff paid compared to what they could earn elsewhere?


Equipment
How many vehicles does the agency have?
How are they deployed?
How many and what type of personal computers does the agency have?
Who uses them and for what purposes?
Are there sufficient peripherals (printers, universal power supplies, modems, air
conditioners, cables, etc.)?
What software does the agency have?  Who uses it, and for what purpose?
What is the availability of office equipment (phones, faxes, photocopiers)?
How adequate is the supply of consumables (paper, diskettes, printer ribbons, pencils,
etc.)

Sample Frame

When was the last census done?
What publications are available, and at what level of disaggregation?
What unit record data are available, and at what level of disaggregation?
What methodological documents are available?
What is the size distribution of the census units?

Client Orientation

What official and de facto data access policies exist?
What fora exist for obtaining feedback from data users?
```

B. Developing a Budget

Few aspects of survey design are less conducive to generic statements than
the development of the survey budget. On top of the country-dependent technical
specificities of each budget item, the shape of the budget itself and the way it is
broken down may be dictated by the national or the donor agencies' accounting
procedures. Obviously the errors and omissions made at this point are extremely
hard to amend later and can have serious consequences for the quality of the
survey.

Table 8.1: Approximate Survey Budgets from Selected Countries[a]

Country	Sample Size	Budget in Millions of US$
Jamaica	2000	.155
Ghana	3200	.819
Morocco	3400	1.178
Pakistan	4800	1.024
Viet Nam	4800	.700
Nicaragua	4200	.781
Nepal	3300	.737
Brazil	4480	3.129

Note: a. These are the main budgets formulated when the projects were proposed, rather than the ex post facto amounts. No adjustments have been made for inflation, although the budgets were done in years between 1987 and 1994.

Actual Survey Budgets

Survey budgets for several of the LSMS surveys are shown in Table 8.1. They vary by a factor of 20-fold, from a low of about US$150,000 for one year of the Jamaican survey of about 2,000 households, to a high of as much as US$3 million for the Brazilian sample of 4,480 households. Several surveys form a cluster, with budgets that range from US$750,000 to US$1,000,000.

The large differences between actual budgets stem from the different number of units of each input needed in each country, their prices, and whether they were included in the budget or left off-budget because they were supplied in kind. The importance of these is illustrated by looking at how three items were handled in the real budgets included in Table 8.1.

TRANSPORT DECISIONS. In Jamaica, no vehicles were included in the budget. The field work plan called for using public transportation or vehicles already owned by the survey agency. In Nepal, four jeeps are included in the budget at a price of about $12,000 each. The rest of the field work will be done in cities accessible by public transport or in remote areas inaccessible to vehicles. In Brazil, the budget calls for fourteen vehicles, one for each team. All are Brazilian made, and will cost about $45,000 each.

PERSONNEL COSTS. No allowance is made in the Viet Namese budget for field staff, since the costs were wholly borne by the statistical agency. In Nepal about $40,000 is allowed; in Nicaragua, about $80,000; and in Brazil, $800,000.

TECHNICAL ASSISTANCE. In Jamaica, most technical assistance was provided by World Bank staff and hence was not budgeted. Only about $50,000 of on-budget technical assistance was used in the first year. In Brazil, the budget allows $158,000 for technical assistance and in Pakistan about $200,000 was budgeted.

Base Case Prototype

Since the actual budgets vary so widely in what was included (as well as in the unit costs and number of units of each item), it is useful to develop a "prototype" budget, which is shown in Table 8.2. It is designed to carry out a one-year, 3,200-household LSMS survey. It is followed by comments on some of the budget items to explain how they can vary depending on local conditions. At the very least the hypothetical budget should be useful as a checklist of the things that should not be forgotten when costing a survey; at best, the comments may serve as guidelines on how to better tailor the budget to the country.

This budget shows all the major inputs that are needed, without regard for whether they must be purchased new for the survey or will be provided in-kind by the statistical or international aid agency that helps to finance the survey. Usually the infrastructure and occasionally staff and vehicles are contributed by the statistical agency. In the past, a large share of technical assistance has been supplied in kind by the World Bank and not included in project budgets. Here we include the costs of such technical assistance in the prototype budget, because increasingly the technical assistance is contracted out. Some of the implications of this are discussed in Box 8.3.

The amounts in Table 8.2 are in a hypothetical common currency suggestive of 1994 US Dollars. Real budgets are usually written both in dollars and in the local currency. Allowance for inflation may be needed in long projects or countries where inflation is high.

SALARIES. The budget in Table 8.2 assumes a full complement of headquarters staff, a project manager, a data manager, a field manager, two assistant managers, a secretary, and an accountant. It also assumes the standard LSMS setup of field operations, where 10 field teams visit 3,200 households in one year. Each team is composed of one supervisor, two interviewers, one anthropometrist, one data entry operator, and one driver. Some surveys make do with fewer core staff. The number of the field teams budgeted here is average, but it can easily be larger or smaller.

189

Table 8.2: Generic, All-Inclusive Budget for a One Year, 3,200-Household Living Standards Survey

Item	No.	Level of effort	Unit amount	Total amount
(1) Base salaries:				**385,300**
Project manager	1	30 months	800	24,000
Data manager	1	30 months	600	18,000
Field manager	1	30 months	600	18,000
Assistant managers	2	30 months	450	27,000
Accountant	1	24 months	450	10,800
Secretary	1	30 months	350	10,500
Supervisors	10	14 months	400	56,000
Interviewers	20	13 months	350	91,000
Anthropometrists	10	13 months	350	45,500
Data entry operators	10	13 months	350	45,500
Drivers	10	13 months	300	39,000
(2) Travel allowance:				**114,400**
Project manager	1	90 days	40	3,600
Data manager	1	60 days	40	2,400
Field manager	1	90 days	40	3,600
Assistant managers	2	60 days	40	4,800
Supervisors	10	200 days	10	20,000
Interviewers	20	200 days	10	40,000
Anthropometrists	10	200 days	10	20,000
Drivers	10	200 days	10	20,000
(3) Materials:				**313,330**
Vehicles	12		15,000	180,000
Fuel	12	13 months	220	34,320
Car maintenance	12	13 months	110	17,160
Data entry computers	10		1,200	12,000
Data entry printers	10		500	5,000
UPS, stabilizers, etc.	12		800	9,600
Air conditioners and safety	12		1,200	14,400
Core team computers	4		1,400	5,600
Computer for analysis	1		6,000	6,000
Core team printer	1		500	500
Laser printer	1		1,500	1,500
Computer supplies	15	13 months	50	9,750
Photocopier	1		4,000	4,000
Fax machine	1		500	500
Stationery, toner, etc.		30 months	50	1,500
Measuring tapes (adults)	10		50	500
Scales (adults)	10		150	1,500
Measuring boards (children)	10		300	3,000
Scales (children)	10		150	1,500
Survey material	10		50	500
(4) Printing and xerox				**16,500**
Questionnaires	4000		2	8,000
Manuals	400		5	2,000
First abstract	1000		4	4,000
Other	500		5	2,500
(5) Consultancy and travel:				**236,500**
Foreign consultants	14	man/months	10,000	140,000
Local consultants	5	man/months	2,500	12,500
International travel	12	trips	4,000	48,000
International per diem	240	days	150	36,000
(6) Other:				**147,000**
Office space		30 months	100,000	100,000
Communications		30 months	200	6,000
Pilot survey			5,000	5,000
Household listing			20,000	20,000
Software			10,000	10,000
Translation			6,000	6,000
SUBTOTAL				**1,213,030**
Contingency			10.0%	121,303
TOTAL				**1,334,333**

Box 8.3: *Contracting Out for Technical Assistance*

In the first eight years or so of LSMS experience, the World Bank provided a good deal of the technical assistance and management oversight of LSMS surveys itself by using staff or consultants on its payroll. More recently, this role is being assigned to technical assistants outside the Bank. This brings the conduct of LSMS surveys closer to that of other kinds of projects (where the Bank provides financing for the country to purchase technical assistance) and allows the Bank to support a larger number of LSMS-type surveys than would be the case if all the technical assistance had to be provided by a small pool of people in the Bank. The Bank is, however, still learning how to contract out to best advantage. Listed here are some of the pitfalls experienced to date so that they may be avoided in future surveys.

Mismatch between Budgets and Desired Product. A very common problem where the implementation of the surveys have been contracted out is that the budget allocated falls very far short of what it would take to produce the desired product. It is not unusual for the allocated budget to be only half of what is realistically required, and in some cases it has been a much smaller fraction. This happens most often and most severely when the idea of doing a survey is slotted into a larger project and the budget is assigned without doing a mission or two to clarify what product is actually wanted and what the existing statistical infrastructure is.

The solution to this is to treat an LSMS survey as any other complex project element and use successive missions to define three levels of issues: 1) The big picture — in addition to a data set, how ambitious will the project be in building capacity for data collection? Sponsoring analysis of the data set? Building capacity for data analysis? 2) The medium picture — what will the basic parameters of the survey look like? Will something like the full set of LSMS questionnaires be used or will they be truncated? Will the field work and data management use the full LSMS procedures? How large will the sample be? and 3) The smaller detail — what are the total requirements for inputs? Who will finance each?

Inadequate Terms of Reference. In several cases the terms of reference have not been sufficiently specific in defining what sort of survey and institutional process was wanted. In some cases the consultants did what seemed reasonable to them, but it was not what the country or the Bank really wanted. In other cases, consulting firms were asked to bid on terms of reference that included making decisions on items that would affect the costs, e.g., how large the sample should be and whether or not to do anthropometrics. This obviously made it difficult for the firms to bid sensibly on the projects.

The solution to this is to write better terms of reference. This means that the task manager must allocate adequate time to the task and above all should consult with other task managers and survey specialists in the Bank about the strengths and weaknesses found in the terms of reference that have been used in various countries to date.

Inadequate Learning from Experience with LSMS Surveys. All too often new LSMS-type surveys are being planned without taking into account the lessons from experience in old surveys. This can result in the above problems of bad budgets and terms of reference, in badly designed questionnaires, in inadequate quality control, etc.

The solutions to this are two-fold. First, the LSMS division in the World Bank is making an effort to make the lessons of experience more widely available. Writing this manual is an important part of the effort. The LSMS division will provide examples of questionnaires, manuals, basic information documents, abstracts, and other key products to those planning new surveys.[75] The division can provide additional support to surveys sponsored by the World Bank. The division sponsors a training course for Bank task managers in how to do LSMS surveys. Also, it spends a portion of its time helping those working on new surveys by critiquing draft terms of reference, budgets, work programs, questionnaires, etc. The other part of

---

75. Those who are planning new LSMS surveys should send an electronic mail message to LSMS@worldbank.org to request these materials.

Box 8.3 continues on next page

Box 8.3 (continued)

the solution, of course, is that those working on new surveys must make the effort to learn from experience. In a surprising number of cases the people in charge of new surveys do not do this.

Interaction between the World Bank and the Technical Assistants. Although the technical assistance is contracted out, World Bank staff or consultants will have to be involved in the development of surveys sponsored by the World Bank, as follows:

In the project identification phase, Bank staff or consultants will help define the project and its budget, write the terms of reference for the technical assistants, and supervise the process of selecting the technical assistants.

In the implementation phase, the Bank staff provide the consultants with the lessons of experience and supervise the work they do. This should include providing two or three days of orientation for the contractor, reviewing successive drafts of the questionnaire, manuals, and data entry program, and participating in the field test. This should also include being "on call" to answer queries about specific issues as they arise.

In the analysis phase, Bank staff and consultants will again be involved to ensure that the survey documentation, calculation of consumption aggregates, and calculation of poverty lines are appropriate. Bank staff will also have a very important role in ensuring that the links between the survey and policy analysis and policy makers are made.

Obviously adequate time and funds must be allowed for both the Bank staff/consultants and for the technical assistants to carry out their respective roles in this collaborative effort. At the time this manual is being written, there have not yet been enough successful experiences to know exactly what the right amount is. The current guess is that this is on the order of 15-25 weeks of staff/consultant time over the 30 calendar months from the beginning of planning the project to the production and distribution of the abstract and documented data sets, of which half or more should take place in the country where the survey is being developed. In the technical assistance contracts, time and travel funds should be made available for those involved in the project to attend the orientation course. The time involved for interactions on each of the specific sub-products (questionnaires, manuals, etc.) will be lumped in with interactions with the other parties involved in each. The successful interaction will require the allotment of both enough days of technical assistance time for each sub-task and enough lead time for each iterative process.

Advantages of Being Simultaneously Technical Assistants, Data Users, Policy Advisers, and Financiers. Finally, it should be realized that there are some advantages to having the Bank simultaneously be technical assistants, data users, and financiers. First, the technical advice the Bank gave was consistent with what it wanted as a data user. Since competent, reasonable survey experts and analysts will differ from each other on some issues, this is not guaranteed when the technical assistance is divorced from the user, even when all of the above problems with using outside technical assistance are solved. Second, in the Bank's role as data user and policy adviser it is often present when policy decisions are being debated. When the same individuals are working on the survey, they can provide an exceptionally good channel for ensuring that the survey adequately addresses policy issues and that the results of the survey are considered in the policy decisions. Third, it can greatly ease and speed implementation if the financiers don't have to be separately tutored, courted, or cajoled into setting budgets and time tables appropriately.

Losing the synergy between roles is probably inherent in contracting out the technical assistance. The impact of the loss may be minimized by providing the following: including terms of reference that clearly specify the analytic requirements of the surveys; providing in the project for feedback mechanisms between data users and survey designers; providing in the project data analysis and information transmission to policy makers; and providing adequate time for the Bank's task manager to supervise the project.

For a one-year LSMS survey, most the field staff salaries should be budgeted for 13 months (the 12 months of field work plus one month of training); but it is wise to allow an extra month for the supervisors, whose participation may be necessary earlier to help in tasks such as the field test of the questionnaire. Core staff salaries should be budgeted for about 30 months to allow for preparatory activities and post-field work analysis and documentation.

Determining appropriate salary levels is almost always a thorny issue. In most countries it is difficult to obtain the level of effort and competence required for a successful LSMS survey at civil service wage rates. Though there are nearly always some diligent, knowledgeable people working in the statistical agency at regular government wages, these few dedicated souls are usually already overburdened with the work that should be done by those in vacant posts. It is unrealistic to expect these people to take on an LSMS survey in addition to their other tasks. It is likewise unrealistic to think that it will be possible to easily hire more such people.

A way has to be found to reward those who work on the survey so that they are willing to accept the difficulties of setting it up and managing it well. The job entails many months of intense work and it is unrealistic to assume that statistical agency officials — always badly paid, even by government standards — will do it well without proper incentives.[76] The problem is that paying high wages to new hires from outside discourages the permanent staff. Paying some of the permanent staff more than others may lead to similar resentment. But relying on permanent staff with no extra rewards will, in most countries, doom the survey to produce low-quality work far behind the hoped-for schedule.

The underlying conundrum of the civil service — low salaries leading to low productivity leading to low salaries — is a much larger problem than can be solved in planning one survey. The survey planner must, therefore, find some solution (usually involving a good deal of compromise) tolerable to the specific country. This problem must be approached with a mixture of creativity, diplomatic skill, and some research into the ways it has been solved previously for similar projects in the country. A typical solution consists of establishing a system of performance-based incentives linked to the extra activities the staff must undertake because of the survey. These incentives might include overtime premia, travel allowances, and production bonuses. In some cases the staff may act as temporary consultants to the project, either corporately or as individuals. The payment problem is often harder to solve for the core team, which is almost always composed of regular staff members of the statistical agency, than for the field staff, who are more often hired externally.

---

76. Survey contractors in the private sector know this very well. A typical call for bids to conduct a marketing research survey usually establishes certain *minimum* levels of remuneration for interviewers and supervisors.

TRAVEL ALLOWANCE. This budget item is very country-specific. Each field team devotes about 40 weeks during the survey year to effective survey work, but how much travel is involved will vary. Some teams will spend a lot of the year visiting households in the same localities where the teams are based, so no travel allowance is necessary. This will be the case for the team based in the capital city. In other cases, the localities will be close enough to the team's headquarters to allow for daily trips from the base station so that a small meal allowance rather that a full *per diem* will suffice. In other cases, as in remote rural areas, much of the year will be taken up in travel. The *per diem* amounts and the number of travel days shown in Table 8.2 are intended to be illustrative averages, but a good budget should be based on some estimate of the proportion of localities that will fall in each of the three accessibility situations mentioned (i.e., in the team's base station itself, close to the base station, and far from the base station). This of course requires some educated guessing and/or prior knowledge of survey work in the country; if none of these are available, it is best to err on the safe side and assume that most localities will require expensive *per diems*.

Generally, no *per diem* differentials are considered within the field team's staff, though in some cases the supervisor may be expected to have an extra "representation" responsibility and given a slightly larger daily amount. The *per diems* of the core team, who also have to travel country-wide for central supervision, are usually much larger[77]

MATERIALS. This budget item considers several groups of expenses.

TRANSPORTATION. The sample budget in Table 8.2 assumes that new cars will be purchased for the survey and that these will be regular two-wheel-drive vehicles. It also assumes that one car will be needed for each of the field teams and that two extra cars will be needed for transportation of the core staff. The prices do not include import duties, as official government development programs almost always benefit from some kind of tax exemption. All these assumptions are, of course, country-dependent. Sometimes the statistical agency may provide vehicles from the existing fleet; in certain countries it may be politically incorrect to suggest that anything less than four-wheel-drive vehicles are suitable for the field teams or that the core staff might travel in cars that are not air-conditioned.

Fuel and car maintenance costs can be estimated from assumptions on the distance to be traveled (usually from 2,500 to 3,000 miles per car per month).

---

77. Remember that travel allowances for the core staff can also be used as a way to increase their base salaries.

COMPUTERS AND PRINTERS. Each field team will need its own data entry computer and printer. Technically, the data entry computers can be very simple,[78] but if new machines have to be purchased it would be unwise to select anything less that the standard entry-level configuration of the moment (as this is being written, this is a 80486-SX 25 megahertz [Mhz] machine with 4 megabytes [MB] of random access memory [RAM] and an 80 MB hard drive). The printers can be narrow-carriage, dot-matrix machines.

Most of the core team's computers can also be entry-level machines, and one simple dot-matrix printer can be shared by all members for most tasks. The data manager's machine, however, should have the largest configuration that can reasonably be acquired (presently, it would be something like a 80486DX 66Mhz or Pentium machine with a 8MB RAM and a 400 MB hard drive, and a fast laser printer). Some form of backup system, such as a cartridge tape drive or Bernoulli box, should be included in the data manager's setup. Individual data entry operations can back up daily onto standard diskettes.

As said before, the field computers should be installed at the field base stations, in reasonably safe premises, with universal power supplies (UPS) and air conditioners. All the core staff machines can share one or two UPSs.

The budget should also ensure a sufficient supply of computer supplies (diskettes, printer paper, ribbons, toner, and so forth) throughout the survey period.

OFFICE EQUIPMENT. At least one photocopier and a fax machine (and in certain cases even basic furniture) should be made available to the project and budgeted for.

ANTHROPOMETRIC EQUIPMENT AND SURVEY MATERIAL. If the survey includes an anthropometric module, each team should be equipped with one set of boards and scales.

PRINTING AND PHOTOCOPIES. This budget item depends on the printing facilities that may be available in house at the statistical agency, as well as on the bulk of the reports to be produced as a direct result of the survey. The only reports included in the budget in Table 8.2 are the preliminary and final statistical abstracts.

---

78. The 1984 Côte d'Ivoire survey was done with standard IBM PCs (8088 machines with 128K RAM and no hard drive).

CONSULTANCY AND TRAVEL. The amount of consultancy will obviously vary widely depending on the statistical agency's capabilities, the amount of training needed, and the amount of analysis included in the project design. As a median, the budget in Table 8.2 includes 14 months of international consultancy and five of local consultancy.

The low end of the range of international consultancy required is about six months. This would be relevant when the survey institute has all the basic technical skills required and needs principally to learn about LSMS surveys themselves. The six months might include: three months of contact with analysts who have helped design questionnaires and write abstracts and documentation from other LSMS surveys; one month of contact with those who have helped arrange the organization and logistics for other LSMS surveys; one month with someone to teach local staff how to customize the LSMS data entry program; and one month for other training and consultations, including the training of the anthropometrists. Several months of local consultancy might be used to hire local policy analysts to draft the questionnaire and to help the statistical agency draft the abstract.

The high end of the range of international consultancy is on the order of 36 months. This would be required where more technical training is desired[79] and where a technical advisor is hired full-time for two years to assist or substitute for the survey manager.[80] The remaining 12 months of short-term consultancy might be used as follows: three months to develop questionnaires; one month to help design the logistics; two months to prepare the data entry program; one month to train the anthropometrists; and five months to provide training in analytic software and assistance in producing the first abstract and documentation. Local consultancies would also be arranged to assist in drafting the questionnaire and abstract and to supplement the training in analytic software.

Depending on the country, some of the required technical assistance may be available locally, especially for the design of special questionnaire modules and the community questionnaire. A small allotment is therefore made in the budget.

International travel and per diem are necessary both for foreign experts travelling to the country and for core staff members travelling abroad for training. In several past surveys, the latter has proved to be a cost-effective way of

_____

79. Consider, for instance, the selection of the localities to be visited by the survey. With a computerized sample frame, an expert can do this in one afternoon. However, if each step of the process has to be explained and discussed didactically, the same task may extend to two weeks or more.

80. Such long-term contracts cost a good deal less than the $10,000/month budgeted for the short-term contracts.

conducting certain tasks such as data entry program development or drafting the first statistical abstract.

OTHER COSTS. There are a number of other costs that are difficult to classify, but important nonetheless.

> OFFICE SPACE. The core team offices are usually provided by the statistical agency, representing one of the national contributions to the project. The agency may or may not also provide the premises to be used as field team headquarters and other amenities such as utilities, furniture, etc., which otherwise would have to be considered in the budget.
>
> COMMUNICATIONS. This item should consider the cost of both national long-distance calls during the survey period and the cost of international calls, e-mail, couriers, and the like, which are especially important to ensure frequent and efficient contact between the local core staff, the international consultants, and the international agencies during the survey preparatory phase.
>
> PILOT SURVEY AND HOUSEHOLD LISTING. The actual cost of these activities depends heavily on local conditions and can vary widely from the amounts indicated in Table 8.2. This listing may not be required at all or may take up as much as a third of the cost of the field work. These activities have been included here mainly as a reminder of their tendency to be accidentally omitted from survey budgets.
>
> SOFTWARE. Operating systems are usually included with computers. If the customized LSMS data entry program is used, it will be tailored to the survey as a part of the project. If a commercially available package is used, enough copies for all the data entry operators and data managers should be purchased. All computers should be equipped with virus detection software. Some additional software, to be used at the core team computers, will also have to be purchased. A major statistical program is essential, as well as several copies or a corporate license of a standard word processor and a spreadsheet. A graphics package, a presentation manager, and some compilers are also useful.

CONTINGENCY. A contingency item should always be appended to any budget and that of an LSMS survey is certainly no exception. Given the uncertainties faced by the survey planner when the budget is being developed, this should be five to 10 percent of the total cost.

The budget should be costed in detail, but when the project is submitted for funding it is safer to keep the details as a technical reference and cluster the budget items into larger groups. This usually makes them conform with the agency reporting requirements and provides the survey managers with more accounting flexibility later.

Discussion

The budget in Table 8.2 may look daunting when compared with the budgets of other surveys previously conducted in the country. The evaluators should consider, though, that this budget is all-inclusive. It takes into account many direct and indirect costs that are often excluded from other budgets. In other words, the budget intends to reflect the total cost of the survey regardless of who provides the financing for different parts of it.

In particular, the total of expenditures for local salaries and travel allowances has been costed; this is an item that can often be covered by the regular budget of the statistical agency. A realistic amount of technical assistance has been explicitly considered in the budget as well. For many surveys this is provided in kind by the sponsoring international agency. In many LSMS surveys part of this was provided in kind by World Bank staff. As the number of new surveys increases and the role of the LSMS division evolves, more technical assistance must come from hired consultants.

It should also be noted that a substantial part of the budget is devoted to the purchase of cars, computers, and other equipment, most of which will become part of the statistical agency assets and be useful for other projects after the survey is finished. Indeed, past projects may have left the agency with similar equipment which can be used in this survey, considerably reducing the costs to be financed. The cost of office space also may well be absorbed in kind by the statistical agency. It is certainly preferable to have the headquarters team present in the main offices of the agency, and if the field teams can take advantage of regional offices, that is useful as well.

Sensitivity Analysis

Table 8.3 shows how the total budget might vary if the sample size and number of years of the survey were changed.

A little over half the budget for a one-year survey is devoted to start-up costs. These are mostly for salaries of the core team during preparation, international consultancies, and purchase of equipment. The cost of the field staff, supplies, and infrastructure during the field work constitutes the difference between the start-up and one-year costs. Thus the additional cost of conducting the survey for a second year is much lower than double the cost for the first year. It includes the extra year of salaries and supplies but less technical assistance than used in the first year. In general, it adds about 60 percent of the cost of the first year's survey.

198

Table 8.3: Sensitivity Analysis on the Budget

Time Period	1600 Households	3200 Households	4800 Households
Start-up Costs only	592,000	717,000	842,000
Start-up plus One Year of Survey	991,000	1,340,000	1,687,000
Start-up plus Two Years of Survey	1,529,000	2,100,000	2,671,000

The fact that so much of the cost of the survey goes to the financing of preparatory activities means that the bulk of disbursements will come early in the work. This should be considered when planning the project's cash flow.

About 40 percent of the total one-year cost is proportional to the sample size. This is the cost of field team salaries, their equipment, and their supplies. Thus, to increase the sample size from 3,200 households to 4,800 households (that is, to increase the number of field teams from 10 to 15), will only increase survey costs by about a quarter. However, the advantages of increasing the sample size at the marginal cost of adding new survey teams should be carefully weighed against the increased managerial complexities this entails.

C. Developing the Work Program

To set up any household survey a large number of people need to undertake preparatory activities in a coordinated way. The situation is even more delicate for LSMS surveys, because they differ from what is considered to be standard statistical practice in most countries. It is therefore essential to establish a plan for all the activities needed to implement an LSMS survey. Though such a plan must of course be tailored to each specific situation, the elements it should include are common to most countries. The length of time needed for some activities may vary; for others it may differ little from country to country.

The timetable in Figure 8.1 is a schematic representation of the most important activities that must be completed to conduct a generic LSMS survey for one year. The time frame is a 30 month period, of which the first 12 months are devoted to preparatory tasks, months 13 to 24 to data collection in the field, and

199

1 MANAGEMENT AND LOGISTICS

MONTHS: 1 2 3 4 5 6 7 8 9 10 11 12 13 14 15

```
1.01 Agreements and institutional environment   ****...
1.02 Appoint core staff                          ****...
1.03 Core staff logistics                        ...**
1.04 Acquire anthropometric equipment            ...********************************...
1.05 Acquire computers                           ...****.........|...****************...
1.06 Acquire survey materials                    ...|...|...|...|**********|...
1.07 Mobility strategy and vehicle acquisition   ...|...******************************...
1.08 Publicity and hh motivation strategy        ...|...********************************...
```

2 QUESTIONNAIRE DEVELOPMENT

MONTHS: 1 2 3 4 5 6 7 8 9 10 11 12 13 14 15

```
2.01 Identify policy-relevant issues             ...****
2.02 Prepare draft of the hh questionnaire       ...|...************...
2.03 Distribute draft of hh questionnaire        ...|...|...|...****...
2.04 Seminar                                     ...|...|...|...|*..
2.05 Finalize the draft and plan the field test  ...|...|...|...|.**
2.06 Field test                                  ...|...|...|...|..****
2.07 Review field test                           ...|...|...|...|..**
2.08 Print household questionnaire               ...|...|...|...|....******
2.09 Prepare community & price questionnaires    ...|...********************************...
```

3 SAMPLING

MONTHS: 1 2 3 4 5 6 7 8 9 10 11 12 13 14 15

```
3.01 Sample design                               ********...
3.02 Develop the sample frame                    ...|...****
3.03 Select sampling units                       ...|...|.*..
3.03 Plan the field assignments                  ...|...|.**
3.04 Dwelling listing & cartographic updating    ...|...|...******************...
3.05 Select dwellings in each CU                 ...|...|...|..********************...
```

4 STAFFING AND TRAINING

MONTHS: 1 2 3 4 5 6 7 8 9 10 11 12 13 14 15

```
4.01 Select and train field test staff           ...|...|...|..*******...
4.02 Prepare supervision procedures and manual   ...|...|...|...|...*******...
4.03 Prepare interviewer manual                  ...|...|...|...|...*******...
4.04 Select interviewers                         ...|...|...|...|...***..*...
4.05 Train interviewers                          ...|...|...|...|...|****...
```

5 DATA MANAGEMENT

MONTHS: 1 2 3 4 5 6 7 8 9 10 11 12 13 14 15

```
5.01 Prepare 1st version of data entry program   ...|...|...|..***********...
5.02 Final version of data entry program         ...|...|...|...|...******...
5.03 Prepare data entry manual                   ...|...|...|...|...*******...
5.04 Install data entry computers for training   ...|...|...|...|...***...
5.05 Train data entry operators                  ...|...|...|...|...|****...
5.06 Install data entry computers in the field   ...|...|...|...|...|.**...
5.07 Data entry in the field (1st month)         ...|...|...|...|...|...****...
5.08 Evaluation and debugging                    ...|...|...|...|...|...**..
5.09 Define data management procedures           ...|...|...|...|...|...|.**
5.10 Data entry in the field                     ...|...|...|...|...|...|..*****>
```

6 FIELD WORK

MONTHS: 1 2 3 4 5 6 7 8 9 10 11 12 13 14 15

```
6.01 Survey in the field (1st month field test)  ...|...|...|...|...|...|****...
6.02 Evaluation of field test                    ...|...|...|...|...|...|.**..
6.03 Survey in the field                         ...|...|...|...|...|...|.******>
```

Figure 8.1 continues on next page

Figure 8.1 (continued)

6 FIELD WORK (continued)

MONTHS

	16	17	18	19	20	21	22	23	24	25	26	27	28	29	30
6.03 Survey in the field	>***********************************									...	...	...	...	...	...
5.10 Data entry in the field	>***********************************									...	...	...	...	...	...

7 DATA ANALYSIS AND DOCUMENTATION

MONTHS

	16	17	18	19	20	21	22	23	24	25	26	27	28	29	30
7.01 Define first plan of tabulations	...	...	********	...	...	...	...	...	...	...	...	...	...	...	...
7.02 Create data sets for first six months	...	...	...	...	**	...	...	...	...	...	...	...	...	...	...
7.03 Prepare preliminary statistical abstract	...	...	...	...	..****	...	...	...	...	...	...	...	...	...	...
7.04 Distribute preliminary abstract	...	...	...	...	...	..**	...	...	...	...	...	...	...	...	...
7.05 Seminar	...	...	...	...	...	...	..*	...	...	...	...	...	...	...	...
7.06 Revise contents of abstract	...	...	...	...	...	...	...	..*	...	...	...	...	...	...	...
7.07 Create complete data sets	...	...	...	...	...	...	...	...	...	**	...	...	...	...	...
7.08 Prepare complete statistical abstract	...	...	...	...	...	...	...	...	...	******	...	...	...	...	...
7.09 Prepare survey documentation	...	...	...	...	...	...	...	...	...	..****	...	...	...	...	...
7.10 Distribute raw data sets to analysts	...	...	...	...	...	...	...	...	...	...	..****************>				

months 25 to 30 to preparation of the statistical abstract and dissemination of data sets and policy analysis based on the survey data.

The tasks are divided into seven main areas: (1) finance, management, and logistics; (2) questionnaire development; (3) sampling; (4) staffing and training; (5) data management; (6) field work; and (7) data analysis and documentation. The first five areas consist mainly of preparatory tasks conducted between months 1 and 15. Field work takes place from months 13-24. Data analysis and documentation take place between months 16 and 30.

Certain activities can be conducted in parallel, but some sequences must be respected. The simultaneous development of several tasks is sometimes precluded by the limited availability of resources (mainly by staff time at the core level), whereas in other cases the sequences are imposed by logical constraints (for example, the data entry program can only be completed after the questionnaire is complete). Two activities are extremely important to the planning process in this regard. One is the field testing of the questionnaire (Activity 2.06 in the timetable) and the other the training of the field teams (Activity 4.05). The real scheduling of preliminary tasks, which consists of assigning actual calendar dates to all activities, is usually done around these two key events.

Following the timetable is an explanation of the activities that are most different from normal survey procedures, or most likely to be overlooked.

Management and Logistics

AGREEMENTS AND INSTITUTIONAL ENVIRONMENT. The main institutional actors in the survey process are the data users, the data producers, the providers

201

of technical assistance, and the financiers.[81] These actors must be identified as early as possible and their relationships clearly agreed upon. Three key items must be agreed upon: financing, access to the data, and mechanisms by which data users provide input into the survey design.

The local data users may include the national planning agency, sectoral ministries, and local universities. International development organizations such as the World Bank, several U.N. agencies, and some bilateral aid agencies are also important data users. In most countries the most natural data collecting organization will be the official national statistical institute, which is often one of the survey initiators. Alternatively, the survey may be conducted by one of the local data users or contracted to a private organization.

Developing new LSMS surveys is easier when it is possible to use experience from past surveys. Although some of this can be done through written documents, much of it requires personal contact; hence the need for international technical assistance. In the first LSMS surveys this was supplied exclusively by World Bank staff and consultants. Increasingly, however, a wider group of individuals and agencies are becoming involved.

Financing for an LSMS survey generally comes from several sources. The World Bank itself may be a major provider, usually through the evaluation component of a larger loan in one of the social sectors. Bilateral or international agencies like the United States Agency for International Development, the Japanese Grant Facility, or the United Nations Development Program may also be interested in supporting the project, especially if it includes an institution-building component. Specialized international agencies may help with specific budget items (for instance, UNICEF may provide anthropometric equipment and training if one of the survey modules assesses child nutrition). The country's own financing is usually an in-kind contribution of office space and personnel.

FINANCING. The first agreements are, of course, those related to the survey financing. These should be established as soon as an initial budget is drafted and should basically make clear who will be paying for what, when, and what administrative procedures will be used for spending the money.

DATA ACCESS POLICY. The next agreement should concern user access to the survey data, as discussed in Chapter 7.

---

81. Sometimes the same persons or agencies can appear in more than one role. In the first surveys, the World Bank was the sole financier and provider of technical assistance and distressingly close to being the only data user. More recently, a variety of agencies have participated in each of these roles.

MECHANISMS FOR USER INPUT INTO THE SURVEY DESIGN. Experience to date suggests that the surveys that have been used the most are those that had the most input from potential users. These mechanisms may be formalized and continuous, as in the case of an official steering committee, more occasional, as through workshops held at key stages, or informal, through consultations throughout the process.

APPOINTMENT OF CORE STAFF. A central core staff, composed of at least the survey manager, data manager, and field manager, must be appointed early in the planning process and be made responsible for running the survey on a day-to-day basis during the preparation period.

PROCUREMENT. The equipment and supplies must be available in time to ensure adequate quality in planning and carrying out the field work. It would not be much of an exaggeration to say that delays or difficulties in obtaining some of the basic items has occasioned more headaches and absorbed more time than some of the more substantive tasks in survey preparation (such as questionnaire design or drawing the sample). Anecdotes of such problems and their consequences are legion, but one here will suffice.

In the first year of the Jamaica survey, original procurement arrangements called for the anthropometrists' scales and measuring boards to be purchased through an international procurement agency. The arrangements languished because of unclear responsibilities, inattention, and bureaucratic delay. Suddenly the training for the anthropometrists and the beginning of field work were only a few days and weeks away, respectively. The consultant engaged to train the anthropometrists happened to have a supply of equipment on hand, but the equipment was calibrated in the English system and the labels on the questionnaires were in the metric system. Although explicit instructions were given during training that the measuring units were to be recorded from the equipment and not converted by the anthropometrists, these instructions were not followed uniformly. In the end, some field workers recorded weights in pounds and others in kilos. Despite several attempts in the ex post facto (not concurrent)[82] data entry to rectify the situation, the anthropometric data from that year had to be discarded.

The procedures for purchasing will vary according to the item, cost, and rules of the country or agency financing the survey. Moreover, the tasks in procurement for LSMS surveys are no different from those for procurement in general. Thus it is not necessary to discuss the "how to" in detail here, but an

---

82. If the survey had been organized using the standard two- round interview and concurrent decentralized data entry, the problem probably could have been caught early enough to solve it in the field. The Jamaican survey, however, uses a single interview, a short period of field work (usually about 10 weeks), and ex post facto data entry.

outline of when the various times will be needed is provided. The survey planner will have to work out the details based on country-specific arrangements.

MAKE LOGISTIC ARRANGEMENTS FOR CORE STAFF. Essential tasks here include obtaining and equipping office premises from which the core team can work and deciding on transportation procedures for these staff.

ACQUIRE ANTHROPOMETRIC EQUIPMENT. If the survey includes an anthropometric module, special equipment must be bought and the procurement procedures initiated well in advance because the suppliers of good quality equipment are few and probably far away. The measuring boards and scales used in clinics are not suitable for field work.

ACQUIRE COMPUTERS. In addition to the computers and printers needed for each field team, a few extra machines will have to be acquired for the core staff in the statistical agency headquarters. The field machines will only be needed at the time of data entry operator training (about two months before the survey starts), but the core staff machines should be available as soon as possible because they will be needed for some early tasks like questionnaire development.

ACQUIRE SURVEY MATERIALS. The interviewers will need standard equipment such as pencils, erasers, clipboards, simple pocket calculators, and briefcases in which to carry the questionnaires. Badges and credentials should be produced so the interviewers can identify themselves. In some countries interviewers may also need items such as boots and raincoats. (For the Côte d'Ivoire LSMS, each team was also provided with a tent and campbeds!) How many and what kinds of items are needed will depend on the climate and the availability of lodgings.

MOBILITY STRATEGY AND VEHICLE ACQUISITION. The decision will have to be made on whether to acquire cars for all teams or if some of them can rely on public transportation. Vehicle procurement is usually a long procedure that should be initiated as soon as possible so that the cars are available before the survey goes to the field. However, even an efficient bureaucracy is unlikely to produce the cars on time for certain pre-survey activities such as the field testing or the household listing operation. Special arrangements may need to be made to have a few vehicles available early on. They may be borrowed from the existing fleet or rented.

If public transportation is to be used, other logistical issues should also be considered. It will have to be decided, for example, how and by whom the transportation budget will be managed (ideally, it should be managed by the team supervisors, but the accounting procedures should be devised so that they are neither too lax nor too bureaucratic). In a few countries, government employees on official business receive reduced or zero fares on public transportation. Where this arrangement is to be used, the appropriate credentials and authorizations should be obtained.

PUBLICITY AND HOUSEHOLD MOTIVATION STRATEGY. The use of mass media and preparation of targeted motivational materials can be developed in parallel with the rest of the preliminary tasks. It is best to initiate these activities early because they tend to require substantial attention from the survey manager.

Questionnaire Development

IDENTIFY POLICY-RELEVANT ISSUES. The main issues to be addressed by the survey should be made explicit as early as possible. Meetings with the various interested parties should be scheduled, either on a short and intense timetable or over a longer period. Often key decisions will be made when the international technical assistants are present on a series of short trips. Decisions on successively more detailed issues can be made on each trip.

PREPARE DRAFT OF THE HOUSEHOLD QUESTIONNAIRE. The hard part of this task is, of course, the intellectual translation of relevant concepts and policy issues into concrete questions, a theme already addressed in Chapter 3. However, the mechanical part of the process — that is, the physical production of a lengthy paper document — cannot be overlooked or, worse, considered to be a clerical job that can be delegated to a secretary. Though it is usually done on a computer, questionnaire drafting is *not* the job of the data manager either. More often than not the survey manager will have to assume this task personally. Efficient word processing software makes drafting the questionnaire easier, but it will probably take two months or more to complete. In fact, the job should be spread over more calendar months to allow comments as needed.

Extra time may be needed for translations. If only the final questionnaire is to be translated into one or more commonly spoken languages, two or three weeks may be sufficient. If translations are needed to facilitate the discussions among local and international members of the team drafting the questionnaire, two to three weeks will be needed just to translate the first draft. Several more days may be needed for each subsequent draft and to update the translation to reflect revisions made in the drafts.

DISTRIBUTE DRAFT OF THE HOUSEHOLD QUESTIONNAIRE. Two weeks to a month should be allowed for international consultants, data users, subject-matter specialists in international agencies, local sectoral ministries, and academics to analyze the draft. The process of revision and comments may be repeated two or three times if necessary.

SEMINAR. Some of the people to whom the draft questionnaire will be distributed will provide written comments, but more feedback can be obtained from a brief seminar of one or two days, conducted one month after the draft is circulated.

FINALIZE THE DRAFT AND PLAN THE FIELD TEST. While the questionnaire draft is being revised (usually for about two weeks, and maybe for two more weeks if it has to be translated at this stage), logistical arrangements for the field test can be completed. These include selecting and briefing a small number of experienced interviewers, who will conduct the field test along with the core staff, and ensuring their transportation, lodging, and communications during the field test. Around 200 questionnaires will have to be reproduced, probably by photocopying rather than printing.

FIELD TESTING THE QUESTIONNAIRE. At least four weeks should be allowed to field-test the questionnaire, with one or two additional weeks to review it in the central office. As explained in Chapter 3, the personal participation of the survey core staff, the survey planner, and experienced consultants in both activities is extremely important. This requires appropriate scheduling to guarantee that their participation is possible.

PRINT HOUSEHOLD QUESTIONNAIRE. It is never a good idea to put too much pressure on a print shop because small flaws in the printing can cause large problems in field work. Plenty of time should be allowed and proper quality control procedures should be agreed on with the printers. There should be frequent, regular monitoring of the work by the core team. About five weeks should be allowed in total.

PREPARE COMMUNITY AND PRICE QUESTIONNAIRES. The community and price questionnaires should be developed in parallel with the household questionnaire. These questionnaires are not a major undertaking, compared with the household questionnaire, but they have a tendency to be overlooked. Some check points on these questionnaires' development should be established during the months of survey preparation. Ideally, these questionnaires should be field tested at the same time as the household questionnaire, though as explained in Chapter 3 constraints in manpower may dictate that they be tested at a different time.

Sampling

SAMPLE DESIGN. This part of the survey planning process is as much a financial and political issue as it is a technical one, and its broader parameters (such as total sample size and stratification) are often decided along with the idea of conducting the survey. If this has not been the case, an early decision must be made on the number of explicit strata and how the sample will be allocated among them. Also, the number of households to be visited in each cluster has to be determined and from it the number of clusters to select in each stratum. The length of time required to reach these decisions depends largely on the difficulty of establishing a consensus. As little as two weeks or as long as two months may be required.

DEVELOP THE SAMPLE FRAME. The actual implementation of this task may vary widely among different countries. If there is no recent census or if the census records are not properly kept, developing a sample frame may take several months and have a substantial impact on the survey budget. In countries with a recent census and strong statistical capabilities, developing the sampling frame may require virtually no work at all.

SELECT SAMPLING UNITS. This consists of sorting the sample frame according to any desired implicit stratification criteria and selecting the required number of primary sampling units in each stratum with probability proportional to size (PPS). This used to be a major undertaking B.C. (before computers), but now it can be done in a few days at most if the sample frame is in a computer file.

PLAN THE FIELD ASSIGNMENTS. The selected clusters need to be distributed among the field teams and the order in which they will be visited throughout the year must be decided. Planning the task assignments can usually be completed in a few full-time days.

DWELLING LISTING AND CARTOGRAPHIC UPDATING. A new listing of dwellings or households will almost always be needed in the selected clusters[83]. The time and resources needed for the dwelling listing are to some extent country-specific, but a first rough estimate can be obtained by considering a yield of 80 dwellings per interviewer-day in urban areas and 50 in rural areas.

The maps of all selected CUs should be made available. Statistical agencies always prepare these maps as a part of the census operations, but they have a tendency to get lost shortly after the census so sometimes new ones will be needed. If this is the case, cartography and the dwelling listing should be planned in parallel to avoid prolonging the survey preparation period.

SELECT DWELLINGS IN EACH CLUSTER. A sample of the same number of dwellings is needed in each cluster. Additional dwellings should be selected to act as reserves in case a dwelling or household has to be replaced, as explained in Chapter 4. This task can be completed in about one full-time month in the central offices, either after the dwelling listing is completed for all CUs or as a parallel activity.

---

83. The 1995 Tunisia survey is an exception. The household listings were available for the whole country in a computer file prepared from the March 1994 census, which was both recent and of a very good quality.

Staffing and Training

SELECT AND TRAIN FIELD TEST STAFF. In addition to the core staff and consultants, a few interviewers should participate in the field test. They should be selected on the basis of their experience, given that they cannot be formally trained (there will be no manuals at that point of questionnaire development). Depending on their performance during the field test, they can be considered for later promotion to survey supervisors.

PREPARE SUPERVISION PROCEDURES AND SUPERVISOR AND INTERVIEWER MANUALS. Preparing the supervisor and interviewer manuals and the supervision forms are the field manager's most important tasks during the two-month period between the field test and interviewer training.

SELECT INTERVIEWERS. A larger number of interviewers than needed should be selected for training, to allow for a final choice after their performance is assessed during the practical part of the training.

The selection process should be initiated three to six weeks before the interviewer training is scheduled. Selection may take longer if the interviewers are to be hired externally rather than from the ranks of the statistical agency. It may also take longer, and even involve decentralized personnel searches, if interviewers with specific geographic, ethnic, or linguistic backgrounds are sought.

TRAIN INTERVIEWERS. Training should be held over four weeks, as explained in Chapter 5. It should include practical sessions of interviewing real households interspersed with classroom work on theory. This means that households that were not part of the field test and will not be part of the final sample must be selected for field training. Transportation must be arranged.

Anthropometric training should be treated as a separate module. A large supply of babies and children is needed for this aspect of training, and a nursery school willing to make its children available should be found near the training headquarters.

Data Management

PREPARE FIRST VERSION OF THE DATA ENTRY PROGRAM. The development of a first version of the data entry program should be started as soon as possible, because in addition to its obvious importance, it is also the first and most important training activity for the data manager. However, even a rough first version of the program cannot be initiated before a relatively developed questionnaire is available. Usually, this happens shortly before the field test.

Two to four weeks should be allowed to develop the first version of the data entry program. Much of this time will be absorbed in on-the-job training in conceptual issues related to data management for LSMS surveys. Thus the required time will not be determined primarily by the programming skill of the data manager but by the manager's experience with such complex surveys. As a part of the training, the questionnaire's organization into sections and modules will be translated into a set of data entry screens and as many of these screens as possible will be designed. Fields and ranges for all variables and the corresponding intra-record checks must be defined for each screen.

FINAL VERSION AND DEBUGGING OF THE DATA ENTRY PROGRAM. While the questionnaire is field tested and finalized, the data manager will complete the design and intra-record check definition for the rest of the screens. It is generally better to postpone the definition and programming of inter-record checks until all or most of the individual screens have reached their final form.

The survey data manager is the main person responsible for testing and debugging the program thoroughly. However, the first real test of the program comes while the interviewers and data entry operators are trained, when actual questionnaires will be completed and entered. Generally still more refining and debugging is necessary after the first month of field operations.

DATA ENTRY MANUAL. The data entry manual can be written in about two weeks.

COMPUTER INSTALLATION AND DATA ENTRY OPERATOR TRAINING. The data entry computers should be initially installed in one large room at the statistical agency central offices or in some other room made available for the training of the data entry operators. It is better to start thinking about the logistical implications well in advance, because finding adequate premises may be harder than it seems (a frequent problem is ensuring a safe and adequate power supply and plugs for all the machines).

The operators are trained at the same time as the interviewers in theoretical and practical sessions. This means the operators enter the data on the questionnaires actually completed by interviewers during the practical part of their training.

When training is completed, the computers must be moved to the teams' base stations throughout the country. It is technically possible for each operator to carry and install the team's own computer personally (this must be part of the training anyway), but in some countries this may void the supplier's guarantee. In this case, different arrangements are needed.

DATA MANAGEMENT PROCEDURES. The task of the data manager is to consolidate all the information arriving from the field,[84] to ensure its completeness (that is, establish that each data entry operator is sending data for all the households the team was supposed to visit), and to prepare the unit record data sets to be released to the survey analysts. Consolidation is usually done on a monthly basis.

It is better to postpone the data manager's training on data set formation until after the field test. The reason is that these operations are very different from the previous task of preparing and debugging the data entry program and they call for different skills (the former requires imagination, whereas the later requires discipline). It is also better to test the central data management procedures with the actual survey data that will be available after the field test.

Field Work

PILOT TEST OF FIELD PROCEDURES. As explained in Chapter 5, a separate pilot test of field procedures is rarely used in LSMS surveys. Instead, a review of the field experience is made after the first month of field work. The review itself will take one to two weeks. If a formal field test before the beginning of field work is planned, it should take place after the questionnaire has been field tested and the data entry program completed, but before the field staff is trained. This may add as much as two months to the preparation period, which could be inserted about month 10 in Figure 8.1.

FIELDING THE SURVEY. The survey should be fielded as soon as possible after interviewers and data entry operators are trained. However, usually at least one week must be allowed for the data entry computers to be moved to and installed at the field teams' base stations. The survey will be in the field for one year.

Data Analysis and Documentation

PRELIMINARY STATISTICAL ABSTRACT. The first plan of tabulations can be made after the survey has been in the field for about four months. The list of tables can be circulated among the users for comment. Then as soon as the first six months' data are available, work can begin on the first statistical abstract. It usually takes about two weeks to prepare the data for analysis and four to six weeks to prepare the abstract. It should be disseminated widely. A month or so after the abstract has been made available, a seminar should be held. This will give the survey further publicity, but more importantly can be used to critique the preliminary abstract so that the final abstract reflects the users' interests.

---

84. Exactly how this is done depends on the software used for data entry. In most of the LSMS surveys conducted so far, each household is kept as a separate file and the information is transferred from the field stations to the central office in lots made by month or by CU.

STATISTICAL ABSTRACT. A polished version of the statistical abstract should be assembled from the full year's data. This can usually be prepared within about three months of the end of field work. The final data will take a week or so to come in from the field. Constructing the complete data sets will then take approximately two weeks. Analysis itself will take about four to six weeks. Note that many of the analytic programs used in the preliminary abstract will require only minor modifications.

DATA SET DOCUMENTATION AND DISSEMINATION. The basic survey documentation should be prepared concurrently with the abstract. This normally takes about two to four weeks. Mechanisms to permanently support the dissemination of the basic documentation and data sets should be set in place.

FURTHER ANALYSIS. More in-depth analysis will continue over months and years. Some may be financed specifically under the project that paid for data collection, more may be sponsored from other sources.

Annex I. Description of Questionnaires from Viet Nam LSMS

Survey Questionnaires

Household Questionnaire

The household questionnaire contains modules (sections) to collect data on household demographic structure, education, health, employment, migration, housing conditions, fertility, agricultural activities, household non-agricultural businesses, food expenditures, non-food expenditures, remittances and other income sources, savings and loans, and anthropometric (height and weight) measures.

For some sections (survey information, housing, respondents for second round, remittances and other incomes, credit and savings) the individual designated by the household members as the household head provided responses. For some others (agro-pastoral activities, non-farm self employment, food expenditures, non-food expenditures) a member identified as most knowledgeable provided responses. Identification codes for respondents of different sections indicate who provided the information. In sections where the information collected pertains to individuals (education, health, employment, migration, fertility) each member of the household was asked to respond for himself or herself, except that parents were allowed to respond for younger children. In the case of the employment and fertility sections it is possible that the information was not provided by the relevant person; variables in these sections indicate when · this is the case.

The household questionnaire was completed in two interviews two weeks apart. Sections 0-8 were administered in the first interview, sections 9-14 in the second interview, and section 15 in both interviews. The survey was designed so that sensitive issues such as savings were discussed near the end. The content of each module is briefly described below.

I. FIRST INTERVIEW

Section 0 SURVEY INFORMATION
   0A HOUSEHOLD HEAD AND RESPONDENT INFORMATION
   0B SUMMARY OF SURVEY RESULTS
   0C OBSERVATIONS AND COMMENTS

The date of the interview, the religion and ethnic group of the household head, the language used by the respondent, and other technical information related to the interview are noted. Section 0B summarizes the results of the survey visits, i.e., whether a section was completed on the first visit or the second visit. Section 0C, not entered into the computer, contains remarks of the interviewer and the supervisor. Since the data on Section 0C are retained only on the

212

questionnaires, researchers cannot gain access to them without checking the original questionnaires in Hanoi.

Section 1 HOUSEHOLD MEMBERSHIP
  1A HOUSEHOLD ROSTER
  1B INFORMATION ON PARENTS OF HOUSEHOLD MEMBERS
  1C CHILDREN RESIDING ELSEWHERE

The roster in Section 1A lists the age, sex, marital status, and relation to household head of all people who spent the previous night in that household and for household members who are temporarily away from home. The household head is listed first and receives the personal ID code of 1. Household members were defined to include "all the people who normally live and eat their meals together in this dwelling." Those who were absent more than nine of the last twelve months were excluded, except for the head of the household and infants less than three months old. A lunar calendar is provided in the questionnaire to help respondents recall the year and month they were born. For individuals who are married and whose spouse resides in the household, the personal ID number of the spouse is noted. This way information on the spouse can be collected by appropriately merging information from the roster and other parts of the survey.

Section 1B collects information on the parents of all household members. For individuals whose parents reside in the household, parents' personal ID numbers are noted, and information can be obtained by appropriately merging information from other parts of the survey. For individuals whose parents do not reside in the household, information is recorded on whether each parent is alive, as well as their schooling and occupation.

In section 1C information is collected for children of household members living elsewhere. This information is only collected for children below thirty years of age. Children who have died are not included. All living children are listed along with the personal ID number of their father and mother (if parents reside in the household). Then information on the age, schooling, and current place of residence of each such child is recorded.

Section 2 SCHOOLING

In Section 2, data were collected on self-reported literacy and numeracy, school attendance, completion, and current enrollment for all household members of creche or pre-school age and older. The interpretation of creche or pre-school age appears to have varied, with the result that while education information is available for some children of pre-school age, not all pre-school children were included in this section. But for ages six and above information is available for nearly all individuals, so in essence the data on schooling can be said to apply to all persons ages six and above. For those who were enrolled in school at the time of the survey, information on school attendance, distance, travel time, expenses, and scholarships was also collected.

Annex I

Section 3   HEALTH

Data on any illness or injury experienced in the 4 weeks preceding the date of interview were obtained for all household members in this section. For those who reported being ill in the past 4 weeks, information was obtained on the duration and type of illness, type of care sought, distance to health provider, travel time, and cost of medication and consultation. All individuals, whether or not ill in the past 4 weeks, were asked if they had been ill in the year before the survey, and if so the total amount they had spent on health care in the previous year. At the request of the World Health Organization, several questions on smoking were asked of all individuals 6 years of age and older.

Section 4   EMPLOYMENT
        4A TYPE OF WORK AND JOB SEARCH
        4B MAIN JOB DURING THE PAST SEVEN DAYS
        4C SECONDARY JOB DURING THE PAST SEVEN DAYS
        4D SEARCH FOR ADDITIONAL EMPLOYMENT
        4E MAIN JOB DURING THE PAST TWELVE MONTHS
        4F EMPLOYMENT HISTORY
        4G SECONDARY JOB DURING THE PAST TWELVE MONTHS
        4H OTHER ACTIVITIES

All individuals age six and older were asked to respond to the economic activity questions in Section 4, beginning with questions on the nature of their work in the last seven days. For persons who did not work in last seven days, data were collected on job search, and reason for not seeking employment. For work in last seven days, information was collected on hours, length of employment, type of employer, taxes, distance and travel time to place of work, money and in-kind compensation, and benefits. Similar questions were asked on the secondary job in the last seven days. Questions were asked on search for additional employment, including the kind of work sought and the lowest acceptable wage. If main work in the last twelve months was different from the main or secondary job in the last seven days, the complete set of questions was answered for that work as well. Type of work and years of experience at any work prior to that of the main job in the last twelve months were collected. Again, if there was a secondary job in the last twelve months different from the other jobs, data on work conditions and compensation were collected. Days and hours spent doing household chores were collected for each household member age seven and older.

Occupation and sector of employment codes are not available in the household questionnaire. These appear in the supervisor's manual.

Section 5   MIGRATION

All household members age 15 or older responded to the questions on migration in Section 5. If not born at current place of residence, respondents

214

were asked whether the place of birth was a village, town, city, or other. The age at which such individuals left their place of birth was recorded, as well as the main reason for leaving. In addition, individuals were asked the main reason for coming to the current place of residence, from what region they had come to the current place, and whether the previous place was a village, town or city. Finally, respondents were asked how many places they had lived for periods of more than three months in their life.

Section 6 HOUSING
6A TYPE OF DWELLING
6B HOUSING EXPENSES
6C HOUSING CHARACTERISTICS

Section 6 contains information on the type of dwelling, housing expenses, and housing characteristics for all households interviewed. Information was collected on the number of rooms in the dwelling, ownership status, wall material, roof material, water source, toilet type, utilities expenses, and square meters of living area. Respondents for all 4,800 households, regardless of whether the dwelling was owned or rented, were asked for the resale value of the dwelling. This section also contains information on type of cooking fuel used, the time and distance involved in collecting wood, and whether it is the primary cooking fuel used by the household.

Section 7 RESPONDENTS CHOSEN FOR ROUND TWO (the second interview)

In Section 7, the principal respondent for Round One was asked to identify: 1) the household member who knows the most about all the agricultural and livestock activities of the household; 2) the household member who shops for food; and 3) the household member who knows the most about the other household expenses, income, and savings of household members. The respondent was also asked to identify the three most important businesses and trades belonging to the household, and the household members who know most about them. Finally, a woman was selected at random from among the women in the household between the ages of 15 and 49 to respond to the fertility module.

In principle, those identified in this section for interviewing in later sections should be the ones who are actually interviewed in those sections. While this is true for many households there are some cases where the respondents for the agriculture, food expense, and non-food expense sections are different from those identified in this section. This is possible if the person identified was not present at the time the section was completed (i.e., during the second visit to the household).

Section 8 FERTILITY
8A FERTILITY HISTORY
8B FAMILY PLANNING

In each household one woman 15-49 years old, randomly selected in Section 7, responded to the questions in Section 8. If a household contained no woman in this age range, Section 8 was not completed. The woman was asked if she had ever been pregnant and, if so, whether she had ever given birth. Women who respond that they have are asked the birth date and sex of all children they have given birth to, including children who did not survive. If the child is not alive the woman is asked how long it survived. The woman is asked about the birth and breastfeeding of her last child, the age at which she was married, and the number of miscarriages she has had. Section 8B gathers information on knowledge, use, source, and cost of six modern and six traditional methods of family planning. In using data from this section it should be kept in mind that unlike the Demographic and Health Surveys and the World Fertility Surveys, interviewers were not necessarily women.

II. SECOND INTERVIEW

Section 9 AGRO-PASTORAL ACTIVITIES
        9A1 AGRICULTURAL LAND
        9A2 FOREST LAND
        9A3 SELLING OR BUYING LAND
        9A4 VACANT LOT, BALD HILL, LAND CLEARING RECLAMATION
        9A5 AGRICULTURAL TAXES
        9B1 PADDY
        9B2 OTHER FOOD CROPS
        9B3 ANNUAL INDUSTRIAL CROPS
        9B4 PERENNIAL INDUSTRIAL CROPS
        9B5 FRUIT CROPS
        9B6 FOREST TREES
        9C CROP BYPRODUCTS
        9D FARM INPUTS
        9E TRANSFORMATION OF HOMEGROWN CROPS
        9F LIVESTOCK
        9G OTHER ANIMAL PRODUCTS
        9H RAISING/PLANTING WATER PRODUCTS
        9I EXTENSION CONTACTS FOR LIVESTOCK
        9J LIVESTOCK EXPENDITURES
        9K HAND TOOLS
        9L FARMING EQUIPMENT

In Section 9 the respondent was the household member identified in Section 7 as the one most knowledgeable about the household's agricultural and pastoral activities. Most questions refer to the past twelve months. This section is by far the largest section of the household questionnaire, with many subsections that contain information on different aspects of agricultural production and related livestock activities — collectively referred to as agro-pastoral activities.

Sections 9A1 to 9A5 collect information on household's control over land of different tenures. These include land allocated by the commune, auctioned land, privately held land, rented/sharecropped land, and swidden land. In each case data are obtained on total land size, size of irrigated land, and payments for use of land. For annual crop land information is also obtained on quality of land. Similar information is obtained on water surface cultivated, forest land controlled, land reclaimed from a bald hill, newly ploughed land, and roadside/riverside land. In these sections data are also obtained on purchases and sales of land, and land taxes paid by the household.

Section 9B1 to 9B6 contain detailed output information for all crops grown by the household. This information is obtained separately for each crop and includes (in most cases) information on quantity produced, value of output, quantity sold in the market and given to the cooperative, quantity kept for seeds, quantity fed to livestock, and quantity given as gifts. In the case of paddy information is obtained, separately, for the summer crop, winter crop, and the autumn crop. It should be remembered that while data is obtained for each crop cultivated by a household, it is not possible to link the information on land tenure (and size) with output information to determine the tenure structure of land on which a certain crop is cultivated — unless a household cultivates only one crop on the land it cultivates. Section 9C contains information on crop byproducts.

Section 9D obtains detailed information on seeds, manure, fertilizer, insecticides, and transportation for all crops cultivated by a household. This information is also crop-specific and can, theoretically, be linked with the output information in the earlier sections by matching the datasets by household codes and crop codes. Information on other inputs such as hired labor, packing and storage costs, etc., are obtained at an aggregated level for each household. Other crop-specific information obtained in this section consists of data on home consumption and on the use of agricultural extension services.

Section 9E contains information on transformation of home grown crops that were subsequently sold. This includes data on output for sale, codes of household members who participated in the production process, number of sales, revenues from these sales, and costs of production. Section 9F collects information on livestock, poultry, and other animals that are either consumed by a household or generate income. These data include an inventory of current numbers possessed, the numbers born, sold, consumed, given away or lost, and the numbers bought by a household. Also included is information on the value of current stocks, revenue from sales, and purchase costs. Section 9G then collects information on animal products such as milk, eggs, silk, manure, etc. Here information is restricted to revenue from sales. In section 9H similar information is collected for water animals (fish, shrimp, etc.).

Section 9I collects information on extension services for livestock, and section 9J contains information on livestock expenditures. Finally, section 9L and 9K collect data on implements and farm machinery owned by the household.

Section 10 NON-FARM SELF-EMPLOYMENT
10A WORKING CONDITIONS
10B EXPENDITURES
10C REVENUES
10D BUSINESS ASSETS

Section 10 gathers data on household businesses for the three most important enterprises operated by the household. The respondent for each enterprise is the household member most familiar with its operation (as identified in Section 7). Data are gathered on the ownership, number of employees, and type of employee compensation for each enterprise. For each business, expenditures over the last twelve months on wages, raw materials, and taxes are collected. The respondent is asked how much, in money and goods, was received from sales and how much of the enterprise's product was consumed by the household since the first interview. Information on ownership, sales and purchases of assets — buildings, land, vehicles, tools and other durable goods — in the last twelve months is also collected.

Section 11 FOOD EXPENSES AND HOME PRODUCTION
11A HOLIDAY EXPENSES
11B NORMAL EXPENSES

In Section 11A the amounts spent on holidays, primarily Tet (New Year), 15th January, 15th July, Moon festival, and Independence day. The range of food items for which such expense information is obtained is smaller than that for which information is obtained in the Section 11B. The main reason for separating holiday expenses from normal expenses, a departure from the standard LSMS survey format, is to take into account the fact that the Tet holiday in Viet Nam often represents significant departures from normal spending patterns — particularly unusually high expenditures.

Section 11B collects detailed information on market purchases and consumption from home production for forty-five food items. Information is obtained for expenses since the interviewer's first visit. For a longer recall period (twelve months) data are obtained on which months (in the preceding twelve months) each food item was purchased, the number of times purchases were made during those months, the quantity purchased each time, and the value per purchase. These four pieces of information can be combined to obtain the total expenditure on food in the twelve months before the date of the interview. Note that this, in effect, is a variable-recall procedure because the time frame for which purchase information is provided by a respondent can differ for two food items, as well as across respondents. Besides market purchases (including barter), information is also collected on consumption from home production. Again data are obtained on which months each item was consumed, but unlike market purchases, the quantity and value of consumption information applies to the whole year.

Section 12 NON-FOOD EXPENDITURES & INVENTORY OF DURABLE GOODS

    12A DAILY EXPENSES
    12B ANNUAL EXPENSES
    12C INVENTORY OF DURABLE GOODS
    12D EXPENSES FOR REMITTANCES

Section 12 collects information on non-food household expenditures from the household member identified in Section 7 as the one most able to answer non-food expenditure questions. In section 12A respondents were asked to recall the amount spent since the first interview (approximately two weeks) on daily expenses such as lottery tickets, cigarettes, soap, personal care products, cooking fuel, matches and candles, and gasoline. In section 12B expenditure data, both in the last two weeks *and* the last twelve months, were collected for shoes, cloth, clothing, home repairs, public transport, paper supplies, kitchen equipment, medical services, domestic servants, jewelry, entertainment, and other goods (see household questionnaire). Purchase price, year of purchase, and resale value of durable goods owned were collected in Section 12C. Relation and location of the recipients of remittances sent out from the household are noted in Section 12D (remittances received by the household are recorded in Section 13A).

Section 13 OTHER INCOME

    13A INCOME FROM REMITTANCES
    13B MISCELLANEOUS INCOME

Section 13 collects data on money and goods that come into the household as remittances or from other sources unrelated to employment, such as employee welfare funds, dowries, sale of consumer durables, rental of buildings, etc.

Section 14 CREDIT AND SAVING

    14A MONEY AND GOODS LENT AND BORROWED
    14B LOANS CONTRACTED
    14C SAVINGS

Section 14 collects information on the amount of indebtedness of household members to people or institutions outside the household. If money or goods have been borrowed, or borrowed and repaid by any household member in the last twelve months, information is collected on those loans, including the source and amount of the loan, interest, side payments, collateral, repayment schedule, reason for borrowing, and number of loans from the same source. The household is asked to list the location of its savings, if any, including bank, housing savings bank, rural savings bank, foreign currency account, other bank accounts, bonds, stocks and home. The respondent is also asked the total value of all savings accounts.

Annex I

Section 15 ANTHROPOMETRICS

Anthropometric measurements are completed for each household member. Data were collected on the household member's age, gender, date of measurement, weight, height, and arm circumference. It was also noted if female respondents were pregnant or breastfeeding. If a person was not measured the reason why is noted.

Community Questionnaire

A Community questionnaire was administered by the team supervisor and completed with the help of village chiefs, teachers, government officials and health care workers. The questionnaire was administered only in rural areas, i.e. commune numbers 1 to 120.

Section 1 (DEMOGRAPHIC INFORMATION) includes the population of the community, a list of principal ethnic groups and religions, the length of time the community has existed and whether or not it has grown. Section 2 (ECONOMY AND INFRASTRUCTURE) questions include a list of principal economic activities, access to a motorable road, electricity, pipe-borne water, restaurant or food stall, post office, bank, daily market and public transport. There are also questions on employment, migration for jobs, and the existence of community development projects. Section 3 (EDUCATION) asks distance to primary and middle schools. For up to three primary schools, the nearest middle school, and the nearest secondary school, information is obtained on whether it is public or private, whether it is for boys or girls, or both, how many classes there are, and when it was built. Enrollment rates and reasons why children do not attend school are also collected. Section 4 (HEALTH) collects data on distance and travel time to the nearest of each of several types of health workers (doctor, nurse, pharmacist, midwife, family planning worker, community health worker, traditional birth attendant and traditional healer) and each type of several types of health facilities (hospital, dispensary, pharmacy, maternity home, health post and family planning clinic). The questions in Section 5 (AGRICULTURE) include the type of crops grown in the community, how often and when they are planted and harvested, and how the harvest is generally sold. This section also includes questions on the availability of an extension center, agricultural cooperatives, and machinery, and questions on the use of pesticides and irrigation. Qualitative data on the last year's rainfall, the local land market, the prevalence of sharecropping, and agricultural and non-agricultural wages in the community are also gathered.

Price Questionnaire

In rural areas (commune numbers 1 to 120), price data were collected by the team supervisor for thirty-six food items, thirty-one nonfood items, nine medicines, seven insecticides/fertilizers, and five types of services from local

220

markets. Three separate observations were made and these did not necessarily involve actual purchases. In some communes fewer than three observations were made, either because of a lack of three distinct markets, or for some other reason. A separate set of prices are available for urban areas (commune numbers 121 to 150). These were collected by the General Statistical Office as part of a separate effort to construct a spatial price index, and their values appear to be comparable to those of the rural prices.

Annex II. Annotated List of Selected References

THE SOCIAL DIMENSION OF ADJUSTMENT SURVEY PROGRAM

Delaine, Ghislaine and others. 1992. *The Social Dimensions of Adjustment Integrated Survey: A Survey to Measure Poverty and Understand the Effects of Policy Change on Households.* Social Dimensions of Adjustment Working Paper No. 14. World Bank, Washington, D.C.
The SDA Integrated Survey is quite similar to the LSMS survey — indeed an outgrow from them. Unlike this manual, the SDA manual gives particular attention to explaining the objectives of the survey, the content of the prototype questionnaire and its analysis. It puts more emphasis on some of the theoretical issues in sampling and data management. However, it was written at the beginning of the SDA survey program, before a body of practical experience had been amassed.

Marchant, Timothy, and Christiaan Grootaert. 1991. *The Social Dimensions of Adjustment Priority Survey.* World Bank, Washington.
The SDA Priority Survey is designed as a lighter survey that uses a much shorter questionnaire and a larger sample to gather information which is less detailed but covers many of the same topics as the LSMS or the SDA IS. This manual contents are analogous to that of the manual on the Integrated Survey.

INSTITUTIONAL ISSUES IN PROJECT DESIGN

Grosh, Margaret E. 1991. *The Household Survey as a Tool for Policy Change: Lessons from the Jamaica Survey of Living Conditions.* Living Standards Measurement Study Working Paper No. 80. World Bank, Washington, D.C.
Using the Jamaican survey as a case study, Grosh discusses seven strategic choices in designing a survey project. Among others, these include how much and how to build institutional capacity, how to involve users in steering the survey, and how much emphasis to put on speed vs quality in data collection.

QUESTIONNAIRE DESIGN

In addition to the references to existing materials provided below, the reader should keep abreast of the results of a major research initiative launched in 1995. It undertakes a complete review and critique of the content of the LSMS questionnaires and will make recommendations for changes that should be adopted.

General Overview

Grootaert, Christiaan. 1986. *Measuring and Analyzing the Level of Living in Developing Countries: An Annotated Questionnaire.* Living Standards Measurement Study Working Paper No. 24. World Bank, Washington, D.C.

This document frequently serves as the description of the LSMS "prototype" questionnaire. Some improvements and many country specific variations have been made since, but only one other nicely annotated questionnaire is available, so this remains a classic reference.

Ainsworth, Martha, Godlike Koda, George Lwihula, Phare Mujinja, Mead Over, and Innocent Semali. 1992. *Measuring the Impact of Fatal Adult Illness in Sub-Saharan Africa: An Annotated Household Questionnaire.* Living Standards Measurement Study Working Paper No. 90. World Bank, Washington, D.C.
The Tanzania survey is one of the most specialized and most ambitious of the LSMS surveys. This questionnaire is interesting not only because it is well documented, but because it goes farther than most in trying to address time use, intrahousehold allocation issues, household dynamics, and behavior related to illness and death. Some parts of it may be too detailed to be of interest in more general-purpose surveys.

Ainsworth, Martha, and Jacques van der Gaag. 1988. *Guidelines for Adapting the LSMS Living Standards Questionnaires to Local Conditions.* Living Standards Measurement Study Working Paper No. 34. World Bank, Washington, D.C.
This discusses how to think about changing sections, emphasis, and wording of the questionnaires used in Côte d'Ivoire and Peru to make them applicable to a new country. The document is a good beginning, though the changes it suggests may not be deep enough. Also, since the document was written early in the history of LSMS surveys, few real-life examples are incorporated.

United Nations National Household Survey Capability Programme (UNNHSCP). 1985. *Development and Design of Survey Questionnaires.* United Nations Department of Technical Cooperation for Development and Statistical Office, New York.
This is a basic primer on issues of measurement, question formulation, and questionnaire formatting. Because the manual tries to address all kinds of surveys, treatment is confined to a rather general level.

Experiences with Specific Modules

Grosh, Margaret E., and Henri-Pierre Jeancard. 1995. "The Sensitivity of Consumption Aggregates to Data Collection Methods: Some Preliminary Evidence from the Jamaican and Ghanaian LSMS Surveys." Poverty and Human Resources Division, Policy Research Department, World Bank, Washington, D.C.
This paper addresses the sensitivity of consumption estimates to three variations in the consumption module: the length of recall period used; the omission of some sub-components; and the use of an alternative point-of-purchase orientation for the questions.

Jolliffe, Dean. 1995. "Review of the LSMS Agricultural Activities Survey Module." Poverty and Human Resources Division, Policy Research Department, World Bank, Washington, D.C.
This paper reviews the experience with the Ghana and Viet Nam LSMS agricultural modules. Minor changes are suggested to the module when its purpose is to measure net farm income. Suggestions are made for much larger reformulations when its purpose is to understand farm behavior.

Scott, Christopher, and Ben Amenuvegbe. 1990. *Effect of Recall Duration on Reporting of Household Expenditures: An Experimental Study in Ghana.* Social Dimensions of Adjustment in Sub-Saharan Africa Working Paper No. 6. World Bank, Washington, D.C.
Analysis of a special experiment shows that for frequently purchased items, recall erodes rapidly over short time periods.

Vijverberg, Wim. 1991. *Measuring Income from Family Enterprises with Household Surveys.* Living Standards Measurement Study Working Paper No. 84. World Bank, Washington, D.C.
After reviewing the data from the Côte d'Ivoire, Peru 1985, and Ghana LSMS data sets, Vijverberg shows that the estimates of enterprise income resulting from different approaches to calculation (profits, net revenues, earnings) are not consistent. He proposes some modifications to the module.

World Bank. 1993. *Indonesia: Public Expenditures, Prices and the Poor.* Report No. 11293-IND. Indonesia Resident Mission, Country Department III, East Asia and Pacific Region, Washington, D.C.
Analysis of a data collection experiment in the Indonesia SUSENAS survey suggests that very short consumption modules can give results very similar to those from much longer and more costly modules. The data chapter also discusses the core and rotating module design of the survey and the choices made in reforming it.

SAMPLING

Cochran, William G. 1977. *Sampling Techniques*, 3rd ed., New York; John Wiley and Sons.

Kish, Leslie. 1965. *Survey Sampling*. John Wiley and Sons: New York.

Azorin Poch, Ernesto. 1967. *Curso de Muestreo y Aplicaciones*. Aguilar S.A.: Madrid.
The above references are among the classics of the field. The drawback is that they were all written before the modern computer age. What is now feasible is different, so some of the recommendations are no longer well justified, and certain branches of the field are underdeveloped.

Verma, Vijay. 1991. *Sampling Methods: Training Handbook.* Statistical Institute for Asia and the Pacific, Tokyo.
This is an excellent Introduction to sampling as it is actually practiced in household surveys, at a level that is deeper than was possible in this manual yet less academic than the classics.

Grosbras, Jean-Marie, and Jean-Claude Deville. 1987. *Algorithmes de Tirage* (in Droesbeke, Jean Jacques, et.al., editors. *Les Sondages.* Economica, Paris.
Provides guidelines to develop algorithms for selecting samples from computerized files (with and without replacement, with PPS, etc.).

UNNHSCP. 1982. *Non-Sampling Errors in Household Surveys (Assessment and Control).* United Nations Department of Technical Cooperation for Development and Statistical Office, New York.
This document reviews the different sources and ways to control non-sampling errors, especially those stemming from inadequate or incomplete sample frames.

UNNHSCP. 1986b. *Sampling Frames and Sample Designs for Integrated Household Survey Programmes.* United Nations Department of Technical Cooperation for Development and Statistical Office, New York.
This manual covers how to design and to maintain sampling frames for integrated household survey programs. The reader may find particularly useful the discussion on listing and updating the sample frame which we passed over lightly in this manual. Extensive treatment is given to the use of master samples.

Scott, Christopher. 1990. *Master Sample: Advantages and Drawbacks.* Inter-stat, March 1990, No.2, 33-42. Eurostat/ODA/INSEE. French version: 1989. *Echantillon-maître: avantages et incovénients.* STATECO, Dec. 1989, No.60, p.91-105. INSEE.
Provides a balanced assessment of the pros and cons of master samples, based on the author's experience in nine Latin-American and Asian countries.

Howes, Stephen, and Jean Lanjouw. 1994. "Making Poverty Comparisons Taking Into Account Survey Design: How and Why." first draft. World Bank and Yale University.
This paper demonstrates the importance of adjusting standard errors for sample design features such as stratification and clustering. Sensitivity analysis is done using data sets from the Pakistan and Ghana LSMS surveys.

Sampling in LSMS Surveys

Coulombe, Harold, and Lionel Demery. 1993. *Household Size in Côte d'Ivoire: Sampling Bias in the CILSS.* Living Standards Measurement Study Working Paper No. 97. World Bank, Washington, D.C.

Household size as measured in the CILSS declined more from 1985 to 1988 than was plausible. The paper examines possible causes and concludes that changes in sampling procedures are the likely culprits.

Scott, Christopher, and Ben Amenuvegbe. 1989. *Sample Designs for the Living Standards Surveys in Ghana and Mauritania/Plans de sondage pour les enquêtes sur le niveau de vie au Ghana et en Mauritanie.* Living Standards Measurement Study Working Paper No. 49. World Bank, Washington, D.C.

After first-stage sampling with probability proportionate to size one can update the size measures and preserve self-weighting by re-allocating workloads: instead of one workload in each primary sampling unit, one allocates none, one, two, or (rarely) three. The paper explains how this was applied to two LSMS surveys.

ANTHROPOMETRICS

UNNHSCP. 1986a. *How to Weigh and Measure Children: Assessing the Nutritional Status of Young Children in Household Surveys.* United Nations Department of Technical Cooperation for Development and Statistical Office, New York.

The standard reference on how to carry out anthropometric measurements.

Kostermans, Kees. 1994. *Assessing the Quality of Anthropometric Data: Background and Illustrated Guidelines for Survey Managers.* Living Standards Measurement Study Working Paper No. 101. World Bank, Washington, D.C.

The sensitivity of estimates of malnutrition to errors in the measurements is simulated using data from the Pakistan LSMS survey. Suggestions are made for the analyst on how to assess the quality of existing data sets. Suggestions are made for survey planners on how to carry out quality control through supervision and data management.

DATA ANALYSIS

Examples of Simple Descriptive Analysis

A number of abstracts published by the governmental statistical institutes are available from the LSMS Division.

Glewwe, Paul. 1987a. *The Distribution of Welfare in Peru in 1985-86.* Living Standards Measurement Study Working Paper No. 42. World Bank, Washington, D.C.

Also available in French and Spanish. Something of an annotated abstract for the survey.

On Measuring Poverty

Ravallion, Martin. 1992. *Poverty Comparisons: A Guide to Concepts and Methods*. Living Standards Measurement Study Working Paper No. 88. World Bank, Washington, D.C.

A detailed primer on how to measure poverty and make comparisons between time periods or regions. Assumes some facility with mathematical notation, but little prior knowledge of the matter at hand.

Howes, Stephen, and Jean Olson Lanjouw. 1994. "Making Poverty Comparisons Taking Into Account Survey Design: How and Why." first draft. World Bank and Yale University.

Most poverty analysis is based on the assumption that the household surveys used are simple random samples of the national population. This is often not true — most are two or three-stage samples, many are not self-weighting, and stratification is common. This paper shows how to correct standard errors for common sample designs. It also provides empirical examples using the Pakistan and Ghana LSMS data. Correct standard errors for well-known poverty measures can be about one-third higher than uncorrected statistics.

Howes, Stephen. 1994. "SAS Dominance Module." draft. software package.

Howes has made publicly available a set of SAS routines to conduct statistical tests on differences between common measures of poverty, welfare, and inequality. The routines can be run using either the PC or mainframe versions of SAS.

Glewwe, Paul, and Jacques van der Gaag. 1988. *Confronting Poverty in Developing Countries: Definitions, Information and Policies*. Living Standards Measurement Study Working Paper No. 48. World Bank, Washington, D.C.

Illustrates the degrees to which different measures of household welfare identify the same households as poor using data from the Côte d'Ivoire LSMS.

Kakwani, Nanak. 1990. *Poverty and Economic Growth: With Application to Côte d'Ivoire*. Living Standards Measurement Study Working Paper No. 63. World Bank, Washington, D.C.

The paper explores the relationship between economic trends and poverty, and develops the methodology to measure separately the impact of changes in average income and income inequality on poverty. The methodology proposed is applied to the data taken from the 1985 Living Standards Survey in Côte d'Ivoire.

Ravallion, Martin, and Gaurav Datt. 1991. *Growth and Redistribution Components of Changes in Poverty Measures: A Decomposition with Applications to Brazil and India in the 1990s*. Living Standards Measurement Study Working Paper No. 83. World Bank, Washington, D.C.

The authors show how to parse changes in poverty measures between growth and redistribution components. Analysis is provided for Brazil and India.

Ravallion, Martin. 1994. "How Well Can Methodology Substitute for Data? Five Experiments in Poverty Analysis." Policy Research Department, World Bank, Washington, D.C.
One of the experiments is an attempt to forecast poverty using aggregate statistics (such as agricultural wages and yields) in the absence of household survey data. The paper finds that one-year forecasts are reasonably accurate, but that sizable drift can occur after just a year or two.

Sophisticated Analysis

The majority of the LSMS Working Papers contain applications of modern econometric modeling to household survey data. Many themes and countries are covered. The reader is advised to look at the full list of papers in the inside covers of recent working papers. The abstracts of the first 59 papers are contained in a booklet compiled by Brenda Rosa, and available from the same location as the LSMS Working Papers.

Deaton, Angus. 1994. "The Analysis of Household Surveys: Microeconometric Analysis for Development Policy." Book manuscript. Poverty and Human Resources Division, Policy Research Department, World Bank, Washington, D.C.
This book is designed as a reference text for the policy analyst new to the sophisticated analysis of household survey data. Although basic knowledge of statistics is assumed, the book goes to considerable effort to explain the intuition and policy relevance of the statistics and econometrics it teaches.

Demery, Lionel, Marco Ferroni, and Christiaan Grootaert. 1993. *Understanding the Social Effects of Policy Reform.* A World Bank Study. World Bank, Washington, D.C.
This is a compendium of thought on how to analyze the effects of policy reform (especially of the kinds of policies that comprise structural adjustment packages) on various social dimensions of welfare. Each chapter treats a separate issue — poverty, employment and earnings, migration, education, health, nutrition, fertility, women, and smallholder agriculture. The chapter authors are among the leading experts in applying household data to the topic at hand.

Annex III. LSMS Working Papers

No.	TITLE	AUTHOR
1	*Living Standards Surveys in Developing Countries*	Chander/Grootaert/Pyatt
2	*Poverty and Living Standards in Asia: An Overview of the Main Results and Lessons of Selected Household Surveys*	Visaria
3	*Measuring Levels of Living in Latin America: An Overview of Main Problems*	United Nations Statistical Office
4	*Towards More Effective Measurement of Levels of Living, and Review of Work of the United Nations Statistical Office (UNSO) Related to Statistics of Level of Living*	Scott/de Andre/Chander
5	*Conducting Surveys in Developing Countries: Practical Problems and Experience in Brazil, Malaysia, and The Philippines*	Scott/de Andre/Chander
6	*Household Survey Experience in Africa*	Booker/Singh/Savane
7	*Measurement of Welfare: Theory and Practical Guidelines*	Deaton
8	*Employment Data for the Measurement of Living Standards*	Mehran
9	*Income and Expenditure Surveys in Developing Countries: Sample Design and Execution*	Wahab
10	*Reflections of the LSMS Group Meeting*	Saunders/Grootaert
11	*Three Essays on a Sri Lanka Household Survey*	Deaton
12	*The ECIEL Study of Household Income and Consumption in Urban Latin America: An Analytical History*	Musgrove
13	*Nutrition and Health Status Indicators: Suggestions for Surveys of the Standard of Living in Developing Countries*	Martorell
14	*Child Schooling and the Measurement of Living Standards*	Bridsal
15	*Measuring Health as a Component of Living Standards*	Ho
16	*Procedures for Collecting and Analyzing Mortality Data in LSMS*	Sullivan/Cochrane/Kalsbeek
17	*The Labor Market and Social Accounting: A Framework of Data Presentation*	Grootaert
18	*Time Use Data and the Living Standards Measurement Study*	Acharya
19	*The Conceptual Basis of Measures of Household Welfare and Their Implied Surveys Data Requirements*	Grootaert
20	*Statistical Experimentation for Household Surveys: Two Case Studies of Hong Kong*	Grootaert/Cheurg/Fung/Tam
21	*The Collection of Price Data for the Measurement of Living Standards*	Wood/Knight
22	*Household Expenditure Surveys: Some Methodological Issues*	Grootaert/Cheung
23	*Collecting Panel Data in Developing Countries: Does It Make Sense?*	Ashenfelter/Deaton/Solon
24	*Measuring and Analyzing Levels of Living in Developing Countries: An Annotated Questionnaire*	Grootaert
25	*The Demand for Urban Housing in the Ivory Coast*	Grootaert/Dubois
26	*The Côte d'Ivoire Living Standards Survey: Design and Implementation (English-French)*	Ainsworth/Munoz
27	*The Role of Employment and Earnings in Analyzing Levels of Living: A General Methodology with Applications to Malaysia and Thailand*	Grootaert
28	*Analysis of Household Expenditures*	Deaton/Case
29	*The distribution of Welfare in Côte d'Ivoire in 1985 (English-French)*	Glewwe
30	*Quality, Quantity, and Spatial Variation of Price: Estimating Price Elasticities form Cross-Sectional Data*	Deaton
31	*Financing the Health Sector in Peru*	Suarez-Berenguela

LSMS Working Papers

No.	TITLE	AUTHOR
32	*Informal Sector, Labor Markets, and Returns to Education in Peru*	Suarez-Berenguela
33	*Wage Determinants in Côte d'Ivoire*	Van der Gaag/Vijverberg
34	*Guidelines for Adapting the LSMS Living Standards Questionnaires to Local Conditions*	Ainsworth/Van der Gaag
35	*The Demand for Medical Care in Developing Countries: Quantity Rationing in Rural Côte d'Ivoire*	Dor/Van der Gaag
36	*Labor Market Activity in Côte d'Ivoire and Peru*	Newman
37	*Health Care Financing and the Demand for Medical Care*	Gertler/Locay/Sanderson Dor/Van der Gaag
38	*Wage Determinants and School Attainment among Men in Peru*	Stelcner/Arriagada/Moock
39	*The Allocation of Goods within the Household: Adults, Children, and Gender*	Deaton
40	*The Effects of Household and Community Characteristics on the Nutrition of Preschool Children: Evidence from Rural Côte d'Ivoire*	Strauss
41	*Public-Private Sector Wage Differentials in Peru, 1985-86*	Stelcner/Van der Gaag/ Vijverberg
42	*The Distribution of Welfare in Peru in 1985-86*	Glewwe
43	*Profits from Self-Employment: A class Study of Côte d'Ivoire*	Vijverberg
44	*The Living Standards Survey and Price Policy Reform: A Study of Cocoa and Coffee Production in Côte d'Ivoire*	Deaton/Benjamin
45	*Measuring the Willingness to Pay for Social Services in Developing Countries*	Gertler/Van der Gaag
46	*Nonagricultural Family Enterprises in Côte d'Ivoire: A Developing Analysis*	Vijverberg
47	*The Poor during Adjustment: A Case Study of Côte d'Ivoire*	Glewwe/de Tray
48	*Confronting Poverty in Developing Countries: Definitions, Information, and Policies*	Glewwe/Van der Gaag
49	*Sample Designs for the Living Standards Surveys in Ghana and Mauritania (English-French)*	Scott/Amenuvegbe
50	*Food Subsidies: A Case Study of Price Reform in Morocco (English-French)*	Laraki
51	*Child Anthropometry in Côte d'Ivoire: Estimates from Two Surveys, 1895-86*	Strauss/Mehra
52	*Public-Private Sector Wage Comparisons and Moonlighting in Developing Countries: Evidence from Côte d'Ivoire and Peru*	Van der Gaag/Stelcner/Vijverberg
53	*Socioeconomic Determinants of Fertility in Côte d'Ivoire*	Ainsworth
54	*The Willingness to Pay for Education in Developing Countries: Evidence from rural Peru*	Gertler/Glewwe
55	*Rigidite des salaires: Donnees microeconomiques et macroeconomiques sur l'ajustement du marche du travail dans le secteur moderne (French only)*	Levy/Newman
56	*The Poor in Latin America during Adjustment: A Case Study of Peru*	Glewwe/de Tray
57	*The substitutability of Public and Private Health Care for the Treatment of Children in Pakistan*	Alderman/Gertler
58	*Identifying the Poor: Is "Headship" a Useful Concept?*	Rosenhouse
59	*Labor Market Performance as a Determinant of Migration*	Vijverberg
60	*The Relative Effectiveness of Private and Public Schools: Evidence from Two Developing Countries*	Jimenez/Cox
61	*Large Sample Distribution of Several Inequality Measures: With Application to Côte d'Ivoire*	Kakwani
62	*Testing for Significance of Poverty Differences: With Application to Côte d'Ivoire*	Kakwani
63	*Poverty and Economic Growth: With Application to Côte d'Ivoire*	Kakwani

LSMS Working Papers

No.	TITLE	AUTHOR
64	*Education and Earnings in Peru's Informal Nonfarm Family Enterprises*	Moock/Musgrove/Steicher
65	*Formal and Informal Sector Wage Determination in Urban Low-Income Neighborhoods in Pakistan*	Alderman/Kozel
66	*Testing for Labor Market Duality: The Private Wage Sector in Côte d'Ivoire*	Vijverberg/Van der Gaag
67	*Does Education Pay in the Labor Market? The Labor Force Participation, Occupation, and Earnings of Peruvian Women*	King
68	*The Composition and Distribution of Income in Côte d'Ivoire*	Kozel
69	*Price Elasticities from Survey Data: Extensions and Indonesian Results*	Deaton
70	*Efficient Allocation of Transfers to the Poor: The Problem of Unobserved Household Income*	Glewwe
71	*Investigating the Determinants of Household Welfare in Côte d'Ivoire*	Glewwe
72	*The Selectivity of Fertility and the Determinants of Human Capital Investments: Parametric and Semiparametric Estimates*	Pitt/Rosenzweig
73	*Shadow Wages and Peasant Family Labor Supply: An Econometric Application to the Peruvian Sierra*	Jacoby
74	*The Action of Human Resources and Poverty on One Another: What we have yet to learn*	Behrman
75	*The Distribution of Welfare in Ghana, 1987-88*	Glewwe/Twum-Baah
76	*Schooling, Skills, and the Returns to Government Investment in Education: An Exploration Using Data from Ghana*	Glewwe
77	*Workers' Benefits from Bolivia's Emergency Social Fund*	Newman/Jorgensen/Pradhan
78	*Dual Selection Criteria with Multiple Alternatives: Migration, Work Status, and Wages*	Vijverberg
79	*Gender Differences in Household Resource Allocations*	Thomas
80	*The Household Survey as a Tool for Policy Change: Lessons from the Jamaican Survey of Living Conditions*	Grosh
81	*Patterns of Aging in Thailand and Côte d'Ivoire*	Deaton/Paxson
82	*Does Undernutrition Respond to Incomes and Prices? Dominance Tests for Indonesia*	Ravallion
83	*Growth and Redistribution Components of Changes in Poverty Measure: A Decomposition with Applications to Brazil and India in the 1980s*	Ravallion/Datt
84	*Measuring Income from Family Enterprises with Household Surveys*	Vijverberg
85	*Demand Analysis and Tax Reform in Pakistan*	Deaton/Grimard
86	*Poverty and Inequality during Unorthodox Adjustment: The Case of Peru, 1985-90 (English-Spanish)*	Glewwe/Hall
87	*Family Productivity, Labor Supply, and Welfare in a Low-Income Country*	Newman/Gertler
88	*Poverty Comparisons: A Guide to Concepts and Methods*	Ravallion
89	*Public Policy and Anthropometric Outcomes in Côte d'Ivoire*	Thomas/Lavy/Strauss
90	*Measuring the Impact of Fatal Adult Illness in Sub-Saharan Africa: An Annotated Household Questionnaire*	Ainworth/and others
91	*Estimating the Determinants of Cognitive Achievement in Low-Income Countries: The Case of Ghana*	Glewwe/Jacoby
92	*Economic Aspects of Child Fostering in Côte d'Ivoire*	Ainsworth
93	*Investment in Human Capital: Schooling Supply Constraints in Rural Ghana*	Lavy
94	*Willingness to Pay for the Quality and Intensity of Medical Care: Low-Income Households in Ghana*	Lavy/Quigley

LSMS Working Papers

No.	TITLE	AUTHOR
95	*Measurement of Returns to Adult Health: Morbidity Effects on Wage Rates in Côte d'Ivoire and Ghana*	Schultz/Tansel
96	*Welfare Implications of Female Headship in Jamaican Households*	Louant/Grosh/Van der Gaag
97	*Household Size in Côte d'Ivoire: Sampling Bias in the CILSS*	Coulombe/Demery
98	*Delayed Primary School Enrollment and Childhood Malnutrition in Ghana: An Economic Analysis*	Glewwe/Jacoby
99	*Poverty Reduction through Geographic Targeting: How Well Does It Work?*	Baker/Grosh
100	*Income Gains for the Poor from Public Works Employment: Evidence from Two Indian Villages*	Datt/Ravallion
101	*Assessing the Quality of Anthropometric Data: Background and Illustrated Guidelines for Survey Managers*	Kostermans
102	*How Well Does the Social Safety Net Work? The Incidence of Cash Benefits in Hungary, 1987-89*	van de Walle/Ravallion/Gautam
103	*Determinants of Fertility and Child Mortality in Côte d'Ivoire and Ghana*	Benefo/Schultz
104	*Children's Health and Achievement in School*	Behrman/Lavy
105	*Quality and Cost in Health Care Choice in Developing Countries*	Lavy/Germain
106	*The Impact of the Quality of Health Care on Children's Nutrition and Survival in Ghana*	Lavy/Strauss/Thomas/de Vreyer
107	*School Quality, Achievement Bias, and Dropout Behavior in Egypt*	Hanushek/Lavy
108	*Contraceptive Use and the Quality, Price, and Availability of Family Planning in Nigeria*	Feyisetan/Ainsworth
109	*Contraceptive Choice, Fertility, and Public Policy in Zimbabwe*	Thomas/Maluccio
110	*The Impact of Female Schooling on Fertility and Contraceptive Use: A Study of Fourteen Sub-Saharan Countries*	Ainsworth/Beegle/Nyamete
111	*Contraceptive Use in Ghana: The Role of Service Availability, Quality, and Price*	Oliver
112	*The Tradeoff between Numbers of Children and Child Schooling: Evidence from Côte d'Ivoire and Ghana*	Montgomery/Kouamé/Oliver
113	*Sector Participation Decisions in Labor Supply Models*	Pradhan
114	*The Quality and Availability of Family Planning Services and Contraceptive Use in Tanzania*	Beegle
115	*Changing Patterns of Illiteracy in Morocco: Assessment Methods Compared*	Lavy/Spratt/Leboucher
116	*Quality of Medical Facilities, Health, and Labor Force Participation in Jamaica*	Lavy/Palumbo/Stern
117	*Who is Most Vulnerable to Macroeconomic Shocks? Hypothesis Tests Using Panel Data from Peru*	Glewwe/Hall
118	*Proxy Means Tests: Simulations and Speculation for Social Programs*	Grosh/Baker
119	*Women's Schooling, Selective Fertility, and Child Mortality in Sub-Saharan Africa*	Pitt
120	*A Guide to Living Standards Measurement Study Surveys and Their Data Sets*	Grosh/Glewwe
121	*Infrastructure and Poverty in Viet Nam*	van de Walle
122	*Comparaisons de la Pauvreté: Concepts et Méthodes*	Ravallion
123	*The Demand for Medical Care: Evidence from Urban Areas in Bolivia*	li
124	*Constructing an Indicator of Consumption for the Analysis of Poverty: Principles and Illustrations with Reference to Ecuador*	Hentschel/Lanjouw
125	*The Contribution of Income Components to Income Inequality in South Africa: A Decomposable Gini Analysis*	Leibbrandt/Woolard/Woolard

Annex IV. Instructions for Price Questionnaire from Kagera Health and Development Survey

VIII. THE PRICE QUESTIONNAIRE

A. General Instructions

You must complete two price questionnaires in each cluster. One questionnaire will be completed at the nearest daily market to every cluster of households, and a second price questionnaire will be completed at the nearest dukas to every cluster. A DAILY MARKET is one that takes place at least six days per week. The price questionnaire should be completed for every cluster, both urban and rural. In most cases there will be a daily market in the village or town being interviewed. If there is no daily market, then the supervisor will find out where the nearest daily market is located and you will visit that market to complete the questionnaire.

The price questionnaire may be completed either during round one or round two. The price questionnaire contains a list of 30 food items, six pharmaceutical products and 13 non-food items. You must collect three prices for each item in the questionnaire. The prices should be obtained from three traders at different locations in the market.

You should begin by explaining to the traders that you do not intend to buy their goods. You are only conducting a survey of prices and the information will not be used for tax purposes. The *first* price quoted by the trader should be recorded. On no account should there be any bargaining. If you bargain for the price, the trader will be annoyed if you make no purchase.

B. Food items

The price of FOOD ITEMS is to be measured by weighing each item and recording both the price and the weight on the questionnaire. For this purpose you will be provided with a food scale. The scale must be kept in working order. Before making each measurement, you should "zero" the scale. This means that you should adjust the scale so that it reads "zero grams" when it is empty. If the food to be measured is in a container, the scale must be "zeroed" with the container empty before the food is added. This procedure must be followed for each food item.

The weight of all food items must be recorded in *grams*. One kilogram is the same as 1000 grams; half a kilogram is 500 grams; one quarter of a kilogram is 250 grams. If a food item weights two kilograms, you must write 2000 grams.

The weight should be recorded to the *nearest 50 grams*. This means that if a food item weighs 375 grams, the anthropometrist should round *up* the weight to 400 grams. If the item weights 370 grams, the anthropometrist should round *down* the weight to 350 grams.

Weight in grams	Weight recorded
25 - 74	50
75 - 124	100
125 - 174	150
175 - 224	200
225 - 274	250
.	
.	
.	
925 - 974	950
975 - 1025	1000

You must *always record the weight of food items in grams, unless the questionnaire instructs otherwise*. For example, if someone is selling bananas by the piece, you should ask the price of one banana, weigh it, and record the weight in grams. If bananas are sold in bunches, you should ask the price of a bunch and weigh a bunch. You should *not* write "1 banana" or "1 bunch" on the questionnaire as this will be entered in the computer as one gram, which is incorrect. If someone is selling potatoes in groups of three, you should ask the price for three potatoes, weigh them and record the price and weight, in grams. You must *not* write "3 potatoes", as this will be entered in the computer as three grams, which is also incorrect.

Everything written on the questionnaire will be recorded into the computer. The weight should be recorded clearly and *without* the unit of measurement. For example, 500 grams of sugar at a price of 100 Tshs should be recorded as follows:

		OBSERVATION	
		GRAMS	PRICE
06	Sugar	500	100

Do *not* write "g" or "gm" after the weight or "Tshs" or /= after the price.

There is only one food item in the price questionnaire that is *not* measured in grams — chicken eggs. You must ask the price of *one* egg. The number 1 is already written in the questionnaire, and it means "one egg" not "one gram". Eggs should not be weighed.

C.   Pharmaceutical products

There are six pharmaceutical products in the price questionnaire. These products should *not* be weighed. The first four items should be measured in tablets. For example, if nivaquine tablets are being sold at two tablets for 25 Tshs, then it should be recorded as:

		1ST OBSERVATION	
		TABLETS	PRICE
33	Nivaquine	2	25

If aspirin tablets are sold one at a time for two Tshs each, then you should record 1 in the column for tablets and 2 in the column for price.

Two of the items — liver salts and milk of magnesia — are not sold in tablet form. You must record the price of one *packet* of liver salts and one *bottle* of milk of magnesia. The amount is already written in the questionnaire; the anthropometrist should only copy the price for these two items.

D.   Non-food items

There are 13 non-food items for which prices must be collected. Most of the non-food items do not have to be weighed. The prices should always correspond to the description of the item in the questionnaire. For example, the price recorded for a battery should always be for one battery of *1.5 volts*. A price should not be recorded for a 4-volt battery. The price for firewood should be for a bunch about one foot in diameter — no smaller, no larger.

The last non-food item is charcoal. This is the only non-food item that must be weighed, in grams. The price should be asked for a *small amount* of charcoal — *not a large sack*.

E.   **Problems**

Sometimes, sellers of food items will not allow their goods to be weighed unless a purchase is made. In this case, you should wait for a customer to make a purchase and record the weight and the price paid.

Occasionally you will have problems finding certain items. For example, smoked fish may not be sold in the markets of mountain villages. When this happens, write "NA" in all of the columns for that item. In this example:

		GRAMS	PRICE	GRAMS	PRICE	GRAMS
25	Smoked Fish	NA	NA	NA	NA	NA

NA means "not available"

You may also find that only one person in the market sells an item. Then you will only be able to get one price. You should record the price from this one vendor, then write in the columns for the second and third prices "NA".

You must make every effort to locate all of the items and to get three prices for each. All cases of "NA" will be examined closely by your supervisor.

Annex V. Calendar of Events in Kagera, Tanzania

Year	Events
1914-18	First World War
1926	Tanganyika partitioned into provinces
1932-34	Immigrants from Burundi into Karagwe, Ngara, and Muleba cause famine
1935-36	Locust swarms destroy crops all over the region
1939-	Second World War
1940	Colonial government repatriates the chiefs to Uganda
1943-	Famine causes people to dismantle their roofing (iron sheets) to exchange for food
1945-	Earthquake
1946	End of Second World War
1948	Tribal political groups
1949-	Political activist — TAR is started
1950-	Cooperative union started
1951-52	Good income from coffee
1952-	Chief of Ihangiro sacked due to swindling coffee from peasants
1953	Union of tribal political group with TAA
1954-	TANU inaugurated
1958-	Partition into districts — Karagwe becomes autonomous
1960-	Colonial government detains TANU leaders
1961-	Complete independence
1962	All chiefs dethroned
1963-	Extraordinarily heavy rains: bridges swept away, rivers flooded
1964-	Zanzibar revolution
1966-	Two days of continuous rain
1967-	Arusha Declaration. The Ihangiro and Karagwe members of Parliament are sacked for opposing the Arusha Declaration
1971-	Ten years of independence
1972-	First of Iddi Amin's aggression wars
1973-74	Famine
1976	Ujamaa villages
1978 October	Beginning of Iddi Amin war
1979 June	End of Iddi Amin war
1981-83	The AIDS disease is coined "Juliana"
1985	The start of President Mwinyi's government

Annex VI. Full Questionnaire
Verification Form Used in Pakistan LSMS

PROVINCE	SUB-UNIVERSE	STRATUM	PRIMARY SAMPLING UNIT	HOUSEHOLD

Sec-tion	Ques-tion	Round One Check	Satis-factory	To be redone	Notes / Remarks
1A	2-5	These questions must be completed for all names in Q.1			
1A	9	All persons were correctly classified as members of the household.			
1A	A-B	A cross was written in column A for all members of the household (code 1 in Q.9) and the age in years was copied from Q.5 to column B.			
2		This section was completed.			
3A		A line is filled in for each household member 5 years or older.			
4A 4B		A line is filled in for each household child 5 years or under.			
4C		A line is filled in for all household members.			
5A		A line is filled in for each household member 10 years or older.			
5B		A line is filled in for each household member 10 years or older.			
6A	1	If the answer is 1 (YES), a line is filled in for each household member 10 years and older. The ID code of the best-informed person is to be transferred to the second page (Summary of survey results).			
6B	1	If the answer is 1 (YES), Q.1-5 for First, Second or Third Enterprise should be filled in. Industry codes of all enterprises must be filled in, and ID codes of best-informed persons must be transferred to the second page (Summary of survey results).			
6C		A line is filled in for each female member 10 years or older.			
M7A		This section is completed.			
M7B	1	If the answer is 1 (YES), then Q.2-43 must be filled up.			
M7C	1	If the answer is 1 (YES), then Q.2-16 must be filled up.			
M7D	1	If the answer is 1 (YES), then Q.2-12 must be filled up.			
M7E	1	If the answer is 1 (YES), then Q.2-28 must be filled up.			

R E S U L T

238

Sec-tion	Ques-tion	Round One Check	RESULT		Notes / Remarks
			Satis-factory	To be redone	
M7F	1	If the answer is 1 (YES), then Q.2-21 must be filled up.			
M7I	5	If the answer is 1 (YES), then Q.6-21 must be filled up.			
M7M	4	All digits 1 to 7 appear once in each column.			
M7M	5	All digits 1 to 6 appear once in the RANK column.			
F7A	1	If the answer is 1 (YES), then the rest of this part should be completed. Review carefully all filter questions (Q.7, 17, 25, 26, 37, 48, 59, 67, 74, 82, 94, 103, 112, 120, 129, and 137). They should all be completed, and if the answer to any of them is greater than 0, then the block of questions that follow should be filled in.			
F7B	1	If the answer is 1 (YES), then the rest of this part should be completed. Review carefully all filter questions (Q.2, 12, 19, and 28). They should all be completed, and if the answer to any of them is greater than 0, then the block of questions that follow should be filled in.			
F7C	1	If the answer is 1 (YES), then the rest of this part should be completed. Review carefully all filter questions (Q.2, 12, 20, and 28). They should all be completed, and if the answer to any of them is greater than 0, then the block of questions that follow should be filled in.			
F7D	1	If the answer is 1 (YES), then the rest of this part should be completed. Review carefully all filter questions (Q.2, 14, 21, and 42). They should all be completed, and if the answer to any of them is greater than 0, then the block of questions that follow should be filled in.			
F7E F7F F7G F7H	1	If the answer is 1 (YES), then the rest of these parts should be completed.			
F7I	1	If the answer is 1 (YES), then the rest of this part should be completed. In this case, a single box (for NO or YES) must be crossed for each biomass fuel, and Q.3-5 must be filled up for each fuel with a cross in the YES box.			
F7J	1	If the answer is 1 (YES), then the rest of this part should be completed.			
F7K F7L		These sections must be completed.			
8		A line is filled in for each household member 15 years and older			

PROVINCE	SUB-UNIVERSE	STRATUM	PRIMARY SAMPLING UNIT	HOUSEHOLD

Sec-tion	Ques-tion	Round Two Check	RESULT Satis-factory	RESULT To be redone	Notes / Remarks
9A	1	Parts A to E should be completed if (and only if) the answer to this question is YES.			
9B1 9B2 9B3	1	A single box (for NO or YES) should be crossed for each crop in the list. If "Other crops" are reported, their codes must be specified. A line must be completed for each crop with a cross in the YES box.			
9B4	1	If the answer is 1 (YES), the rest of this part should be completed.			
9C	1	If the answer is 1 (YES), Q.2-4 should be filled in.			
9C	7	If the answer is 1 (YES), Q.8-9 should be filled in.			
9D	1	If the answer is 1 (YES), crops and corresponding crop codes should be specified in Q.2, and Q.3 to 5 should be completed.			
9D	6	If the answer is 1 (YES), Q.7-22 should be filled in following skip patterns correctly.			
9D	25	If the answer is 1 (YES), Q.26-30 should be filled in.			
9D	32	If the answer is 1 (YES), Q.33-35 should be filled in.			
9D	36	If the answer is 1 (YES), the rest of this section should be completed.			
9D	37	A single box (for NO or YES) should be crossed for every equipment in the list. A line must be completed for every item of equipment on the list.			
9E	1	If the answer is 1 (YES), the rest of this part should be completed.			
9F	1	If the answer is 1 (YES), the rest of this part should be completed.			
9G	1	If the answer is 1 (YES), the rest of this part should be completed.			
9H	1	If the answer is 1 (YES), the rest of this part should be completed.			
10A	1	If the answer is 1 (YES), the rest of this section should be completed.			
10B 10C		Every line should have a cross mark on either YES or NO column. For every line with a YES, Q.1-8 should be filled in following skip pattern correctly.			
10D		A line should be completed for every enterprise.			

Section	Question	Round Two Check	Satisfactory	To be redone	Notes / Remarks
11A 11B	1	Every line should have a cross mark on either YES or NO column. For every line with a YES, the rest of the line should be completed.			
11C	1	Every line should have a cross mark on either YES or NO column. For every line with a YES, one or more items should appear in Q.2, with the corresponding code, and Q.3 to 7 should be completed.			
12A	1	Every line should have a cross mark on either YES or NO column. For every line with a YES, Q.2-9 should be filled in.			
12B	1	If answer is 1 (YES), the rest of this part should be be completed.			
12B	2	Every line should have a cross mark in either YES or NO column. For every line with a YES, Q.3-7 should be filled in, following skip pattern correctly.			
12B	3	If the answer is 2 (NO), Q.4 should be filled in.			
13A 13B		Information was asked of each woman 14 years or older.			
13C		Information was asked of each woman who ever married from age 14 to 50 years with maternity experience.			
13D		This section must be completed for each woman with a child 3 years and younger.			
13E		Information was asked of all men 14 years and older.			
14		All lines are filled for children under 5 years and their mothers.			
15A	1	If the answer is 1 (YES), Q.2 and part 15B should be completed.			
15A	3	If the answer is 1 (YES), Q.4 and part 15C should be completed.			
16A 16B	1	If the answer is 1 (YES), Q.2-12 should be filled in.			
17	1	Every line has a cross mark on either YES or NO column. For every line with a YES, Q.2 should be filled in.			

SUPERVISOR:_____   DATE

Annex VII. Inter-Record Checks in the Romania Integrated Household Survey

Consistency Checks

Presence of household level sections

The following sections must be present in all households:

- Section 0 (The cover page)
- Sections 1A and 1B (The family roster and basic demographic data)
- Section 2 (Education)
- Section 3 (Migration)
- Sections 4A, 4B and 4C (Dwelling and Assets)
- Section 5 (Current occupational status)
- Section 12 (Food consumption)
- Section 13 (Non-food expenditures)
- Section 14 (Expenditure on services)
- Section 16 (Health)
- Section 19 (Balance of incomes)
- Section 20 (Balance of expenditures)

The program flags an error whenever any of these sections is missing; an exception is made for those households where the interview could not be conducted (as reported in a specific question on the cover page) for which only the cover page should be completed.

Household size as reported in different sections

The household size is reported explicitly in question 4 in Section 4A (Dwelling), and implicitly in Section 1 (the list of all household members, present and absent). These data must be consistent.

Presence of individual level sections

Each household member must be present in the following sections:

- Sections 1A and 1B (The family roster and basic demographic data)
- Section 2 (Education)
- Section 3 (Migration)
- Section 16 (Health)

Also, members 14 years and older should be present in Section 5 (Current occupational status), women 14 years and older should be present in Section 18 (Fertility), and children under 6 years old should be present in Section 17

242

(Anthropometrics). Members under 14 years old should not be present in Section 11 (Job history).

Age and birth date

The age of each person, reported in Section 1A (The family roster), must be consistent with the age deducted from the birth date (in Section 1B) and the date of the interview (on the cover page).

Age and schooling allocation

Only members 18 years old and younger can report schooling allocations in Section 2 (Education).

Disability of mutes

People who cannot speak at all, as reported in Question 2 (Mother tongue) in Section 2 (Education), should also report a permanent disability in Section 16 (Health).

Consistency of occupational status

The current occupation of each person should be consistent between Section 1 (the family roster) and Section 5 (Occupational status).

Wages of wage-earners

People who report to be working for wages in Section 1 (the family roster) or Section 5 (Occupational Status) should also report wages in Section 6 (Wage activities).

Employers and employees

A person who reports to be an employer in Sections 1 or 5 should also appear as the first member of a family enterprise that pays wages to non-family members in Section 7.

Self-employment and family enterprises

People who report to be self-employed in Sections 1 or 5 should also appear as workers in one of the family enterprises in Section 7.

Farmers and farms

People who report to be farmers in Sections 1 or 5 should also report to be working on a household farm in Section 7. Also if one of the family enterprises in Section 7 is a farm, income from farming should be reported in Section 19 (Balance of Incomes).

Housewives and wages

Housewives (as reported in Sections 1 or 5) should not report income in Section 5.

Military

People reported in the armed forces in Sections 1 or 5 cannot be absent from the household for other than institutional reasons (on Question 11 in Section 1). Also, only males 20 to 40 years old can be in the military.

Job history of former workers

People who stopped working after 1989 (as reported in Question 14 in Section 5) should also report a job history in Section 11.

Illness and medical allocations

People who report to receive medical allocations in Section 5 (Occupational status) should also report an illness in Section 16 (Health).

Demographic consistency of spouses

According to Question 6 (Spouse ID code) in Section 1B (Demographics), spouses should be of different genders, and linked to each other.

Demographic consistency of mothers

According to Question 7 (Mother ID code) in Section 1B, a person's mother should be a woman 15 to 45 years older.

Demographic consistency of fathers

According to Question 8 (Father ID code) in Section 1B, a person's father should be a man at least 15 years older.

Date of the anthropometric measure

The date of the last anthropometric measure (reported in Section 17) should not be earlier than the child's birth date.

Breast-feeding

Only children under 2 years old should be reported as currently being breast-fed in Section 17 (Anthropometrics).

Anthropometrics

Anthropometric measures should be consistent regarding weight-for-age, length-for-age and weight-for-length.

It is important to keep in mind that the purpose of these tests is simply to detect probable recording or data-entry errors; not to assess nutritional status. The raw weight, length and age data will be kept in the files, to let the latter be performed in due time, and with more refinement at the analytical stage.

To check data consistency, the program uses the Means plus and minus three Standard Deviations from the World Health Organization standard tables. Linear interpolation between a few key points in these tables is used to approximate intermediate values. The following key points were selected:

Weight (kg.) for age (months)							
Males				Females			
Minimum		Maximum		Minimum		Maximum	
mo.	kg.	mo.	kg.	mo.	kg.	mo.	kg.
0	2.0	0	4.8	0	1.8	0	4.3
4	3.7	4	9.4	8	5.3	4	8.6
6	4.9	15	14.4	13	6.6	12	12.7
12	7.1	59	25.6	30	9.1	59	25.8
24	8.6	60	29.2	84	13.6	60	29.2
84	15.0	84	38.8	132	18.2	78	31.8
132	18.6	180	100.3	180	29.2	132	73.6
168	27.0	204	111.0	216	34.8	156	86.2
216	41.9	360	140.0			180	92.8
						360	108.0

Length (cm.) for age (months)							
Males				Females			
Minimum		Maximum		Minimum		Maximum	
mo.	cm.	mo.	cm.	mo.	cm.	mo.	cm.
0	43.6	0	57.4	0	43.4	0	56.4
6	59.8	3	69.0	6	58.0	3	67.0
12	68.0	6	75.9	15	68.9	7	75.6
48	90.2	24	97.7	36	86.3	16	87.8
168	137.0	59	123.1	48	92.4	59	121.0
204	156.0	60	130.1	132	123.9	60	128.7
		108	155.3	168	140.3	108	158.2
		156	188.3	216	145.8	156	181.6
		180	195.0				
		216	199.6				

Weight (kg.) for length (cm.) Males and females			
Minimum		Maximum	
cm.	kg.	cm.	kg.
48.0	2.0	48.0	4.5
110.0	13.8	110.0	25.0
150.0	25.0	130.0	40.0
200.0	65.0	150.0	60.0
		160.0	90.0
		170.0	130.0
		180.0	180.0

Children data on Fertility and on the roster

• Children with a mother ID code in Section 1B (Demographics) should also be reported in Section 18 (Fertility).

• The number of children reported should be equal to the number of children ever been given birth to by each woman.

• The gender and age of those children reported in Section 18 (Fertility) who have a household ID Code should be consistent with the same data in Section 1B (Demographics).

• Children should be sorted by birth date in Section 18 (Fertility), and the age of the eldest should be consistent with the age of the mother.

Age and gender-specific illnesses

Illnesses coded 30 to 50 can only affect women. The program is prepared to perform other tests regarding the demographic specificity of certain illnesses in Section 16 (Health).

Non-agriculture family enterprises

Non-agriculture family enterprises reported in Section 7 should also be reported in Section 8 (Income and expenses of non-farming family enterprises).

Farms

Farms reported in Section 7 (Family Enterprises) should not report income or expenses in Section 8; instead, detailed information on farming should be present for the household in Section 9. Conversely, if Section 9 is present, at least one farm should be reported as a family enterprise in Section 7.

Wage employees

Expenditure on wages should be reported in Question 6 in Section 8 if — and only if — wage employees are reported in any of the family enterprises in Question 21 of Section 7 (Family enterprises).

Internal consistency of added lines

Lines for totals are included for certain columns used to record monetary values in various sections. The program checks that the totals add up correctly in the following cases:

- Section 8 (Income and expenses of non-farm family enterprises); Columns 2 to 8; Line "Total" should be equal to the sum of lines 1 to 6.

- Section 9A (Agriculture surfaces); Columns 2 to 6; Line "Total" should be equal to the sum of lines 1 to 5.

- Section 10 (Cattle); Columns 2 to 6; Total number of bovines (line 03) should be equal to the sum of bulls, cows and veal (lines 04 to 06).

- Section 12 (Food consumption); Columns 2 to 14; Line number 186 (Total food) should be equal to the sum of lines 101 to 185 (food items).

- Section 12 (Food consumption); Columns 2 to 14; Line number 190 (Total) should be equal to the sum of lines 186 (Total food) and 187 to 189 (animal fodder and wool).

- Section 19 (Balance of incomes); Column 2; Line number 32 (Total cash) should be equal to the sum of lines 01 to 31.

- Section 19 (Balance of incomes); Column 2; Line number 34 (Total cash and in-kind) should be equal to the sum of lines 32 and 33.

- Section 19 (Balance of incomes); Column 2; Line number 40 (Total income) should be equal to the sum of lines 34 to 39.

- Section 19 (Balance of incomes); Column 2; Line number 42 (Total balance) should be equal to the sum of lines 40 and 41.

- Section 20 (Balance of expenditures); Column 2; Line 521 (Total expenses) should be equal to the sum of lines 501 to 520.

- Section 20 (Balance of expenditures); Column 2; Line 527 (Total outputs) should be equal to the sum of lines 521 to 526.

- Section 20 (Balance of expenditures); Column 2; Line 529 (Total balance) should be equal to the sum of lines 527 and 528.

Groups of animals

Some lines in Section 10 (Cattle) represent subgroups of animals in other lines. The program checks that the quantities in columns 2 to 6 are not smaller in the totals than in the subsets:

- Line number 07 (Ovine si caprine) should be at least equal to line number 08 (Oi si capre)

- Line number 09 (Porcine) should be at least equal to line number 10 (Scroafe).

- Line number 11 (Pasari) should be at least equal to line number 12 (Pasari ouatoare).

Land rented by farmers

The surface of rented farming land should be reported in Question 5 of Section 9A (Agriculture surfaces) if — and only if — a rental amount is reported also for some crops in Question 5 of Section 9B (Farm production).

Land farmed or owned in association

The surface of land worked or owned in association should be reported in Questions 4 or 6 in Section 9A (Agriculture surfaces) if — and only if — production from that land is also recorded in Section 9D.

Expenditure on medicines

Expenditure on medicines must be reported as item 294 in Section 13 (Non-food purchases) if — and only if — they are also reported for a specific illness in Question 19 in Section 16 (Health). (The amounts do not necessarily need to match.)

Expenditure on utilities

Expenditure on the following utilities must be reported in Section 14 (Expenditure on services) if — and only if — the presence of those utilities is also reported in Section 4A (Dwelling):

Item in Section 14	Questions in Section 4A
430 Rental	05 (Codes 2 or 3)
431 Tap water	20 and 21 (Codes 1 or 2)
432 Electricity	14 and 18 (Code 1)
433 Thermal energy	15 (Codes 1 or 2)
434 Gas	15 (Codes 2 or 3), 18 (Code 2).

Health-related expenditures

Expenditure on health-related services must be reported as items 420 (Medical) or 421 (Dental) in Section 14 (Expenditure on services) if — and only if — they are also reported in Questions 14 (First consultation), 16 (Second consultation), 17 (Analysis) or 18 (Treatments) in Section 16 (Health). (The amounts do not necessarily need to match.)

Also, if a taxi (Code 3) was reported as the means of transportation to reach a health center in Question 11 in Section 16 (Health), the corresponding expenditure should also be reported as item 441 in Section 14 (Expenditure on services). If public transportation (Code 3) was used, then an expenditure should be reported for at least one of the other transportation services (Items 439 to 445) in Section 14.

Income items

The presence of various sources of income should be reported consistently in Section 19 (Balance of Incomes) and in other parts of the questionnaire. The program checks that the amounts for the following items are mentioned in Section 19 if they are also mentioned elsewhere (though actual quantities may be different):

- Wages must appear on line 01 in Section 19 if — and only if — they are also reported for household members in Question 12 in Section 6 (Wage earning activities).

- Bonuses and benefits must appear on line 02 in Section 19 if — and only if — they are also reported for household members in Questions 13 and 14 in Section 6 (Wage earning activities).

- Medical and maternity allocations must appear on lines 03 or 04 in Section 19 if — and only if — they are also reported for household members in Question 11 in Section 6 (Wage earning activities).

- Income from self-employment must appear on lines 19 to 22 or 24 in Section 19 if — and only if — it is also reported in Question 2 in Section 8 (Income and expenses of non-farm family enterprises).

- Scholarships must appear on line 08 in Section 19 if — and only if — they are also reported in Question 9 in Section 2 (Education).

- Student allocations must appear on line 07 in Section 19 if — and only if — they are also reported in Question 11 in Section 2 (Education).

- Income from rental of land or housing must appear on line 22 in Section 19 if — and only if — it is also reported in Section 4D.

- Dividends to shareholders must appear on line 23 in Section 19 if — and only if — they are also reported in Section 4D.

- Income from various kinds of pensions must appear on lines 09 to 17 in Section 19 if — and only if — the corresponding pension codes are also reported for household members in Questions 16, 18, 20 or 22 in Section 5 (Occupational status).

- In-kind payments must appear on line 33 in Section 19 if — and only if — they are also reported in Question 18 in Section 6 (Wage earning activities).

- Income from farming must appear on lines 25 or 26 in Section 19 if — and only if — it is also reported in Question 15 in Section 9B (Farm production).

- Income from selling cattle must appear on line 27 in Section 19 if it is also reported in Question 6 in Section 10 (Cattle).

- "Other income" must appear on line 31 in Section 19 if renting-out animal traction is reported in Question 12 in Section 10 (Cattle).

- Sales of farm production must appear on line 26 in Section 19 if — and only if — it is also reported in Question 10 in Section 12 (Food consumption).

Expenditure items

The presence of various expenditure items should be reported consistently in Section 20 (Balance of Expenses) and in other parts of the questionnaire. The program checks that amounts for the following items are mentioned in Section 20 if they are also mentioned elsewhere (though actual quantities may be different):

- Payments for unemployment insurance must appear on line 511 in Section 20 if — and only if — it is they are also reported in Question 15 in Section 6 (Wage earning activities).

- Payments for supplementary pension must appear on line 510 in Section 20 if — and only if — they are also reported in Question 16 in Section 6 (Wage earning activities).

- Taxes on wages must appear on line 512 in Section 20 if — and only if — they are also reported in Question 17 in Section 6 (Wage earning activities).

- Expenditure on veterinary services must appear on line 509 in Section 20 if they are also reported in Question 14 in Section 10 (Cattle).

The actual amounts of other expenditure items must be identical in Section 20 and in other sections of the questionnaire:

- Food purchases (line 501 in Section 20) must be equal to the sum of columns 4 and 6 on line 186 in Section 12 (Food consumption).

- Expenditure on animal fodder (line 503 in Section 20) must be equal to the sum of columns 4 and 6 on line 187 in Section 12 (Food consumption) and column 7 on line 14 in Section 10 (Cattle).

- Non-food purchases (line 502 in Section 20) must be equal to column 3 on line 314 in Section 13.

- Expenditure on services (line 509 in Section 20) must be equal to column 2 on line 457 in Section 14.

Nutritive value of food consumption

The program uses the daily per capita energy provided by each food item in Section 12 (Food consumption) to perform various tests on the likelihood of the reported data. As in the case of the anthropometric controls, the only purpose of these tests is to detect probable reporting or data entry errors, not to assess nutritional adequacy at this stage. The raw data will be kept untouched in the files, to let analysts develop this task in due time.

The basic formula used is:

$$
\begin{bmatrix} \text{Energy provided} \\ \text{by a food item} \\ (Kcal/person/day) \end{bmatrix} = \begin{bmatrix} \text{Food} \\ \text{intake} \\ (gr) \end{bmatrix} \times \begin{bmatrix} \text{Energy value} \\ \text{of 1 gr. of food} \\ (Kcal) \end{bmatrix} \div \begin{bmatrix} \text{Number of} \\ \text{person days} \end{bmatrix}
$$

The food intake is taken from Column 13 (Food consumed by humans) on Section 12 (Food Consumption). The number of person-days is computed by multiplying the household size by the number of days in the reference month and adding the number of guest-days in the month (reported on the single Question in Section 4C). The energy value of 1 gram of food is taken from the food composition table below, where food items are divided into three main groups:

```
┌─────────────────────────────────────────────────────────────────────────┐
│                        Group I: Starchy staples                           │
│                                                                           │
│   Food                                              Energy value          │
│   Code   Rumanian name            English name        (Kcal/gr)           │
│                                                                           │
│   101    Grau si secara           Wheat & rye            3.57             │
│   102    Porumb                   Maize                  3.55             │
│   103    Faina                    Flour                  3.33             │
│   104    Malai                    Maize-flour            3.68             │
│   105    Paine                    Bread                  2.43             │
│   106    Alte produse franzelarie Ot kind of bread       2.46             │
│   109    Paste fainoase           Pasta                  3.69             │
│   110    Orez                     Rice                   3.60             │
│   111    Gris                     Ot milling (semolina/barley) 3.54       │
│   113    Fasole boabe leguminoase Beans                  1.18             │
│   114    Cartofi                  Potatoes               0.87             │
└─────────────────────────────────────────────────────────────────────────┘
```

```
┌─────────────────────────────────────────────────────────────────────────┐
│             Group II: Meat, animals, milk, alcohol, oil                   │
│                                                                           │
│   Food                                              Energy value          │
│   Code   Rumanian name            English name        (Kcal/gr)           │
│                                                                           │
│   141    Ulei comestibil          Edible oil             8.84             │
│   142    Margarina                Margarine              7.20             │
│   152    Vin                      Wine                   1.37             │
│   153    Produse din vin          Wine products          1.37             │
│   154    Bere                     Beer                   0.42             │
│   155    Tuica si rachiuri        Plum/Ot brandy         1.53             │
│   156    Alte bauturi alcoolice   Ot alcohol bever       2.31             │
│   158    Carne de bovine          Beef                   3.49             │
│   159    Carne de porcine         Pork                   2.61             │
│   160    Carne de oaie si capra   Mutton/Goat            1.86             │
│   161    Carne de pasare          Fowl                   1.90             │
│   162    Alte feluri de carne     Ot meat (Rabbit/Hunt etc) 2.16          │
│   163    Specialit prep din carne Ham etc                3.49             │
│   164    Salamuri/Cirnati         Sausage                3.69             │
│   165    Alte preparate din carne Ot meat preparat       3.09             │
│   166    Conserv de carne si carne Tinned meat           1.62             │
│   167    Slana cruda              Bacon?                 5.93             │
│   168    Untura                   Grease                 8.84             │
│   169    Peste proaspat & congelat Fresh/Frozen fish     1.05             │
│   170    Peste sarat uscat afumat Salted/Dried fish      2.90             │
│   171    Conserve din peste       Tinned fish            1.69             │
│   172    Lapte de vaca si bivolita Cow's milk            0.61             │
│   173    Lapte de oaie si capra   Sheep/Goat milk        0.89             │
│   174    Lapte praf               Powdered milk          3.63             │
└─────────────────────────────────────────────────────────────────────────┘
```

The program performs the following tests:

- The total daily per capita energy provided by all foods should not be less than 800 Kcal/person/day or more than 4,000 Kcal/person/day.

- Each individual food in Group I should not provide more than 3,500 Kcal/person/day.

- Each individual food in Group II should not provide more than 2,500 Kcal/person/day or more than 66.7% of the total energy intake.

- Each individual food in Group III should not provide more than 1,500 Kcal/person/day or more than 33.3% of the total energy intake.

```
                              Group III
          Fruit, vegetables, sugar, bakery, cheese, yogurt, eggs, other diary

     Food                                                    Energy value
     Code    Rumanian name            English name            (Kcal/gr)

     107     Biscuiti                 Biscuits                  3.64
     108     Specialitati panificatie Bakery specialties        2.95
     112     Alte prd morarit si panif Ot bakery (cornflakes etc) 3.93
     115     Morcovi sfecla radacinoas Carrots/Beets           0.38
     116     Alte radacinoase consumab Ot edible roots          0.38
     117     Tomate                   Tomatoes                  0.19
     118     Patlagele vinete         Eggplants                 0.26
     119     Ceapa uscata             Onion                     0.34
     120     Usturoi uscat            Garlic                    1.49
     121     Ardei si gogosari        Green/bell pepper         0.25
     122     Fasole verde             Green beans               0.31
     123     Varza dulce si conopida  Cabbage/Cauliflow         0.24
     124     Verdeturi proaspete      Green spices              0.33
     125     Alte legume proaspete    Ot vegetables             0.42
     126     Muraturi si varza acra   Pickles                   0.11
     127     Bulion                   Tomato paste              0.84
     128     Conserve de legume       Tinned vegetables         0.42
     129     Pepeni verzi si galbeni  Melon/watermelons         0.32
     130     Nuci in coaja            Nuts                      6.42
     131     Mere                     Apples                    0.59
     132     Pere                     Pears                     0.59
     133     Visine/Cirese            Cherries                  0.61
     134     Caise/Piersici           Apricots/peaches          0.46
     135     Prune                    Plums                     0.60
     136     Struguri                 Grapes                    0.71
     137     Capsuni/Zmeura           Straw/Black-berry         0.41
     138     Alte fructe proaspete    Ot fresh fruits           0.54
     139     Citrice/Fructe merid     Citric                    0.46
     140     Fructe deshidratate      Dehydrated fruits         2.96
     143     Compot de fructe         Stewed fruit              1.07
     144     Dulceata/Gem/Peltea/Marm Sweetness                 2.72
     145     Sirop de fructe          Fruit syrup               2.72
     146     Zahar                    Sugar                     3.85
     147     Ciocolata                Chocolate                 5.07
     148     Rahat/Halva              Turkish delight           5.33
     149     Alte zaharoase           Other sweets              4.37
     150     Cafea                    Coffee                    0.00
     151     Cacao                    Cocoa                     2.20
     157     Bauturi nealcoolice      Non-alcoh beverag         3.90
     175     Lapte batut/Iaurt        Buttermilk/Yogurt         0.51
     176     Branza (telemea) vaca    Spiced cheese             3.76
     177     Branza de oaie           Sheep cheese              4.66
     178     Branza proaspata de vaca Fresh cream cheese        1.03
     179     Conserve                 Preserves                 2.50
     180     Alte feluri de branza    Other cheese              3.56
     181     Unt                      Butter                    7.17
     182     Oua                      Eggs                      1.40
     183     Miere de albine          Honey                     3.05
     184     Sare si condimente       Salt and spices           1.00
```

Annex VIII. Table of Contents from Abstract of Pakistan Integrated Household Survey

CONTENTS

I. Introduction

A. Design of the Survey
B. Management and Field Implementation
C. Sample Design
D. The Questionnaires

II. Statistical Tables

    A.   Demography
    B.   Fertility and Family Planning
    C.   Migration
    D.   Health and Child Survival
    E.   Literacy, Education, and Training
    F.   Employment
    G.   Housing and Social Infrastructure

III. Annex I: List of Field Staff

LIST OF TABLES

INTRODUCTION

A. DEMOGRAPHY

B. FERTILITY AND FAMILY

C. MIGRATION

D. HEALTH AND CHILD SURVIVAL

E. LITERACY, EDUCATION, AND TRAINING

F. EMPLOYMENT

G. HOUSING AND SOCIAL INFRASTRUCTURE

LIST OF FIGURES

A. DEMOGRAPHY

B. FERTILITY AND FAMILY PLANNING

Annex IX. Table of Contents from Abstract of the 1993 Jamaica Survey of Living Conditions

Contents

Preface

The data made available by the Survey of Living Conditions since its inception in 1988 provide an important measure of the manner in which houschold welfare has been affected by the macro-economic policies associated with structural adjustment. The survey gleans houschold data from a subset of the population covered by the Labour Force Survey. Information is collected on consumption, health, education, nutrition, housing, demographic characteristics, and the food stamp programme.

The 1993 Report presents a descriptive analysis of the findings of the survey. In addition to the perspectives mentioned above, this survey collected data on Employment and Time Use. This additional module will be analysed in other papers.

Gratitude is owed to the Ministries of Health, Education, Labour and Welfare, the University of the West Indies, and the World Bank for their contributions to the publication of the report. In addition, the co-operation of the households which participated in the survey is greatly appreciated.

The SLC is a joint effort of the Planning Institute of Jamaica (PIOJ) and the Statistical Institute of Jamaica (STATIN).

Marjorie Henriques
Director General
The Planning Institute
of Jamaica
March 1995

Vernon James
Director General
The Statistical Institute
of Jamaica
March 1995

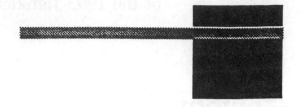

Acknowledgements

The contribution of all those who helped to prepare this document is gratefully acknowledged.

Special mention is due to the staff at the Statistical Institute of Jamaica (STATIN) in the Surveys and Computer Systems Divisions and, in particular, to Mr. Pattisapu Murthy, Mr. Hubert Sherrard and Ms. Isbeth Bernard. Staff from the Social and Manpower Planning Division of the Planning Institute of Jamaica (PIOJ) also contributed significantly, including Dr. Dennis Brown, Mr. Colin Williams, Mrs. Aldrie Henry-Lee, Mrs. Heather Ricketts, Ms. Terry Ranglin and Miss Ann Marie Chandler; contribution was also made by Ms. Pauline McHardy, a Consultant. The work of editing and desktop publishing was done by the Research, Publication and Documentation Division of the Planning Institute.

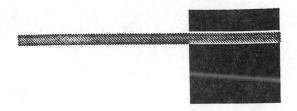

List of Chapter Tables

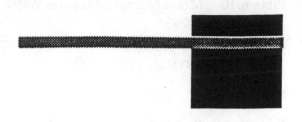

List of Figures

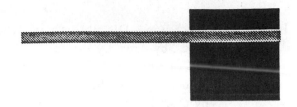

List of Standard Tables

Annex X. Calculating Basic Consumption Aggregates

Introduction

One of the most important uses of household data sets is to analyze poverty and the distribution of welfare. The very first step in this analysis is the construction of a basic measure of monetary welfare that will make it possible to rank households by their welfare level and to assess what progress alternative policies are having in reducing poverty.

In this annex, we provide an overview of the general steps taken in calculating a monetary welfare measure based on consumption. The intent here is to make the reader aware of the initial steps needed in order to use the data collected for welfare analysis. We do not provide detailed formulas and algorithms. Individual researchers in statistical institutes, other Government agencies, and other private and public institutions looking for detailed practical instructions for the actual calculation of consumption aggregates should refer to some of the recent work done in the LSMS division (Lanjouw and Lanjouw 1996, Hentschel and Lanjouw 1996) and to some upcoming work to be completed in 1996. The construction of total income or savings and the definition and calculation of poverty lines are not covered in this appendix. The reader interested in getting advice on constructing income aggregates should consult Johnson, McKay and Round (1990). The reader interested in advice on the setting of poverty lines or on the methods for making comparisons should refer to the excellent documentation in Ravallion (1994) and Demery, Ferroni, and Grootaert (1993).

This appendix is organized in five main sections. First, the rationale for working with a welfare measure based on consumption is explained. Next, the main methodological issues dealing with the construction of consumption aggregates are discussed. In particular, all the components needed for constructing the consumption aggregates using current and implicit expenditures are outlined. Each one of them is reviewed and the main problems and difficulties that can be encountered in their calculations are explained. These include expenditures on food, housing, other housing expenditure, transport, education, health, other non food expenditure, and the flow of services derived from the use of own durable assets. In the third and fourth sections, the major issues in building regional and time price deflators and in making adjustments to take family size and composition into account are outlined. Finally, other important implementation issues, like the treatment of missing values, the adjustment for missing values, and programming are reviewed.

Why use Consumption as a Measure of Welfare?

The aim of the exercise is to obtain an interpersonally comparable monetary measure of welfare on which assessments of the impact of policies can be based and for which there will be reasonably wide public agreement about the conclusions drawn. The first issue is to decide what we mean by welfare and how we propose to measure it.

Economists want welfare measurements to be consistent with the consumption choices made by people on the assumption that the evaluation of somebody's level of welfare should be based on their subjective choices. This theory is based on the fact that the combination of commodities that are consumed by individuals, given their budget constraint, is an expression of their utility function. In fact, if we assume that consumers make rational choices (derived from a well-defined set of preferences), then the commodities that they consume represent those choices for a given set of prices, family composition, and so on. Following the economist's paradigm, we would like to measure the utility level that is an expression of their level of satisfaction or happiness. Under standard conditions (common tastes, complete markets, and flexible prices), it has been proven that the minimum cost of a given utility level (the consumer's cost function) represents the monetary measure of utility, which can be measured by the actual expenditure on consumption. Following this approach, one is aiming to estimate the "value" to each person of the commodities (goods and services) that were "consumed" in a given period of time (Pollack 1991, Deaton and Muellbauer 1980, Varian 1978).

There are several caveats and limitations that have to be taken into account when using this approach to derive a monetary measure of welfare. First of all, we have to decide which commodities enter in the utility function. This list will depend not only on the inclination of the analyst but also on the availability of data and resources. We also have to adjust the welfare measure to take into account differences in the cost of living and household size and composition. Some special adjustments may also need to be made to take into account market imperfections, transaction costs, and rationing, all of which might preclude access to all commodities. Lastly, there are other factors that are very important for determining the well-being of individuals that might not be easily quantified in one comprehensive index, like their nutritional, health, and education status. As a matter of fact, what we propose to measure is a narrowly defined measure of welfare, but it is the starting point for welfare analysis. The most important thing at this stage is to obtain the proper ranking of the households. Once we are confident that this has been obtained, then it is possible to expand the analysis to other dimensions of poverty and see how they relate to the welfare ranking that was previously obtained. (A good introduction to the different approaches is in Ravallion 1994.)

The school of thought presented here, which is shared by the poverty analysts in the LSMS division of the World Bank, uses current total consumption as the measure of consumption. There is also another school of thought that uses total income as the basic measure of welfare. Even though from a conceptual point of view we believe that income could also be the basis for calculating welfare, we contend that for several reasons consumption is a better measure of welfare.

First, income does not benefit the household until it is used for consumption purposes (in other words, saving or borrowing do not enter the definition of utility). Consumption is often regarded as providing a better representation of lifetime welfare, since households often smooth their consumption in response to variations in their income earnings. In such cases, using income would overlook the role played by consumption in reducing variation in the household welfare over time (Deaton 1992, Chaudhuri and Ravallion 1994). This is also especially true given that data are collected over a short period of time and cannot cover a long retrospective period.

We also have more confidence that data collected on consumption and expenditure are more accurate than data collected on income. To calculate total income, it is necessary to add the revenues from wage employment and net revenues from private and agricultural enterprises. In order to calculate these net revenues, it is necessary to collect detailed information on businesses and agricultural production, which increases the possibility that inaccuracies will affect the data. When we want to measure the well-being of the poor, for example, we are likely to find consumption to be much easier to estimate than income, since households essentially consume basic foods and non-food items while their income may come from a myriad of sources at different periods. There is also the well-founded assumption that the interviewee will not declare all his or her income for fear of having to pay income tax.

Methodological Aspects of Calculating Total Consumption

It is surprisingly difficult to provide specific recommendations on how to construct consumption aggregates in practice. This is partly due to the fact that only a few references exist in some World Bank and UN publications (Delaine and others 1992, Johnson, McKay, and Round 1990, and UN Publications 1989 among others) and because there is a lack of consensus among economists about how to apply the principles derived from economic theory in practice. In addition, each questionnaire is unique (even LSMS questionnaires are quite different from each other). The general overview provided here draws from a pool of methodologies and experiences that have been used in calculating consumption aggregates in several countries and that have been proved to be relatively non-controversial. Other more complicated methodologies could always be used to calculate specific components if this is deemed to be necessary by the analyst.

When considering alternative approaches, it is important to realize that there are several trade-offs to consider that may or may not have an impact on the ranking of the households. For example, there is the trade-off between the amount of data it would be desirable to collect and the resources available to collect it and the trade-off between complexity and transparency. The more assumptions that are used to calculate the components of the aggregates, the more difficult it will be to justify and explain all the assumptions needed to carry out the analysis, and thus ultimately the credibility of the methodology might be questioned (Hentschel and Lanjouw 1996).

What to Include

Total actual consumption, which is the monetary measure of welfare that we describe here, can be calculated as the sum of the values of all goods and services used by the households in a given time period and deflated by a price index and a measure of household size and composition. What is actually going to be calculated is a measure of total actual and implicit expenditures necessary to acquire those goods and services. Expenditure is measured by the quantity consumed times the price. Where the quantity is "consumed," it is destroyed by use at that instant. The prices are the price paid by the consumers at the exact point in space and time at which consumption occurred. With some unavoidable averaging over time and space, as determined by the data, one will end up with a reasonably conventional measure of "expenditure" on consumption.

The first basic step towards calculating total consumption is to define clearly the sub-aggregates of commodity groups to be considered and the expenditure items that are going to be used to estimate it. This list of expenditure aggregates does not have to be the same in every situation but can differ from country to country, depending on the particular issues to be analyzed and the availability of the required variables. Having said that, there are some general guidelines that should be followed in determining the expenditure aggregates to be considered.

One fundamental point to keep in mind is that total expenditure is composed of actual physical expenditures and imputed expenditures, which reflect the value of goods and services used by the households that have been received for free or that have been produced by the households themselves. Actual expenditure should be evaluated at the current prices faced by the households. By current prices, we mean the actual price paid by the household. In most available surveys, only expenditure data are available; however, in more recent surveys, both quantities and expenditures are reported. In these cases, it is possible to calculate the unit values, which are equal to the value divided by the quantity. In any case, prices are different across different groups — spatially, temporally, or through rationing (Hentschel and Lanjouw 1996). This is a point to keep in mind later on when we will discuss the evaluation of specific commodities and the creation of regional price indices.

The value of goods and services received for free have to be included in the calculation of welfare to be sure that the ranking among households reflects the actual differences in their standards of living and not the differences in their access to free commodities or in the local price structures. Therefore, when households use goods or services that are available for free or that are produced by the household and are not paid for, we want to make sure that we estimate the value of those goods and services if we think that adding their value to the measure of welfare will change the ranking of the households with respect to their standards of living.

One special case in which goods and services are received for free is the use of public goods. In principle, we would like to include the value of all public goods used, but in practice, this process is quite difficult, because we would need to know the cost of these commodities and the exact use made of them by the household. In some cases, if some services are delivered only to a group of (better-off) people and not to another group of (worse-off) people who have to pay high market price for it, we want to make sure that we evaluate these goods and services to quantify the differences that exist between the two groups in terms of welfare (Hentschel and Lanjouw 1996). In other cases, for example, the use of public roads, it would be quite difficult to assess the actual value used by each households, even though we might suspect that wealthier people, who drive in their own cars, make more use of the roads than poorer people who use buses. One way to find out who benefits the most from the use of public goods is to perform incidence analysis and find out from which welfare class (calculated without subsidies) come those who actually make the most use and, therefore, derive the most benefit from public services. This is a way of assessing how the subsidies affect the distribution of total welfare and who would benefit or lose from privatization or cost recovery policies.

The value of time spent on leisure and other household activities should, in theory, also be included in the welfare measure. Not only should leisure be considered as a component of the utility function but also of household activities, such as cleaning, cooking, and taking care of the children, which are important economic activities usually performed by women that should be taken into account. This is seldom done in practice and is not recommended here because of theoretical and practical difficulties, for example, how do we value time? Which wage or reservation wage rate should be used? Do we have available detailed data on time use?

All expenditure items that have no impact on the level of current welfare or that represent investments in the household's production should be excluded, since we want to calculate the total value of the consumption that will determine the household current level of welfare. Some examples of items that do not increase the welfare of the households include expenditure on taxes, transfers to other households or individuals, and repayment of loans. It should be clear that, even though these items are not going to be included in the calculation of the welfare measure, they should be included in the survey questionnaire and their amounts calculated. In fact, it would be interesting to know what is the share of taxes paid by the households given their level of total expenditure. Similarly, transfers cannot be included in the welfare calculation because they do not provide additional consumption to the remitting household. In addition, if we account for the recipient's expenditure of the transfer, the same expenditure would be recorded twice, once in the remitting household and then again in the recipient household. Still, as in the case of taxes, it is important to calculate the level of transfers and assess how much of a burden they are on the remitting individuals.

All expenditures on inputs for or other investments in the production of the household's commodities should also be excluded to avoid double counting. Generally, the distinction between consumption and investment items is very clear. Take, for example, farm inputs; including them would lead to an increase in the level of welfare above the real value of the production used for home consumption. The expenses of renovating a home should be excluded because they represent an investment in the assets owned by the household. Occasionally, the distinction is not clear. A good example is expenditure for education, which is commonly included as a current expenditure, but it could also be interpreted as an investment in the child's future.

In conclusion, the complete list of items and groups to be included in the calculation of welfare does not have to be predetermined exactly. In any case, we suggest defining one or more aggregate measures of welfare and then performing some sensitivity analysis on the ranking of the households to determine whether the alternative calculation methods matter or not.

The next step toward the calculation of total expenditure is to identify and locate in the questionnaire the variables that represent the items in which we are interested. This task can be very simple when all the sections containing expenditure variables are in clearly separated modules. However, it gets more complicated when the components of other expenditure variables that are included in other modules have to be added to the expenditure groups that have been identified. For example, the variables relating to education expenditure might be located in the education module or in the other household expenditure section, and the expenditure on electricity, water, and other housing might be included in the housing section, or in the other monthly expenditure section.

One additional problem is that, once all the main expenditure variables have been identified, it is still possible that some other variables relating to the same or similar expenditure items are present in different sections of the questionnaire. This raises the issue of choosing one variable over the other or excluding part of a variable in order to avoid double counting. For example, the value of food received from other sources reported in the food expenditure section should be comparable to the value reported in the wage employment section. If, in fact, the value of food reported in the wage section exceeds the amount reported in the food section, the difference should be added to the welfare measure.

Several of the problems mentioned above arise from decisions that were taken when the questionnaire was designed. What we suggest for future surveys is to prepare a note on the calculation of total income and expenditure before the questionnaire is finalized. This should be detailed enough to make explicit reference to the specific variables that can be obtained. This exercise can help to determine whether all of the variables that are needed are going to be collected and if there are any overlaps among them.

Food

Food expenditure is one of the most important consumption items for a large part of the population and especially for poor households in the poorest countries. In fact, food consumption is one of the fundamental basic needs, and, according to some economists the percentage of total expenditure allocated to food represents an important indication of poverty (Lipton 1983 and 1988). An accurate measure of food consumption should include the value of items derived from actual purchases and the estimation of the consumption of food commodities derived from own production or received in form of gifts, remittances, or wage payments.

Ideally, to estimate the value of the consumption of a commodity in a given time interval, we would like to get the actual expenditure for the quantity consumed of that item in that given reference period. Sometimes the choice of the reference period might be crucial in determining the resulting calculations. This can be illustrated by looking at the difference between the purchasing pattern of perishable commodities (milk, for example) and storable commodities (such as rice). Perishable commodities are purchased on a daily or a weekly basis, and a one or two week recall question will yield the right values. Storable commodities, on the other hand, might be purchased every two or three months. If, for example, the household purchases a sack of rice weighing 50 kilos every two months, the amount purchased during the last two weeks might not give an accurate measure of rice consumption, which will be closer to 12 kilos than to 50 kilos. Therefore, longer periods of recall or flexible recall methods are preferable to shorter recall periods. To overcome these potential problems, the analyst should verify the recall period used and the specific instructions that were given to the interviewers (for example, were they supposed to prorate the quantities purchased to a meaningful time period?). If possible, the questionnaire should be designed to include provisions for dealing with such occurrences. (For an example of the implication of the confusion about the item interval used, see Lanjouw and Lanjouw 1996. They show that the imperfect matching of recall period to the item purchased can undermine the whole Engel curve approach to poverty analysis — which is implicit in all the poverty measurement work that is usually done.)

In any event, even if the analyst wants to use actual consumption values, commodities should be valued at the actual purchase price faced by the household when available. The general rule of thumb is to use the observed price closest to the household. In other words, if we know the price paid by the household, we would use that price to value the consumption of those commodities When available, these prices are referred to as unit values. The main difference between unit values and prices is that the former reflect the quality choice made by the household. Not only are they a direct indication of the choice made by the household, but they may also contain other indications of the consumer's behavior. The only problem with using unit values is that they are more difficult to use to calculate price deflators (Deaton 1992).

The quantities of food received from other sources or produced by the households should be valued at the price that the household is more likely to face. We suggest the following alternatives in the order of preference: a) the price that the household would have had to pay for the same item; b) the median price paid by the households by cluster; c) the median price paid by the households by sub-region; d) cluster prices from the community questionnaire; and e) medians of cluster prices from the community questionnaire; and so on up to national level aggregates if necessary.

Housing and Shelter

All researchers agree that housing is an important component in the bundle of goods and services consumed by the households and that it should be included in the calculation of total expenditure. Some households rent the dwelling they live in while others live in a dwelling of their own. Those who rent their dwelling are incurring current expenditures for their housing. For those who live in their own house, there are no equivalent payments to be made, yet these people are still consuming housing services. Thus, to yield comparable estimates of the welfare generated by the consumption of housing services, all households should be treated in the same way with respect to housing services.

When it comes to the actual measurements to be used to estimate the value of owner-occupied housing, various alternatives have been used by different researchers depending on their particular inclination, on which country is being analyzed, and on how much data is available. The first alternative is to use the estimate given by the household itself on the value of the rent that they would have to pay to live in that same dwelling if they did not own it. This alternative is feasible only when there is an actual rental market and when the information given in the questionnaire and the data are judged to be of reasonably good quality.

The second alternative is to estimate the value of rent using the results from an econometric analysis based on the characteristics of the house itself. The rental value paid by renters (either in nominal or log form) is regressed on housing (not household) characteristics such as number of rooms, type of roof, type of floor, type of sanitation and services available, location and so on. The results are then used to predict the rental values for the households that own their dwelling. This alternative is acceptable when there is an actual rental market for properties.

The third alternative is to use the value of the houses (or estimates if values are not available) of owner-occupied households and use the ratio between value of the houses and the rent paid in a similar area for a similar house to estimate the value of the rent. If most of the households report a resale value for their property, then this task is reduced to estimating the values of houses when a value is not available. In this case, an hedonic regression analysis technique similar to the one described above should be used. Here, the value of housing (or its log) is regressed on the characteristics of the dwelling, and the results are used to estimate the values of housing for non-reporting households.
In this case some analysts suggest using the Heckman correction technique to correct for selection bias between renters and non-renters when estimating the regression of the renters to be used to extrapolate the values for the non-renters (for examples, see Glewwe 1987b and Kozel 1990).

Other Housing Expenses

These expenditures, sometimes referred to as utilities (not to be confused with the utility function), in general, include expenses necessary for the functioning of the dwelling such as electricity for lighting, heating, cooking, water, gas, wood for cooking, and so on. In most questionnaires, these expenses are recorded individually in a separate sub-section in the housing section. We also want to make sure that the value of own-produced commodities and of goods and services received for free only by a specific group of households are included.

We want to make sure that, in dealing with this type of expenditures, items are not included more than once (in other words, they are not double-counted). The risk of double counting is particularly acute in this case. To avoid this problem, the first thing to do is to separate rental costs from other housing expenses and evaluate them separately. When these expenditures are bundled together (for example, in apartment complexes, water and electricity may be paid in one single payment to a maintenance company, the municipalities, or even to the government), they should be compared to expenditures reported as single items.

Not all housing expenditures are made directly by the household. In some instances, as in the case of water and fuel for cooking, households receive these for free or collect them themselves. The value of these goods and services should be included in the measure of welfare. Sometimes this is not done because the amounts involved are very small and do not vary across welfare categories. On other occasions, this procedure is deemed to be too difficult. To include them, the analyst should evaluate either the amount that the households would have paid to purchase those items or the cost in terms of time that the household spent to collect the water or the wood. The first alternative is preferable if the amounts of the wood or water consumed are available and if there is a local market for these commodities that can be used to derive unit prices. If such a market does not exist, then the value of the time of the household members should be used to estimate the cost of water and wood, assuming that estimates of the time spent in these activities are available.

When estimating the value of household time, in theory, we want to determine either the opportunity cost to the household members or the amount that should have been paid to someone else to perform the same activity. The two measurements are not necessarily the same. Aside from the important theoretical debate on the inclusion of the value of household members' time spent on producing household commodities mentioned above, we recommend using a wage rate that reflects some type of estimate of the minimum wage currently used in the area. Not estimating the value of time from these activities would exaggerate the poverty gap.

The last issue to deal with is the case in which only few households are receiving some services free of charge or at very low cost, while others have to pay a very high price for it. In these cases, it is important to determine the value of the subsidy by imputing the value of the services that are delivered free of charge to those households in order to make their level of welfare comparable. Here, the estimate of these costs should be based on the unit prices observed in the market. These unit prices may be very high. Therefore, the value of the services delivered expresses the maximum amount of the subsidy that is provided to people who have access to the service with respect to the people who have to pay for it. In practice, the imputation of utility consumption might be done using some type of regression analysis involving an estimation of the quantity and use of utility services. An interesting case on the estimation of water costs is in Hentschel and Lanjouw (1996).

Besides the housing expenses mentioned above, local property taxes and maintenance expenses can also be reported and identified in the questionnaire. They can be identified by all the households that own their dwelling and are usually included in the rental fee paid to the landlord by renting households. Therefore, they should be reflected in the estimates of the rental value for homeowners.

Transport

All the variables relative to different transport expenses in the different expenditure sections should be added together, provided that they have not been included already. Expenses for transport are usually available from two or more sections of the questionnaire. They are reported in the category of own-car expenses (fuel, repairs, insurance and so on), or of public transport expenses.

In addition, the transport expenses incurred by household members in going to school or to work may be reported in the education or the dependent work sections, and some of these costs might even be subsidized by the employer. Some people argue that transport expenditure to go to work should be regarded as an input that adds to the utility of the individual rather than as a "regular" consumption expenditure.

Education

Information on education expenditures can be found in the summary expenditure and the education sections. Detailed information is usually available for tuition and other school expenses for each member of the household. The only task here is to add up the values of all the individuals and to calculate household totals.

Health

Information on health expenditures can be found in two places. Recall expenditure for medical services and medicines are collected for the households as a unit and separately for the individual household member for the past two or four weeks in case a medical consultation has taken place. Our suggestion is to add up all the actual expenses for medical goods and services reported in the household section, provided that they are consistent with the sum of the total expenses of all the individuals as reported in the individual section. While individual expenses are larger and probably more accurate, they cover a limited time frame.

Other Non-Food Expenditures

After all the main components of total expenditure have been calculated, there may still be some other important aggregate items in the survey that are relevant for policy analysis in that specific country. Otherwise, we are left with the task of combining together the remaining expenditure items into one generic category.

Durables

Consumer durables provide a flow of services over a period of time, and a measure of their value should be included to capture the correct level of welfare of the households, especially if the ownership of consumer durables is more prevalent for one particular group of households than for other groups. One way to include the value of consumer durables is to evaluate the stream of consumption services that arise from the ownership of durable commodities, or in other words to calculate their user value in the 12 months preceding the interview.

Several different methodologies can be used to perform the actual evaluation of the value of use of durables (Katz 1983 and 1989 and Kozel 1990). The choice will depend on the availability of data needed to carry out this evaluation. Information on consumer durables is collected in almost all surveys, but the variables may not necessarily be the same. They may include the type of commodity, the purchase price, the years of use, the current resale value, the location of acquisition, and so on.

A very simple methodology consists of estimating the yearly value of the good by dividing the actual replacement cost of the new commodity by the average lifetime for that type of commodity. The average lifetime can be calculated by multiplying the average time of ownership by two if we assume that the distribution of the years of life of the items is uniformly distributed. The only data needed is the actual replacement value at the time of the interview and the age of the item in years.

A more sophisticated and more data intensive method is to calculate the user value by using the actual depreciation rate calculated using the value and the age of each item. This approach is more correct and also has the advantage of taking into account the opportunity cost of keeping the item or selling it and investing the money at the real interest rate. However, it might not be applicable due to a lack of data.

Price Deflators Over Regions and Over Time

Price deflators should be calculated to adjust the welfare measure based on expenditure in order to be able to compare welfare levels across geographical areas and across time if we suspect that the prices faced by households are very different from area to area or if the data have been collected over a period of time during which inflation was high. In rural areas, for example, the cost of living is usually lower than in urban areas or metropolitan areas. The standard alternatives suggested are to take into account the differences in the cost of living either by calculating different poverty lines or by deflating the welfare measure by the appropriate cost of living index. In this section, we present the methodology to calculate regional price deflators.

To simplify the analysis we suggest focusing on a limited number of geographical locations that are pertinent to the analysis and where we suspect that major differences might exist. Of course, the choice of these areas depends on the geographical characteristics of the country and on the patterns of transportation costs. Once these areas have been chosen, a few tests can be run using the prices of some specific commodities to verify the existence of the differences and whether they matter. At the end of this exercise we would like to obtain one deflator for each period and for each of the geographical locations previously identified to measure the average difference in prices from the national average at one given point in time. This deflator is a composite index that takes into account the prices of all of the commodities purchased by the households.

The procedure to calculate the general price index consists of calculating a price index for different commodity groups or components of the budget shares of the population for each time period. The price indices of the different commodity groups are then combined in one single index using the average national budget shares of a particular group of the population. One possibility is to use the budget shares of the bottom 40 percent of the population. Another, better alternative is to use the budget shares of the poor population. In this way, the prices of the commodities that are consumed in large quantities by poor people receive a bigger weight and are more prominent in the composition of the index and are not affected by the regional purchasing patterns.

In practice, there are several issues to consider when calculating price deflators for commodity groups. First, we must consider the type of prices that are available. In this case, cluster or store prices are preferable to the price reported by the households (referred to before as unit values) since they incorporate quality characteristics. If local prices for standard commodities are available, price indices by commodity groups can easily be calculated. If the only prices that are available are the unit values (derived by dividing actual expenditure by quantities), then we have to define the methodology to be used to calculate price indices by commodity group and consider whether we want to adjust them to take into account quality differences (see Deaton 1992 and, for an example of a method of adjusting for quality differences, see Ravallion and Chen 1996). In this case, we have to calculate the average regional price for a commodity group for a particular region at a particular time, in other words, to compare the actual total cost of the bundle of commodities purchased by the reference population in an area to the actual cost of the same commodity group (even if in different quantities) in another area. The difference (ratio) from the national average will yield the commodity group regional index (for a useful example on the use of different price indices for China, see Howes and Lanjouw, forthcoming).

One alternative is to convert the prices of each commodity for each household into indices that represent the deviation from the average national price paid at a given time. These prices can then be combined into meaningful commodity group prices using the budget shares of a reference population. Once commodity group prices have been obtained for each household, regional indices can be calculated by taking the average of all of the observations on each given area for each given time or by regressing the prices observed on the location, time variable, and other characteristics and then using the results from the coefficients to derive the indices. When dealing with the prices of food and other commodities, using averages is easier, but to compare prices that may differ because of qualitative characteristics, such as the price of housing, then it is advisable to use econometric analysis. The resulting price indices take into account only the effect of location, excluding the effect for quality differences for any given type of commodity group, housing for example (Berndt 1991).

Once price indices for food, housing, and personal and other food expenditures have been calculated, they can be combined in one price index using the budget shares of the bottom 40th percentile of the population. In some cases the prices for some commodity groups will not be available. The best thing to do in these cases is to assume that they are the same as the average commodity price index they represent. In other words, they can be excluded from the calculation as long as the weights used include only the budget shares of the other commodities.

Per Capita or Per Adult Equivalent?

Welfare measures are usually calculated by adding up the total household expenditure during the reference period. The data, in fact, are collected at the household level and contain several expenditure items that are made for all the members of the households. We are interested in the level of individual welfare, which will depend on the number of people that are sharing the resources available. Therefore, we have to adjust the level of welfare calculated at the household level to take into account the number of people in the household. The simplest way to correct for household size and composition is to calculate per capita expenditure levels, obtained by dividing the total household expenditure by the household size.

There are other alternative methodologies suggested in the literature on how to adjust for family size and composition. They take into account not only the number of people but also their consumption capabilities and economies of scales generated by the presence of more individuals in the household (Deaton and Muellbauer 1980, Deaton 1992, Lanjouw and Ravallion 1995, and Browning 1992). The choice of method, once again, will depend on the particular country situation and on the specific assumptions made by the analyst. Our suggestion is always to start with a straight per capita measure that should be reported and compared with the alternative adult equivalent adjusted measure to evaluate the differences in the welfare ranking of the individuals.

Other Implementation Issues

There are several other detailed issues and adjustments that might need to be made in calculating aggregate consumption. We will briefly touch on some of these issues.

Missing Values and Outliers

There are a large number of variables that are used in calculating the welfare measure. If missing values are not treated, every missing value in any of the components might cause the elimination of the household in question from the analysis. Sometimes this item might represent only a small percentage of the total expenditure. Therefore, it advisable to replace missing values either with a zero consumption value or with estimates of the median or means by specific categorical variables, like cluster, location, regions, or any other relevant classification if you know that the household consumes a quantity greater than zero. Outliers can be treated similarly, provided that all values outside a certain range are first set to missing and then replaced as suggested above. The issue then becomes: what are the criteria to clean the data and screen outliers? (see Box 7.4).

Ad Hoc Adjustments to Avoid Double Counting

The possibility of double counting is always present. This is not only a conceptual issue dealing with the classification of commodities as inputs of other consumption items, as described above, but also a practical issue of combining different sections of the questionnaire together. The recommendation here is to run a few comparison checks at the time when all the different components are pulled together. For example, if the total household transportation expenditures reported in the expenditure section include expenses for travel to work or school, the values from those other sections should not simply be added to the others. (Simple check: total transport expenditures should be larger than the expenses for transportation reported in the employment and education sections together).

Programming

The amount of programming and data manipulation needed to combine large data sets from different levels of aggregation and from different sections of the questionnaire can be overwhelming. One suggestion is to use a statistical package with good data management capabilities that can be used with batch programs.

In our experience, we have found that it is useful to create a clear programming structure or programming tree to keep track of the flow of programs and output files. This structure should be documented clearly and should explain how the programs are able to manipulate the original files, which more or less replicate different components of the questionnaire, and to create the total expenditure variable and its different components. If these programs are prepared clearly, not only can they be rerun when changes are made to the original data sets or to the assumptions to the calculation of some specific components, but they can also provide the detailed transparent documentation on the steps used to make the calculations.

The function of the main program is pull in the files created from the different subprograms, and to make the necessary adjustments to reduce the possibility of double counting.

Ideally, what we want to have as a final output of this exercise is a set of files at the household level that contain all of the expenditures for the major groups of commodities and the total expenditure at the household level on a monthly or yearly basis. An additional file should contain the main household expenditure for the main food groups. These two files can be the basis for calculating the expenditure shares. Note that at this stage it is extremely important that a clear distinction is made between missing values and zero consumption values. The values for all the items that are not consumed by the household should be equal to zero, if not otherwise noted.

Conclusions

The first step in the analysis of welfare and poverty is the construction of a basic measure of monetary welfare. For a variety of reasons mentioned above, the best measure of welfare is a measure of the individual (household) consumption aggregates, as expressed by current per capita (or adult equivalent) expenditure deflated by an appropriate price index. The actual process of constructing this aggregate is not trivial and requires a great deal of detailed analysis. The different expenditure components have to be specified and identified. Investment items have to be carefully excluded, and care should be taken not to double count items as inputs and consumption values.

In addition, some of the items are expressed at the actual price, and items received for free or from own production have to be evaluated at a given price. The prices themselves are collected in different ways and can vary greatly from month to month or from area to area. Many assumptions and adjustments have to be made to ensure that the ranking of the households reflects the actual differences in standards of living.

The task of constructing aggregates is difficult and time-consuming, and should be carried out with great care. The results will depend also on the interest of the analyst, the particular issues to be analyzed in that particular country, and the availability of the variables. We suggest that the analyst should reflect on the main policy issues in the country with respect to poverty and welfare before the data are collected. This should yield insights into how to use the data to carryout poverty and policy analysis. Then the analyst should lay out the main objectives in the construction of consumption and expenditure aggregates. The insights from this analysis should provide important feedback on the design of the questionnaire. This process will ensure that the welfare measure used reflects the needs of the analysts in the country.

Finally, we strongly recommend documenting this process clearly and in such a way that everybody who uses the data and the analysis is aware of the specific assumptions made and of their implication on the results.

Bibliography

Ainsworth, Martha. 1989. *Socioeconomic Determinants of Fertility in Côte d'Ivoire*. Living Standards Measurement Study Working Paper No. 53. World Bank, Washington, D.C.

_____. 1990. "The Demand for Children in Côte d'Ivoire: Economic Aspects of Fertility and Child Fostering." Ph.D. Dissertation in Economics. Yale University.

_____. 1992. *Economic Aspects of Child Fostering in Côte d'Ivoire*. Living Standards Measurement Study Working Paper No. 92. World Bank, Washington, D.C.

_____, Godlike Koda, George Lwihula, Phare Mujinja, Mead Over, and Innocent Semali. 1992. *Measuring the Impact of Fatal Adult Illness in Sub-Saharan Africa: An Annotated Household Questionnaire*. Living Standards Measurement Study Working Paper No. 90. World Bank, Washington, D.C.

_____, and Juan Munoz. 1986. *The Côte d'Ivoire Living Standards Survey: Design and Implementation*. Living Standards Measurement Study Working Paper No. 26. World Bank, Washington, D.C.

_____, and Jacques van der Gaag. 1988. *Guidelines for Adapting the LSMS Living Standards Questionnaires to Local Conditions*. Living Standards Measurement Study Working Paper No. 34. World Bank, Washington, D.C.

Azorin Poch, Ernesto. 1967. *Curso de Muestreo y Aplicaciones*. Aguilar S.A.: Madrid.

Benefo, Kofi, and T. Paul Schultz. 1994. *Determinants of Fertility and Child Mortality in Côte d'Ivoire and Ghana*. LSMS Working Paper No. 103. World Bank, Washington, D.C.

Berndt, Ernst. 1991. *The Practice of Econometrics: Classic and Contemporary*. Reading, MA: Addison-Wesley Publishing Company.

Browning, Martin. 1992. "Children and Household Economic Behaviour." *Journal of Economic Literature*, 30:1434-1475.

Chaudhuri, Shubham, and Martin Ravallion. 1994. "How Well Do Static Indicators Identify the Chronically Poor?" *Journal of Public Economics*, 53:367-394.

Cochran, William G. 1977. *Sampling Techniques*. 3rd ed. New York: John Wiley and Sons.

Coulombe, Harold, and Lionel Demery. 1993. *Household Size in Côte d'Ivoire: Sampling Bias in the CILSS*. Living Standards Measurement Study Working Paper No. 97. World Bank, Washington, D.C.

Cox, Donald, and Emmanuel Jimenez. 1993. "Private and public safety nets—transfers between households." *Outreach*. No. 13 (September 1993). Policy Research Department, World Bank, Washington, D.C.

Deaton, Angus. 1992. *Understanding Consumption*. Oxford: Clarendon Press.

Deaton, Angus. 1994. "The Analysis of Household Surveys: Microeconometric Analysis for Development Policy." Book manuscript. Poverty and Human Resources Division, Policy Research Department, World Bank, Washington, D.C.

_____, and Dwayne Benjamin. 1988. *The Living Standards Survey and Price Policy Reform: A Study of Cocoa and Coffee Production in Côte d'Ivoire*. Living Standards Measurement Study Working Paper No. 44. World Bank, Washington, D.C.

_____, and John Muellbauer. 1980. *Economics and Consumer Behavior*. New York: Cambridge University Press.

Delaine, Ghislaine and others. 1992. *The Social Dimensions of Adjustment Integrated Survey: A Survey to Measure Poverty and Understand the Effects of Policy Change on Households*. Social Dimensions of Adjustment Working Paper No. 14. World Bank, Washington, D.C.

Demery, Lionel, Marco Ferroni, and Christiaan Grootaert. 1993. *Understanding the Social Effects of Policy Reform*. A World Bank Study. World Bank, Washington, D.C.

_____, and Christiaan Grootaert. 1993. "Correcting for Sampling Bias in the Measurement of Welfare and Poverty in the Côte d'Ivoire Living Standards Survey." *The World Bank Economic Review*, 7(3):263-292.

Deming, William Edwards. 1950. *Some Theory of Sampling*. Dover Publications: New York.

Gertler, Paul, and Jacques van der Gaag. 1990. *The Willingness to Pay for Medical Care: Evidence from Two Developing Countries*. Johns Hopkins University Press: Baltimore, MD.

Glewwe, Paul. 1987a. *The Distribution of Welfare in Peru in 1985-86*. Living Standards Measurement Study Working Paper No. 42. World Bank, Washington, D.C.

_____. 1987b. *The Distribution of Welfare in the Republic of Côte d'Ivoire in 1985*. Living Standards Measurement Study Working Paper No. 29. World Bank, Washington, D.C.

_____. 1990. *Investigating the Determinants of Household Welfare in Côte d'Ivoire*. Living Standards Measurement Study Working Paper No. 71. World Bank, Washington, D.C.

_____. 1991. "Investigating the Determinants of Household Welfare in Côte d'Ivoire." *Journal of Development Economics*. April.

_____, and Gillette Hall. 1992. *Poverty and Inequality during Unorthodox Adjustment: The Case of Peru, 1985-90*. Living Standards Measurement Study Working Paper No. 86. World Bank, Washington, D.C.

_____, and Hanan Jacoby. 1992. *Estimating the Determinants of Cognitive Achievement in Low-Income Countries: The Case of Ghana*. Living Standards Measurement Study Working Paper No. 91. World Bank, Washington, D.C.

_____, and Jacques van der Gaag. 1988. *Confronting Poverty in Developing Countries: Definitions, Information and Policies*. Living Standards Measurement Study Working Paper No. 48. World Bank, Washington, D.C.

Grootaert, Christiaan. 1982. *The Conceptual Basis of Measures of Household Welfare*. Living Standards Measurement Study Working Paper No. 19. World Bank, Washington, D.C.

_____. 1986. *Measuring and Analyzing the Level of Living in Developing Countries: An Annotated Questionnaire*. Living Standards Measurement Study Working Paper No. 24. World Bank, Washington, D.C.

_____. 1994. *The Determinants of Poverty in Côte d'Ivoire in the 1980s*. World Bank, Washington, D.C.

_____, and Ravi Kanbur. 1990. *Policy-Oriented Analysis of Poverty and the Social Dimensions of Structural Adjustment: A Methodology and Proposed Application to Côte d'Ivoire, 1985-88*. Social Dimensions of Adjustment (SDA) Working Paper. World Bank, Washington, D.C.

Grosbras, Jean-Marie, and Jean-Claude Deville. 1987. "Algorithmes de Tirage." in Droesbeke, Jean Jacques and others, editors. *Les Sondages*. Economica, Paris.

Grosh, Margaret E. 1991. *The Household Survey as a Tool for Policy Change: Lessons from the Jamaica Survey of Living Conditions*. Living Standards Measurement Study Working Paper No. 80. World Bank, Washington, D.C.

_____, and Paul Glewwe. 1995. *A Guide to Living Standards Measurement Study Surveys and Their Data Sets*. Living Standards Measurement Study Working Paper No. 120. World Bank, Washington, D.C.

_____, Qing-hua Zhao, and Henri-Pierre Jeancard. 1995. "The Sensitivity of Consumption Aggregates to Questionnaire Formulation: Some Preliminary Evidence from the Jamaican and Ghanaian LSMS Surveys." Poverty and Human Resources Division, Policy Research Department, World Bank, Washington, D.C.

Hansen, Morris H., William N. Hurwitz, and William G. Madow. 1953. *Sample Survey Methods and Theory*. John Wiley and Sons: New York.

Hentschel, Jesko, and Peter Lanjouw. 1996. *Constructing an Indicator of Consumption for the Analysis of Poverty: Principles and Illustrations with Reference to Ecuador*. Living Standards Measurement Study Working Paper No. 124. World Bank, Washington, DC.

Howes, Stephen. 1994. "SAS Dominance Module." draft. software package.

_____, and Jean Olson Lanjouw. forthcoming. *Making Poverty Comparisons Taking Into Account Survey Design: How and Why*. Living Standards Measurement Study Working Paper. World Bank, Washington, D.C.

Johnson, Martin, Andrew C. Mckay, and Jeffery I. Round. 1990. *Income and Expenditure in a System of Household Accounts: Concepts and Estimation*. Social Dimensions of Adjustment Working Paper No. 10. World Bank, Washington, D.C.

Jolliffe, Dean. 1995. "Review of the LSMS Agricultural Activities Survey Module." Poverty and Human Resources Division, Policy Research Department, World Bank, Washington, D.C.

Kakwani, Nanak. 1990. *Poverty and Economic Growth: With Application to Côte d'Ivoire*. Living Standards Measurement Study Working Paper No. 63. World Bank, Washington, D.C.

Katz, Arnold J. 1983. "Valuing the Services of Consumer Durables." *Review of Income and Wealth*, 29(4):405-427.

Keyfitz, Nathan. 1951. "Sampling with Probabilities Proportional to Size: Adjustment for Changes in the Probabilities." *Journal of the American Statistical Association*, No. 46.

Kish, Leslie. 1965. *Survey Sampling*. John Wiley and Sons: New York.

Kostermans, Kees. 1994. *Assessing the Quality of Anthropometric Data: Background and Illustrated Guidelines for Survey Managers*. Living Standards Measurement Study Working Paper No. 101. World Bank, Washington, D.C.

Kozel, Valerie. 1990. *The Composition and Distribution of Income in Côte d'Ivoire*. Living Standards Measurement Study Working Paper No. 68. World Bank, Washington, D.C.

Lanjouw, Jean O., and Lanjouw, Peter. 1996. *Comparing Poverty with Non-Identical Consumption Aggregates: Theory and Illustrations from Ecuador and Pakistan*.

Lanjouw, Peter, and Martin Ravallion. 1995. "Poverty and Household Size." *Economic Journal*, 105(433):1415-1434.

Lipton, Michael. 1983. *Poverty, Undernutrition, and Hunger*. World Bank Working Paper No. 597. World Bank, Washington, D.C.

_____. 1988. *The Poor and the Poorest: Some Interim Findings*. World Bank Discussion Paper No. 25, World Bank, Washington, D.C.

Marchant, Timothy, and Christiaan Grootaert. 1991. *The Social Dimensions of Adjustment Priority Survey: An Instrument for the Rapid Identification and Monitoring of Policy Target Groups*. Social Dimensions of Adjustment (SDA) Working Paper No. 12. World Bank, Washington, D.C.

Montgomery, Mark, and Aka Kouamé. 1995. "Fertility and Child Schooling in Côte d'Ivoire: Is There a Tradeoff?" in *The Tradeoff between Numbers of Children and Child Schooling: Evidence from Côte d'Ivoire and Ghana*. LSMS Working Paper No. 112. World Bank, Washington, D.C.

Newman, John, Steen Jorgensen, and Menno Pradhan. 1992. "How Did Workers Benefit?" in Steen Jorgensen, Margaret Grosh, and Mark Schacter, eds., 1992. *Bolivia's Answer to Poverty, Economic Crisis, and Adjustment: The Emergency Social Fund*. World Bank Regional and Sectoral Studies Series. Washington, D.C.

Oliver, Raylynn. 1995a. *Contraceptive Use in Ghana: The Role of Service Availability, Quality, and Price*. LSMS Working Paper No. 111. World Bank, Washington, D.C.

_____. 1995b. "Fertility and Child Schooling in Ghana: Evidence of a Quality/Quantity Tradeoff" in *The Tradeoff between Numbers of Children and Child Schooling: Evidence from Côte d'Ivoire and Ghana*. LSMS Working Paper No. 112. World Bank, Washington, D.C.

Pakistan Integrated Household Survey Project (PIHS). 1992. *Pakistan Integrated Household Survey: Final Results, 1991*. Islamabad, Pakistan.

Peabody, John W., Omar Rahman, Kristin Fox, and Paul Gertler. 1993. *Public and Private Delivery of Primary Health Care Services in Jamaica: A Comparison of Quality in Different Types of Facilities*. March.

Ravallion, Martin. 1991. *Growth and Redistribution Components of Changes in Poverty Measures: A Decomposition with Applications to Brazil and India in the 1980s*. Living Standards Measurement Study Working Paper No. 83. World Bank, Washington, D.C.

_____. 1992. *Poverty Comparisons: A Guide to Concepts and Methods*. Living Standards Measurement Study Working Paper No. 88. World Bank, Washington, D.C.

_____. 1994. "How Well Can Methodology Substitute for Data? Five Experiments in Poverty Analysis." Policy Research Department, World Bank, Washington, D.C. November.

_____, and Benu Bidani. 1993. "A Regional Poverty Profile for Indonesia." *Bulletin of Indonesian Economic Studies*, 29(3):37-68.

_____, and Benu Bidani. 1994. "How Robust is a Poverty Profile?" *The World Bank Economic Review*, 8(1):75-102.

_____, and Shaohua Chen. 1996. "Data in Transition: Assessing Rural Living Standards in Southern China." Policy Research Department, World Bank.

_____, and Gaurav Datt. 1991. *Growth and Redistribution Components of Changes in Poverty Measures: A Decomposition with Applications to Brazil and India in the 1990s*. Living Standards Measurement Study Working Paper No. 83. World Bank, Washington, D.C.

Republic of Ghana. 1981. *1984 Population Census: Enumerator's Manual*. Census Office, Accra, Ghana. November.

Republica de Nicaragua. no date. *Encuesta de Medicion de Nivel de Vida*. Instituto Nacional de Estadisticas y Censos.

Schafgans, Marcia. 1991. *Fertility Determinants in Peru: A Quantity-Quality Analysis*. World Bank Discussion Paper No. 116, Washington, D.C.

Scott, Christopher. 1990. *Master Sample: Advantages and Drawbacks*. Inter-stat, March 1990, No.2, 33-42. Eurostat/ODA/INSEE. French version: 1989. *Echantillon-maître: avantages et incovénients*. STATECO, Dec. 1989, No.60, p.91-105. INSEE.

_____ and others. 1988. "Verbatim Questionnaires Versus Field Translation or Schedules: An Experimental Study." *International Statistical Review*, 56(3):259-278.

_____, and Ben Amenuvegbe. 1989. *Sample Designs for the Living Standards Surveys in Ghana and Mauritania/Plans de sondage pour les enquêtes sur le niveau de vie au Ghana et en Mauritanie*. Living Standards Measurement Study Working Paper No. 49. World Bank, Washington, D.C.

_____, and _____. 1990. *Effect of Recall Duration on Reporting of Household Expenditures: An Experimental Study in Ghana*. Social Dimensions of Adjustment in Sub-Saharan Africa Working Paper No. 6. World Bank, Washington, D.C.

Statistical Institute of Jamaica (STATIN) and World Bank. 1988. *Preliminary Report: Living Conditions Survey, Jamaica*. draft. Kingston, Jamaica. October.

Statistical Institute of Jamaica (STATIN), and Planning Institute of Jamaica (PIOJ). 1989. *Jamaica Survey of Living Conditions, 1989*. Kingston, Jamaica.

_____, and _____. 1994. *Jamaica Survey of Living Conditions, 1992*. Kingston, Jamaica.

_____, and _____. 1995. *Jamaica Survey of Living Conditions, 1993*. Kingston, Jamaica.

Tufte, Edward R. 1983. *The Visual Display of Quantitative Information*. Cheshire, Connecticut: Graphics Press.

UNNHSCP (United Nations National Household Survey Capability Programme). 1982. *Non-Sampling Errors in Household Surveys (Assessment and Control)*. United Nations Department of Technical Cooperation for Development and Statistical Office, New York.

_____. 1985. *Development and Design of Survey Questionnaires.* United Nations Department of Technical Cooperation for Development and Statistical Office, New York.

_____. 1986a. *How the Weigh and Measure Children: Assessing the Nutritional Status of Young Children in Household Surveys.* United Nations Department of Technical Cooperation for Development and Statistical Office, New York.

_____. 1986b. *Sampling Frames and Sample Designs for Integrated Household Survey Programmes.* United Nations Department of Technical Cooperation for Development and Statistical Office, New York.

_____. 1989. *Household Income and Expenditure Surveys: A Technical Study.* United Nations Department of Technical Cooperation for Development and Statistical Office, New York.

Varian, Hal R. 1978. *Microeconomic Analysis.* New York and London: WW Norton and Company.

Verma, Vijay. 1991. *Sampling Methods: Training Handbook.* Statistical Institute for Asia and the Pacific, Tokyo.

Vijverberg, Wim. 1991. *Measuring Income from Family Enterprises with Household Surveys.* Living Standards Measurement Study Working Paper No. 84. World Bank, Washington, D.C.

Wold, Bjorn. 1995. *Community Surveys.* Human Resources Division, Technical Department, Africa Region, World Bank, Washington, D.C.

World Bank. 1993. *Indonesia: Public Expenditures, Prices and the Poor.* Report No. 11293-IND. Indonesia Resident Mission, Country Department III, East Asia and Pacific Region, Washington, D.C.

_____. 1994a. *Jamaica: A Strategy for Growth and Poverty Reduction — Country Economic Memorandum.* Report No. 12702-JM. Country Department III, Country Operations Division 2, Latin America and the Caribbean Region, Washington, D.C.

_____. 1994b. *Viet Nam Poverty Assessment.* Report No. 13442 VN. September 23. Country Operations Division, Country Department I, East Asia and Pacific Region, Washington, D.C.

_____. 1995a. *Ecuador Poverty Report, Part I: Components of a Poverty Alleviation Strategy.* green cover draft, confidential. Report No. 14533-EC. Country Operations Division I, Country Department III, Latin America and the Caribbean Region. June 30.

_____. 1995b. *Republic of Tunisia: From Universal Food Subsidies to a Self-Targeted Program.* draft. Report No. 11946-TUN. Agriculture Operations Division, Maghreb and Iran Department, Middle East and North Africa Region, Washington, D.C.

LSMS Working Papers

No.	TITLE	AUTHOR
1	*Living Standards Surveys in Developing Countries*	Chander/Grootaert/Pyatt
2	*Poverty and Living Standards in Asia: An Overview of the Main Results and Lessons of Selected Household Surveys*	Visaria
3	*Measuring Levels of Living in Latin America: An Overview of Main Problems*	United Nations Statistical Office
4	*Towards More Effective Measurement of Levels of Living, and Review of Work of the United Nations Statistical Office (UNSO) Related to Statistics of Level of Living*	Scott/de Andre/Chander
5	*Conducting Surveys in Developing Countries: Practical Problems and Experience in Brazil, Malaysia, and The Philippines*	Scott/de Andre/Chander
6	*Household Survey Experience in Africa*	Booker/Singh/Savane
7	*Measurement of Welfare: Theory and Practical Guidelines*	Deaton
8	*Employment Data for the Measurement of Living Standards*	Mehran
9	*Income and Expenditure Surveys in Developing Countries: Sample Design and Execution*	Wahab
10	*Reflections of the LSMS Group Meeting*	Saunders/Grootaert
11	*Three Essays on a Sri Lanka Household Survey*	Deaton
12	*The ECIEL Study of Household Income and Consumption in Urban Latin America: An Analytical History*	Musgrove
13	*Nutrition and Health Status Indicators: Suggestions for Surveys of the Standard of Living in Developing Countries*	Martorell
14	*Child Schooling and the Measurement of Living Standards*	Bridsal
15	*Measuring Health as a Component of Living Standards*	Ho
16	*Procedures for Collecting and Analyzing Mortality Data in LSMS*	Sullivan/Cochrane/Kalsbeek
17	*The Labor Market and Social Accounting: A Framework of Data Presentation*	Grootaert
18	*Time Use Data and the Living Standards Measurement Study*	Acharya
19	*The Conceptual Basis of Measures of Household Welfare and Their Implied Surveys Data Requirements*	Grootaert
20	*Statistical Experimentation for Household Surveys: Two Case Studies of Hong Kong*	Grootaert/Cheurg/Fung/Tam
21	*The Collection of Price Data for the Measurement of Living Standards*	Wood/Knight
22	*Household Expenditure Surveys: Some Methodological Issues*	Grootaert/Cheung
23	*Collecting Panel Data in Developing Countries: Does It Make Sense?*	Ashenfelter/Deaton/Solon
24	*Measuring and Analyzing Levels of Living in Developing Countries: An Annotated Questionnaire*	Grootaert
25	*The Demand for Urban Housing in the Ivory Coast*	Grootaert/Dubois
26	*The Côte d'Ivoire Living Standards Survey: Design and Implementation (English-French)*	Ainsworth/Munoz
27	*The Role of Employment and Earnings in Analyzing Levels of Living: A General Methodology with Applications to Malaysia and Thailand*	Grootaert
28	*Analysis of Household Expenditures*	Deaton/Case
29	*The distribution of Welfare in Côte d'Ivoire in 1985 (English-French)*	Glewwe
30	*Quality, Quantity, and Spatial Variation of Price: Estimating Price Elasticities form Cross-Sectional Data*	Deaton
31	*Financing the Health Sector in Peru*	Suarez-Berenguela

LSMS Working Papers

No.	TITLE	AUTHOR
32	*Informal Sector, Labor Markets, and Returns to Education in Peru*	Suarez-Berenguela
33	*Wage Determinants in Côte d'Ivoire*	Van der Gaag/Vijverberg
34	*Guidelines for Adapting the LSMS Living Standards Questionnaires to Local Conditions*	Ainsworth/Van der Gaag
35	*The Demand for Medical Care in Developing Countries: Quantity Rationing in Rural Côte d'Ivoire*	Dor/Van der Gaag
36	*Labor Market Activity in Côte d'Ivoire and Peru*	Newman
37	*Health Care Financing and the Demand for Medical Care*	Gertler/Locay/Sanderson Dor/Van der Gaag
38	*Wage Determinants and School Attainment among Men in Peru*	Stelcner/Arriagada/Moock
39	*The Allocation of Goods within the Household: Adults, Children, and Gender*	Deaton
40	*The Effects of Household and Community Characteristics on the Nutrition of Preschool Children: Evidence from Rural Côte d'Ivoire*	Strauss
41	*Public-Private Sector Wage Differentials in Peru, 1985-86*	Stelcner/Van der Gaag/ Vijverberg
42	*The Distribution of Welfare in Peru in 1985-86*	Glewwe
43	*Profits from Self-Employment: A class Study of Côte d'Ivoire*	Vijverberg
44	*The Living Standards Survey and Price Policy Reform: A Study of Cocoa and Coffee Production in Côte d'Ivoire*	Deaton/Benjamin
45	*Measuring the Willingness to Pay for Social Services in Developing Countries*	Gertler/Van der Gaag
46	*Nonagricultural Family Enterprises in Côte d'Ivoire: A Developing Analysis*	Vijverberg
47	*The Poor during Adjustment: A Case Study of Côte d'Ivoire*	Glewwe/de Tray
48	*Confronting Poverty in Developing Countries: Definitions, Information, and Policies*	Glewwe/Van der Gaag
49	*Sample Designs for the Living Standards Surveys in Ghana and Mauritania (English-French)*	Scott/Amenuvegbe
50	*Food Subsidies: A Case Study of Price Reform in Morocco (English-French)*	Laraki
51	*Child Anthropometry in Côte d'Ivoire: Estimates from Two Surveys, 1895-86*	Strauss/Mehra
52	*Public-Private Sector Wage Comparisons and Moonlighting in Developing Countries: Evidence from Côte d'Ivoire and Peru*	Van der Gaag/Stelcner/Vijverberg
53	*Socioeconomic Determinants of Fertility in Côte d'Ivoire*	Ainsworth
54	*The Willingness to Pay for Education in Developing Countries: Evidence from rural Peru*	Gertler/Glewwe
55	*Rigidite des salaires: Donnees microeconomiques et macroeconomiques sur l'ajustement du marche du travail dans le secteur moderne (French only)*	Levy/Newman
56	*The Poor in Latin America during Adjustment: A Case Study of Peru*	Glewwe/de Tray
57	*The substitutability of Public and Private Health Care for the Treatment of Children in Pakistan*	Alderman/Gertler
58	*Identifying the Poor: Is "Headship" a Useful Concept?*	Rosenhouse
59	*Labor Market Performance as a Determinant of Migration*	Vijverberg
60	*The Relative Effectiveness of Private and Public Schools: Evidence from Two Developing Countries*	Jimenez/Cox
61	*Large Sample Distribution of Several Inequality Measures: With Application to Côte d'Ivoire*	Kakwani
62	*Testing for Significance of Poverty Differences: With Application to Côte d'Ivoire*	Kakwani
63	*Poverty and Economic Growth: With Application to Côte d'Ivoire*	Kakwani

LSMS Working Papers

No.	TITLE	AUTHOR
64	Education and Earnings in Peru's Informal Nonfarm Family Enterprises	Moock/Musgrove/Stelcner
65	Formal and Informal Sector Wage Determination in Urban Low-Income Neighborhoods in Pakistan	Alderman/Kozel
66	Testing for Labor Market Duality: The Private Wage Sector in Côte d'Ivoire	Vijverberg/Van der Gaag
67	Does Education Pay in the Labor Market? The Labor Force Participation, Occupation, and Earnings of Peruvian Women	King
68	The Composition and Distribution of Income in Côte d'Ivoire	Kozel
69	Price Elasticities from Survey Data: Extensions and Indonesian Results	Deaton
70	Efficient Allocation of Transfers to the Poor: The Problem of Unobserved Household Income	Glewwe
71	Investigating the Determinants of Household Welfare in Côte d'Ivoire	Glewwe
72	The Selectivity of Fertility and the Determinants of Human Capital Investments: Parametric and Semiparametric Estimates	Pitt/Rosenzweig
73	Shadow Wages and Peasant Family Labor Supply: An Econometric Application to the Peruvian Sierra	Jacoby
74	The Action of Human Resources and Poverty on One Another: What we have yet to learn	Behrman
75	The Distribution of Welfare in Ghana, 1987-88	Glewwe/Twum-Baah
76	Schooling, Skills, and the Returns to Government Investment in Education: An Exploration Using Data from Ghana	Glewwe
77	Workers' Benefits from Bolivia's Emergency Social Fund	Newman/Jorgensen/Pradhan
78	Dual Selection Criteria with Multiple Alternatives: Migration, Work Status, and Wages	Vijverberg
79	Gender Differences in Household Resource Allocations	Thomas
80	The Household Survey as a Tool for Policy Change: Lessons from the Jamaican Survey of Living Conditions	Grosh
81	Patterns of Aging in Thailand and Côte d'Ivoire	Deaton/Paxson
82	Does Undernutrition Respond to Incomes and Prices? Dominance Tests for Indonesia	Ravallion
83	Growth and Redistribution Components of Changes in Poverty Measure: A Decomposition with Applications to Brazil and India in the 1980s	Ravallion/Datt
84	Measuring Income from Family Enterprises with Household Surveys	Vijverberg
85	Demand Analysis and Tax Reform in Pakistan	Deaton/Grimard
86	Poverty and Inequality during Unorthodox Adjustment: The Case of Peru, 1985-90 (English-Spanish)	Glewwe/Hall
87	Family Productivity, Labor Supply, and Welfare in a Low-Income Country	Newman/Gertler
88	Poverty Comparisons: A Guide to Concepts and Methods	Ravallion
89	Public Policy and Anthropometric Outcomes in Côte d'Ivoire	Thomas/Lavy/Strauss
90	Measuring the Impact of Fatal Adult Illness in Sub-Saharan Africa: An Annotated Household Questionnaire	Ainworth/and others
91	Estimating the Determinants of Cognitive Achievement in Low-Income Countries: The Case of Ghana	Glewwe/Jacoby
92	Economic Aspects of Child Fostering in Côte d'Ivoire	Ainsworth
93	Investment in Human Capital: Schooling Supply Constraints in Rural Ghana	Lavy
94	Willingness to Pay for the Quality and Intensity of Medical Care: Low-Income Households in Ghana	Lavy/Quigley

LSMS Working Papers

No.	TITLE	AUTHOR
95	*Measurement of Returns to Adult Health: Morbidity Effects on Wage Rates in Côte d'Ivoire and Ghana*	Schultz/Tansel
96	*Welfare Implications of Female Headship in Jamaican Households*	Louant/Grosh/Van der Gaag
97	*Household Size in Côte d'Ivoire: Sampling Bias in the CILSS*	Coulombe/Demery
98	*Delayed Primary School Enrollment and Childhood Malnutrition in Ghana: An Economic Analysis*	Glewwe/Jacoby
99	*Poverty Reduction through Geographic Targeting: How Well Does It Work?*	Baker/Grosh
100	*Income Gains for the Poor from Public Works Employment: Evidence from Two Indian Villages*	Datt/Ravallion
101	*Assessing the Quality of Anthropometric Data: Background and Illustrated Guidelines for Survey Managers*	Kostermans
102	*How Well Does the Social Safety Net Work? The Incidence of Cash Benefits in Hungary, 1987-89*	van de Walle/Ravallion/Gautam
103	*Determinants of Fertility and Child Mortality in Côte d'Ivoire and Ghana*	Benefo/Schultz
104	*Children's Health and Achievement in School*	Behrman/Lavy
105	*Quality and Cost in Health Care Choice in Developing Countries*	Lavy/Germain
106	*The Impact of the Quality of Health Care on Children's Nutrition and Survival in Ghana*	Lavy/Strauss/Thomas/de Vreyer
107	*School Quality, Achievement Bias, and Dropout Behavior in Egypt*	Hanushek/Lavy
108	*Contraceptive Use and the Quality, Price, and Availability of Family Planning in Nigeria*	Feyisetan/Ainsworth
109	*Contraceptive Choice, Fertility, and Public Policy in Zimbabwe*	Thomas/Maluccio
110	*The Impact of Female Schooling on Fertility and Contraceptive Use: A Study of Fourteen Sub-Saharan Countries*	Ainsworth/Beegle/Nyamete
111	*Contraceptive Use in Ghana: The Role of Service Availability, Quality, and Price*	Oliver
112	*The Tradeoff between Numbers of Children and Child Schooling: Evidence from Côte d'Ivoire and Ghana*	Montgomery/Kouamé/Oliver
113	*Sector Participation Decisions in Labor Supply Models*	Pradhan
114	*The Quality and Availability of Family Planning Services and Contraceptive Use in Tanzania*	Beegle
115	*Changing Patterns of Illiteracy in Morocco: Assessment Methods Compared*	Lavy/Spratt/Leboucher
116	*Quality of Medical Facilities, Health, and Labor Force Participation in Jamaica*	Lavy/Palumbo/Stern
117	*Who is Most Vulnerable to Macroeconomic Shocks? Hypothesis Tests Using Panel Data from Peru*	Glewwe/Hall
118	*Proxy Means Tests: Simulations and Speculation for Social Programs*	Grosh/Baker
119	*Women's Schooling, Selective Fertility, and Child Mortality in Sub-Saharan Africa*	Pitt
120	*A Guide to Living Standards Measurement Study Surveys and Their Data Sets*	Grosh/Glewwe
121	*Infrastructure and Poverty in Viet Nam*	van de Walle
122	*Comparaisons de la Pauvreté: Concepts et Méthodes*	Ravallion
123	*The Demand for Medical Care: Evidence from Urban Areas in Bolivia*	li
124	*Constructing an Indicator of Consumption for the Analysis of Poverty: Principles and Illustrations with Reference to Ecuador*	Hentschel/Lanjouw
125	*The Contribution of Income Components to Income Inequality in South Africa: A Decomposable Gini Analysis*	Leibbrandt/Woolard/Woolard

Distributors of World Bank Publications

Prices and credit terms vary from country to country. Consult your local distributor before placing an order.

ALBANIA
Adrion Ltd.
Perlat Rexhepi Str.
Pall. 9, Shk. 1, Ap. 4
Tirana
Tel: (42) 274 19; 221 72
Fax: (42) 274 19

ARGENTINA
Oficina del Libro Internacional
Av. Cordoba 1877
1120 Buenos Aires
Tel: (1) 815-8156
Fax: (1) 815-8354

AUSTRALIA, FIJI, PAPUA NEW GUINEA, SOLOMON ISLANDS, VANUATU, AND WESTERN SAMOA
D.A. Information Services
648 Whitehorse Road
Mitcham 3132
Victoria
Tel: (61) 3 9210 7777
Fax: (61) 3 9210 7788
URL: http://www.dadirect.com.au

AUSTRIA
Gerold and Co.
Graben 31
A-1011 Wien
Tel: (1) 533-50-14-0
Fax: (1) 512-47-31-29

BANGLADESH
Micro Industries Development
Assistance Society (MIDAS)
House 5, Road 16
Dhanmondi R/Area
Dhaka 1209
Tel: (2) 326427
Fax: (2) 811188

BELGIUM
Jean De Lannoy
Av. du Roi 202
1060 Brussels
Tel: (2) 538-5169
Fax: (2) 538-0841

BRAZIL
Publicações Tecnicas Internacionais
Ltda.
Rua Peixoto Gomide, 209
01409 Sao Paulo, SP.
Tel: (11) 259-6644
Fax: (11) 258-6990

CANADA
Renouf Publishing Co. Ltd.
1294 Algoma Road
Ottawa, Ontario K1B 3W8
Tel: 613-741-4333
Fax: 613-741-5439

CHINA
China Financial & Economic
Publishing House
8, Da Fo Si Dong Jie
Beijing
Tel: (1) 333-8257
Fax: (1) 401-7365

COLOMBIA
Infoenlace Ltda.
Apartado Aereo 34270
Bogotá D.E.
Tel: (228) 212940
Fax: (228) 217492

COTE D'IVOIRE
Centre d'Edition et de Diffusion
Africaines (CEDA)
04 B.P. 541
Abidjan 04 Plateau
Tel: 225-24-6510
Fax: 225-25-0567

CYPRUS
Center of Applied Research
Cyprus College
6, Diogenes Street, Engomi
P.O. Box 2006
Nicosia
Tel: 244-1730
Fax: 246-2051

CZECH REPUBLIC
National Information Center
prodejna, Konviktska 5
CS – 113 57 Prague 1
Tel: (2) 2422.9433
Fax: (2) 2422.1484
URL: http://www.nis.cz/

DENMARK
SamfundsLitteratur
Rosenoerns Allé 11
DK-1970 Frederiksberg C
Tel: (31)-351942
Fax: (31)-357822

ECUADOR
Facultad Latinoamericana de
Ciencias Sociales
FLASCO-SEDE Ecuador
Calle Ulpiano Paez 118
y Av. Patria
Quito, Ecuador
Tel: (2) 542 714; 542 716; 528 200
Fax: (2) 566 139

EGYPT, ARAB REPUBLIC OF
Al Ahram
Al Galaa Street
Cairo
Tel: (2) 578-6083
Fax: (2) 578-6833

The Middle East Observer
41, Sherif Street
Cairo
Tel: (2) 393-9732
Fax: (2) 393-9732

FINLAND
Akateeminen Kirjakauppa
P.O. Box 23
FIN-00371 Helsinki
Tel: (0) 12141
Fax: (0) 121-4441
URL: http://booknet.cultnet.fi/aka/

FRANCE
World Bank Publications
66, avenue d'Iéna
75116 Paris
Tel: (1) 40-69-30-56/57
Fax: (1) 40-69-30-68

GERMANY
UNO-Verlag
Poppelsdorfer Allee 55
53115 Bonn
Tel: (228) 212940
Fax: (228) 217492

GREECE
Papasotiriou S.A.
35, Stournara Str.
106 82 Athens
Tel: (1) 364-1826
Fax: (1) 364-8254

HONG KONG, MACAO
Asia 2000 Ltd.
Sales & Circulation Department
Seabird House, unit 1101-02
22-28 Wyndham Street, Central
Hong Kong
Tel: 852 2530-1409
Fax: 852 2526-1107
URL: http://www.sales@asia2000.com.hk

HUNGARY
Foundation for Market
Economy
Dombovari Ut 17-19
H-1117 Budapest
Tel: 36 1 204 2951 or
36 1 204 2948
Fax: 36 1 204 2953

INDIA
Allied Publishers Ltd.
751 Mount Road
Madras - 600 002
Tel: (44) 852-3938
Fax: (44) 852-0649

INDONESIA
Pt. Indira Limited
Jalan Borobudur 20
P.O. Box 181
Jakarta 10320
Tel: (21) 390-4290
Fax: (21) 421-4289

IRAN
Kowkab Publishers
P.O. Box 19575-511
Tehran
Tel: (21) 258-3723
Fax: 98 (21) 258-3723

Ketab Sara Co. Publishers
Khaled Eslamboli Ave.,
6th Street
Kusheh Delafrooz No. 8
Tehran
Tel: 8717819 or #716104
Fax: 8862479

IRELAND
Government Supplies Agency
Oifig an tSoláthair
4-5 Harcourt Road
Dublin 2
Tel: (1) 461-3111
Fax: (1) 475-2670

ISRAEL
Yozmot Literature Ltd
P.O. Box 56055
Tel Aviv 61560
Tel: (3) 5285-397
Fax: (3) 5285-397

R.O.Y. International
PO Box 13056
Tel Aviv 61130
Tel: (3) 5461423
Fax: (3) 5461442

Palestinian Authority/Middle East
Index Information Services
P.O.B. 19502 Jerusalem
Tel: (2) 271219

ITALY
Licosa Commissionaria Sansoni SPA
Via Duca Di Calabria, 1/1
Casella Postale 552
50125 Firenze
Tel: (55) 645-415
Fax: (55) 641-257

JAMAICA
Ian Randle Publishers Ltd.
206 Old Hope Road
Kingston 6
Tel: 809-927-2085
Fax: 809-977-0243

JAPAN
Eastern Book Service
Hongo 3-Chome,
Bunkyo-ku 113
Tokyo
Tel: (03) 3818-0861
Fax: (03) 3818-0864
URL: http://www.bekkoame.or.jp/~svt-ebs

KENYA
Africa Book Service (E.A.) Ltd.
Quaran House, Mfangano Street
P.O. Box 45245
Nairobi
Tel: (2) 23641
Fax: (2) 330272

KOREA, REPUBLIC OF
Daejon Trading Co. Ltd.
P.O. Box 34
Yeoeida
Seoul
Tel: (2) 785-1631/4
Fax: (2) 784-0315

MALAYSIA
University of Malaya Cooperative
Bookshop, Limited
P.O. Box 1127
Jalan Pantai Baru
59700 Kuala Lumpur
Tel: (3) 756-5000
Fax: (3) 755-4424

MEXICO
INFOTEC
Apartado Postal 22-860
14060 Tlalpan,
Mexico D.F.
Tel: (5) 606-0011
Fax: (5) 606-0386

NETHERLANDS
De Lindeboom/InOr-Publikaties
P.O. Box 202
7480 AE Haaksbergen
Tel: (53) 574-0004
Fax: (53) 572-9296

Private Mail Bag 99914
New Market
Auckland
Tel: (9) 524-8119
Fax: (9) 524-8067

NIGERIA
University Press Limited
Three Crowns Building Jericho
Private Mail Bag 5095
Ibadan
Tel: (22) 41-1356
Fax: (22) 41-2056

NORWAY
Narvesen Information Center
Book Department
P.O. Box 6125 Etterstad
N-0602 Oslo 6
Tel: (22) 57-3300
Fax: (22) 68-1901

PAKISTAN
Mirza Book Agency
65, Shahrah-e-Quaid-e-Azam
P.O. Box No. 729
Lahore 54000
Tel: (42) 7353601
Fax: (42) 7585283

Oxford University Press
5 Bangalore Town
Sharae Faisal
PO Box 13033
Karachi-75350
Tel: (21) 446307
Fax: (21) 454-7640

PERU
Editorial Desarrollo SA
Apartado 3824
Lima 1
Tel: (14) 285380
Fax: (14) 286628

PHILIPPINES
International Booksource Center Inc.
Suite 720, Cityland 10
Condominium Tower 2
H.V dela Costa, corner
Valero St.
Makati, Metro Manila
Tel: (2) 817-9676
Fax: (2) 817-1741

POLAND
International Publishing Service
Ul. Piekna 31/37
00-577 Warzawa
Tel: (2) 628 6089
Fax: (2) 621-7255

PORTUGAL
Livraria Portugal
Rua Do Carmo 70-74
1200 Lisbon
Tel: (1) 347-4982
Fax: (1) 347-0264

ROMANIA
Compani De Librarii Bucuresti S.A.
Str. Lipscani no. 26, sector 3
Bucharest
Tel: (1) 613 9645
Fax: (1) 312 4000

RUSSIAN FEDERATION
Isdatelstvo <Ves Mir>
9a, Kolpachniy Pereulok
Moscow 101831
Tel: (95) 917 87 49
Fax: (95) 917 92 59

SAUDI ARABIA, QATAR
Jarir Book Store
P.O. Box 3196
Riyadh 11471
Tel: (1) 477-3140
Fax: (1) 477-2940

SINGAPORE, TAIWAN, MYANMAR, BRUNEI
Asahgate Publishing Asia
Pacific. Pte. Ltd.
41 Kallang Pudding Road #04-03
Golden Wheel Building
Singapore 349316
Tel: (65) 741-5166
Fax: (65) 742-9356
e-mail: ashgate@asianconnect.com

SLOVAK REPUBLIC
Slovart G.T.G. Ltd.
Krupinska 4
PO Box 152
852 99 Bratislava 5
Tel: (7) 839472
Fax: (7) 839485

SOUTH AFRICA, BOTSWANA
For single titles:
Oxford University Press
Southern Africa
P.O. Box 1141
Cape Town 8000
Tel: (21) 45-7266
Fax: (21) 45-7265

For subscription orders:
International Subscription Service
P.O. Box 41095
Craighall
Johannesburg 2024
Tel: (11) 880-1448
Fax: (11) 880-6248

SPAIN
Mundi-Prensa Libros, S.A.
Castello 37
28001 Madrid
Tel: (1) 431-3399
Fax: (1) 575-3998
http://www.tsai.es/mprensa

Mundi-Prensa Barcelona
Consell de Cent, 391
08009 Barcelona
Tel: (3) 488-3009
Fax: (3) 487-7659

SRI LANKA, THE MALDIVES
Lake House Bookshop
P.O. Box 244
100, Sir Chittampalam A.
Gardiner Mawatha
Colombo 2
Tel: (1) 32105
Fax: (1) 432104

SWEDEN
Fritzes Customer Service
Regeringsgaton 12
S-106 47 Stockholm
Tel: (8) 690 90 90
Fax: (8) 21 47 77

Wennergren-Williams AB
P.O. Box 1305
S-171 25 Solna
Tel: (8) 705-97-50
Fax: (8) 27-00-71

SWITZERLAND
Librairie Payot
Service Institutionnel
Côtes-de-Montenon 30
1002 Lausanne
Tel: (021) 320-2511
Fax: (021) 320-2514

Van Diermen Editions Techniq
Ch. de Lacuez 41
CH1807 Blonay
Tel: (021) 943 2673
Fax: (021) 943 3605

TANZANIA
Oxford University Press
Maktaba Street
PO Box 5299
Dar es Salaam
Tel: (51) 29209
Fax: (51) 46822

THAILAND
Central Books Distribution
306 Silom Road
Bangkok
Tel: (2) 235-5400
Fax: (2) 237-8321

TRINIDAD & TOBAGO, JAM.
Systematics Studies Unit
#9 Watts Street
Curepe
Trinidad, West Indies
Tel: 809-662-5654
Fax: 809-662-5654

UGANDA
Gustro Ltd.
Madhvani Building
PO Box 9997
Plot 16/4 Jinja Rd.
Kampala
Tel/Fax: (41) 254763

UNITED KINGDOM
Microinfo Ltd.
P.O. Box 3
Alton, Hampshire GU34 2PG
England
Tel: (1420) 86848
Fax: (1420) 89889

ZAMBIA
University Bookshop
Great East Road Campus
P.O. Box 32379
Lusaka

ZIMBABWE
Longman Zimbabwe (Pte.)Ltd
Tourle Road, Ardbennie
P.O. Box ST125
Southerton
Harare
Tel: (4) 662711
Fax: (4) 662716